THE FOREIGN POLICIES OF EASTERN EUROPE:
DOMESTIC AND INTERNATIONAL DETERMINANTS

East-West Perspectives, 4

Under the auspices of
The EAST-WEST FOUNDATION,
An International Research Organization

THE FOREIGN POLICIES OF EASTERN EUROPE: DOMESTIC AND INTERNATIONAL DETERMINANTS

edited by

James A. Kuhlman

associate professor
Department of Government and
International Studies
The University of South Carolina, USA

1978
A.W. Sijthoff – Leyden

327.47
F714

ISBN 90 286 0577 0

Printed in The Netherlands.
79-153

FOR MY MOTHER AND FATHER

PREFACE

The challenge of teaching and researching a multi-national
milieu such as Eastern Europe in the framework of the logic of
comparative inquiry is great indeed. One approach to this task
has been the country-by-country study, which, even when done
well, leads to the narrowness and lack of perspective common
to all case studies. Another approach has been the attempt to
focus upon specific policy inputs and outputs, comparing these
variables cross-nationally. While providing needed perspective,
area specialists argue that inevitably a shallowness of insight
results from this latter approach.
    Utilizing the advantages and counter-balancing the disadvantages
of the two schools, scholars in the context of multi-national and
multi-methodological working groups have found it easier to cope
with the complexity inherent in a multi-variate research field
such as Eastern Europe. All of the contributors to this volume
are faced with the teaching challenge and research problem posed
by the "socialist commonwealth of nations". Given foreign policy
as a central concern, it was decided to organize a working
conference and confront the logic of comparative approaches to
communist studies.
    On December 3-5, 1970, a core group met at the University of
South Carolina for a Workshop Conference on the Comparative
Study of Communist Foreign Policy.* Given a broad introductory
framework as suggestive to comparative foreign policy analysis

-----

* This core group is represented in this volume in the chapters by
Farkas, Jamgotch, Kuhlman, Morrison, Pirages, Socianu and Váli. The
chapters by Farlow, Mallinckrodt and Starrels, and Potter have been
added for their contribution to the methodological and area breadth
of the volume.

of the bloc, each author brought to bear particular methods and emphases in his approach to the various systems under scrutiny.

The editor's introductory chapter to the volume posits a general model in which influences upon bloc-wide foreign policy are categorized into historical-cultural, socio-economic, institutional, and elite determinants, which are seen as conditioning bloc impact or the resultant relationships (consensus, adaptive, integrative and disintegrative conflict) among East European nations.

Each subsequent chapter stressed certain categories of variables as determinative of foreign policies and bloc relations. Professor Jamgotch analyzes the Soviet position in Eastern Europe, stressing the importance of Soviet ideology and rules for the conduct of international relations in the bloc. Professor Pirages, on the other hand, attempts to show the strong influence of socio-economic variables in the determination of Czechoslovakia's political behavior and position within the socialist community.

Professors Mallinckrodt and Starrels and Professor Váli, viewing East Germany and Hungary, respectively, emphasize the institutional and elite features of communist regimes, while also acknowledging the potential contradictions of these determinants with national values historically evident in those systems. Historical-cultural interrelationships with communist elite characteristics are again given prominence in the chapters on Poland by Professor Morrison and Romania by Dr. Socianu.

Chapters eight and nine by Professors Farlow and Farkas, respectively, given added emphasis to the special roles played by Romania and Yugoslavia within socialist international relations. The Romanian model of partial alignment, emphasizing elite manipulation of system variables as described by Farlow, is an interesting contrast to the non-aligned program of Yugoslav foreign policy. The special position of Yugoslavia vis-à-vis the bloc is interpreted by Professor Farkas with reference to the role of each variable-category in the estimate of system capabilities.

Though foreign policy analysis at any moment runs the risk of time, much of the analysis in this volume retains its immediacy as the European eyes focus attention on the follow-up to the Helsinki Conference on Security and Cooperation in Europe, concluded in July, 1975. The concluding chapters on innovative behavior in East European foreign policies by Professor Potter provides an appropriate focus on change within the socialist community as a means to projecting stability-instability in the European future. Recent and imminent changes in leadership across Europe and the international system certainly demand a mobilization of social scientific resources to chart such change in as understandable and empirical a fashion as possible.

The multiplicity of concerns in an edited volume such as this at the very least may bring the not always recognized complexity of Eastern Europe to the attention of students, scholars, and decision-makers. As an additional intent, the editor also hopes this awareness of complexity leads to an acceptance of the multiplicity of approaches, a necessary reciprocity in any scholarly undertaking. A subsequent volume in preparation in the East-West Perspectives series will deal with the integrative-disintegrative continuum in the Soviet/East European sub-system, thus proceeding to a concentration upon relationships among socialist states' policy orientations on the basis of the present attention to determinants of those policies.

As any editor, I am indebted most of all to the contributors to this volume. Many of the participants in the conference have responded enthusiastically to the "working" nature of the original meetings and continue currently with their cooperative inquiry into East European events. The combined conference essays and subsequently contributed chapters allow the reader to observe trends and patterns, as well as shifts and reversals, in the analysis of East European foreign policies to a greater extent than do the commonplace current events materials so readily and abundantly available.

Of course such efforts require generous administrative and financial assistance. I would like to thank in particular James E. Larson and Robert D. Ochs, who, as Chairman of Political Science and Dean of Arts and Science, respectively, gave much moral and material support to the original workshop. Expertly assisting in many personal and professional ways were graduate assistants Nancy Eldridge Morgan, Kirk Johnson and Arthur Tarleton. Finally, another personal and professional note of appreciation must be given to my colleague Richard P. Farkas, without whose insights and efforts the undertaking would not have reached fruition.

James A. Kuhlman

Washington, D.C.
June, 1976

TABLE OF CONTENTS

xiv

LIST OF TABLES

xvi

LIST OF FIGURES

LIST OF CONTRIBUTORS

JAMES A. KUHLMAN is an Associate Professor of Government and International Studies at the University of South Carolina. He holds BS, MA, and Ph.D. degrees from Northwestern University, and earned an MA in Public and International Affairs while with the Institute for Sino-Soviet Studies of the George Washington University. He has co-edited *The Future of Inter-Bloc Relations in Europe* (1974) and *Changes in European Relations* (1976), and has edited a forthcoming study on *Regional Integration: Theory and Research on Eastern Europe* (1976).

RICHARD P. FARKAS is an Associate Professor of Political Science at De Paul University. He earned his Ph.D. in International Studies from the University of South Carolina. He has authored *Yugoslav Economic Development and Political Change* (1975) and is co-authoring forthcoming volumes on comparative communist state systems and the social sciences in Eastern Europe.

ROBERT L. FARLOW is Chairman of the Department of Political Science at Muskingum College. He received his MA and Ph.D. degrees from Case Western Reserve University. He has widely published in journals and is co-author of *Comparative Patterns of Foreign Policy and Trade: Communist Balkans in International Politics* (1976).

NISH JAMGOTCH, JR. is an Associate Professor of Political Science at the University of North Carolina at Charlotte. He holds MA and Ph.D. degrees from Claremont Graduate School. Among his many publications is *Soviet-East European Dialogue: International Relations of a New Type?* (1968).

ANITA M. MALLINCKRODT is an Adjunct Professor of Public and
International Affairs at the George Washington University where
she earned her Ph.D. in political science and has served as
Associate of "Deutsche Welle" of the International Radio Voice of
West Germany. She has authored *Wer Macht die Aussenpolitik der DDR?*
(1972) and co-authored *Politics in the German Democratic Republic*
(1975).

JAMES F. MORRISON is a Professor of Political Science at the
University of Florida. He received his MA and Ph.D. degrees from
Standford University. He has published widely in journals and is
author of *The Polish People's Republic* (1968) and co-author of
Politics and the International System (1971).

DENNIS C. PIRAGES is an Associate Professor with the Department
of Government and Politics at the University of Maryland. He holds
a Ph.D. in political science from Stanford University. He has
authored numerous books on socialist politics and science, technology and public affairs, among them *Modernization and Political
Tension Management: A Socialist Society in Perspective*, *A Case
Study of Poland* (1972), *Ark II: Social Response to Environmental
Imperatives* (1974), and *Managing Political Conflict* (1976).

WILLIAM C. POTTER is a Lecturer in the Department of Political
Science at the University of California, Davis. He is a specialist
in comparative foreign policy and arms control and disarmament. He
has contributed to *Papers of the Peace Science Society (International)*, *Journal of Politics* and *Policy Studies Journal*.

HORIA SOCIANU has served on the Romanian desk of the Voice of
America. He holds a Ph.D. from the School of Public and International Affairs of the George Washington University where he has
been a Lecturer in the Institute for Sino-Soviet Studies. He was
formerly an Assistant Professor of Law in Bucharest.

JOHN M. STARRELS is an Assistant Professor of Political Science
and International Affairs with the George Washington University.
He holds a Ph.D. from the University of California, Santa Barbara.
He has contributed several chapters to volumes on German politics
and international relations and is co-author of *Politics in the
German Democratic Republic* (1975).

FERENC A. VÁLI is a Professor Emeritus of the Department of
Government at the University of Massachusetts. He holds a Ph.D.
from the University of London. Among his many standard works in
the field are *Rift and Revolt in Hungary* (1961), *Bridge Across the
Bosphorous: The Foreign Policy of Turkey* (1971), and *The Turkish
Straits and NATO* (1972).

Chapter I

COMPARING COMMUNIST FOREIGN POLICIES

James A. Kuhlman

Through a matter of debate currently, the positing of "adaptive politics" as a new field has underlined a significant thrust in all comparative political studies, namely that of approaching the actor either in terms of its environmental variation or its external behavior. (1) The fact that these two alternative emphases in foreign policy studies have produced sets of hypotheses both autonomous and even incompatible now confronts the scholar attempting comparative analysis. It should be pointed out that what is mandatory for theoretical advances are comparative foreign policies. The existence of the latter phenomena would indeed end the argument over whether the field itself exists or does not exist. But linkage between sets of internal and external data must be established before any determination can be made as to whether truly comparative foreign policies are or are not a reality in the international system. The linkage problem is met herein on two levels of analysis, one theoretical and the other substantive. Theoretically, this introduction attempts to use both the systems and issue-processing approaches or theories to establish linkage between internal and external variables in the communist foreign policy-making process. Substantively, this analysis attempts to view the Soviet/East European bloc as a sub-system within the international system, thereby facilitating use of the afore-mentioned approaches. (2) The limitations of Western social science models in analysis of communist political processes has been generally acknowledged. (3) What the general approach implied in systems theory can offer policy analysis, however, offsets potential drawbacks when combined with elemental features of the issue-processing approach. While the former allows the researcher to outline specific inputs and the process of feedback based upon authoritative outputs, the latter emphasizes the issues being processed and the resultant impact on the nature of the policy-making system. Figure 1.1 at the end of this introductory chapter represents this combined approach, or a model of the bloc policy process.

Such a model, it is hoped, will provide for an awareness of the congruence or incongruence between national goals and bloc goals, on the one hand, and for determination of the types of events, activities, and issues which condition relationships in the bloc on the other hand. The particular issue area of bloc relations provides an ideal framework within which to view the stresses and strains of national goals upon the bloc sub-system. Furthermore, it is hoped that this approach will provide a basis for innovative and empirical hypotheses concerning integration problems in the bloc. At the very least the introductory framework should aid in interpreting the broad range of materials presented in the country chapters to follow.

Use of this approach is enhanced by the existence of the sub-system indentified as the Soviet/East European bloc (Bulgaria, Czechoslovakia, East Germany, Hungary, Poland, Romania and the Soviet Union). It is the intention of the model to be constructed here to organize data for this specific sub-system of seven states, though events and issues surrounding the socialist systems of Albania and Yugoslavia are analytically integrated within the model. The contention implied is that the process which enables such a sub-system to exist in a systemic one of communication and control. (4) Feedback processes allow nation-state participants to achieve types of inter-relationships at the decision-making levels. With this conceptual framework in mind, and through the use of the approaches mentioned above, the following analysis hopes to provide for comparative study of communist foreign policies on an empirical basis.

Policy Determinants

The comparative study of Communist Party-state policy-making has been considerably altered in recent years. (5) Dimensions of communist political behavior which formerly had become almost an obsession for many political analysts have lost attention as explanatory variables. Elements of the political system once viewed only situationally have been highlighted by the new comparative focus. The potential for systematic comparative inquiry that accompanies the employment of the various communist polities as units of analysis has begun to be acknowledged. Yet such considerations as elite roles, leadership characteristics and perceptions, not to mention ideology, are becoming the residual categories of much comparative communist analysis.

The reasons for clarifying the main dimensions of elite behavior and elevating the priority attached to them by students of compar-

ative communist studies are obvious due to the nature of the systems
under consideration. At this stage I intend to demonstrate the
necessity for a clearer conceptualization of the role of elites
vis-à-vis other variables in comparative communist policy studies.
Although it is a somewhat vague generalization, the overview of
comparative communist studies literature asserts the need for investigating the nations' historical and socio-economic environments
in order to explain varying frequency and intensity in policy outputs or even events. When the variables made salient by the hierarchical Party and/or governmental structures are the only ones
employed to explain policy, simplistic and often misleading assumptions are bound to gain acceptance. Model building necessitates
the opening of previous theoretical boundaries to include variables
of the social and economic environment.

Almost without exception students of Communist Party-state
politics have warmly greeted the admission of the comparative
communist studies sub-field into the more systematic parent field
of comparative political systems, evidenced, for example, in the
work or development theorists. Comparative policy analysis itself ·
seems to have been applied more systematically and scientifically
to such areas as the American state systems than to foreign political systems, probably because of politics and data availability.
Several objections have been raised to the appropriateness of the
bloc Party-states as primary units of analysis but the notion of
a sub-system in the international system is predicated upon that
basis. One must, of course, remain cautions of attempts to broaden
the boundaries of inquiry into new and different levels of analysis,
particularly in a case such as the regional sub-system under
consideration here, since such a framework could devalue the relevance of national political systems and governmental structures
to foreign policy. In any event one most assuredly can question
the explanatory power of the various indices of political systems
and governmental structures that have been employed to date in
comparative studies of Communist Party-state behavior.

However, as new methods of measurement are increasingly applied
to communist and other "area" studies, there might well be discovery
of facets of Parties and structures that are crucial or marginal to
the policies adopted within the Soviet/East European bloc. Even if
one were to concede a marginal contribution for political and
institutional variables to the policy processes of the countries
involved, while still recognizing and investigating the contribution of socio-economic determinants, it remains a necessity
to develop an awareness of the multi-variability and multi-dimen-
sionality of the model which this comparative sub-field is attempting to construct. One of the obvious points made by the collective
efforts in this volume is that one simply cannot account for most
of the variance in policy across Communist countries with a list
of economic and social statistics unless one is totally ignorant
of existing elite studies.

Findings that assert that the policies of the Communist Party-

states are for the most part the result of universal laws of
social and economic behavior are as disturbing for their normative
implications as are traditional hypotheses that Communist elites
operate within their own ideological vacuum. Such arbitrary exclusion of questions of perception, judgment and leadership would
be possible only with a set of hypotheses as deterministic as some
that Marxists themselves claim, which to my knowledge does not
yet exist. Any model constructed must consider here the nature of
the relationship of socio-economic/policy variables and other
determinants, and further, to place in perspective their implications for other determinants of policy-making by Communist Party-
state elites.

The crucial question, then, is to what extent are the policy-
making elites in Communist countries, assuming that one can
readily identify those who are formally and functionally endowed
with that power, agents free from the influence of historical-
cultural, socio-economic and institutional variables? Communist
foreign policies are the result of deliberate actions by these
elites, but none of the studies of relationships between socio-
economic and other variables and the policy output have come close
to closure on the search for determinants of foreign policies.

Due to inaccessibility of hard data concerning communist elite
behavior, measurement of their actual "impact" has traditionally
deferred to assessment of "influence" based upon assumptions about
"communism". Even many scholars of the new school have attempted
to define elite roles in foreign policy-making by explaining
some variance according to historical-cultural, socio-economic,
and institutional factors, and then assuming the left-over,
unexplained variance must be accredited to elite variables.

The first task for both "traditional" and "behavioral" scholar,
then, is to establish linkage between sets of variables accounting
for the frequence and intensity of certain foreign policy outputs.
This involves not only the question as to how one category of determinant affects another, but also to what degree should one
category rather than another be considered as salient on a given
foreign policy issue. Linkages must be defined between Party-
states for certain variables and between variables for certain
Party-states. The position afforded elites in any policy-making
model for the socialist community should conform to conventional
wisdom as well as to confirmed empirical generalizations. Contrary
to the emphases of comparative policy analysis of state systems
in the United States, policy studies in communist systems have
traditionally underestimated importance of socio-economic factors.
Yet the character of elite emphasis in these latter studies has
been such as to contribute little to understanding the linkage
with other determinants.

Two major problems present themselves in the attempt to specify
the relevant dimensions of national policy-making elites: one
concerns the identification of elite characteristics as related
to specific issues and as related to other variable categories,

while the other concerns the conceptualization (and eventual operationalization) of those elite factors. The strength of the present efforts in those directions, however, rests in its inventiveness but not in the clarity with which the central concepts have been operationalized. That strength, of course, is also the greatest weakness: those who construct their models minus presentation of their data are bound to invite criticism of their methods and theories. Though this introduction builds a model temporarily bereft of data, it attempts to be careful concerning any pretense of theory.

Not only the spatial but the temporal dimensions of the model are bound to affect the correlations of societal and political indicators. In attempting to assess the strength of relationship, for instance, between historial-cultural and elite variables in any given issue area under consideration, the strength of relationship itself becomes a variable in the policy-making process. Though virtually no work has been done on the problem of which factors condition that relationship (event data analysis seems to prefer to ignore the problem completely by the simple device of using events as independent rather than dependent variables), one aspect that seemingly must account for differing degrees of strength is the issue area itself. It is probably overly simplistic to assume that elite perceptions of non-political factors alone account for those factors' importance in policy-making. Some as yet unidentified facets of an issue area may bring forth factors independent of perceptions and nevertheless significant in policy-makers' behavior.

Even with the gradual systematization of elite studies in recent comparative communist systems literature, one should resist studying this variable category in a vacuum. A great deal of so-called conventional wisdom has been re-evaluated, and yet aggregate data on social background characteristics and content analysis data on elite perceptions have revealed little explanation of the nature of socio-economic/political relationships in the policy process. As amply argued in the field of comparative politics as a whole, and only accentuated by area studies' results, the mounting body of discrete hypotheses enhances empiricism, not necessarily understanding. Admittedly one level of research must complement the other, multi-national data bases must be followed by multi-variate strategies, but (even) primitive model building should direct the approach of both -- hopefully data would be organized along comparable indices and provide for testing by replication. Patterns of historical, economic and institutional development have been correlated with foreign policy output sufficiently in the chapters to follow to suggest the need for further investigation. But the delineation of the linkages in the network of variables, including elite behavior, that determine foreign policy behavior has eluded most inquiry. It could be argued that much of the unexplained variance in Communist Party-state foreign policies rests in the elite sector of the model in Figure 1.1 at

the end of this introductory chapter. Though only a preliminary
formulation as to the how and why of ideological and other elite
variable impact on the policy process is sketched, it is hoped
the requirements for further analysis in the fields are clarified.

What is required is a model including awareness of historical-
cultural variables, socio-economic variables, institutional and
elite behavior variables in the policy formation process. The
following general typology of inputs could be envisioned as
determinants of policy in the Soviet/East European sub-system:
1) historical/cultural determinants, for example linguistics and
   ethnicity, nationalism, salient events such as world wars,
   foreign occupation, disputed territory, etc.;
2) socio-economic determinants, for example the agricultural-
   industrial balance in the economic sector, private to state
   ratio in ownership in each sector, growth rates, resources, etc.;
3) institutional determinants, for example the governmental
   structure, importance of trade and other unions, constitutional structure, interest group formation, etc.; and
4) elite behavior determinants, for example the social background
   characteristics, beliefs, perceptions and factions existing
   within an elite, etc.
Five factors account for variation among the types of determinants, or for variations in determinants across bloc participants.
Each of the five dimensions are pertinent to the degree of determination in policy-making afforded the four variable categories
mentioned above:
a) values and attributes -- these may define historical traditions and cultural norms of actors in the bloc policy
   process, attitudes prevalent at certain socio-economic
   development levels, opinions of certain specialized groups
   within the society, and beliefs held by elites;
b) levels and stratification -- these factors could account
   for degree of cultural or national consciousness operative
   in the policy process, the relevance of certain occupational
   sectors in policy considerations, the status of pressure
   groups, and the level of leadership involved;
c) area and function -- these might account for differing
   impact of issues with respect to nationalities within a
   participant nation, or to certain economic issues across
   nations, to the involvement of specific groups within and
   between nations, or to elite stratifications in both Party
   and State channels;
d) natural boundaries -- these factors refer to possible de-
   limitation of policy according to national power relations,
   economic capability, lack of articulated interests, or to
   such variables as elite education and experience; and
e) codified or formalized roles -- such factors could appear
   in the form of legal recognition of certain historical
   events or cultural groups, established procedures for
   planning, constitutional guarantees for groups and organi-

zations, and formalized administrative procedures with regional policy-making bodies.

One might easily argue that the categorization of non-political variables into three discrete sectors in the model is unnecessary and even confusing. Obviously, historical-cultural settings condition the social and economic structure of the Party-states, but, analytically speaking, it becomes useful to distinguish them on the grounds of their mutual interdependence. Likewise the institutions developed in any country are to a great degree dependent upon socio-economic conditions, and yet it would be instructive to analytically acknowledge when institutions arise that are not reflective of economic capabilities or social structure. Equally interesting in a cross-national context would be the effort to outline occurences when Party-states with similar historical happenings and cultural orientations develop differing social structures, or when similar geographical and resource characteristics end up with distinct economic mechanisms.

All of these situations could determine to a greater or lesser degree the type of issue considered by policy-makers. The typology of such determinants in the model explicitly recognizes that all policy-making is to some extent a function of historical background and cultural conditions. Yet the analytical model used must be prepared to direct research investigating the possible direct impact of socio-economic variables upon foreign policy and not really be concerned with how these variables came to be structured as they are. The independent role of each sector in the model necessitates their analytic separation. For instance institutional behavior may directly affect decision-making independently of socio-economic determination and sometimes in contrast to it. Special status, however, has been afforded the last sector prior to policy conversion. No actions may be taken, and no analysis undertaken, without passing through the elite sector. Any definition of policy-making automatically implies deliberate action by a designated elite, varying of course on levels of analysis. The calculation of policy determinants may differ from issue to issue, time to time, location to location, but elite behavior itself is necessary in some form. While necessary, it should be remembered elite behavior is hardly sufficient for foreign policy-making.

Given the difficulty of accession to and measurement of elite behavior variables in communist systems, there is still the danger of considering these factors as residual in our empirical research. This difficulty is compounded and the danger increased because the relationship between any of the other sectors with the elite sector are the most subtle to distinguish. Much of comparative communist studies already indicates that one of the best ways to consider the model in application would be to begin with elite variables and work backwards through the historical-cultural, socio-economic and institutional sectors. Indeed, policy-making as a process indicates greater importance is attached to the

elites and their institutional environments than to the more
diffused determinants of the first two sectors. Indicators
such as elite socialization could much more readily ascertain the
policies of the leader who, for example, might shift the natural
economic resources of an underdeveloped nation into an industrialization program, than those identified by proceeding "logically"
from history and culture through socio-economic to elite behavior.

Once again, however, as is particularly the case with the concept "ideology" in communist studies, certain elite associated
terms have been used in such rigid and deterministic fashions by
students of these systems that one has to be cautious about the
director of research backward through the model. Also, similar
decisions may have dissimilar consequences in countries with
varying socio-economic conditions.

The relationships among sectors of the model as discussed thus
far have emphasized the direct and reciprocal (or feedback)
phenomena. One could study the direct impact of socio-economic
variables upon a nations' elite, irrespective of history, culture,
and mass behavior. One might also wish to study the same two-
sector relationship in a reverse direction. Furthermore, the most
productive research has been and may continue to be centered on
hypotheses about these direct relationships. As research proceeds
beyond description and classification, however, inferences from
data collection of these direct relationship alone must appear
deceptively simple.

Once the researcher is faced with the problem of similar sectors
in cross-national perspective producing dissimilar policies, the
possible incremental or cumulative relationships have to be
recognized. Polycentrism, as a concept describing a very loosely
structures "policy arena" in Eastern Europe, is a consequence in
bloc relations determined by a complex accumulation of variables
from all sectors. The routes through the model explaning such a
consequence are limited only by the number of variables the
researcher wishes to consider. The calculation of probability of
certain outcomes in bloc relations would ultimately have to consider the reciprocal relationships among sectors (e.g., culture/
elite/culture/institutional) and how this would affect the incremental plotting of determinants. The infinity of permutations
in the model suggests that predictability is hardly even implied
at our present stage of research. The possible explanations of
policy-making are merely expanded in this framework, hardly
delimited. Specific independent/dependent variables' association
will be discovered for the most part in uni-directional search
for some time to come.

Overtly the parameters of this model diagram single issue determination of policy-making. Given a Party-state with a pre-WWII
history of economic growth, significant reserves of key minerals,
a developing managerial class with political participation in elite
decision-making bodies, all factors associated with industrialization, and at the same time supporting a regional economic policy

of locating agricultural specialization in pastoral countries, one could easily assume all sorts of causal connections through the model. However, one could also determine other variables in correlation with the same policy. Thus in addition to the single issue structure of the model, a sub-structural network might exist and should be acknowledged in the policy framework. This sub-structural framework might at any given time assume greater or lesser significance than the issue under consideration, as in the case with industrialization in the example above. Perhaps education or nationalism as issues could elicit variables in each sector that might relate positively or negatively with the policy examined.

Yet again the temporal dimension introduces further variability into the task of determining bloc policy. The sub-structural networks may witness the political relevance of certain environmental phenomena rising and falling from time to time in relation to the policy output. Consider the modifying influence of the changing international system upon the variables in the sectors determining the bloc policy. Sub-structural networks on a longitudinal analysis could produce interesting insights into determinants that are genuinely comparable.

The environmental, dynamic, systemic and other shared characteristics of comparative politics models authored by Apter, Easton, Spiro and others, as pointed out by Welsh in his essay cited previously, are again incorporated (or hopefully so) into the framework formulated here. The sub-structural variations in the policy environment just mentioned alert one to the developmental, dynamic aspects of the model. The overall systemic orientation of the diagram is clarified further in the discussion that will follow on "policy relationships". Additionally, this model also seems to provide for analysis of individual Party-state's behavior as being either functional or dysfunctional for the bloc sub-system in that system maintenance is implied in the approach. In other words as one moves vertically (or cross-nationally) in the sectors, obvious discrepancies can alert the researcher to types of relationships in the sub-system that will occur on the output side of the model.

Moving horizontally in the model, as time changes, one may confirm such findings by noticing when certain variables increase or decrease in importance within a Party-state. One could conceive of the Breshnev Doctrine, for instance, as an incident which for variable duration has changed the ground rules for bloc policy-making. National or international facets of the environment, as with the case of Sino-Romanian interaction, can become relevant to policy-making for specified periods of time. The "group" perspective of the political process, pointed out by Welsh as common to the major models, is also stressed in the role of the elite sector in this model and can be investigated in the uni-directional hypotheses relating the socio-economic/institutional and institutional/elite sectors in particular.

It is appropriate here to consider some of Welsh's criticisms

of the comparative models of Easton and Spiro, since the systems
and issue-processing approaches are quite explicit in the model
diagrammed at the end of this introduction. The ideas of sub-
structural variation according to issue area and permeability of
the boundaries of the model are extremely important in answering
many of the questions raised by Welsh. With some degreee of disagreement on the list of "characteristics" of East European
political behavior, I have attempted to account for processes
in some manner (perhaps frequency of certain behavior in some
instances and perhaps intensity of behavior in others) peculiar
to those systems. The incrementalism of the model should provide for some attention to Welsh's challenge of identifying sub-
system (or variable sectors in the model here) overlap, rather
than just analytically account for sub-system interaction and
autonomy. Overlap between the sectors still does not, however,
excuse the analytical necessity of pointing out the potential
for independent or inter-dependent relations among the variable
categories.

Extent of sub-system (or sector) autonomy, as discussed by
Welsh, is itself highly questionable in East European political
behavior. Admittedly we do not know the intra- or extra-systemic
influences upon such outcomes as Hungary 1956 or Czechoslovakia
1968, but if the boundaries of the model are considered permeable,
we may at least be aware of either influence. And this permeability is not thought of as subject to random events in the international system, but rather is related in a more generic way to the
variable sectors in the model. Events such as World Wars may be
at any point in time considered as politically relevant and therefore permeate the boundaries of the model, but it would be much
more relevant to view such events as elemental to the historical-
cultural sector. This also implies that what at one time may be
simply a policy-relevant issue may in another context become a
stable part of the policy-making process.

Welsh's fourth characteristic of East European political behavior,
that of the persistent tendency towards orthodox interpretations
of socio-economic change on the part elites, raises the question
as to how to specify origins and directions of change in those
systems. Again, the ability to work backwards, along a value or
ideological dimension for instance, from the elite sector to the
other determinents could account for an awareness of this continuing phenomenon.

While agreeing with Welsh almost completely concerning the
inapplicability of Apter's social stratification approach, the
input-output nature of the model presented here obviously finds
utility for the approach of Easton. Despite the rigid hierarchical
and "closed" aspects of the East European political systems, and
the resultant lack in society-wide feedback, one could argue
those characteristics themselves dictate an analytical separation
of inputs and recognition of each sector's independent role. As
has been discussed above, specific paths of formulation in the

policy process will vary with the issue at hand. Relative impact of sectors will also vary accordingly. The stability as well as the complexity of sub-structural networks in policy may also be a function of issues. The dynamic requirements of any model of the political process, unless one assumes nothing dynamic in Eastern Europe is occuring, necessitates many features of the systems model. As socio-economic determinants of policy gain or lose impact in the policy area, some analytical distinction apart from purely political variables must be maintained in order to measure those fluctuations.

This is not to say that stable sub-structural characteristics cannot temporarily or permanently disappear. The pattern of social and political activity following Khrushchev's de-Stalin-ization and recognition of "separate roads to socialism" might well have been significantly altered by the Brezhnev Doctrine and might well again be shifted after a European Security Conference. Welsh argues that the extent of congruence between societal and political goals presents problems for Easton's framework because it does not outline the possibility of political output which may have little or no impact on the environment, while the converse is made quite explicit by Easton. Again the issue area and issue processing approach accounts for such behavior. Internal reforms of the Party and elite turnover many times has litte effect on the surrounding environment in Communist systems. Yet it is still important to investigate the origins of such change and, I would submit, it is not overly naive to assume some environmental input into and impact from such changes. Even if leadership turnover is initiated only due to elite perceptions of that necessity, the present model simply need proceed backwards through the other sectors to locate the objects of those perceptions.

Even if one were to agree with the general observations of some policy analysts in other comparative fields of study, that aggregate statistics on the environment have explained little of the policy variance across political systems, this would indicate further emphasis on comparative elite studies, not an erasure of the analytical boundaries between the sectors in the model pre-sented here. Moving horizontally along a goal or value oriented dimension, one would be able to identify the incongruity between cultural and socio-economic values and the institutional and elite goals of the political system. Even modest methods of measurement available to us at present could indentify many such inconsistencies in communist political behavior. The importance of those findings for bloc relationships in certain policy areas is self-evident.

One result of early empirical generalizations arising from such research could be a typology of issue areas which could in turn lead one to formulate working hypotheses applicable from one class of policy to another. It is much easier at this stage of our knowledge to identify types of relationships in a regional sub-system than to identify the types of issues that give rise to such interactions. The issue processing approach, however, also

12

has many problems in the communist context, problems which
features of the input-output model may help to solve. For instance
it is typical of all elites to keep certain issues out of consideration, either consciously or unconsciously. Obviously not
all issues, not even most issues from an objective assessment,
reach the point of conversion. Elites and institutions are in-
tricately structured to filter out such issues whenever possible.

How one measures so-called "non-decision", which analytically
speaking, may have a vast impact on the environment, is a considerable task. Unless there is an analytical separation of political
system from its environment, as in the Eastern framework, little
chance of identifying and measuring issues not brought to the
attention of the political system is possible. Despite the characteristics of communist polities, which are likely to have more
"non-decisions" than most Western systems, it is nevertheless
important to be able to point out new issues as they enter the
model. The idea here is not to choose between concepts provided by
different models, but rather to borrow freely and inventively until
a new model begins to fit the systems under consideration. The
difference between communist systems and other political systems
itself indicates the necessity of some sort of original synthesis.
It has been shown here that issues are quite relevant to the sub-
structural variation that may occur in the policy-making process.
The permutations of that sub-structure will also affect the nature
of issues being considered by policy-makers. One could imagine
situations confronting the bloc which present both research problems simultaneously. Economic and cultural issues bring forth
quite different levels and areas of the model. A Soviet "mobilization of bias" against the raising of certain issues in CMEA
or Warsaw Pact meetings is quite frequently noted.

Most comparative policy analysis, across national and
methodological boundaries, has emphasized the inputs rather than
the outputs. It is often easier to decide or "guestimate" the
why of a particular action than to infer the nature of impact of
a given action. Since the bloc is the focus of the model presented
here, relationships along the primary units of analysis, the Party-
states, should receive our attention next. The time has long since
passed, if it ever existed, when it was considered possible to
assume the nature of the bloc sub-system on the basis of its
"communist" inputs. If comparative analysis across varying inputs
is necessary to explain the range of policy-making in the bloc,
then a similar approach should be employed to discern the results
of those policies. A typology of inter-nation (and perhaps
other?) relationships in the sub-system at least begins completion
of the model.

I have attempted to use some of the current conceptualization
in comparative policy analysis to show the necessity of a comparative framework with an emphasis on elites, and to offer a means
for integrating the growing number of autonomous sets of hypotheses
that are being produced in the comparative communist studies area.

These approaches are seen as necessary both to explain the linkages
between national characteristics and foreign policies of the region,
and to begin reducing the variance which is still unexplained.

Policy Relationships

The next obvious objective is to consider what impact the policy
formation processes have upon the bloc structure and function in
policy-making. Rather than proceed immediately to typologies of
events or actions in foreign relations, as suggested by some scholars, the model for policy-making in the Soviet/East European sub-
system must provide for resultant relationships among units in
the sub-system. The following analysis attempts to acknowledge
the nature of the bloc sub-system with respect to types of relationships formed in the conversion or policy-making process.

The effort here is directed toward the long range goal of em-
ploying empirical research within an area of study long subjected
to, and necessarily so, more speculative forms of analysis under
the general rubric of "Kremlinology", "Sovietology", or "national
versus international communism". (6) After presenting four types
of inter-nation behavior in bloc policy-making, which represent a
continuum covering most of the possible relationships running
from consensus policy-making to disintegrative conflict, two tasks
loom before the researcher: 1) operationalization of, and testing
for relationships among, the variables; and 2) completion of the
model for policy-making in the Soviet/East European bloc.

Beginning within the context of a sub-system, in particular
the Soviet/East European sub-system or socialist commonwealth of
nations, within the international systems in general, it is hoped
that the typology developed and model consequently constructed
will provide a more solid and empirically grounded framework for
Communist foreign policy analysis. Too often the enthusiasm for
theory building has precluded the obligations to relate hypotheses
to international political realities. While this analysis will
borrow freely from established theoretical works in the field of
the comparative study of foreign relations, it will be selective
in the knowledge that hypothetical relationships ought to be based
equally on reasoned observation as aon abstract reasoning.

As noted previously, studies in Communist foreign policy may
be divided into two categories, those dealing essentially with the
formation of foreign policy in Communist states and those dealing
with foreign policy relations of international Communism in general. (7) It is with respect to a third category that this section
hopes to make a contribution. This focus is upon the foreign policy
process of the Soviet/East European community of nations. While
the works by Professors Brzezinski, Jamgotch, McNeal, Triska and
others all present impressive grasps of Communist international
behavior, they often provide more competitive than complementary
frameworks within which research may proceed. The attempt at this

point is to establish the viability and nature of the bloc as a
foreign policy formulating and executing body of nations, while
still retaining an awareness of the variability of nation behaviors
within the bloc.

Brzezinski's standard volume on the Soviet bloc in the main
offers simply a historical classification of four phases in bloc
relations: 1) The People's Democracy: Institutional and Ideological
Diversity; 2) Stalinism: Institutional and Ideological Uniformity;
3) From Thaw to Deluge: Institutional and Ideological Diversity;
and 4) The Communist Commonwealth: Institutional Diversity and
Ideological Uniformity. His unifying concepts are those of
"ideology" and "power", which offer a firm foundation for his
approach andemphasis on politico-historical events, but these
hardly foster an empirical understanding of the interrelationships
among bloc nations. Also, both concepts seems to stress the Soviet
variable as sole cause for bloc resolution in policy-making.

As a consequence of these conceptual limitations, the reader
may assume too easily that Soviet ideology and Soviet power were
the only important variables in bloc development. While one certainly could argue for their status as significant, or even most
significant, variables, the titles for historical stages used by
Brzezinski in themselves indicate an awareness of new relationships evolving in bloc politics which would involve additional
variables. The concepts of diversity and uniformity, undefined
empirically, especially indicate the need for explication. The
typology constructed in this section of the chapter attempts to
posit relationships running from consensus to disintegrative conflict in policy-making, a somewhat parallel continuum to that
implied by Brzezinski's analysis, yet also concerned with operationalization of labels for relationship falling somewhere between
these polar types.

In Triska's edited volume on Communist Party-States, the emphasis
rests upon the world Communist system, not upon an operational
policy-making community. The inclusive concept is that of the
Party-State, rather than bloc or commonwealth, thus the analyses
include nations not under consideration in this chapter. It might
be feasible to extend the applicability of the types envisioned
here to all fourteen Communist Party-States after repeated testing
and refinement of the original construct, but for present purposes
the Soviet/East European community is the focus of analysis. (8)

The concept of integration provides unity for most of the Triska
book. Where these authors work at one level, that of international
Communism, and attempt to establish its reality by observing the
behaviors of all Party-States, the analysis here desires to investigate the practicality and/or reality of the approach to the
Soviet and East European states at the bloc level by observing
their inter-nation relations. Assumptions based upon the studies
found in Triska clarify Party-State behavior within the "world
communist system". Assumptions based upon the model undertaken in
this chapter would have the intention of clarifying bloc behavior

by empirically observing types of inter-nation behavioral patterns
in policy-making. Closest to this approach to the comparative
study of Communist foreign policy are the articles in Triska
utilizing coalition theory and related works on "regionalism" and
"alliance". (9)

The "special" nature and "exclusiveness" of the international
relations among Communist systems are stressed by Professor McNeal.
Much as Brzezinski saw a dichotomy of relations in uniformity and
diversity, so McNeal determines, "Theirs is a closed network of
alignments and antagonisms". (10) Nowhere in his volume of analysis
with documents, however, does hij specify the nature of bloc interrelationships beyond the two-fold nominal classification of inter-
Party relations and inter-State relations on the one hand, and
multi-lateral and bi-lateral relations on the other hand. McNeal
does enumarate issues at stake in the international system of
Communist states, but does not extend the discussion to relate
these issues (ideological, territorial, economic, tactical and
domestic) and processes in bloc policy-making.

The notion of the Soviet/East European bloc as a sub-system
within international Communism and the general international system
is developed in the recent work by Professor Jamgotch, in which
he posits a "qualitative differences between Soviet-East European
relations and those within the rest of the system". (11) With his
explicit postulation of a potential policy-making role for the
bloc, Professor Jamgotch presents us with the concrete task of
ascertaining the present and predictable policy patterns of the
Communist commonwealth. (12)

The typology of inter-nation relationships in the bloc policy
processes attempted here may alleviate the burden of approaching
the comparative study of Communist foreign policy from the present
options of national or international system levels, and proceed
with sub-system processes. The traditional concerns of Sovietology
are hardly ignored in this approach, "for the future of the Soviet
political process as we know it, and of communism as a political
ideology, with universal application, may well depend upon the
outcome of precisely all these new relations among the sub-system
nations of Eastern Europe." (13)

Policy-making in the bloc sub-system may be seen in the form
of typology of relationships or outcomes, specifically a four-fold
scheme of interaction. Each type of relationship varies according
to five procedurally oriented factors persistent in the policy
process. Before delineating this second typology in the model,
however, the use of typology should be considered briefly. All
concepts in social science are generalizations; that is, they
imply abstraction and reduction, the process of typification.
Typologies are the constructs of formal inquiry. Comparative
analyses by necessity involve the conceptualization of new constructs
which organize previously unrelated phenomena. (14) This study is
concerned with variables that express the dimensions of a typology
generally identified as the Soviet/East European bloc. The limita-

tions of "ideal types" have been debated since the term was first invoked by Max Weber, but this analysis must once again acknowledge the understanding that, "There is no such thing as a type independent of the purposes for which it was constructed." (15) Thus the types of determinants outlined in the first section are for the purpose of identifying categories of inputs into the bloc policy-making process. Here we are concerned with types of relationships arising from the conversion process. Our typologies aid only in the analysis of a specific body of data to which we refer in the literature as the Soviet bloc nations, the socialist commonwealth of nations, or the East European sub-system. This author readily receives the implications for this study of the empirical error criterion as fundamental to the critique of the typological appraoch and analysis.

The four types of inter-nation interaction involved in the bloc policy process are as follows:

consensus policy-making; (16)
adaptive policy-making; (17)
integrative conflict; (18) and
disintegrative conflict. (19)

The factors accounting for variations in each of the four types are five in number, These factors or variables allow the researcher to distinguish among the types of interaction in bloc policy processes:

a) ideologies and social background characteristics of national leaderships: a structural dimension in the typology -- the continuum here would be from a homogeneous bloc elite to a heterogeneous leadership. (20)

b) levels of decision-making units involved in specific policy issues or areas at hand: a functional dimension in the typology --- the continuum here is from the highest organs of Party to lower levels in non-Party hierarchies involved functionally with the problems at hand. (21)

c) impact area of policy issue with respect to national political governmental and societal structures or sub-system components: a spatial dimension in the typology -- the continuum here would be from nation-wide impact for all members to sub-national impact. (22)

d) natural boundaries of bargaining imposed by relative power relationships among bloc members, aside from formally acknowledged special status: a relational dimension -- the continuum here would run from a preeminent role for country to the levelling off of all members' role in the policy process. (23)

e) nature of formalized, administrative rules associated with bloc organizations, or the particular regulatory machinery under auspices of which the policy is considered: a structural-functional dimension -- the continuum would start with explicit roles and functions and proceed to undefined situations. (24)

The details of this typology must be pursued in the application to real events in the bloc relations of the Soviet Union and Eastern Europe. The four types for present purposes will serve only to provoke discussion with respect to issues of concern among bloc participants. This model only proposes an approach by which further study of these relations may be taken in a more empirical, and thus more comparative, fashion. The superficial imposition of types to real events here in conclusion represents initiation of this approach, and not a refinement of the model as shown in Figure 1.1.

Consensus policy-making might imply a fairly homogeneous group of higher Party and state organ personnel, involving and affecting their hierarchies, following routine policy procedures, enjoying flexibility in their deliberations, and open to change on various issues at hand. Perhaps one could consider the bloc position with respect to the European Security Conferences as an example of this type of policy relationship. Overall indices of treaties and treaty-making could serve as the means of measurement in this category.

A second type, that of adaptive or more accurately accommodative policy-making, involves a decisional elite with differing orientations and experiences, composed of middle range yet important Party and state personnel, usually representing functional aspects of the issue and involved in real negotiation, with some pressures being applied in various areas, and whose decisions will in conclusion set the scene for a reasonable period of time. Bi-lateral and multi-lateral agreements on cultural relations or scientific cooperation could represent this type. The chapter on "Technical Coordination" in this study posits the thesis type of interaction as most salient in future bloc integration.

Integrative conflict involves actors with value conflicts, usually arising from special interests, having an impact in functional spheres within the political system but also including outside interests, and inducing conflict of a particular nature. The integrative aspect of this conflict comes into being when new areas of policy are opened up for discussion. The strain upon existing administrative structures is considerable, yet formality prevails and decisions within that context are likely to set patterns for the future. The ambivalence of this type may be presented by the policy concerns of CMEA and the role of Romania within that structure. Economic indices of interaction are the means to measurement of this type of policy relationship.

Disintegrative conflict evidences an antagonistic decisional unit, including lower level participation of various sub-national groupings, which confront an irreconcilable issue. The inflexibility of the rules of the game in this instance may often lead to disassociation by various members. The implications for the bloc policy are long range. The August Events in Prague and the Warsaw Pact structure could represent the type here. It is important to note that the experimental model of the Warsaw Pact invasion process, introduced in this example, allows empirical analysis to investigate the many questions concerning the bloc policy-making in that event. This author hesitates to accept the ready made explanations by some scholars that the invasion was purely a question of Soviet power politics. Though the Soviet role should be shown as significant, the wide-ranging and contradictory interpretations of this bloc foreign policy action in themselves lend credence to an approach more empirical in nature. Political-military-diplomatic indices are crucial in the estimation of this type of relationship.

The approach and inquiry of this study may simply evidence that much remains to be done bringing comparative Communist studies, the sub-field, into the more rigorous framework of the field of comparative political analysis:

> There appears to be two reasons for this failure:
> (1) there have been relatively few attempts to
> apply these 'modern trends' to the study of communist
> systems, and (2) many of those social scientists who
> have made the attempt can easily be indicted for having
> done 'bad science'. (25)

This study makes such an attempt. I can hardly hope to reverse Professor Fleron's attitude on the second point. (26)

The ongoing process of comparative research in the social sciences involves both inductive and deductive reasoning. Theoretical orientations and conceptual schemes provide initial suggestions as to what type of data to collect. Such ways of approaching the political world do not always constitute a precise model, specifying exact or even probablistic relationships between clearly conceptualized and operationalized variables, nor are they often precide enough to enable the deduction of specific hypotheses. But by analyzing the data collected through suggestion by a conceptual scheme can serve as a basis for inductive reasoning, the results of which is a more precise model. More specific hypotheses may then be deduced and tested. Though no multivariate scheme can ever be a substitute for systematic theoretical work, it seems reasonable to suggest that any one may be employed in both the inductive and deductive phases of research. The model sketched in Figure 1.1 is put forth with that principle in mind.

Figure 1.1 illustrates the key features of the model. Policy determinants are seen as "funneled" into the policy-making or "conversion" portion according to degree of significance. (27) In other words a general indication of variable importance in socialist foreign policy is implied in the proximity of the four sectors to the point of conversion. Thus elites and institutions are given greater weight than socio-economic variables, which in turn are considered more significant than historical-cultural variables (see the direction of "concentration" as diagrammed in the model).

Nevertheless it is also recognized in various sector relation-ships that certain issues might reorder the salience of specific variables in determining policy on those issues. Therefore, not only cumulative or incremental building up of influences on policy may take place, but some key historical events or ethnic diversities may directly limit or expand the range of issues determined as policy relevant. The model also attempts to provide for a horizontal view of the multi-variate process in a single Party-state, while at the same time providing a vertical view of cross-national comparison on a single dimension.

Again emphasizing that Figure 1.1 presents a preliminary diagram of the model, useful only for hypothesis generation and not theory building, emphasis is next given to the effect "projected" by the nature of policy determinants. (28) The specific independent/ dependent relationships of variables in the conversion sector are not insignificant, but simply not a matter of concern here. Testing of hypotheses related to policy input and output of an organization such as CMEA, for instance, involve matters not within the scope of our discussion though obviously of central concern in any full explication of policy-making in the Soviet/East European sub-system. More simply put the model sketched in Figure 1.1 outlines the conditions and consequences of such policy-making.

Types of relationships (or consequences), rather than specific policy outputs, are stressed on the projector side of the model since the bloc or sub-system impact is the concern of the model. Individual or Party-state position in that typology will vary accordingly with the issues involved. Vertically viewed, one may discern the bloc-wide impact of a single issue.

On this projector side of the model, the types of relationships become progressively "polycentric" as sectors move away from the point of conversion (see the direction of "diffusion" as diagrammed). The open-endedness of the funnel and projector visually depict the feedback dynamics of any system-oriented model. For example a disintegrative relationship could result in an event which finds its way back into the model as a salient historical determinant of future bloc policy-making.

As a final caution, it should be outlined that the metaphorical uses of the funnel and projector should not be carried to the extreme. They aptly serve to focus our attention on those factors conditional and consequential to Soviet/East European bloc behavior, but cannot at this primitive stage serve as predictors of future political acts. The discussions and data in the chapters to follow might be viewed more systematically with the aid of the model, while certainly the model may be made more sensitive to the realities of Soviet/East European politics with the assistance of several authors.

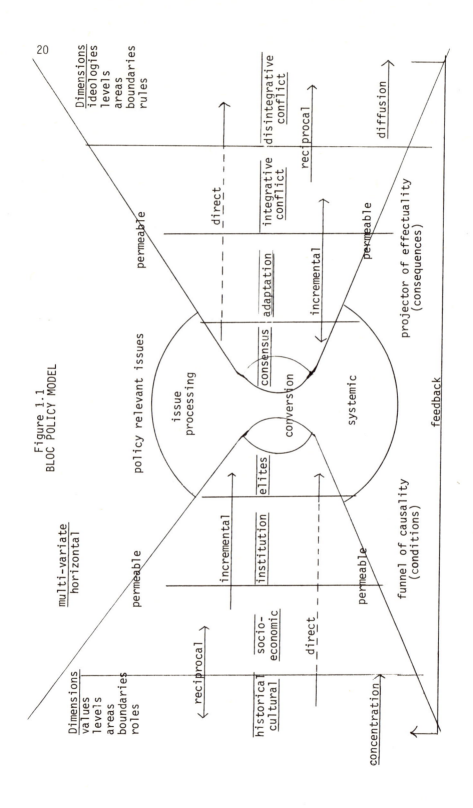

Figure 1.1
BLOC POLICY MODEL

NOTES

1. The parent field to comparative communist foreign policy has
   produced a massive amount of theoretical materials during recent
   years. One need only survey the major contributions to become
   bewildered at the working hypotheses yet to be tested in con-
   crete contexts. There is the theory of linkage found in
   James N. Rosenau, ed., *Domestic Sources of Foreign Policy* (New
   York: The Free Press, 1967), 340 pages; and in *Linkage Politics:
   Essays on the Convergence of National and International Systems*
   (New York: The Free Press, 1969), 352 pages. The factors for
   effectiveness are stressed in F.S. Northedge, ed., *The Foreign
   Policies of the Powers* (New York: Frederick A. Praeger,
   Publishers, 1969), 299 pages. The central theme of Western and
   Non-Western modes of foreign relations is found in Joel Larus,
   ed., *Comparative World Politics:Readings in Western and Pre-
   modern Non-Western International Relations* (Belmont, California:
   Wadsworth Publishing Company, Inc., 1964), 274 pages. The
   Western democratic patterns of foreign policy are discussed in
   Kenneth N. Waltz, *Foreign Policy and Democratic Politics, The
   American and British Experience* (Boston: Little, Brown and
   Company, 1967), 331 pages. One of the most innovative attempts
   at a systematic framework for comparative foreign policy
   analysis is David O. Wilkenson, *Comparative Foreign Relations:
   Framework and Methods* (Belmont, California: Dickenson Publishing
   Company, Inc., 1969), 191 pages. For an overview of competitive
   approaches to foreign policy analysis see Harold Karan Jacobson
   and William Zimmerman, eds., *The Shaping of Foreign Policy*
   (New York: Atherton Press, 1969), 214 pages.

2. See P. Terry Hopmann, "International Conflict and Cohesion in
   the Communist System", *International Studies Quarterly*, 11, 3
   (September, 1967), pages 212-36, for empirical justification of
   this unit. See also a theoretical discussion of the utility of
   this approach in Thomas W. Robinson, "Systems Theory and the
   Communist System", *International Studies Quarterly*, 13, 4
   (December, 1969), pages 398-420.

3. See William A. Welsh, "The Usefulness of the Apter, Easton,
   and Spiro Models in the Study of Communist Systems in Eastern
   Europe", *Newsletter on Comparative Studies of Communism*, V. 4
   (August, 1972), pages 3-20.

4. See Michael P. Gehlen, "The Integrative Process in Eastern
   Europe: A Theoretical Framework", *Journal of Politics*, 30, 1
   (February, 1968), pages 90-114.

5. The general field of comparative communist studies has produced
   a series of studies far too numerous for mention here. Witness
   to the progress of this new sub-field of comparative politics

are the *Newsletter on Comparative Studies of Communism* (sponsored)
by the Planning Group on Comparative Communist Studies of the
American Council of Learned Societies and edited by Frederic
J. Fleron, Jr., of the State University of New York at Buffalo)
and the quarterly *Studies in Comparative Communism, An Inter-
disciplinary Journal* (published for the School of Politics and
International Relations of the University of Southern California).
An excellent review of the recent literature may be found in
Paul Shoup, "Comparing Communist Nations: Prospects for an
Empirical Approach", *American Political Science Review*, LXII,
1 (March, 1968), pages 185-205.

6. The empirical approach to area studies in the comparative communist field must be approached with caution. For an understanding yet critical appraisal of this empirical thrust see the
review of Frederic J. Fleron, Jr., ed., *Communist Studies and
the Social Sciences* (Chicago: Rank McNally & Company, 1969),
481 pages, by Frederick C. Barghoorn in *Slavic Review*, 29, 3
(September, 1970), pages 539-42.

7. A traditional approach in this former category is represented
by Kurt L. London, *The Making of Foreign Policy: East and West*
(Philadelphia: J.B. Lippincott Company, 1965) 358 pages, while
a more recent, empirical attempt may be found in R. Barry
Farrell, "Foreign Policy Formation in the Communist Countries
of Eastern Europe", *East European Quarterly*, 2, 1 (March, 1967),
pages 39-74. With respect to the latter category see the standard work by Zbigniew K. Brzezinski, *The Soviet Bloc:Unity and
Conflict* (New York: Frederick A. Prager, Publishers, revised
edition, 1965), 470 pages. Several empirical approaches for
this category may be found in Jan F. Triska, ed., *Communist
Party-States:Comparative and International Studies* (Indianapolis:
Bobbs-Merrill Company, Inc., 1969), 392 pages. Two additional
studies have appeared on international relations of communist
states, one by Robert H. McNeal, ed., *International Relations
Among Communists* (Englewood Cliffs, New Jersey: Prentics-Hall,
Inc., 1967), 191 pages; and the other by Nish Jamgotch, Jr.,
*Soviet-East European Dialogue:International Relations of a
New Type?* (Stanford: Hoover Institution on War, Revolution
and Peace, 1968), 165 pages.

8. For an attempt to bring countries outside the bloc into analytic
perspective of the international unity implied by the Soviet
bloc, see David Ronfeldt and Daniel Tretiak, "Cuba's Integration
into the World Communist System, 1962-1966: A Preliminary
Assessment" in Triska, op. cit., pages 189-216. Along these
lines see also the articles stressing integration processes
among party states by Robert C. North, "On Integration: Some
Pre-theoretical Observations", pages xvii-xxxv; David O. Finley,
"Integration Among the Communist Party States: Comparative Case

Studies", pages 57-81; and Edward L. Miles with John S.
Gillooly, "Processes of Integration Among the Fourteen Communist
Party States: An Exploratory Essay", pages 106-135.

9. See R. Judson Mitchell, "A Theoretical Approach to the Study
   of Communist International Organizations" in Triska, op. cit.,
   pages 81-106, wherein an attempt is made to lay an empirical
   foundation for predicting communist international goal realization, behavior of the organizer and other units in making strategic choices, rate of integration, changes in allocation of
   resources and functions, changes in distribution of economic
   and political power within the coalitions, and response by the
   organizations to major changes outside the sub-system. For
   thorough discussion of the concepts regionalism and alliance,
   respectively, see Louis J. Cantori and Steven L. Spiegel, eds.,
   The International Politics of Regions: A Comparative Approach
   (Englewood Cliffs, New Jersey: Prentice-Hall, Inc., 1970),
   432 pages; and Julian R. Friedman, Christopher Bladen and
   Steven Rosen, eds., *Alliance in International Politics* (Boston:
   Allyn and Bacon, Inc., 1970), 383 pages.

10. McNeal, op. cit., p. 175.

11. Jamgotch, Jr., op. cit., p. 128.

12. See Jamgotch, Jr., op. cit., p. 128: "The impossibility of
    reconciling communism in one country with existing doctrine
    need not prevent concerted Soviet efforts toward establishing
    communism in one bloc or subsystem, a goal which is at least
    plausible and perhaps attainable, but by no means inevitable."

13. Jamgotch, Jr., op. cit., p. 129.

14. For a clear and concise explication of the process of typifica-
    tion and structural-functional aspects of typologies, see John
    T. Doby, ed., *An Introduction to Social Research* (New York:
    Appleton-Century-Crofts, second edition, 1967), chapters by
    John C. McKinney on "Constructive Typology: Explication of a
    Procedure", pages 213-30; and on "Constructive Typology:
    Structure and Function", pages 230-44.

15. McKinney in Doby, op. cit., p. 217.

16. Both the hegemonic and consensus types are put forth as models
    for entire historical periods in bloc development in a recent
    article by Vernon V. Aspaturian, "Patterns of Variation in
    Foreign Policies of Communist States", delivered to the Sixty-
    sixth Annual Meeting of the American Political Science Associa-
    tion, September 8-12, 1970. Aspaturian applies his consensus
    model to bloc relations during the period 1956-1968. While this

classification may serve to organize bloc development in general during those years, as presented in this study, the type includes several variables that would preclude the use of that type alone for such duration.

17. See James N. Rosenau, "Foreign Policy as Adaptive Behavior: Some Preliminary Notes for a Theoretical Model", *Comparative Politics*, 2, 3 (April, 1970), pages 365-89.

18. See Robert C. North, Howard E. Koch, Jr., and Dina A. Zinnes, "The Integrative Functions of Conflict", *Journal of Conflict Resolution*, IV, 3 (September, 1960), pages 355-74.

19. See Michael P. Gehlen, "The Integrative Process in East Europe: A Theoretical Framework", *Journal of Politics*, 30, 1 (February, 1968), pages 90-113. Integration in the Soviet bloc is constructed as a process of regulation and thereby denotes the necessity for an integrative/disintegrative continuum in relationships.

20. Such empirical data may be collected as found in R. Barry Farrell, ed., *Political Leadership in Eastern Europe and the Soviet Union* (Chicago: Aldine Publishing Company, 1970), 359 pages.

21. See H. Gordon Skilling, "Interest Groups and Communist Politics", *World Politics*, XVIII, 3 (April, 1966), pages 435-52. Also see his "Leadership and Group Conflict in Czechoslovakia" in Farrell, op. cit., pages 276-94.

22. See Lloyd Jordan, "Scientific and Technical Relations Among Eastern European Communist Countries", *Minerva*, VIII, 3 (July, 1970), pages 376-95.

23. See Thomas W. Wolfe, *Soviet Power and Europe, 1945-1970* (Baltimore: The John Hopkins Press, 1970), 534 pages.

24. Two of the most helpful studies with respect to this set of variables are Kazimierz Grzybowski, *The Socialist Commonwealth of Nations: Organizations and Institutions* (New Haven: Yale University Press, 1964), 300 pages; and Michael Kaser, *Comecon: Integration Problems of the Planned Economies* (London: Oxford University Press, second edition, 1967), 279 pages.

25. Frederic J. Fleron, Jr., "Soviet Area Studies and the Social Sciences: Some Methodological Problems in Communist Studies", *Soviet Studies*, XIX, 3 (January, 1968), pages 313-39.

26. Recent articles on the state of comparative communist studies and methodological underdevelopment in this field are John A.

Armstrong, "Comparative Politics and Communist Systems: Introductory Remarks"; Alfred G. Meyer, "The Comparative Study of
Communist Political Systems"; John H. Kausky, "Communism and
the Comparative Study of Development"; Dan N. Jacobs, "Area
Studies and Communist Systems"; and Robert S. Sharlet, "Systematic Political Sciences and Communist Systems", a symposium in
Slavic Review, XXVI, 1 (March, 1967), pages 1-29; Alex Inkeles,
"Models and Issues in the Analysis of Soviet Society", *Survey*,
60 (July, 1966), pages 3-18; Robert S. Sharlet, "Concept Forma-
tion in Political Science and Communist Studies", *Canadian
Slavic Studies*, I, 4 (Winter, 1967); and Robert C. Tucker, "On
the Comparative Study of Communism", *World Politics*, XIX, 2
(January, 1967), pages 242-58.

27. Special mention must be made here of the entire field of compar-
    ative policy analysis in the American states as found in the
    writings of Thomas R. Dye, Richard I. Hofferbert and Ira
    Sharkansky, among others. "The funnel of causality" utilized
    in this model is based upon the original conceptualization pro-
    vided by Angus Campbell, Philip E. Converse, Warren E. Miller
    and Donald E. Stokes in their *The American Voter* (New York:
    John Wiley & Sons, Inc., 1960). In particular the discussion
    throughout this introduction of the relationships among sectors
    in the funnel must give credit to the work of Hofferbert and
    his "Elite Influence in Policy Formation: A Model for Compara-
    tive Inquiry" delivered to the American Political Science Asso-
    ciation Annual Convention, Washington, D.C., September 2-7,
    1968. To this author's knowledge, the projector of effectuality
    as a completion of the policy-making model is wholly his own
    and reflects that obvious deficiency.

28. Perhaps "pre-theory" in Rosenau's meaning of the term found in
    James N. Rosenau, "Pre-theories and Theories of Foreign Policy"
    in R. Barry Farrell, ed., *Approaches to Comparative and Inter-
    national Politics* (Evanston, Illinois: Northwestern University
    Press, 1966), pages 27-92.

Chapter II

SOVIET FOREIGN POLICY PERSPECTIVES

Nish Jamgotch, Jr.*

To understand the politics of Eastern Europe one must first know Soviet foreign policy. Having determined very early after World War II that Eastern Europe must have Marxist-Leninist public order systems patterned closely on the Soviet model, Stalin and his successors arrogated to themselves the right to intrude in all Eastern European affairs even remotely touching upon communist security -- both regime and territorial. Through highly diversified policies, often belatedly justified by doctrinal elaborations, Soviet leaders proved that no international system of states since World War II has been more forcefully and continuously influenced by the conspicuous intervention and manipulation of superpower. Surprisingly, so innured has the world become to Soviet interventionism in Eastern Europe that even blatant political pressures and military coercion are widely regarded as commonplace, unavoidable, and legitimate within the contemporary understandings of power politics.

Historically strategic to the defense of the USSR, Eastern Europe by the mid-fifties had acquired even greater significance in terms of four closely related Soviet priorities: 1) the ideological commitment to the realization of Marxism-Leninism on an international plane; 2) the military pledge to regard any threat to a Warsaw Pact signatory a threat to the Soviet Union itself; 3) the Soviet Union's need to protect its great-power status and the future of its socio-economic system maturing at home, but only in somewhat earlier stages in Eastern Europe; and 4) international organizations for concerted political and economic integration designed to prepare the way for a "simultaneous entry into communism within one and the same historical epoch" with, of course, special doctrinal allowances for the admittedly nebulous character of this process.

The purpose of this study is to review the perspective from which

Soviet foreign policy toward Eastern Europe is best examined. The objective is to show that the continuous development of the above priorities has necessitated a reordering of Soviet foreign policies and the elaboration of explanatory Marxist-Leninist categories collectively called "international relations of a new type". The truth is that the expression "international relations of a new type" really signifies the failure to unify world-wide communism and make of it a global system subservient to Soviet interests. This has elevated the importance of the Eastern European sector of the international communist system of fourteen ruling-party states, making it a highly specialized communist sub-system, a Soviet core interest, and the only area of the world which has been consistently rendered pliant for essential security objectives. A related idea is that the Soviet Union's security effort is not only global and widely diversified, but also increasingly pressed to devise East European policies according to a variety of challenges in Asia.

International Relations of a New Type

The idea of international relations of a new type, i.e. among socialist states as distinct from ordinary relations among bourgeois states, was officially expressed in the Soviet Union's *Diplomatic Dictionary* in 1960. The importance of the idea warrants a rather full quotation.

The new type of diplomatic relations is free of antagonism based on the principle of proletarian international-ism and brotherly cooperation in the name of common objectives, i.e. complete respect for sovereign rights and the national interests of each socialist country. At a time when the political relations among the capitalist countries even allied by treaty are marked by antagonistic competition and rivalry (if not attempts to gain hegemony by one over the other), the political relations among the socialist countries exclude such antagonisms and establish relations of friendship and close brotherly mutual coop-eration on the basis of equality.

To maintain such relations, socialist countries employ new methods of constructive activity which facilitate unity and the coordination of measures for defense and general peace. The methods of socialist diplomacy employed in the mutual relations among socialist countries sponta-neously develop into organizational forms and joint efforts of united free peoples throughout the world who are for the general principles of building communism and preserving world peace. (1)

Analyzed further in 1964 by two Soviet specialists in world affairs, the foreign policies of Marxist-Leninist states were said to be characterized by : 1) political cooperation firmly based upon

Marxism-Leninism with its objective laws for both international
and domestic development; 2) maintenance of individual national
independence and sovereignty; 3) sincerity and honesty, rooted
in the power of socialism; 4) solidarity of socialist countries,
which serves the interests of all peaceful peoples by restraining
aggressive circles and maintaining the forces for peace; and
5) recognition of the Soviet Union's definitive role in the peace
efforts of our time. (2)

In reality these statements are samples of a highly utopian
theory purporting to show that multi-lateral relations -- economic,
political, ideological, cultural, and international-legal -- among
the fourteen communist party states are conducted on an ethically
exaulted plane based on uncommon mutual trust, deference, and
obligations. It is not without purpose that frequent official
testimonials emphasize socialist internationalism, respect for
individual national sovereignty, and agreements founded upon
friendship and cooperation, despite abundant evidence that such
values have little operational significance in Eastern Europe's
foreign policies at all. It is, however, in the nature of aging
Marxist-Leninist movements that as they becomes less radical and
more willing to revise revolutionary success. (3) It is also true
that as communist ideology becomes less activist and more historical, its hortatory function is gradually superceded by the imperative to preserve and extend a mythology to which communist
ideologues cling tenasiously, not because they believe in it un-
reservedly but because myths die hard and it is always extremely
difficult to discard ideas to which years of dedication and
loyalty have been given.

In practice international relations of a new type actually en-
compass at least five distinct political phenomena prominent in
Soviet-Eastern European relations in the past decade -- none of
them anticipated or deliberately planned, all of them contrary to
original Marxist-Leninist tenets, and all of them underscoring the
indispensability of Eastern Europe for Soviet political, ideological, and military purposes. Each of the following constitutes a
realistic perspective from which Soviet foreign-policy formulators
view Eastern Europe's relevance to Soviet security interests.

First, the idea of international relations of a new type is a
patent admission that worldwide communism as envisioned by Marx
and Lenin is a vain hope. The East European states of the Council
for Mutual Economic Cooperation (CMEA) and the Warsaw Treaty Organization (WTO) constitute the only genuine context for the realization of international communism on any level subject to the leadership of the Soviet Union. The result is an ongoing subsystem of
highly specialized exchanges and interdependence based on shared
political origins of Eastern Europe's ruling communist party states,
excepting of course Yugoslavia and Albania which for special historical, geographical, and political reasons continue to operate
outside the mainstream of East European politics dominated by the
Soviet Union. The essential countries are Poland, Czechoslovakia,

Hungary, Romania, Bulgaria, and the GDR. Even though more limited
in geographical scope, the example of this East European subsystem
is proof that continuous efforts toward international communism
are apparently viable, doctrinally sound, and realizable. The
orientation in this first perspective is dictated by the practical
realities of a more limited operational scope for Communist activities under Soviet influence. Such activities are characterized by
excessive ideological verbage and ostentatious demonstrations of
unity which, however exaggerated or unrealistic, nevertheless
satisfy the need for collective expressions stressing the international commitments of the CPSU and the most loyal East European
communist parties.

It is especially difficult for non-communists to understand
that as an ideologically oriented great power and the first Marxist-
Leninist state, the USSR is unusually dependent upon its political
transplants in Eastern Europe. Frequent crossnational exchanges
among government and party personnel, coupled with appropriate
doctrinal interpretations, function to preserve something of the
weathered and fragmented political faith in international communism. Granted that Soviet hopes may be far too ambitious and
visionary in their commitment to the highest form of Marxist-
Leninist relationships as yet unrealized; the fact remains that
it is precisely this Soviet vision that constitutes much of the
foundation of an operational East European communist subsystem
with a unifying raison d'etre of its own. Of course, the Soviet
Union has become unusually dependent upon its political fulfillment
but also as periodic confrontations with Chinese communism neces-
sitate reliable allies plus frontier peace and security in Europe.

Second, from a strictly theoretical viewpoint, international
relations of a new type mark a transitional historical era in
which a number of socialist states are presumably laboring to
enter communism more or less simultaneously. The idea of a
simultaneous entrance into communism was originally expressed by
Nikita Khrushchev whose view it was that true communism is an
international condition of the future to be realized through
increasing social, economic, and political cooperation, including
eventual economic equalization and abundance. Phrased in Khrushchev's inimitable style:

Comrades, we are working hand in hand with you to build
communism. The Soviet people will come to communism together with you, the working people of Hungary. It is out
of the question that we, Communists and internationalists
of the Soviet Union, the first to seize power and to
engage in the great cause of communist construction,
should come to communism alone, and, to use a figure of
speech, should eat ham every day while the rest look on
and lick their chops. That would be wrong.

Where would the proletarian solidarity, the internationalism, of that socialist country be then? The country
with the more developed economy, capable of raising the

living standard of its people still higher, must by all
means help the other socialist countries to level out with
time. All the countries will rise to the level of the foremost ones, which are also not going to mark time. We must
enter the Communist world all together. (4)

Since Khrushchev's ouster in 1964 there has been considerable
speculation about revisions in Soviet policy toward Eastern Europe.
There is as yet no evidence that either the theoretical or practical commitments to the entry into communism have been officially
abandoned. Such a decision of course would signal the end of the
international communist system as we know it. The idea of more-or-
less simultaneous entry appears permanent, for it is crucial not
only to the internationalist pretensions of the CPSU but more
particularly to the continued legitimacy of individual East
European communist parties as well. Having evolved beyond socialism
in one country, Marxism-Leninism is required to explain the existence of four socialist countries (USSR, Czechoslovakia, Yugoslavia,
and Romania) plus ten states in lesser stages of economic and
political development, all ostensibly experiencing a higher order
of relationships, but necessarily short of ultimate fulfillment on
an international level. Thus, in this second perspective international relations of a new type are interim and transitional,
emphasizing the international communist system's current place in
an extended historical continuum between communist revolution in
one country (1917) and its highest political, economic, and social
operation in two or more countries, yet to be realized.

Third, if one views the whole history of Soviet policy toward
Eastern Europe, international relations of a new type signify a
doctrinal accommodation to polycentric communism and the ideologically unaccounted for challenges to the Soviet Union's capacity
to control absolutely the international communist movement.
Decisive watersheds in this evolution would include Tito's successful bolt in 1948, the Polish and Hungarian bids for greater independence in the fall of 1956, markedly independent Albanian and
Romanian diplomacy since 1961, and the growth of self-sufficient,
self-assertive communism in the People's Republic of China,
seriously challenging the Soviet Union's ideological legitimacy and
leadership. The resultant relations have included greater diversity
among communist states, limited domestic independence, more fluid
international alignments and alliance mobility, varying degrees
of destalinization designed to humanize communism, and a modicum
of self-imposed restraints on excessive Soviet intrusions in
Eastern European affairs. The ideological underpinnings for these
developments were outlined by Nikita Khrushchev at the 20th Party
Congress in 1956 when he accomplished a theoretical adjustment to
fact and spoke approvingly of many paths to socialism.

Fourth, ever since the late 1950s, the Soviets have tried to
cope with the dynamics of a genuinely operative East European
subsystem by stressing problem solving through integration and
functional international organizations. Activity has been dominated

by commitments to coordinate and integrate defense planning and command and also to industrialize and modernize lagging economies in some cases in accordance with rational cost-prize indices, modern marketing techniques, more efficient economic management, and personnel and wage policies long prevalent in capitalist economics. In this sense, international relations of a new type mean rational and pragmatic international organizational under-takings, based on CMEA and WTO, emphasizing the largest volume of multi-lateral exchanges in the international communist system, considerable institutional flexibility, and individual participation based more or less on national self-interest.

Fifth, international relations of a new type can signify the military dimension of the Soviet Union's keenly felt international-ist duty which culminated in the unprecedented Brezhnec Doctrine of November 12, 1968. This is not to say that the policy is new, for the Soviets have in practice since the early 1950s had an implicit policy of maintaining their hegemony in Eastern Europe by military force when necessary. Harkening back to at least the time of the Hungarian Revolution, this developing commitment has been expressed as follows:

Comrades! Believe me, the decision was difficult, but we could not stand by indifferently when brazen fascist elements began to brutally attack workers, peasants, Communists and other fine representatives of the Hungarian working people . . . when the counter-revolution tried to drown the socialist gains of the Hungarian people in the blood of the people . . .

In giving aid to the Hungarian people in routing the forces of counter-revolution, we fulfilled our international duty. (5)

Today the whole world has had an opportunity to be assured that anyone who dares to encroach upon the inviolability of the Soviet Union's borders as well as those of other socialist countries, will receive a crushing rebuff. The Warsaw Treaty Organization is based on the principle of all for one and one for all. The Soviet government has frequently stated that the borders of all its true friends -- the socialist countries -- will be defended by the Soviet Union exactly as if they were its own borders. This is how we under-stand proletarian internationalism, and this is how all the peoples of the socialist countries understand it. (6)

. . . An atmosphere was created that was absolutely unacceptable to the socialist countries. In this situation it was necessary to act, and act purposefully and resolutely, without losing time. It was precisely for this reason that the Soviet Union and other socialist states decided to satisfy the request by the C.S.R. party and state figures to render the fraternal Czechoslovak people urgent assistance, including assistance with armed forces.

The defense of socialism in Czechoslovakia is not only the internal affair of that country's people but also a problem of defending the positions of world socialism. It is for this reason that we are rendering support to the peoples of Czechoslovakia in defense of the gains of socialism. In giving fraternal internationalist support to our Czechoslavak Communist comrades and the entire Czechoslovak people, we are discharging our internationalist duty to them and to the international Communist workers' and national-liberation movement. For us this duty is the highest of all. (7)

There is no doubt that the peoples of the socialist countries and the Communist Parties have and must have freedom to determine their country's path of development. However, any decision of theirs must damage neither socialism in their own country nor the fundamental interests of the other socialist countries nor the worldwide workers' movement, which is waging a struggle for socialism. This means that every Communist Party is responsible not only to its own people but also to all the socialist countries and to the entire Communist movement. Whoever forgets this in placing sole emphasis on the autonomy and independence of Communist Parties lapses into one-sidedness, shirking his internationalist obligations.

The Communists of the fraternal countries naturally could not allow the socialist states to remain idle in the name of abstract sovereignty while the country (Czechoslovakia) was endangered by antisocialist degeneration. (8)

One of the most authoritative Soviet scholars in the field of foreign policy has offered the following analysis deriving from Leninist sources:

The Socialist countries base their relations on principles of complete equality, respect for territorial integrity, state independence and sovereignty and non-interference in one another's affairs. *These are vital principles. However, they do not exhaust the essence of relations between them. Fraternal mutual aid is part and parcel of these relations. This aid is a striking expression of Socialist internationalism.*

In a definition of the tasks facing the Comintern in developing international relations of a Socialist type, Lenin wrote: "The Communist international policy in the sphere of relations within the state *cannot be restricted to the bare, formal, purely declaratory and actually noncommittal recognition of the equality of nations to which the bourgeois democrate confine themselves -- both those who frankly admit being such and those who assume the*

34

name of Socialists. This means that in defining policy
in relations between nations, between states, Marxist-
Leninist parties are guided above all by the class interests of the working people, the task of preserving
revolutionary gains and strengthening Socialism. "Which
should be put first, the right of nations to self-
determination, or Socialism?" Lenin asked and right
there replied: "Socialism should." (9)
Several times in the 1950s and 60s -- most dramatically in
Hungary in 1956 and in Czechoslovakia in 1968 -- Soviet armies
were called upon to temper or reverse the course of national
particularism, liberalization, and democratization in some of
Eastern Europe's Marxist-Leninist regimes. It was, however, in
the specifically military applications of the Soviet Union's
"internationalist duty" in Czechoslovakia plus an explicit
theoretical follow-up in the Brezhnev Doctrine that something unprecedented was added. The new emphasis was overwhelmingly military, interventionist, retaliatory, and punitive, and then linked
to a widely publicized Soviet policy legitimizing intervention by
Marxist-Leninist states in one another's domestic affairs if
dangers of anti-socialist degeneration are perceived. In this fifth
sense, international relations of a new type are genuinely new and
worth of close attention because they are underpinned by a theoretical elaboration explicitly restricting the doctrine of "many
paths to communism" dating from the 20th Congress of the CPSU, 1956.

Peking, Prague, and Soviet Security -- the Broader View

It is perhaps because of the Soviet Union's intense historical
preoccupation with East European security that the widely reported
large-scale military encounters with the Chinese in early 1969
came as such a surprise. At least one result of the openly publicized campaigns in the Far East was the reminder that the Soviet-
Chinese frontier is the world's longest and that the Soviet Union
whatever its size and wealth, will always be stretched between
two very formidable power centers -- West European and East Asian.
Kremlin policies toward Eastern Europe and Asia have been developed to enhance Soviet territorial and regime security and simultaneously shore up unity in the East European system by stressing:
1) the unacceptable consequences of the 1968 reformist ploys in
Czechoslovakia, and by implication for the future in the rest of
Eastern Europe as well; 2) the Marxist-Leninist duty to close ranks
behind a fraternal Southeast Asian ally waging a war of national
liberation; 3) the reckless deviationist activities of China's
Maoist leadership, thus necessitating greater solidarity among the
Soviet Union's most loyal allies; and 4) the attack by an outside
power (probably China) -- a responsibility specifically built into
the Treaty of Friendship, Cooperation, and Mutual Aid Between the
USSR and the Czechoslovak Socialist Republic, signed May 6, 1970.

It is as if the old fear of simultaneously facing enemies in the
East and West has been rejuvenated from the historical Russian
subconscious. One historian has highlighted the demographic and
cultural dimensions of persistent Soviet wariness as follows:

> In ways that foreigners can hardly appreciate, Russians
> fear the threats they see developing simultaneously from
> an ideologically resurgent China and an economically re-
> surgent Western Europe -- both regions confronting Russia
> with a cultural self-confidence which she envies and po-
> tential population pressures that she fears. (10)

Especially since the mid-sixties, tense relations and military
clashes with Peking along the Sinkiang-Kazak frontier and at the
Ussuri River, plus political and military threats in Europe owing
to the 1967-68 program of liberalization in Czechoslovakia, required that the Soviets devise mutually reinforcing policies which
haveon balance been highly productive investments. Not the least
of these has been the carefully measured pipeline of aid to the
Democratic Republic of Vietnam, the result of which has been to
sustain the Soviet Union's responsibility to a fraternal communist
ally, divert U.S. attention from Europe, and force Peking to stand
alert for a possible confrontation with U.S. troops in Southeast
Asia, thereby presumably dampening her ardor for pursuits along
the Siberian frontier. The success of such a policy depended upon
a reversal of the Soviet Union's general attitude of aloofness
toward general developments in Southeast Asia. However, as relations with China progressively worsened and the scope and intensity of the U.S. presence escalated, Soviet diplomatic activity and
aid, both economic and military, to the D.R.V. grew unmistakably.
For the post-Khrushchev leadership, the period initiated by the
U.S. bombing of North Vietnam in February 1965 and continuing
into 1966, posed the most crucial decisions for an appropriate
Asian policy toward the United States and China.

Far more significant is the point that despite predictions that
expansive American military action in Vietnam would precipitate a
closing of ranks among dissident Marxist-Leninist allies and even
restore monolithism to the communist camp, (11) quite the opposite
took place. The stance of the D.R.V. against the world's foremost
superpower took place against a background of mutual recriminations
between the USSR and China regarding such matter as insufficient
military aid, deliberately obstructed overland supply routes
through China, and unconscionable sellouts in collusion with U.S.
imperialism. Without demeaning nationalist and doctrinal rivalries,
or entering into the merits of whether the acrimony has been more
a consequence than a cause of embittered Sino-Soviet relations,
it is at least safe to say that too little scholarly attention has
been devoted to the paradox that the Vietnam imbroglio actually
inflamed the rift at all. (12)

The war's exact impact on the Chinese order of battle and domestic troop deployments may never be known. It is, however, undeniable
that the proximity of around a half million American troops and

billions of dollars in military plant and equipment, including
supersonic jets, at the very least necessitated extreme caution
in Peking, although its characteristically exaggerated vocabulary
suggested otherwise. Aside from spreading, diverting, and attracting China's military forces, the U.S. presence highlighted the em-
barrassingly small Chinese support relative to that of the USSR.
Doubtless in any final analysis of accusations regarding disloyalty
to the D.R.V., the Soviets would emerge far more respectably; for
it is they who delivered the lion's share of sophisticated military hardware, stealing Hanoi's capacity to carry on the war,
isolating Peking and giving the lie to its charges of Soviet high
treason against the communist world.

Focusing the klieg light of official condemnation on a multitude
of Mao Tse-tung's heresies, the Soviets have fueled an Asian war
of national liberation which is ideologically sound and simultaneously exploited its possibilities to show that the Chinese are
sabotaging communist unity and pursuing a reckless course fraught
with danger to proletarian and socialist internationalism. In
this important sense Hanoi's desperate military and economic
problems forced the communist giants to be hostages. Hanoi expected that if declarations of proletarian and socialist internationalism were to have any meaning, smaller ruling-party states
of the international Communist system must be protected against
territorial losses. Consequently, the decisibe credentials for
leadership in the communist world would naturally accrue to the
power which would do the most to defend the weaker members --
especially the D.R.V. besieged by communism's top-priority military and ideological enemy, the United States.

Of course, Soviet policy-makers know that even if the war in
Vietnam has failed to forge unity among all fourteen ruling-party
states, it has at least served as a focus of cohesion and a sorely
needed topic for expressions of resolve among the most significant
pro-Soviet allies within the strategically vital subsystem of
proximate Eastern Europe. Periodic CMEA and WTO conferences which
muster special words of praise and cooperative aid for the North
Vietnamese thereby help to keep the self-proclaimed internationalist role of the CPSU alive and purposeful, and that of the
other "loyal" parties as well.

Like the policy of checking China through sustained military
aid to the D.R.V., the Kremlin's decision to intervene in Czechoslovakia against the Dubcek-Cernik program of democratization
was clearly motivated by deep security concerns both with quite
different priorities and determinants; for if the reasons underlying aid to the D.R.V. were rooted in the need to enhance Soviet
ideological and political authority, and fix primary Chinese and
U.S. military attentions in Southeast Asia, the policy toward
Prague emanated from the belief that East European defenses and
the character of the Soviet Union's own Marxist-Leninist public
order system were being threatened by unrestrained political and
social experimentation in Czechoslovakia. Among the many factors

promoting the controversial decision to deploy the Soviet Army in August 1968, at least the following should be noted.

Military Security

Although a downgrading of Eastern Europe's military signifi-cance logically followed the revolutionary development of nuclear weaponry and the missile age, the Soviets nevertheless have since the mid-fifties considered the area a security priority comparable to the USSR itself. Contrary to popular conceptions, however, certain parts of Eastern Europe tend to be more sensitive than others. Accordingly, the locating of Czechoslovakia made its move toward selective independence potentially more dangerous than, say those of Romania, whose foreign and domestic policies, whatever their newsworthiness, did not pose a threat to either the terri-torial or regime security of the Soviet Union. Romania's common frontier with the USSR is not only very large, thus making access easier, but it is also situated on the southern flank of Eastern Europe -- not athwart the highly sensitive central region which Stalin once referred to as the corridors through which foreigners historically march to Russia. Czechoslovakia's location is far more strategic because it fronts both Germanies and bifurcates the whole of the Soviet Union's East European defenses. Obsessed by presumed West German schemes to subvert Czechoslovakia through diplomatic overtures and economic penetration, the Soviets re-sponded forcefully to forestall a chink in their defense system. Supporting this move, *Pravda* on August 27, 1968, made it clear that "the Soviet Union and Czechoslovakia (would) continue to deal a resolute rebuff to militarists, revanchists, and neo-Nazi forces seeking to revise the results of the second world war and to breach to inviolability of the border existing in Europe". (13)

Regime Security

Eastern Europe's indispensibility to the Soviet Union's strate-gic defense perimeter must also be viewed in the perspective of political requirements -- especially regime security. Obviously the communist "wave of the future" must never be permitted to recede in a client state, for this would cast serious doubt upon doctrinal predictions and undermine the leadership and legitimacy of the USSR's own exclusive Party. Thus a state once Marxist-Leninist and ruled by a Communist Party must not be permitted to become anything else. In this connection the reasons for a mili-tary commitment to the anti-liberal forces in Czechoslovakia in 1968 were remarkably similar to the crucial decision affecting Castro's Cuba in the fall, 1962, and the D.R.V. since the mid-sixties. Soviet doctrine is simply incapable of withstanding the disappearance of a Marxist-Leninist state behind a "neo-imperialist curtain".

Another factor relevant to regime security is that obviously
Walter Ulbricht's rule in the German Democratic Republic is not
interminable. If the Soviets wish to influence his succession
decisively, no proximate East European state can be permitted to
slip away and regularize freedoms inimical to the public order
system in the GDR. Such a development would not only energize
East German nationalism, but also jeopardize the Soviet Union's
bargaining position in an ultimate solution of the two-Germanies
question.

As the reforms in Czechoslovakia became more bold -- especially
freedom of press and the rumored multiplication of political
parties -- Soviet leaders were forced to ponder the ramifications
of tolerating democratic practices in a bordering East European
state but not at home. (Why, one may ask, should the Soviets
tolerate freedom of press in Prague when they do not tolerate it
in Moscow?) Unwilling to brave an expanding wave of nonconformity,
they acted in August 1968 to preempt further liberalization which
the euphoria of a pending Czech Party Congress and 50th anniversary celebration would most assuredly have sustained. Displeasure
with Professor Ota Sik's unorthodox economic views -- some of
which came close to capitalist principles -- reinforced all of
these developments in underpinning Foreign Minister Gromyko's
explanation to the United Nations General Assembly on October 3
that the Soviet Army's movement across the Czech frontier was an
internal matter and that the countries of the socialist commonwealth constitute . . .

an inseparable entity cemented by unbreakable ties,
the like of which history has never before known. The
socialist states cannot and will not allow a situation
where the vital interests of socialism are infringed
upon and encroachments are made on the inviolability
of the boundaries of the socialist commonwealth and,
therefore, on the foundation of international peace. (14)

This statement based on the now famous article by Kovalev in
Pravda, "Sovereignty and the Internationalist Obligations of
Socialist Countries", September 26, 1968, clearly undermined the
concept of sovereignty and Khrushchev's 1956 dispensation legitimizing many paths to socialism.

Timing

In the absence of hard evidence, one can only hypothesize that
two geographically far-removed developments in the early fall,
1968, made the Soviet Union's disciplinary intervention most
timely. This is not to minimize the crucial factors in Eastern
Europe and the intense Soviet-Czechoslovak dialogue itself. (15)
First, strong predictions of Republican victory in the United
States could not have but alerted the Soviets to mend political

fences in Eastern Europe in preparation for a potentially more militant U.S. foreign policy, perhaps harkening back to the most tense years of the Cold War. Certainly the Soviets wanted no fissures into which an invigorated Republican Administration might seek to drive a wedge; and in any case, it would be far preferable to negotiate with a new American president on large East-West questions and even the Middle East, assured that their East European preserve would remain reliable and orderly.

Second, the fall '68 prospects of liquidating the war in Vietnam suggested to the Soviets the danger of stepped-up Chinese probes along the Siberian frontier and possible renewed American vitality in Europe, thus pressaging a future of two pressing fronts and very demanding tests for Soviet diplomatic and military policies. Less fearful in the fall of 1968 of exposure to its two greatest enemies (the U.S. and China) directly or indirectly along two vulnerable frontiers, the Soviet Union succeeded in exploiting the continuing distraction of the Vietnam war to remove a highly unstable and unpredictable situation in Czechoslovakia. Soviet military pressures on Czechoslovakia were increased precisely when the threshold of risk was relatively low -- with form clued, however, that long delays might easily be met by increased risks.

At first the Soviets miscalculated in thinking that the liberal Dubcek-Cernik regime could be conveniently replaced by a subservient government. (None could be found.) But the ensuing dialogue forcing the Czechs to back down in the face of a juggernaut succeeded. Failing politically, the Soviets aimed for gains through military threats and finally managed to nullify the challenge to their security by translating overwhelming physical power into political pressure.

In retrospect the outcome is doubly instructive because President Johnson's expression on July 18, 1968, the Soviet armed intervention would imperil deliberations on nuclear arms control had little if any apparent restaining effect. Gromyko's U.N. message in the fall hinted that the Czech crisis and arms control need not be related, and since then discussions on a whole range of security issues have taken place as the crisis recedes into historical memory. It means that diplomatic rhetoric notwithstanding, disciplinary operations to guard the status quo in Eastern Europe need not significantly affect negotiations between the Soviet Union and the United States when it is clearly in their interest to have them. Signing the Nuclear Non-proliferation Treaty and the SALT talks in Vietnam were proof of this.

Competing with these measures of success in maintaining East European security is a wide range of costs and setbacks. Contrary to the Hungarian experience in 1956, pressure for liberalization and democratization came primarily from within the Czech Communist Part; and charges of counterrevolution in liason with imperialism, which had to be addressed to the Czechoslovak communists themselves, were lacking in credibility, to say the least. Furthermore, having superceded the doctrine of multiple paths to socialism, the

Brezhnev Doctrine really signaled that Soviet weapons may well be used again and that countless affirmations pledging respect for territorial sovereignty and noninterference in one another's internal affairs are a sham. As demonstrated in the June '69 World Conference and elsewhere, European communist unity received a sharp setback due to varying degrees of sympathy and support for the Czechs by the Romanians, Yugoslavs (who boycotted the Conference), the Hungarians, and the large French and Italian Communist Parties. That the Soviets initially incurred the resentment of some of Europe's staunchest and most prestigious communists was the costliest legacy of a security policy which understandably placed the Soviet Union's own welfare ahead of international communist unity.

Rumored prospects of a potentially strong NATO revival must also have weighed heavily in deliberations to intervene, and certainly Soviet military strategists had to be watchful for signs of renewed life and purpose. There are, however, a number of reservations about the utility of NATO in the face of selective Soviet surprises. How effective would the Alliance be in the event of an incursion into Berlin, Romania, or Yugoslavia? And what would the United States' response be? If the NATO powers were galvanized into a greater appreciation of the Soviet Union's East European presence, there are also lingering doubts about the American sense of balance after having been drawn into the Vietnam vortex at the expense of West European interests.

Few things alienate a people more quickly and profoundly than an invasion of their territory. If the Czechs, Moravians, and Slovaks had no burning issue before 1968, they now have one; and along with the Hungarians and Romanians, whose loyalties have traditionally been directed elsewhere, their strained submission provokes gnawing doubts about reliability in a future crisis, perhaps involving more than East European powers. Herein lies a genuine sleeper. Because the Czechs chose passive rather than active resistance, a whole generation of youthful leaders was not destroyed or lost in emigration as happened in Hungary in 1956. Presently this leadership is intact and perforce quite -- a reservoir of latent discontent and further challenge. There is little pertaining to Soviet foreign policy that should trouble the Kremlin more.

The Romanian Exception

Even though history will probably note that true Soviet policy toward Eastern Europe in the late sixties was characterized by the explicit Brezhnev Doctrine and punitive intervention against Czechoslovakia, the Romanian experience has exemplified an acceptable range of diplomatic independence, largely contingent upon the maintenance of certain domestic political requisites. At best Soviet attitudes have been tolerant of East European foreign policy

initiative if they appear to reinforce Soviet diplomacy and at
the very least if such initiative do not jeopardize the security
of the USSR (the Czech experience clearly violated this tenet)
and if local East European political developments continue to
reflect Marxist-Leninist orthodoxy. The difficult feat is to hit
precisely upon an acceptable mix of Marxist-Leninist continuity,
desirable changes in the name of national self-interest, and adequate respect for the Soviet Union's current assessment of foreign
policy priorities.

More than any other Eastern European nation contiguous to the
Soviet Union, Romania has demonstrated that its diplomatic initiatives, however nettlesome to Moscow, have not as of this writing
posed a security threat. At least since the summer of 1963 and the
initiation of her own industrialization campaign, Romania has
steadfastly insisted upon the practice -- not merely the theory --
of sovereign independence for all communist parties. Opposing
Soviet projects for supranational planning CMEA and all forms of
economic cooperation that might impinge on national sovereignty,
the Romanians have managed to maintain somewhat of a hybrid regime
-- quasi-Stalinist domestic political system, complied with an
exceptionally versatile and independent foreign policy.

Attracting the world's attention to brilliantly executive
foreign policy decisions, the Romanians have proved the persistence
of nationalist preference within the precarious limits of Soviet
toleration. The record includes deft maneuvers in the maintenance
of correct relations with the People's Republic of China, Albania,
and the more orthodox people's democracies; improvements in economic and cultural ties with Western Europe; the maintenance of
diplomatic relations with both Germanies; initiatives toward economic preferment with the United States, underscored by President
Nixon's visit to Bucharest in July 1969; and finally a firm but
apparently sensitive attitide toward the Soviet Union, highlighted
by considerable diplomatic sparring and numerous forthright declarations, culminating in the signing of the Friendship and
Mutual Aid pact in Bucharest on July 7, 1970.

It was hardly surprising that the pact's provisions reflected
the modus vivendi and accommodation so characteristic of Soviet-
Romanian relations since the early sixties. Although General
Secretary Brezhnev's absence at the signing showed Soviet displeasure and a refusal to grant the full international communist
friendship that such an event would normally warrant, Mr. Kosygin
did show considerable sensitivity for Romania's staunchly defended
principle of sovereignty and national independence.

Conspicuous for its contrast with the Soviet-Czechoslovak Treaty
of Friendship, Cooperation, and Mutual Aid signed two months
earlier, the Romanian version did not incorporate the following:
1) the Brezhnev Doctrine of limited sovereignty which gives
signatories the right to intervene in a Warsaw Pact country if
its communist system is deemed in danger; 2) provisions for the
further integration of CMEA economies (Article 2 merely says that

the parties will promote economic ties and cooperation within the framework of CMEA); and 3) the pledge to pursue a joint foreign policy. The two parties agreed to consult on important international questions with the objective of agreeing on their positions. This is considerably more lenient than the stringent Soviet-Czech treaty in which the parties agreed to pursue a foreign policy "from their common position agreed upon in the interests of both states". It should be noted that Article 8 of the Soviet-Romanian treaty provides that in the event of an attack against one of the parties by any state or group of states, the other will render it immediate support -- including military assistance. It is not explicit whether the Soviet Union expects this provision to be activated by an attack from China. Since Romania has steadfastly refused to be drawn into the Soviet quarrel with the Chinese, there were undoubtedly deep reservations about any such provision; which is probably why the treaty's preamble carries a specific geographical limitation by referring to Warsaw Pact commitments "in answer to the NATO threat".

In the past, at least five factors have weighed heavily in complicating decisive Soviet actions against Romania's independent foreign policy decisions: 1) a well-organized and unified Romanian communist party which, in an uncommonly smooth transition from the Gheorghiu-Dej to the Ceausescu leadership in the spring of 1965, demonstrates exceptional cohesion and self-confidence; 2) the continued potential for intrasystem diplomatic alignments due to Sino-Soviet conflicts and their currently uncertain future; 3) Yugoslavia's successful example which remains a model for all aspiring East European independents -- a model which the Soviets do not wish to see emulated; 4) the appearance of more activist diplomatic and economic policies from the West especially in the form of West Germany's initiatives toward general European detente; and 5) the consummate political skills of Ceausescu who from all indications is both highly popular in his country and firmly in command of its politics.

Whatever the newsworthiness of Romania's feats of national independence, she has in her own national way operated as a dedicated and relatively conservative Marxist-Leninist state within the framework of East European politics. The problem is not merely one of an independent stance or deviation from a Soviet position but rather precisely how far a deviation can go without eliciting Soviet reprisals. To be successful, the Romanians must keenly sense the limitations of nationalist bravado and the rational limits of their admittedly assertive and often demanding stance. So far, their political acumen and diplomatic agility have been superlative.

The Soviets for their part know that the stakes for East European security are very high. What is evident in their reactions to Romania's initiatives is a cautious attitude that the Romanians must not be pushed into reckless demonstrations of independence which the logic of international communist system developments

since Stalin have naturally allowed them. One must always recognize that from the outside, even measured dissidence within
the relatively closed East European subsystem invariably denotes
heresy and disintegration, while to those inside, expressions of
independence denote deep changes to be sure, but not necessarily
destructive ones. The pattern of East European interaction is
thereby more complicated and volatile, thus requiring greater
efforts toward accommodation and more sophisticated policies for
balancing particularistic interests in the name of collective
security and ultimate Marxist-Leninist fulfillment.

In contrast to Romania's decision-making record, Czechoslovak
policy in 1968 failed on a number of counts all crucial for their
challenge to the limits of Soviet toleration. Romania's surprisingly successful exchange of diplomatic representation with Bonn
in 1967 could not have but highlighted the direction of specific
national interests in Eastern Europe, thus hardening the Soviets
to any further breakthroughs toward Central European detente without their own leadership. In this sense Czechoslovak policy coming
so soon after the Romanian example erred because it seemed to reinforce an ominous trend and also served to upstage the Soviets
precisely when they were not yet prepared to undertake reconciliation with West Germany. Moreover, by moving directly toward Bonn,
the Czechs evaded and offended the Soviets, thereby inadvertently
strengthening Walter Ulbricht's charges of collusion and imminent
catastrophy. In contrast, the West Germans under Chancellor
Brandt's leadership moved directly toward Moscow, the effect of
which was to allay Soviet suspicions, isolate Ulbricht, and produce a highly significant treaty acknowledging Europe's existing
frontiers and launching Soviet/West German relationships in a new
direction. Based on available evidence, the key points are that
if the Czechs had channeled their initiatives toward West Germany
through Moscow they might have learned that the Soviets were not
yet ready to proceed on such a wide range of issues. In fact, the
Soviets did not proceed until Willy Brandt became Chancellor and
inaugurated his Ostpolitik. What was essential in changing Soviet
minds was the difference between the Kiesinger and Brandt attitudes toward the Soviet Union.

Underlying the Soviet and East European desire for rapproache-
ment with West Germany is the desperate need for superior technical
and industrial skills. But in no case can the Soviets afford these
if their effect is to threaten the East European security system
and forge a constellation of European states around West Germany.
A new regrouping is possible only if the USSR is part of it and
dictates it scope and pace so as not to weaken Eastern Europe's
defense system as was the case with the defection of Yugoslavia
and Albania and the ambivalent military policies of Romania. In
responding to Chancellor Willy Brandt's Ostpolitik, the Soviets
have evinced a desire to accomplish two vital objectives simultaneously: enlarge their economic and technical cooperation with
West Germany and extend the stabilization of the Western front

while working out their tindery relationship with the Chinese.

Specific Soviet-Czechoslovak treaty provisions of May 6, 1970 requiring the Czechs to aid the USSR in the event of an attack by a third party are the most explicit recognition to date that for the Soviet Union the northern tier WTO members are a defense not merely against the old Cold War enemies of Europe but against the much newer and bellicose communist enemy in Asia. In short, the requirement to defend the Soviet Union serves notice to the Czechs that there is much more to the East European defense establishment than Europe. Yet whatever the imperatives of territorial security, it is not in the specific military power of Czechoslovakia that Soviet security against Chinese lies: it is rather in the unchallenged stability and legitimacy of Eastern Europe frontiers and in the more or less orthodox Marxist-Leninist political systems of Eastern Europe, all of which would be subjected to potentially interminable flux and irretrievable losses were Czechoslovakia to renew its liberalization drive.

It could, of course, be said that the intensity of the demands upon Czechoslovakia should logically drive the Soviets to strike at Yugoslavia which is after all the heart of successful ideological deviation and the most persistent example of small-power communist sovereignty in Eastern Europe. That the Soviets cannot have the best of the East European world does not however mean they would settle for the worst. Given the strong possibility that a disciplinary expedition against Yugoslavia would lead to protracted warfare across a number of states, the Soviet objective has been to maintain a balance between restricted pluralism and selfdetermination on the one hand and territorial and regime security on the other. Thus, by sparing Yugoslavia, Albania, and at least thus far Romania, the Soviets have prudently rejected Stalinist garrison-state solutions and settled instead for a mode of operations subject, it is true, to frequent pressures by indigenous forces for liberalization.

In the final analysis, liberalization in Eastern Europe is a highly complex process which has always to be sensitive to Soviet interests: how will Soviet leaders view various reforms and their plausible threats to Soviet security? What is intriguing about recent experiences in Czechoslovakia and Romania is that it is not only a problem of what specific institution or practice is liberalized but also the processes and impact of communicating this to Soviet decision-makers. Since it obviously makes a difference who perceives what political developments in which East European states, it would be essential to know the sources and processes of data collection and the mode of transmission to Soviet decision-makers. Who, for example, are the Soviet Union's chief Poland, Czechoslovakia, or Romania watchers? What specific social and psychological factors influence their perception and sorting of data for evaluation and transmission? What local contacts and sources of intelligence information do they rely on? How current are their assessments of East European developments? And what

access do they have to top officials in the Soviet Ministry of
Foreign Affairs and the Politburo? Answers to such questions
would doubtless lead to greater sophistication in our understanding of how Soviet leaders assess change and continuity in Eastern
Europe as they relate to territorial and regime security. Obstacles to acquiring such information (and they are understandably
very great) should not rule out dedicated efforts to explore
potential breakthroughs, for as long as we lack mastery of the
Soviet Union's diplomatic and even intelligence activity in each
East European nation, our capacity to foretell specific Soviet
initiatives and reactions will be severely hampered.

International Organization as an Instrument of Soviet Policy

Although marked by numerous deficiencies in view of intentions,
the Council for Mutual Economic Cooperation and the Warsaw Treaty
Organization continue to be the most significant international
agencies for formalizing the Soviet Union's presence and influence
in Eastern Europe. On the economic side, the record has not lived
up to Soviet expectations, largely because of one unavoidable
fact: it is in the nature of economic integration that while powerful and affluent nations must provide financial capital and natural
resources to support integrative efforts, the presence of a dis-
parately large member, i.e. the Soviet Union, in practice hampers
success. Thus from CMEA's very inception a true dovetailing of
economies, including a common market and rational division of
labor, was made impossible by the emmense CNP of the USSR, second
largest in the world and more than the total of all the other
CMEA signatories together. Programs for integrating several frag-
ile East European economies and the Soviet Union's selfsufficient
economy could only mean extreme dependency at best and absorption
at worst.

Speaking on behalf of Soviet economic interests, the most
authoritative commentator on CMEA affairs, O. Bogomolov, has been
critical of a number of deficiencies: lagging coordination
between international planning and investment; too low prices
paid for Soviet raw materials; lack of modernity in a number of
East European fuel supplies; and continued problems of currency
convertibility which he suggested would be alleviated by gearing
a CMEA "collective currency" to world dollar prices. (16) Highly
significant was his estimate that the East European demand for
Soviet raw materials -- especially fuel -- would increase by 50%
in the period 1970-75.

Yet CMEA has performed useful work in more narrowly defined
cooperative projects such as the Friendship Oil Pipeline, the
Peace Electric Power Grid, the Brotherhood Gas Pipeline, a rail-
road freightcar pool, the CMEA Bank, and numerous exchanges of
scientific and technical personnel. Such efforts receive highly
enthusiastic and frequently exaggerated coverage in the monthly

magazines, *International Affairs* and *World Marxist Review*, as well as in newspapers and periodical literature addressed specifically to Soviet readers. For example:

The leaders of the Communist and workers' parties and the heads of government of the CMEA countries have repeatedly emphasized the need to enhance still further the role of CMEA and all its bodies in making economic, scientific and technical cooperation between the member countries more efficient. The Communist and workers' parties have been collectively elaborating methods for developing co-ordination which corresponds to the concrete stage of Socialist and Communist construction and the level of productive forces attained in the CMEA countries.

This kind of collective elaboration of concrete tasks at each particular stage of cooperation, and their practical solution on a bilateral basis and within the CMEA framework (hence on a multilateral basis) represent a creative development of Lenin's ideas regarding the new type of international economic relations. Success is ultimely assured by the common aims pursued by the CMEA countries, which are the construction of Socialism and Communism, their common interests, and strong bonds of international Socialist solidarity.

Analyzing in his work the processes within the world economy and also the first few steps in Socialist construction in the Soviet republic, Lenin wrote: "All economic political and spiritual life is becoming more and more international", and will be entirely internationalized by Socialism. "The whole of society must become a single workers' cooperative . . . Now all we need is a single will to enter with an open heart that single world cooperative".

The prospects for the evolution of allround relations between the Socialist countries naturally extend over a relatively long historical period. However the present stage already makes it possible to speak of the international economic relations of the CMEA countries developing precisely as indicated by Lenin. (17)

Although any detailed analysis of Soviet trade with other CMEA members is beyond the purview of these observations, even a brief look at figures for 1968-69 shows that the greatest volume of Soviet economic transactions take place with the East European economies, with the GDR first in overall volume of exchange. (18)

TABLE 2.1

Soviet Foreign Trade Turnover, 1968-70
(billions of rubles: current prices)

	1968 final	1969 provisional	1970 expected
Total	18.0	19.8	. .
Socialist countries	12.2	12.9	. .
incl. CMEA	10.4	11.2	. .
Bulgaria	1.7	1.7	1.8
Czechoslovakia	1.8	2.0	2.2
GDR	2.8	3.0	3.2
Hungary	1.2	. .	1.4
Poland	1.9	2.0	2.3
Romania	0.8	. .	1.0
Non-socialist countries	5.9	6.9	. .
developed	3.9	4.4	. .
developing	2.0	2.5	. .

In an interview published in *Novoye vremya*, No. 15, 1970, N.S. Patolichev, Soviet Minister of Foreign Trade, gave some preliminary data on foreign trade in 1969 and reiterated expected turnover totals with some socialist countries in 1970 based upon existing protocols. These are set out above, together with the known totals for 1968, published in *Vneshnaya torgovlya, SSSR, Za 1968 god*, pp. 10, 12.

This is not to say that exchanges of goods of themselves necessarily entail Soviet controls over East European life; but if one adds the economic dependency of less diversified and self-sufficient East European economies to the somewhat informal controls resulting from CMEA organizational meetings and enterprises, then the scope and intensity of Soviet pressures can become very great indeed. In short, it is not merely in the economic realm that CMEA's achievements have been registered. Periodic multilateral contracts through which the Soviet Union's primary interests are defended and collective affirmations of unity and purpose are communicated have considerable political significance. It is in this manner that the Soviet exercise organizational controls -- addressed

primarily to CMEA's membership and thus to the membership of the
East European subsystem -- by emphasizing acceptable limits of
national independence and deviation, preferred objectives for collective support, and economic preferment to those who resist
offending Soviet political sensitivities.

Shifting to the military side, WTO was originally conceived as
a unified defense command against NATO and especially the threat
that West Germany might seek to revise the results of World War II.
Understandably, the organization's primary significance lies in
its inextricable relationship to the Soviet Union's own defense
policy apart from which it has little independent identity and no
military significance. Periodic formal gatherings serve primarily
as forums for the expression of joint approaches to defense problems, with the Soviet Union delegated as chief spokesman. As
expected, individual national armies have been fully subordinated
to the dominant power of the Soviets and although there are
frequent affirmations about a fully integrated international
command and higher forms of organization and cooperation, there
are as yet no firm indicators that these projections have materi-
alized. The organization's chief contemporary significance would
appear to be as follows: 1) it is a formalized effort to unite
the states of Eastern Europe in a common purpose, primarily
against the threat of agression; 2) it serves to limit the exercise of some aspects of their sovereignty, particularly in matters
of self-defense; 3) it provides extra opportunities to articulate
ostentations unanimity and support of Soviet policies on issues
of common interest -- on the one hand condemnation of American neo-
imperialist efforts, say, in Vietnam and the Middle East, and on
the other, repeated proposals for an all-European conference to
discuss security and East-West cooperation, dismantling of foreign
military bases and withdrawal of troops, a scaling down of all
armed forces, the creation of denuclearized zones (including the
nonaccess to nuclear weapons by West Germany), and the recognition
of two German states; 4) finally, WTO provides the aura of an
international command through which the Soviet Army can exercise
punitive and retaliatory policies as if they were genuinely
cooperative defense policies against threats to East European
security. In this sense, WTO is the most significant multi-
lateral organ through which the Soviets can exercise their internationalist duty against unacceptable political deviations in
Eastern Europe.

The World Conference as a Policy Forum

Culminating almost a decade of Soviet efforts to convene a
world conference, seventy-five communist parties met in Moscow,
June 5-17, 1969, to ventilate problems and forge unity. Neither
objective was fully realized because they are mutually exclusive:
ventilating problems weakens unity; and forging unity restricts

the ventilation of problems. It is, however, worthwhile to look
back on the achievements of the conference and emphasize their
connection to the Soviet Union's need to legitimize three widely
separate initiatives: military intervention in Czechoslovakia;
an imperative aid commitment to North Vietnam; and military and
political skirmishes with Peking.

Years of plans for a conference on the model of 1957 and 1960
had reinforced the view that the Soviets were bent on exploiting
a forum to anathemize the Chinese and read them out of the international Communist system altogether. But all through the months
after the Soviet Army's punitive expedition into Czechoslovakia
in August, 1968, there were persistent indicators that significant
European communists had been alienated by Soviet military brazen-
ness and that, therefore, the conference idea would have to be
shelved indefinitely. Nevertheless, even in the face of signals
that an international gathering might fail or degenerate into
propaganda battles, the resolve of the Soviet leadership to strike
out for sizeable gains in public relations proved decisive.

What was significant about the June 1969 conference was that
the primary emphasis fell upon an excoriation of imperialism and
only secondly on the persistently divisive problems of the international Communist system, due entirely (if one is to believe the
Soviet accounts) to the unreasonableness of the Chinese leadership.
This emphasis tended to spare the Soviets the worst effects of
their high-handedness toward the Czechs. The Soviets spoke their
anti-imperialist piece and then went on to a trenchant criticism
of the unrepentant and absent Chinese which gave the appearance
of exonerating the Soviet Union by pointing a finger at another
communist power that had presumably been doing worse things. As
General Secretary Brezhnev described it:

> The facts testify that the Chinese leadership only
> talks about a struggle against imperialism while in
> practice it directly or indirectly helps imperialism.
> It helps it by seeking to split the unified front of
> socialist states. It helps it by playing an instigatory
> role at times of acute international crises and by
> blocking the relaxation of international tensions. It
> helps it by striving to impede the consolidation of a
> broad anti-imperialist front and by seeking to split
> the mass international organization . . .

> Naturally, the imperialists are making use of Peking's
> present foreign-policy orientation as one of their
> trump cards in the political struggle against world social-
> ism and the liberation movement.

> And so: an attack against the Soviet Union on all
> lines, lying propaganda, slander against the Soviet
> people and against our socialist state and our Com-
> munist Party, the fanning of hatred for the Soviet
> Union among the Chines people, and now even the use
> of arms; intimidation and blackmail with respect to

the other socialist states and the developing countries;
flirtation with the major capitalist powers, including
the F.R.G. -- this is what the foreign policy line of
today's China looks like! (19)

For their part several European parties criticized the Brezhnev
Doctrine as a specious and belated justification for military
pressures on Marxist-Leninist neighbors and an intolerable
impingement on sovereignty. The Italians pointedly condemned
Soviet policies toward Prague and signed only Part Three (on anti-
imperialism) of the final conference summation's four parts.
Pleading reservations, the Romanians nevertheless signed it all,
thus countering their walkout performance at the preparatory
Budapest meeting in February 1968. Most of the disgruntled were
uncommonly vocal and got a little of what they wanted, which is
what conferences are for. This list of seventy signatories
revealed conspicuously that residual pro-Soviet loyalties had
won out and that the Soviet leaders gambled correctly in hosting
the gathering which attracted seventy-four other parties to
Moscow to hear the case against the Chinese "splitters".

There are after all minimum and maximum objectives of policy.
Admittedly there was no chance for another Comintern or Cominform,
and no realistic expectations for the restoration of the old camp
spirit of 1957 or even 1960. Yet in the face of unprecedented
disunity and challenges against Soviet influence, the outcome of
the conference amounted to a major watershed in the international
communist movement. The Soviets gave the appearance of relinquishing supremacy and agreed that the speeches of dissident party
leaders would be published in *Pravda* and they were. More important,
an atmosphere of flexibility seemed to take hold, encouraging
franker expression and greater independence of views. Officially
pronounced:

All parties have equal rights. At this time when there
is no leading center of international communist movement,
voluntary coordination of the actions of parties in order
effectively to carry out the tasks before them acquires
increased importance. (20)

Understandably, the final summation was sufficiently vague and
lacking in binding commitments. Scattered with doctrinaire
platitudes and exhortations, it stressed the mainstays of minimum
cohesion: the historic significance of Vietnam as a beleaguered
outpost of socialism in Asia; the struggle against imperialism --
especially U.S. and West Germany; socialist and proletarian inter-
nationalisms; international relations of a new type; and finally,
more of the perennial dedication to peaceful coexistence and
greater vigilance against bourgeois ideology. The greatest surprise
was the absence of any word in the summation about the feud with
China and the disciplinary action against Czechoslovakia. Indeed
the most profound challenges to the Soviet Union and international
communist unity -- Peking and Prague -- were relegated to the
status of unmentionable, there to mark the Soviet Union's security

poles 5000 miles apart.
   Since the conference, vestiges of the Dubcek-Cernik reforms in
Czechoslovakia have been systematically purges; the offended
communist parties of Europe -- especially the French and Italian
-- have returned to their former pro-Soviet positions on international questions; and the Soviets have pursued a variety of
national security policies both in Europe and the Far East:
   1) Attempts have been made to keep the Chinese off balance by
creating positions of strength among China's likely geographical
enemies -- i.e. India, Japan, Taiwan, Korea, and Vietnam -- and
to link these positions more closely to Soviet diplomacy.
   2) The possibility of multiple front military confrontations
has been reduced by dissuading the Chinese from pursuing gambits
based on presumed Soviet weakness in Eastern Europe. The European
sector of Soviet policy has included: stern responses to potentially disruptive liberalization in proximate Eastern Europe states
(plus warnings for the future); increased military presence in the
Middle East; and efforts to normalize relations with the Federal
Republic of Germany and NATO, including such possibilities as a
joint security pact with the Warsaw Treaty.
   3) There have been initiatives and understandings with the
United States regarding the Vietnam war, the non-proliferation of
nuclear weapons, arms reduction, and the control of MIRV's and
ABM systems. All such bilateral efforts tend to keep China guessing
and diplomatically isolated.
   4) Although secret talks about Asian frontier problems have been
going badly, the Soviets have expressed willingness to discuss
border claims and grievances. Meanwhile they have made conspicuous
shows of forces in the Far East and Middle East, and stepped up
their programs of economic development in Siberia.
   5) Finally, the Soviets have manifested a more conciliatory
stance toward world tensions and have resisted the temptation to
ostracize the Chinese from the international communist system.
The purpose has been to show that China has been the aggressor in
the frontier dispute and that Chinese policies inflame international tensions, due to reckless and misguided leadership.
   It is probably true that no world conference of communist parties can ever restore the prestige and undisputed leadership of
the Soviet Union to their former height. Nevertheless the Soviets
have demonstrated that even in periods of considerable dissension,
intensified by intervention against the Czechs and warnings of
even future interventions, international gatherings can serve to
enunciate Soviet attitudes on major world questions before an
audience that can generally be counted on for support; for as long
as the USSR remains the overwhelmingly powerful member of the East
European subsystem, no combination of power can challenge her
effectively. Herein lies the key to the Soviet Union's utilization
of conferences as vehicles of foreign policy. Conferences can be
places where general international communist positions are advanced as if they are specific Soviet policies and specific Soviet

policies as if they are unquestionably sound international communist positions.

No loyal communist could disagree with the major themes of
General Secretary Brezhnev's conference address: a) The Present-
Day International Situation and the Tasks of the Anti-Imperialist
Struggle; b) Some Problems of the International Communist Movement
and the Unity of Action in the Struggle Against Imperialism; and
c) the CPSU Is Faithful To Its International Duty. More specifically, Brezhnev appraised the conference idea and performance as
follows:

> The Meeting's success was, unquestionably, predetermined
> by the profoundly democratic and candid atmosphere that
> marked its proceedings. Cooperation on an equal footing,
> wide publicity, which made it possible to keep the world
> public constantly informed and, lastly, the decision to
> send the materials of the Meeting to Parties not attending
> it, show that the Leninist code of democratic and prin-
> cipled discussion is deeply rooted in our movement. It is
> also added proof of our movement's strength and viability.

> We can safely say that this form of work, world Com-
> munist meetings, has become an important means of collec-
> tive discussion of pressing tasks and collective elabora-
> tion of an integral program of common action. For us,
> these meetings are valuable as a Marxist-Leninist school
> of political experience and revolutionary action; as a
> forum for a broad exchange of opinions and views and a
> means for charting a policy that takes fuller account of
> the interests of the working masses and enables us more
> actively to fight for these interests.

> Throughout its history, the CPSU has founded its
> policy on the Leninist concept of proletarian inter-
> nationalism. We have always been guided by the well-known
> Leninist definition that to be an internationalist is to
> do "the utmost possible in our country for the develop-
> ment, support and awakening of the revolution in all
> countries". The CPSU has always striven to make full use
> of all inner potentialities to strengthen and promote
> socialism and communism to the utmost in the Soviet Union
> and, at the same time, to support and develop the revolu-
> tionary struggle throughout the world. Such is our approach
> to our international duty to the world Communist and
> working-class movement. (21)

Conclusions

The Soviet Union has utilized a wide spectrum of sophisticated
strategies and tactics designed to regularize its hegemony in
Eastern Europe and simultaneously thwart China. Joined together
by various conventions, treaties, and agreements of a political,

military, economic, and cultural character, the international communist system has, in the period 1968-70, experienced strong Soviet military responses in Czechoslovakia and along the Siberian frontier in East Asia. At the same time there have been international gatherings of CMEA and WTO, and the major world conferences in June 1969, demonstrating institutionalized cooperation, mutual benefits, franker exchanges, difficult adjustments and compromises, and the usual doctrinaire expressions of anti-imperialist unity -- indeed a highly complex pattern of international behavior with special significance for the Soviet Union and contiguous Eastern Europe.

Faced with the enormous economic costs and military risks in expanding the international communist system, the Soviets have instead concentrated on system maintenance; and especially the maintenance of their East European subsystem. As a minimum this much must be preserved if Soviet rule is to retain its essential characteristics. The narrowing of international communism's organizational scope and practical application to the manageable part of Eastern Europe has helped to perpetuate some key myths of early revolutionary thought. It has fortified what is left of the Soviet Union's ideological commitment beyond the realm of absolute territorial security. As a byproduct the Soviet public order system is provided with a source of legitimacy. Subsystem maintenance also militates toward the stability and legitimacy of frontiers in Eastern Europe's security systems. It is no accident, of course, that Eastern Europe's multilateral relations are collectively the instruments for accomplishing all these objectives simultaneously. Contrary to traditional Soviet interpretations, herein lies the true imperative of international relations of a new type and the Soviet Union's self-declared internationalist duty.

It is from this vantage point that the case for orthodoxy vis-à-vis China is best made. The ideological thrust of Lin Pao's political message in August 1966 and Chinese claims ever since has been that the revolutionary center of gravity has shifted from Marx's industrialized and presumably proletarian Western Europe to Lenin's agrarian Russia -- the weakest link the chain of international capitalism -- and now finally to the villages and peasant populations of Asia where Peking claims special leadership rights. But if Mao Tse-tung insists that most of Asia under Chinese leadership is the new repository of truth, revolutionary initiatives, and ultimate Marxist-Leninist success, the Soviets can counter with Eastern Europe, a living example of socialist internationalism and international relations of a new type -- indeed the most mature and sophisticated organizational efforts on behalf of international communism to date.

Of course, none of these observations are meant to diminish the strategic significance of Soviet-American relations, including periodic talks about ABM's, MIRV's, and mutual reductions of military investments, hardware, and deployments across the board. Yet it is precisely the resolution of frontier insecurities -- Asian

54

and East European -- that bulk largest in the Soviet purview.
Detente with the United States can proceed realistically only in
conjunction with the Soviet conviction that pressures on its
borders have abated or that a new round with the Americans will
have a positive impact on frontier enemies. It is from this
perspective highly questionable that the Soviets would prefer to
see the Vietnam war ended without compensatory gains vis-à-vis
China or commensurate advances elsewhere. Thus, President Nixon's
expectations were not fulfilled. Neither Soviet scholars nor
official Party spokesmen have conceded that it is in the USSR's
interest to help extricate the United States from Vietnam.

Even assuming a settlement of major East-West security questions
with the United States or a hypothetical installation of impregna-
ble defenses all along the Soviet Union's frontiers, still Eastern
Europe would continue to be of central importance for Soviet
planning and projections; for as long as the Soviet Union maintains
its Marxist-Leninist system with an exclusivist, monopolistic, and
futuristic political party, underpinned by a strongly internationalist doctrine. the East European nations will at least potentially constitute an indispensable source of both regime security and
ideological fulfillment at the international level. Uncommon
though this interdependence may be, it is a prevalent, if monoto-
nous, theme of official exchanges between Moscow and the other
East European subsystem members and constitutes the most durable
perspective from which the politics and foreign affairs of Eastern
Europe must be seen. Which is to say, that any considerable liberalization of East European life adjacent to the Soviet Union must
await some markedly liberal transformations in the Soviet Union's
own one-party political system -- a plausible but not too likely
prospect in the foreseeable future.

NOTES

* The author wishes to express appreciation to the Foundation,
   University of North Carolina at Charlotte, for research support.

1. A.A. Gromyko, (Chief Editor) *Diplomaticheskii Slovar*, Vol. I
   (Moscow: Gosudarstvennoe Izdatelstvo Politicheskoi Literatury,
   1960), pp. 467-468.

2. M.B. Airpetian and V.V. Sukhodeev, *Novyi tip mezhdunarodnykh
   otnoshenii* (Moscow, 1964), pp. 157-158.

3. For the best analysis of this phenomenon, see Robert Tucker,
   "The De-radicalization of Marxist Movements", *American Political
   Science Review*, LXI, No. 2 (June, 1967).

4. "Speech at Meeting of Csepel Iron and Steel Works During Stay
   in Hungary of Soviet Party and Government Delegation", April 9,

1958, in *For Victory in Peaceful Competition With Capitalism* (New York: E.P. Dutton and Co., 1960), p. 327.

5. N.S. Khrushchev, "Speech in Budapest During Soviet Party and Government Delegation Visit", April 7, 1958, *Pravda*, April 8, 1958.

6. *Pravda* Editorial, May 14, 1960.

7. *Pravda* Editorial, August 22, 1968.

8. Sergei Kovalev, "Sovereignty and the Internationalist Obligations of Socialist Countries", *Pravda*, September 26, 1968.

9. Sh. Sanaloyev, "Proletarian Internationalism: Theory and Practice", *International Affairs*, No. 4 (April, 1969), pp. 11, 14.

10. James N. Billington, "Force and Counterforce in Eastern Europe", *Foreign Affairs* (October, 1968), p. 28.

11. See, for example, Hans J. Morgenthau, "Russia, the U.S., and Vietnam", *The New Republic* (May 1, 1965), p. 13.

12. For one of the few accounts of the Vietnam war in the perspective of Sino-Soviet relations, see Donald S. Zagoria, *Vietnam Triangle: Moscow/Peking/Hanoi* (New York: Pegasus, 1967).

13. During a visit to Moscow's Institute of Law in the summer of 1969 this writer witnessed a highly emotional and impassioned oration in response to questions about the Soviet Union's military reaction to Czechoslovak events. Twenty million casualties and poignant reminders of World War II were repeatedly cited as an irreducible justification for the Soviet Union's resolute military response to what was construed as Czechoslovak tinkering with East European security. My reference to a larger ongoing trade between other East European countries and West Germany or even Romania's diplomatic relations with Bonn had no apparent effect on numerous representatives of the Soviet Union's political science community. Czechoslovakia simply falls into a special category.

14. *Christian Science Monitor*, October 4, 1968.

15. For a highly refined and perceptive analysis, see Richard Lowenthal, "The Sparrow in the Cage", *Problems of Communism*, XVII, No. 6 (November-December, 1968).

16. O. Bogomolov, "The Theoretical Heritage of Lenin and Economic Integration of the Socialist Countries", *Mirovaya ekonomika i*

56

mezhdunarodnye otnosheniya, April 1970, pp. 55-66.

17. I. Ikonnikov, "CMEA's Role in Cooperation Between the Socialist Countries", *International Affairs*, No. 4 (April, 1969), p. 66.

18. It should be pointed out that although there can be disagreements over the meaning of statistics and economic trends, at least one authoritative Soviet observer projected that trade within CMEA during 1966-70 was expected to total about 140 billion rubles of which around one-third would be with the Soviet Union. See T.V. Ryabushkin (ed.), *Ekonomika yevropeiskikh stran-chlenov SEV* (Moscow: Izdatelstvo Nauka, 1968), p. 34. Note also that in overall Soviet trade the percentage share of the industrialized capitalist countries rose from 20,6% in 1967 to 21.3% in 1968 while the share of the communist countries fell from 67.8% in 1967 to 67.4% in 1968.

19. L.I. Brezhnev, "For Strengthening the Solidarity of Communists, For a New Upswing in the Anti-Imperialist Struggle", *Pravda*, June 8, 1969.

20. "Basic Document Adopted by the International Conference of Communist and Workers' Parties in Moscow, June 17, 1969", *Pravda*, June 18, 1969.

21. L.I. Brezhnev, "Fresh Upsurge of the Communist Movement", *World Marxist Review*, XII (August, 1969), p. 4, p. 9.

Chapter III

RESOURCES, TECHNOLOGY, AND FOREIGN POLICY BEHAVIOR:
THE CZECHOSLOVAK EXPERIENCE

Dennis C. Pirages

    In many ways Czechoslovakia's foreign policy behavior is more
easily explained than that of other members of the socialist
commonwealth. Yugoslavia and Romania are seemingly quite independent of Soviet influence in foreign policy and Hungary quitely
goes about her own business and ignores many Soviet guidelines.
While Poland and East Germany carefully read Moscow's signals,
only Bulgaria and Czechoslovakia are closely clutched in the
Kremlin's grasp. Especially since the events of August 1968, one
only need know the policy attitudes of the members of the Politburo of the Communist Party of the Soviet Union to predict how
Czech decision-makers will act on important issues. (1) Since we
don't have access to the personal opinions of Soviet Politburo
members, however, and as Czechoslovakia, unlike Bulgaria, is not
a developing country heavily dependent on Soviet favors, the
Russian guidance of Czech foreign policy provides an intriguing
case study.
    A glance at an Eastern European map yields geographic data of
immediate importance in understanding the origins of Czechoslovakia's contemporary difficulties. Unlike other socialist countries, Czechoslovakia's "sprawls" through the center of Europe
from West Germany to the Soviet Union. Hungary also fronts a non-
socialist country and shares a short stretch of frontier with the
Soviet Union, but Austria is politically neutral and hardly represents the threat to security Soviet leaders perceive to emanate
from West Germany. Additionally, however, Czechoslovakia, with her
relatively small population of 14.5 million, enjoys the dubious
distinction of bordering six different nations. Four of these
countries are ruled by "fraternal" parties taking a great interest
in Czech affairs since her remaining borders from the western
frontier of the socialist camp.

58

Political History and Culture

Every people with a tradition as a nation develop patterns of political beliefs and values that can be referred to as the nation's political culture. (2) Many factors are important in shaping a political culture including historical experiences, geographic location, social, economic, and religious structures. The peculiar mix that has developed into the Czech political culture can only be explained by another look at the map of Europe with a history book in hand. Unlike neighboring Poland with her wide open and indefensible frontiers, Czechoslovakia possesses moderately defensible borders. Unfortunately, the most insurmountable barriers have historically pointed in the wrong direction. While Czechoslovakia has not shared Poland's fate of being periodically flattened by armied moving from East and West, she has shared exposed frontiers with Austria and Hungary and both nations have done much to limit Czech freedom of action. It wasn't until 1918 that the three segments composing contemporary Czechoslovakia were first united under one government. (A fourth segment, Ruthenia, was lost to the Soviet Union after World War II.)

Czechoslovakia, perhaps more than any other Eastern European country, just merits the description of being "caught between West and East". Quite apart from Austro-Hungarian domination, in cultural tradition she has traditionally gravitated toward the West while language and military necessity have forced a turn to the East. The largely impenetrable mountain ranges to the north and east have precluded a close alliance with Poland or Russia, but Russia has still been viewed as a military power that could perhaps be counted upon to offset the pressures from imperialistic neighbors to the south and west.

Although the Czech* nation was not granted independence until 1918, the tutelage of the neighboring states could best be described as benevolent, particularly in Bohemia and Moravia. Only Slovakia suffered outright domination and exploitation at the hands of the semi-feudal Hungarians. During most of history the Czechs have managed to maintain some internal freedoms in exchange for subservience in foreign policy. While bordering states spent most of their time engaging in military plots and adventures the Czechs were denied this pleasure and have earned the reputation as "cowards of Europe" among their more aggressive Eastern European neighbors. While Czechoslovakia certainly possesses a checkered military past, she has survived the decimation that has accompanied more aggressive foreign policies even though she is a natural "invadee". Unlike Poland, nearly obliterated in both World Wars, or Hungary, unable to correctly calculate permissable levels of autonomy from Soviet control in 1956, Czechoslovakia gained her independence as a result of World War I, suffered only light casualties in World War II and survived a full-scale invasion of hostile troops in 1968 with a minimum of bloodshed. Through cleverness, common sense, or just plain good luck, the Czechs have survived the machinations of the great powers clustered around her borders, no mean accomplishment in an era when thoughtless aggression was glorified as intelligent foreign policy. (3)

The historic division of Czechoslovakia between Austria and Hungary has been responsible for the creation of two distinct political cultures. The Western provinces, Bohemia and Moravia, belonged to Austria while Slovakia and Ruthenia fell under the domination of the less industrial Hungarians. As a result Bohemia and Moravia became highly industrialized areas closely tied to the polically sophisticated Habsburg Empire while the eastern sectors languished in semi-feudal agriculture under Hungarian demination. This split has produced two distinctly different political cultures as each section has differing traditions, experiences, and economic needs. The industrialized west has pushed a highly centralized state since independence in the hopes of maintaining industrial dominance and political hegemony. The Slovaks, on the other hand, have preferred a decentralized federation more amenable to preservation of cultural autonomy and industrial progress.

Aside from the realism and pacifism that has pervaded the Czech political culture, history has created these unity problems that have recently become more manifest in Czech politics. Unlike their Polish neighbors to the north, the Czechs have not been gifted with a unified and homogenous population. When the state was founded after World War I there were at least four nationally distinct groups. The Czechs, freed from Habsburg dominance in the industrial provinces of Bohemia and Moravia, provided a majority of the citizenry. Having been dominated by the Hungarians for centuries the Slovaks had needs and desires of their own that were not necessarily in accord with those of the more highly industrialized Czechs. To complicate matters even further the boundaries as drawn for the new nation encompassed substantial groups of Germans, Hungarians, and Poles. The settlement of World War II eliminated some of the minority problems through the large-scale transfer of populations, but friction between the Czechs and the Slovaks has not been eliminated and continues to be a very important factor in contemporary politics. Additional unity problems have been created by the split between the Catholic Church and the Protestant reformers which has been exacerbated by its coincidence with the Czech-Soviet nationality problem. (4)

Current misunderstandings between the two nationalities result from more than linguistic and religious differences. Bohemia and Moravia are among the most industrialized areas of Europe while Slovakia trails far behind in industrial progress. These economic factors have had important divisive consequences in the formation of domestic and foreign policies. The Germans were first to use divide and rule techniques based on the split with success during World War II and the lesson has not been lost on the Soviet leaders who are not above exploiting these possibilities once again. The Russians backed both Gottwald and Novotny in their slighting of Soviet concerns and it wasn't until Dubcek, a Slovak, attained power that the Slovaks had a real voice in policy-making. Just as Romania has balked at the idea of being the breadbasket of CMEA, Slovakia despises any plans that designate her as Czechoslovakia's barnyard.

Another important mark left on the political culture by history has been some admiration for both the Soviet Union and socialist ideals, although the events of 1968 have done much to erase both. Of all of the Eastern European countries Czechoslovakia has the greatest reason to regard the Soviet Union as a genuine liberator. She is geographically far enough removed from Soviet territory so that there have been few opportunities for mutual hostilities. Czechoslovakia's problems have come from the south and west and both France and the Soviet Union have been regarded as potential counterbalances against Austro-Hungarian designs. While Yugoslavia and Romania united with Czechoslovakia for mutual protection after World War I the leaders have felt that only the might of a major power could guarantee independence in this imperialism-prone neighborhood.

Religiously and culturally Czechoslovakia has favored a strong alliance with western powers, but recent history has disabused her of any faith that she might have held in western commitments. To understand this distrust one only need recall the dismemberment of the country at German hands in 1938, while France and her allies looked on. While to the Czech, liberated by advancing Soviet troops, an unholy alliance with the Kremlin against Germany offered real hope for post-war autonomy. While all of this has obviously been re-evaluated since 1968, it does go far to explain how an industrialized nation with a semi-democratic political history could endure twenty years of Soviet tutelage without reacting violently. Stood up in a moment of crisis in 1938, Czechoslovakia has not been about to cast her lot with distant foreign powers one more time.

In addition to the unique view of the Soviet Union as liberator, the Czech nation has had no quarrel with socialist doctrines. It has been claimed that socialist tendencies are deeply entrenched in the Czech culture beginning as far back as the Hussite reformation of 1400. (5) Throughout history there have been both rich Czechs and poor Czechs but the class difference and cleavages have never been as deep as in neighboring countries. Perhaps due to religion or to an unusual intellectual tradition a phobic fear of socialism has never been a siginficant attribute of the political culture.

A final important aspect of Czech political culture that can't be ignored is the democratic tradition that flowered briefly during the interwar period. The iron-fisted dictatorships that have flourished in other European countries are largely absent in Czech history. Ironically, it is this tradition that permitted the parties of the left to win fifty percent of the vote in the May,

1946 elections (the Communists got thirty-six percent) and gave
Moscow its most nearly valid claim to a legal seizure of power.
This same democratic tradition forced its way to the surface
again in 1968 when a group of socialist democrats under the
leadership of Alexander Dubcek challenged the Kremlin-dictated
definition of democracy.

It was not matters of alliance or ideology that drove a wedge
between the Soviet Union and Czechoslovakia in 1968. Rather, it
was the fact that Czechoslovakia was well on her way to becoming
a mature industrial nation and faced organizational problems that
Soviet leaders could not understand. The crisis of 1968 did not
begin as a crisis of faith in the Soviet alliance. At no time did
the Czechs think of turning to the west for help. They knew
better. Unfortunately, the Soviet leaders could not understand
the nature of the problems facing the Czech Party and the resulting events have left the Czechs isolated from the socialist
commonwealth save only her former Little Entente allies.

Socio-Economic Pressures

The events of the late sixties are illustrative of how socio-
economic pressures act as important domestic determinants of
foreign policy behavior in industrial societies. Czechoslovakia
emerged from World War II as the most industrialized of the
socialist countries with neighboring East Germany dismembered, but
not far behind. Using per capita figures the Soviet Union ranked
far below both of these states in level of industrial development.
The unfortunate aspect of this situation is that the "leading
industrial state in the communist system has not been permitted
to pioneer new techniques of economic organization and has been
forced to rely on those applicable in less industrial societies.
The Soviet Union, in its self-selected role as ideological leader
will not admit that anyone other than Soviet theoreticians could
make a worthwhile contribution to Marxist-Leninist economic
theory. This intellectual chauvinism wreaked havoc on the Czech
economy for twenty years as the Soviets forced the adoption of
gross inefficiencies as evidence of ideological loyalty.

The impact of Soviet "guidance" on Czech foreign and domestic
policies cannot be overstressed. Key figures in the Kremlin,
handicapped by Stalinist ideological blinders, decreed that the
Soviet model of societal management be followed in all fraternal
party-states. This meant the implementation of the economic model
that was developed during the harsh era of Stalinist mobilization
in each socialist country without regard for differing individual
needs or levels of industrialization. This "old fashioned" mobilization model fits best in less developed countries like Romania
and Bulgaria and has least relevance in highly industrial
Czechoslovakia.

Full appreciation of the consequences of this anomoly requires familiarity with the relationship between levels of industrial development and types of societal guidance mechanisms. The Stalinist model was developed under conditions of economic stress when the Soviet leaders were facing both external and internal pressures. There is nothing in Marx's writings that sanctions this hierarchical control model as the only one appropriate to a socialist society. The model's command aspects, a tightly controlled Party structure with a small elite making all important social, political, and economic decisions, resulted from a combination of Lenin's principles of organization and Stalin's assessment of the Herculean tasks that his Party faced. Under conditions of great social stress when a nation faces invasion or starvation men need no additional incentives to produce. They are willing to follow the orders of others to insure survival irrespective of whether or not they are permitted to play a role in the decisional process. This control model is not unattractive for developing countries where the energies of nationalism can be successfully tapped by a small modernizing elite. For many reasons this model breaks down when it is grafted onto an industrialized country that is not facing a manpower-motivating crisis. (6)

The appropriateness of different types of co-ordination models for advanced levels of industrialization has been underscored by a well-established research tradition linking economic modernization to changes in social and political structure. Seymour Martin Lipset is credited with initially offering the observation that democracy and political stability seem to regularly occur at advanced levels of modernization. (7) While his initial proposition has been frequently amended it is clear that systematic changes occur in mature industrial societies producing pressures for modification of social structure, modes of social control, and economic organization. Industrial societies require different types of incentives to optimize worker contribution and political leaders unwilling to permit needed reforms suffer the consequences in reduced economic output.

Fundamental variables underlying this relationship are connected with human motivation and the production of energy required to sustain industrialization. Every nation's productivity is heavily influenced by possession and intelligent exploitation of natural resources and the development of a sophisticated societal guidance mechanism capable of optimizing the use of human resources. During initial or crisis stages of industrialization the major task is the accumulation of energy and capital to adequately exploit existing natural resources. The tasks that need to be performed in the energy-development stage of industrialization don't require highly skilled managerial personnel or sophisticated decisional models. Weak minds and strong backs are much more functional than a well-educated white collar class. When high levels of performance cannot be maintained by nationalism or crisis, sanctions can be applied to coerce workers to fill quotas of very observable energy materials. Piece-rate incentives and modified Stakhanovite

techniques can also be employed to keep blue collar workers moderately content. (8)

Socialist economists have recognized the nature of this fundamental shift from brutal exploitation of natural resources to
creation of sophisticated incentive and production models. Ota Sik,
attempting to explain how socialist production grew rapidly for
years in Czechoslovakia and suddenly growing, made a distinction
between "the quantitative expansion of inputs, i.e. the volume of
means of production and the number of productive workers, and ...
the qualitative development of factors increasing the social
productivity of labor, i.e. the technical improvement of means of
production, increase in knowledge, abilities, and experience of
the productive workers and leading personnel ..." Sik goes on to
identify scientific knowledge and its application to technology
as a productive factor that has frequently predominated in the
development of all industrial countries. Although he uses different terms to describe these underlying variables, his "extensive"
economic development is akin to brute expansion of inputs while
"intensive" development refers to incentive, innovation, and
sophisticated guidance models. According to Sik, Czechoslovakia's
economy developed problems because of the heavy concentration on
extensive development and the neglect of intensive factors. (9)

Data also reveal that countries in initial stages of industrialization are normally net exporters of energy which is exchanged
for capital goods and much needed technical assistance. On the
other hand almost all the advanced industrial nations are running
short of vital resources and seek out sources of additional
"extensive" inputs. Production statistics reveal a strong correlation between high levels of industrialization and large energy
deficits which normally are remedied by importation from less
developed countries. Nearly all developed industrial countries
including most European countries, are net importers of energy.

The need to satisfy energy demands at advanced levels of economic development is a powerful motivating force in international
relations. (10) Those nations in strong competitive positions in
the international market make favorable exchanges of finished
goods and technology for the energy-producing raw materials that
they require. Great Britain and Switzerland offer classic examples
of countries that have fared extremely well in overcoming recourse
deficits by astute activity in the international marketplaces. On
the other hand, Czechoslovakia and other industrialized members
of the Communist System have fared much less well in their search
for "extensive" energy inputs due to the constraints placed on
their independence by the Soviet Union.

Sustained industrialization is associated with more than a
need to seek out new sources of raw materials. While initial
industrialization is propelled by "extensive" factors such as new
efficiencies in energy conversion aided by the accumulation of
capital, the simple addition of new machines and the building of
factories it soon reaches a point of saturation. The second or

"intensive" round of industrialization is heavily dependent upon
development of human resources and the free circulation of technical information. Even the most dedicated and intelligent technocrats cannot make intelligent decisions in the face of a restricted
flow of information. (11) Thus, in addition to the obvious need to
seek outside energy sources, leaders of maturing industrial societies are subjected to pressures for international contracts to
augment societal technology. No single nation possesses a monopoly
on scientific information and those that remain isolated from the
mainstream of international exchange of technological information
are doomed to suffer serious competitive disadvantages.

The Czechs clearly had a much better appreciation of these
needs than their Soviet counterparts. The Action Program of the
Czech Communist Party is filled with references to the "political"
constraints on economic advancement. The Czechs claimed to have
"entered another stage of development" at the end of the fifties
in which "methods of direction and organization hitherto used in
the national economy are outdated ... It will be necessary to
prepare the country for joining in the scientific-technical revolution in the world ... A broad scope for social initiative, frank
exchange of views and democratization of the whole social and
political system becomes virtually the condition for the dynamics
socialist society". It is these aspects of the proposed new
control model that most upset the Soviet leaders. Playing around
with a free market and supply and demand relations is one thing,
a full scale liberalization of thought and control is quite another. (12)

A model of societal control appropriate to an advanced economy
is one that both disperses and upgrades decision-making authority.
Not only are there more critical decisions to be made in the complex society with much smaller margin for errors, but a more sophisticated work force is much more easily motivated by the knowledge that there is an opportunity to play a role in decision-
making. The successful or high performance industrial state is one
that is characterized by free internal flow of information, extensive international contacts, appropriate dispersion of decisional
authority, and some rational system of social advancement and
reward based upon performance. (13) Thus, Lipset's hypothesis works
in two ways. Higher levels of economic development create pressures
for more democratic decisional systems while open decisional systems seem requisite for continued economic progress in advanced
industrial societies.

The events in Czechoslovakia occurring between 1960 and 1968
make a strong argument for the prepotent role of economic factors
in foreign policy behavior. Having surmounted most of the basic
problems of industrialization prior to World War II, Czechoslovakia
emerged from the conflict with comparatively limited destruction
of her industrial base and ready to re-organize sustained industrial growth based upon sound methods of societal co-ordination
including free flow of information, democratic decision-making,

and renewed contacts with external sources of energy and information. At one point she even expressed willingness to become a
recipient of Marshall Plan aid, an initiative that was hurriedly
squelched by Soviet pressures.

In the immediate aftermath of the War the pressures were not
"intensive" development that would later become important were
not readily apparent. The Nazis were removed from Czech territory
with Russian help and both nationalistic and pro-Soviet feelings
ran very high. There was little difficulty in motivating people
to repair the war damage and get the economy back on its feet.
After the deprivations of six years of occupation minimal rewards
were required to insure motivated citizen participation. Gottwald
and then Novotny were able to keep the economy stable and political
tensions were minimal in spite of Soviet tutelage by concentrating
on cheap "extensive" development that was extremely awkward in an
industrialized nation.

Political pressures traceable to economic problems first
appeared in the early 50s and were manifest in the demonstrations
of 1953. A series of events delayed the onset of serious crisis
for several years. The deaths of Gottwald and Stalin provided the
masses with some hope that long overdue changes would be made,
but Novotny proved to be no more responsive to the developing
pressures than his predecessors. The wave of de-Stalinization
that began after the Twentieth Party Congress in the Soviet Union
also delayed the inevitable confrontation between outmoded economic policies and domestic necessities. Disillusionment and a stagnation became manifest only after de-Stalinization had passed with
no fundamental reforms having taken place. Fledgling attempts to
develop new economic models in the late 50s were remarkably unsuccessful and were clearly overshadowed by the adoption of a new
constitution in 1960 which took entire passages from Stalin's
constitution of 1936.

By 1960 Soviet pressures to maintain the orthodox patterns of
control had turned Czechoslovakia into a natural laboratory for
the study of social pathology and despair. The Czechs seemed the
subjects of a macabre experiment in political frustration and
human endurance. Forbidden to seek out profitable markets for
their goods or the cheapest sources of raw materials, industries
slipped into a malaise that left them in poor competitive position
on the world market. Trade with the Soviet Union, carried out
under extremely unfavorable terms, had increased well beyond the
point of diminishing returns by 1963. It has been reliably estimated that Czechoslovakia's enforced isolation from natural markets in many cases forced her to pay twice as much for imports as
those paid by her counterparts in the European Free Trade Association. Export prices have also been estimated at far below normal
market values. (14) Czechoslovakia was receiving the bulk of raw
materials, oil, timber, and iron, from the Soviet Union at inflated
prices and returning machinery and consumer goods at less than
world market price, a condition that over time could bankrupt the

most efficient of economies.

The first indications of the true depth of the economic problems could be detected in 1961. Economic figures for this period
are displayed in Table 3.1. As late as 1960 the labor force still
exhibited a healthy six percent yearly productivity increase. The
subsequent leveling, then decline, in productivity requires little
additional comment. It isn't only coincidental that trade turnover
with the Soviet Union peaked during the period of negative economic growth. The Czech economy nearly collapsed in the early 1960s
as net national product per capita peaked in 1962 and then followed the same pattern of decline. The economies found in the
initial "extensive" stages of the industrial revolution had been
completely exhausted. No longer could a tired and frustrated
people be squeezed for higher output and fundamental organizational
reforms were clearly required to avert economic disaster. The
economic failure was translated directly into the standard of
living. While energy consumption per capita had risen continuously
in almost all countries, between 1964 and 1967 it decrease 300
calories in Czechoslovakia. Obviously this type of situation is
an almost automatic spur to serious demands for basic reforms.

TABLE 3.1

Indicators of Czech Economic Growth (15)

Labor Productivity-1963 = 100

1960	1962	1964	1966	1968
95	101	101	113	126

Per Capita Net National Product-1964 = 100

1960	1962	1964	1966	1968
97	103	100	113	126

The Novotny regime, however, was not about to adopt radical
new programs that would incur the wrath of Soviet leaders. The
Kremlin, not being in a position to comment on the problems of
industrial societies, has never been willing an advocate of political and economic reforms. Far from being a dynamic and innovative leader, Novotny was much more intent on plugging economic
loopholes and remaining in power than in experimentation. Top
Party officials must have been aware of the urgent need for
change as early as 1960 but no blueprint was approved until the

Thirteenth Party Congress in 1966 and implementation didn't begin until 1967. The new model abolished some of the overly centralized planning of the Stalinist era while maintaining many of the same political controls. Novotny obviously hoped to maintain political power by making a minimal economic compromise with his internal validators while not disturbing the more orthodox neighbors. The Czech reforms of 1967, as initially planned, didn't go much further than those previously implemented in other socialist countries.

Liberalization and Counterpressures

That the initial small scale economic reforms would turn into a full-scale economic, social, and political democratization was not at all clear in early 1968 and even Novotny's ouster as President of the Republic in March failed to stir much comment. Many less enthusiastic observers attributed the power shift to half-measures and pointed out that his replacement by retired army general Svoboda, heavily decorated by the Soviet Union in World War II, was hardly a great improvement. Domestic economic "need" to reform, Slovak desires to oust the Prague chauvinists, the growing realization that Czechoslovakia was being left behind in international trade, and the charismatic personality of Alexander Dubcek combined to uncork pent-up pressures for fullscale change, that eventually changed the course of Czech foreign policy. As power fell increasingly into the hands of reformers, the new liberal leadership was forced to trace a delicate path between the internal demands from the masses and external pressures from leaders of surrounding states who were less than enthused by the new experiment. To follow the dictates of the unleashed masses meant certain intervention in Czech domestic affairs by outside powers. To play it safe by established rules of socialist conduct meant to risk the economic and political vitality of fourteen million people.

Because of the organizational peculiarities of the Communist System, the industrially most advanced states have not had a big voice in the making of bloc policies and the Russians, responsible for the lion's share of decision, don't always consider the impact of their policies on other states. The leadership of the Communist Party of the Soviet Union has rarely been noted for radicalism or innovative leadership. There have been few domestic threats to the iron-fisted leadership of the CPSU since Stalin's purges of the 30s and a business-like attitude has characterized party leaders. Since the economies of scale characteristic of the first or "extensive" round of industrialization can still be successfully exploited in the Soviet Union, little interest has developed in the problems of advanced socialist states and Soviet leaders have been unwilling to tamper with existing decisional models.

This conservative attitude becomes a foreign policy input for

Eastern Euoprean states because the Kremlin insists that all loyal
party leaders copy the essentials of their true "Marxist-Leninist
co-ordination model". Differing histories, interpretations of
Marxism-Leninism, and domestic popularity of party leaders combine
to create a unique political and economic situation in each Party-
state, but these differences have gone unrecognized. While Dubcek
could feel relatively secure in abandoning a tight command decisional model, similar action by Soviet leaders might well have
swept them from power in a tide of democratization.

Beginning with the secret speech at the Twentieth Party
Congress in 1956, each of the Party-states has been permittedto
engage in limited economic decentralization to ameliorate some of
the excesses of the Stalinist model. This has not given party
leaders licenses to "democratize" their decisional systems. The
Worker's Parties are still to be the leading force in society
even though the workers themselves may not support Party policies.
It has been reported that in the Soviet Czech negotiations at
Cierna Dubcek informed Brezhnev that his program had the support
of nearly all the working people to which Brezhnev retorted "this
only proves that your Party has abandoned its leading role". (16)
The Russians and their close ideological supporters in Poland and
East Germany support limited liberalization but draw the line
short of any moves toward real democracy. The fuzzy borders between liberalization and democratization is difficult to define,
a fact that Dubcek learned under most difficult conditions.

The domestic and foreign policies of all the members of the
Communist System are very closely linked. It is not merely a propaganda exercise when Soviet leaders remark that threats to
socialism in any country must be dealt with in a resolute manner.
Initially the iron curtain did an effective job of keeping un-
wanted information from capitalist countries from being circulated.
Since it has been dismantled, the socialist citizen has learned
that events in the West are of little importance as domestic
policy inputs. Whereas political changes outside the Communist
system have a muffled impact in the socialist countries, events
taking place closer to home have a quite different reception.
Changes occuring within the socialist commonwealth are widely
reported, by tourists if not officially, and a democratization of
political processes in Czechoslovakia is big news in socialists
capitols. In Warsaw young Poles reason that if Dubcek is permitted to change his Party structure there is not excuse for
Gomulka or Gierek not to do the same. Major domestic policy
changes in any socialist country automatically become foreign
policy considerations for leaders in other countries because of
their likely impact on domestic politics.

One needs only minimal familiarity with socio-economic development and the societal guidance models of the socialist countries
to guess where the heaviest pressures for intervention against the
Czech Action Program originated. (17) In keeping with the theory
outlined above, that leaders in more industrialized states are

pressured to turn outward for energy and to democratize internally,
East Germany would be expected to voice the greatest complaint
about the Czech events. The available evidence indicates that both
Ulbricht and Gomulka were key figures behind the decision to
invade. (18) One of the earliest meetings of "fraternal" parties
took place in Dresden in March, 1968, where Dubcek and others were
called on the carpet to explain their anti-socialist reforms.
East Germany faced production problems of her own and Ulbricht
clearly saw the Czech events to be threatening domestic stability.
He felt that he faced an impossible task in managing an increasingly restive citizenry while full scale democratization was taking
place in neighboring Czechoslovakia.

In Poland Gomulka also viewed the events with deep reservations.
Since the Polish thaw in 1956, which placed Poland at the pinnacle
of liberalization achieved in the Communist System to that point,
Gomulka backtracked in an effort to pacify both conservative
elements in his own party and the edgy businesslike leadership in
the Kremlin. Since the late 50s were filled with thaw and reform,
the return to "normalcy" in the 60s didn't meet with great enthusiasm from the masses. The "normalization" issue came to a head
in late 1967 when students went on a rampage in Warsaw that left
scars in many places on "New World" street. The boundary between
Poland and Czechoslovakia is long, the languages are similar, and
contract between peoples is heavy. There is little doubt that the
events in Czechoslovakia spilled over into the volatile Polish
political mix and it led to Gomulka's replacement by Gierek after
extended rioting stemming from a clumsy attempt at economic reform.

Just as de-Stalinization could not be limited in the late 50s,
Dubcekization could not be isolated in the late 60s. Each Party
leader is involved in the delicate business of managing political
tensions that are a natural result of the non-responsiveness
characteristic of the Soviet hierarchical model. The higher the
level of domestic tensions the more likely the Party leaders are
to react toward events in other socialist countries in a paranoid
manner. To some leaders a Czech liberalization represented little
threat because they felt secure in power while others felt it had
to be eliminated at all costs.

Two Decisions

These economic pressures shape the background for an analysis
of two key foreign policy decisions that will shape Czech foreign
affairs for the next decade. The first decision is that of the
Kremlin to invade in 1968, and the second is the Czech decision
not to offer military resistance. An analysis of these decisions
ties the above discussion together and illustrates the internal
and external constraints within which Prague policy makers
operate.

The events of 1968 perplexed and divided the Soviet leadership.

For years Novotny had run a very tight ship and the Czechs had
carefully followed the Soviet line in both domestic and foreign
policy. They were entrusted with the defense of the western frontier against West Germany and no Soviet troops were stationed on
Czech soil. By contrast, East Germany, Poland, and Hungary all
were forced to support substantial Russian garrisons. The ouster
of Novotny certainly stirred sensitive political antennae in
Moscow and other capitals and the events that followed only served
to deepen Russian concern.

In spite of the growing complexity of the problem there was
little indication that the Soviet Union would make the fateful
decision to intervene. The Kremlin had spent many years polishing
the tarnished image received during the bloody invasion of Hungary.
Many thought that Russia had learned a lesson and wouldn't be so
foolish as to flaunt world opinion one more time. An atmosphere
of detente filled the air in East-West relations and the Czech
spring served as an additional sign of mellowing in Soviet foreign
policy. In addition, of all the Soviet Politburo members making
the fateful Hungarian decision only Suslov still remained in power.

As the Prague summer unfolded an intervention seemed less and
less likely. Dubcek indicated that he would abide by socialist
rules and gave no indication that he had any intention of over-
throwing communism or taking Czechoslovakia out of the Warsaw
pact. Soviet troops were reported maneuvering on the Polish-Czech
border, but is time passed without resolute action the crisis
seemed to dominish. Based on past performance the Soviet leaders
were expected to act quickly if they were going to act at all.
The Kremlin has never believed in waiting for world opinion to
mount anti-Soviet campaigns. The conference at Cierna, July 29-
August 1, apparently facilitated a frank exchange of views and
diminished some of the existing tensions. The fact that three
weeks of Soviet military maneuvers took place before the intervention indicates that the decision to invade was not taken
lightly and that the Russian Politburo was undoubtedly deeply
divided on the subject.

As late as July military affairs expert R. Rockingham Gill
wrote in conservative *East Europe* that the chances of a Soviet
invasion of Czechoslovakia were much less than they had been in
Hungary. He pointed out that the strategic situation had markedly
changed in the last decade. The Soviet army had been trimmed from
five to three and one-quarter million men. The Czechs had an exposed western border with ready access to German and American
troops should they be requested. In 1956 the Russians were not
faced with the problem of an aggressive China at the back door.
When all factors were added together very few thought that Soviet
decision-makers would take such a risk without graver Czech provo-
cations. (19)

The invasion of August 20 signalled the crystallization of many
dormant factors in Soviet-East European relations. Perhaps analysts
paid too little attention to reciprocity aspects of Soviet rela-

tions with Eastern European leaders. There is much to indicate
that persistent prodding by Ulbricht and Gomulka as well as their
willingness to provide troops for the venture were very vital factors in tipping the balance in favor of intervention. (20) Not
that the Soviet leaders are ordered about by the periphery, but it
does seem that pressures from allied can be important in carrying
an issue in a divided Politburo.

Another important factor in the invasion decision that has
received scant attention is a "sphere of influence" understanding
that seems to have arisen in the aftermath of the Cuban missile
crisis. Intelligent speculation suggests that Soviet ships approaching the American blockade of Cuba turned around because Soviet
leaders have tacitly recognized United States hegemony over countries near her borders. In return, the Kremlin expects American
reciprocity in matters affecting Eastern European countries. Following this logic, the United States did not intervene and is not
expected to intervene in the future in what are considered to be
matters of internal organization of the socialist camp. During
the intervention the United States hardly raised more than a
whimper, a stark contrast with American protestations during the
Hungarian episode.

The possibility that Soviet leaders might have panicked into
hasty action because of lack of relevant information should also
not be discounted. The issuance of the Soviet Press Group's propaganda booklet justifying the invasion has been ridiculed in the
West, but there are recurrent themes in it that indicate true
Soviet concern over the seriousness of the Czech events. Complaints
are voiced in the booklet that Czech youth was being subverted by
western films, that the press was "misrepresenting" the truth
about Soviet-Czech economic relations, and that the Communist
Party of Czechoslovakia was on the verge of dissolution. A cogent
argument can also be made that the Soviets were concerned for the
safety of the exposed western frontier. From the western point of
view all of the Soviet charges appear absurd, but to the decision-
makers in the Kremlin, possessing limited and perhaps distorted
information from embassy personnel, the issues undoubtedly appeared to be of great importance. (21)

The Soviet decision to invade caused a parallel crisis in the
Czech Politburo. Dubcek was far from naive in his relations with
Soviet leaders and attempted to play within what he thought were
established rules. Key figures removed from power in the long
overdue de-Stalinization of the Party were treated with kid gloves
although public opinion would have sanctioned imprisonment or
worse. All reforms made were thoroughly discussed with interested
parties during the series of conferences held in the pre-invasion
period. No threats were ever officially uttered against the
Warsaw Pact or CMEA and domestically the Communist Party reached
the apex of popularity. Dubcek was also scrupulous in international affairs, even holding former Little Entente allies, Romania and
Yugoslavia, at arm's length. Reports that Russian airplanes would

be landing in Prague in the morning of August 21 came as a shock
to Czech Politburo members.

The decision to only passively resist the Russians was a product of both domestic historical-cultural factors and foreign real-
politik. Historically the Czech nation has been forced to endure
many occupations and betrayals. A small nation with only semi-
protected borders cannot easily deal with major powers from a
position of strength. The passive resistance in the "Schweikian"
tradition is representative of the unique Czech response to foreign
invasion. When an enemy has more than enough men and equipment to
anihilate the entire nation passive resistance is the only realistic possibility. The occupied nation reacts by either ignoring
the invaders completely or else goads them repeatedly to a point
just short of explosion. (22)

Quite aside from historical-cultural and geographic factors,
Czech policy makers were hardly independent agents in making a
decision of this magnitude. To be able to make independent decision a nation must possess adequate means to defend itself against
those that wish to influence the decisions. In the case of the
invasion it is clear that constraints on Czech actions were even
greater than usual and the only real decision that remained to
the Politburo was whether to annonce a pre-emptive mobilization
in the hope of frightening the Russians with the prospects of
another Hungarian-type bloodbath. There was no real possibility
of appealing to western nations for help. Dubcek had precluded
that when he made his initial decision to play be established
rules and gamble against Russian intervention. To call for western
help would automatically terminate the game and offer a real justification for Soviet invasion. Based on past performance the
Russians gambled that the Czechs would not mobilize and resist
and they proved to be correct.

A comparative assessment of military strength reveals that the
Czechs could have done little else but wait for the Russians to
take over. The Czech army, while certainly not a pushover, num-
bered in the vicinity of only 200,000 men while the best estimates
of numbers of foreign troops in the first wave of the invasion are
around 500,000. The defenders could have mobilized as many as 600
planes against the combined air forced of the invading powers but
there is no way that they could have prevailed. Czech airfields
are few in number and in exposed locations. While Dubcek could
have forced the Russian into a bloody struggle with numerous casualties on both sides, this type of irrational action has never
been characteristic of Czech foreign policy and in the end a
greater victory over the Russians was achieved through the passive
resistance which subjected the Russians to international ridi-
cule. (23)

This example of foreign policy decision-making, while illustrative of the type of constraints the Kremlin can place on Czech
independence, should not be taken to mean that the Czechs have
absolutely no freedom of decision. There are always minor issues

in which the Soviet Union chooses not to intervene although these
have been much fewer in number since the Russian invasion. The
principle that seems to apply in the case of the Soviet intervention and the reason that Czechoslovakia has lost a great deal
of leverage vis-à-vis the Kremlin is that the Poles and the East
Germans have been steadfastly opposed to Czech liberalization.
Had the Kremlin been faced with a unified Eastern Europe opposing
an invasion of Czechoslovakia at the time the decision was made it
is much more likely that the Dubcek policies would have succeeded.
If there is a general foreign policy rule to be learned from this
it is that Eastern European countries, Czechoslovakia included,
can only remain semi-independent in foreign policy when all of the
socialist countries are unified in their opposition to a Soviet
demand. When there are important defections to the Soviet side,
the Communist Party of the Soviet Union feels much more secure in
forcing its will on others.

Problems for the Future

The events of 1968 have now passed into history and analysis
of post-crisis political change does not yield an optimistic outlook for the future of independent Czech foreign policy. Now that
the Soviet Union has taken the drastic steps required to "normalize'
the situation there are no indications that she is unwilling to
finish the job. In light of the risks taken and the international
humiliation suffered, the Kremlin is not about to let the Czechs
develop independent domestic foreign policies in the near
future. (24)
The first item on the "normalization" agenda was a purge of
less loyal Party personnel. The occupation forces opted to move
slowly because of the great domestic popularity of the liberal
leaders. Little was changed in the Party structure in the waning
days of 1968, but in early 1969 the classic purge techniques became obvious. Soviet officials managed to organize enough opportunities within the Czech Party to secure necessary petitions, anti-
Dubcek speeches, and denunciations of the new course. The critical
mass of collaborators have been collected, the full scale cleans-
ing preceded. The Fourteenth Party Congress, scheduled to be held
in late 1968, was postponed indefinitely as were national elections
since the results of both could have been embarrassing to the
Soviet Union.
During the peak of purge activities in 1969 hardly a day passed
without announcement of leading figures being removed from positions of power. Government ministers, journalists, academics, and
provincial Party leaders were carefully replaced by figures closely tied to Soviet attitudes. In order to eliminate undesirables
among the rank-and-file all Party cards were recalled to be re-
issued only to those judged worthy. Need for "Party discipline"
and reassessment became stock phrases in Party leaders' speeches.

Most ominous, however, was the rehabilitation of old conservative "comrades" like Vasil Silak and Alois Indra.

Of greatest importance for future foreign policy decision-making are the changes that have taken place among top policy makers. The removal of Dubcek and his associates represented a very delicate problem. The liberal leaders had managed to unite the Czech populations behind the Party for the first time in twenty years and they had to be removed from public view without provoking serious anti-Soviet turmoil. Federal Assembly chairman Smrkovsky was the easiest target and was removed from office without ceremony in October of 1969. Party Secretary Dubcek proved to be more difficult to handle as he was a personal symbol of the democratization. He was first removed as Party First Secretary and replaced by Gustav Husak, a Slovak with more conservative credentials. He initially retained his seat in the Central and on the Politburo, but was removed from top posts in September of 1969. Then he was quitely exiled to Istanbul, where he served as ambassador to Turkey until removed from all offices after an extended campaign against him in 1970.

Prime Minister Cernik survived longer than Dubcek by recanting his support of the liberalization, but he also was axed in 1970 and replaced by the more conservative Lubomir Strougal. Only Svoboda has survived the storm in his position as President, a fact that can best be explained by his wartime decorations from the Soviet Union as well as his appointment as Minister of Defense under Stalin. Thus, those responsible for making foreign and domestic policies for the next decade, having been handpicked by Moscow, represent a different political point of view and are not about to exercise more than a modicum of independent judgment. While these individuals will never enjoy the support of the masses, the Party apparatus has been thoroughly cleansed and will ratify their actions.

A further indication of future Czech subservience in foreign policy lies in the great number of visits exchanged with less friendly socialist states during the first year of "normalization". Aside from formal conferences, Prague and Moscow exchanged high visits monthly. Prague and Warsaw exchanged high level delegations every ninety days and Bulgaria and East Germany followed close behind in frequency. These visits indicate that almost all important measures taken in Czechoslovakia must win the approval of the socialist guardians.

The armed occupation of Czechoslovakia has spawned new doctrines detailing mutual responsibilities among socialist countries. Sovereignty concepts have been completely redefined since the invasion. Immediately after the August events *Pravda* outlined a new theory of socialist commonwealth which details that:

1) Each socialist state has the right to self-determination as long as it doesn't harm the interests of others.

2) Each state is co-responsible to the other socialist state as well as to its own people.

3) Every state can choose its own path to socialism, but can't depart from communism.
4) Sovereignty is not absolute. Its class base must always be considered. (25)
It isn't clear how much of this doctrine was created as an expedient to justify the invasion and how seriously it is to be taken as a new cornerstone of Soviet foreign policy. The important point is that the precedent has now been set and ideological justification for invasion is available should any member of the socialist commonwealth again step out of line.

It now appears that the Soviet leaders can invoke the new sovereignty doctrines for any number of reasons. The Czech events indicate that the Kremlin will not permit any socialist state to give real power to an electorate or to remove media censorship. (26) The possibility of permitting loyal opposition forces to develop within or outside a ruling party will not be considered. The issues that haven't yet been clearly resolved concern the types of economic reforms that are permissable. Dubcek's reforms obviously went too far, especially when they were coupled with political initiatives, but the Hungarians have been permitted to quitely carry out many of the same economic programs. The uncertainty that results from policy shifts and the unclear limits on innovation create docility among Eastern European decision-makers and serve as effective deterrent to independent action. When Party leaders are uncertain about the rules in force a much more conservative course is likely to be followed.

For Czech Party leaders the harsh realities of 1968 have again raised the spectre of economic collapse that haunted them in the early 60s. The masses have lost faith in the Party's ability to deal with the situation and this has been reflected both in lagging productivity figures and short supplies of consumer goods. Recent reports indicate that in addition to cutbacks in energy consumption, long lines are found in front of retail outlets as citizens attempt to lay in supplies before the expected economic crash. Workers are so alienated from Party leaders that they have reportedly thrown conservative Politburo members out of factories during attempted visits. Conditions are much worse now than they were in the early 60s because the Party's subservience to Moscow is now so apparent. (27)

Facing the next decade Czech decision-makers find themselves stymied by the same problems. They still are not permitted to seek out vitally important sources of cheap energy materials and foreign markets for Czech products. Latest reports indicate still greater Soviet domination of foreign trade as the Russian share will grow ten percent to one-third of the total in the next few years. Since normalization exports have decreased twelve percent and foreign currency reserves have disappeared, industry becomes more non-competitive daily as both outmoded technology and worker apathy contribute to economic decay. Moscow visibly directs Czech foreign and domestic policies and isn't about to alter course in

the near future. Given the existing constraints it is inevitable
that further industrial progress will be extremely difficult to
attain as Party leaders and policies continue to inspire only
minimal public confidence.

NOTES

* Unless otherwise specified the word Czech is used as a
  shortened form of Czechoslovakia in this chapter.

1. Although Politburo and Presidium are used in each country at
   different times to denote the small ruling innercircle in the
   Party, in this chapter Politburo is consistently used to refer
   to the Party group in all countries.

2. For further explanation of the political culture concepts see
   Lucian W. Pye and Sidney Verba, *Political Culture and Political
   Development*, (Princeton, N.J.: Princeton University Press,
   1969), especially Chapter 12.

3. A good general discussion is provided in Milton Mayer, "A
   Study of the Czech Resistance: The Art of the Impossible",
   Center Occasional Paper, Vol. II, No. 3, April 1969.

4. A readable Czech history with more detailed explanations is
   S. Harrison Thomson, *Czechoslovakia in European History*,
   (Hamden, Conn.: Archon Books, 1965). For a good discussion of
   Party history see Edward Taborsky, *Communism in Czechoslovakia
   1948-1960*, (Princeton, N.J.: Princeton University Press, 1961).

5. Mayer, op. cit., pp. 9-12

6. For a more complete discussion of modernization and decisional
   models in socialist society see Dennis Pirages, "Modernization: New Decisional Models in Socialist Society", in *Political
   Leadership in Eastern Europe and the Soviet Union*, ed.
   R. Barry Farrell, (Chicago: Aldine Publishing Co., 1970),
   p. 249.

7. See inter alia Seymour M. Lipset, *Political Man*, (Garden City:
   Doubleday & Co., Inc., 1960), Chapter 2. Philips Cutright,
   "National Political Development: Measurement and Analysis".
   American Sociological Review, April 1963. Dankwart A. Rustow,
   "Transitions to Democracy: Toward a Dynamic Model", *Compara-
   tive Politics*, April, 1970.

8. A relevant "two round" model of socialist industrialization
   has been suggested in Jan F. Triska, "Political Response of
   One Party States to Economic Affluence and Social Complexity:

Eastern Europe", presented at the American Political Science Association meeting in Chicago, September, 1967.

9. The most detailed English treatise on problems in the Czech economy is found in Ota Sik, *Plan and Market Under Socialism*, (Prague: Academia, 1967). See especially p. 47 ff.

10. Robert C. North in collaboration with Nazli Choucre, "Population and the Future International System", paper delivered at the American Political Science Association meeting in Los Angeles, September, 1970.

11. This argument is further developed in Amitai Etzioni, *The Active Society*, (New York: The Free Press, 1968), Part II.

12. Czech social scientists were well aware of these needs and the Czech *Action Program* includes many more such references throughout the text. See Paul Ello, ed., *Czechoslovakia's Blueprint for Freedom*, (Washington: Acropolis Books, 1968). Especially pp. 95-96 and 148-150.

13. See Jan Triska, "Czechoslovakia: A Case Study of Social and Political Development", in *The Changing Face of Communism in Eastern Europe*, ed. by Peter Toma, (Tuscon: Arizona Press, 1970), Chapter 6.

14. George Feiwel, *New Economic Patterns in Czechoslovakia*, (New York: Frederick A. Praeger Publ., 1968), pp. 42-43. Also Alfred Zauberman, *Industrial Progress in Poland, Czechoslovakia, and East Germany 1937-1962*, (London: Oxford University Press, 1964), passim.

15. Source: *Yearbook of Labor Statistics 1969*, (Geneva: United Nations International Labor Office), p. 509.

16. Reported in Zdenek Suda, *The Czechoslovak Socialist Republic*, (Baltimore: John Hopkins Press, 1969), p. 138.

17. For more detailed information see Dennis Pirages, "Socioeconomic Development and Political Access in the Communist Party-states", in *Communist Party States*, ed. Jan Triska, (New York: Bobbs-Merrill Co., Inc., 1969), p. 249.

18. Suda, *op. cit.*, pp. 128-139.

19. R. Rockingham Gill, "Czechoslovakia: Will the Soviet Army Intervene?", *East Europe*, July, 1968.

20. Jan Triska, "Political Change in Czechoslovakia and the Soviet Intervention", *Czechoslovakia: Intervention and Impact*, (New

78

York: N.Y. University Press, 1970), Chapter I, ed. W. Zartmen.

21. See Press Group of Soviet Journalists, "On Events in Czecho-slovakia", Moscow, 1968.

22. Mayer, op. cit., pp. 29-39.

23. Gill, op. cit., p. 3. Philips Windsor and Adam Roberts, *Czecho-slovakia 1968: Reform, Repression, and Resistance*, (Toronto: Clark, Irwin, & Co., 1969), pp. 105-108.

24. Suda, op. cit., p. 174 ff.

25. For analysis see Michael Ball, "Soviet Policy in Eastern Europe", *East Europe*, February, 1969, pp. 20-24.

26. Vernon Aspaturian, "The Soviet Union and Eastern Europe: The Aftermath of the Czechoslovakian Invasion", *Czechoslovakia: Intervention and Impact*, ed. W. Zartman, (New York: N.Y. University Press, 1970).

27. Reported in *East Europe*, January, 1969, pp. 41-42.

Chapter IV

EAST GERMAN FOREIGN POLICY

John M. Starrels and
Anita M. Mallinckrodt

Several years ago Henry Kissinger noted that little attention
had been devoted to the impact and influence of domestic factors
in foreign policy making. In his words, "The domestic structure
is taken as a given; foreign policy begins where domestic policy
ends". (1) Since the late 1960s, however, a number of writers in
the international relations field have attempted to deal realistically with the challenge and problem of developing analytical
frameworks capable of simultaneously integrating both sets of
variables in the study of foreign policy making. R. Barry Farrell's
seminal collection of articles in this area, *Approaches to Compa-*
rative and International Politics (1966), (2) was soon followed
(if not accompanied) by a variety of important contributions from
Paul Hammond, Wolfram Hanrieder, Herbert Kelman, and James
Rosenau. (3)
    Rosenau's interest in studying the interrelationship between
domestic and foreign policy has taken an especially interesting
turn. Known as "linkage theory", his writing tends to focus on
how national political systems have become integrally involved
with foreign policy events and processes. "In short", he argues:
    the need for linkage theory in multidimensional. The
    examples suggest that political analysis would be greatly
    facilitated if propositions that link the stability,
    functioning, institutions, and goals of national political
    systems to variables in their external environments could
    be systematically developed. They also indicate that much
    would be gained if hypotheses linking the stability, func-
    tioning, and organizations of international systems to
    variables within their national sub-systems were avail-
    able ... (there) is the need to trace linkages in which
    national and international systems function in such a way

as to continuously reinforce each other. (4)
Building on an emerging theory of "linkage", this discussion
attempts to contribute to an understanding of foreign policy
making in the German Democratic Republic in terms of domestic
variables. In line with recent "external" events and developments
in West Germany and the Soviet Union, a new look at domestic
factors work in the foreign policy making process of the GDR (an
abbreviation used throughout) is certainly justified, if not long
overdue. (5) Though an exploratory study of domestic forces at
work in GDR foreign policy cannot immediately posit empirical sets
of "linkages" between domestic and external variables, the long-
run goals moves in that direction.
    Four general factor are systematically touched upon in the
study:
    1) Historical-cultural trends shed initial light on background
variables conditioning the foreign policy process. As boundary-
setting and maintaining factors, historical-cultural conditions in
the GDR provided necessary insight into how environmental factors
surround analyses of domestic-foreign policy linkages in East-
Germany. (6)
    2) Socio-economic questions have conditioned the development
and maintenance of East German political institutions. On the domestic front, the New Economic System has been used to provide a
framework of political legitimacy for the East German regime; externally, the GDR's complex relationship with the Soviet Union, and
other socialist states in Eastern Europe, turns on a variety of
socio-economic agreements which provide direct and indirect inputs
into the domestic foreign policy making process of the GDR. (7)
    3) Institutional considerations occupy important roles in the
formation and execution of foreign policy directives. The ruling
communist party of the GDR, the SED (Socialist Unity Party),
instruments of government authority, the Ministerial and State
Council's, and institutionalized interest groups, are important
foreign policy actors. (8)
    4) Background characteristics of the GDR elite supply a final
means of understanding its foreign policy behavior. Building on
earlier work in this area, social-psychological variables suggest
an additional way of looking at foreign policy matters. (9)

Historical-Cultural Determinants

    Historical-cultural patterns have played important roles in
East German foreign policy making. Looking backward, the all-
German past has provided positive and negative models for contemporary East German elites. As in West Germany, the GDR has attempted
to "digest the past" with varying degrees of success. With these
issues in mind, five aspects of historical-cultural development
are dealt with.
    1) *Administrative-authoritarianism* -- Is there a typical German?

Journalists and social scientists have devoted an extravagent
amount of time and effort attempting to deal with this question.
Few "hard" or reliable answers have emerged. Perhaps the absence
of a precise and critical focus has been responsible for this
failure to carefully delineate the "modal" German. (10) In other
words, "what kind of German, or ... Germany, are we looking for?"
Current geographocal divisions within the German nation provide a
realistic vantage point for answering the question.

The GDR covers an area of 41,659 miles, or about 23 percent
of the area of the German Reich of 1937. On the north, the
GDR is bordered by the Baltic Sea; on the south, by Czechoslovakia; on the west, by the Federal Republic. On the
east, the Oder and Neisse rivers from the boundary with
Poland. (11)

Geographical boundaries aside, however, historical parellels
between East Germany and the Prussian state of the 17th century
throw comparative light on the existence of administrative-author-
itarian values.

The Prussian state won the acceptance, and eventually the
loyalty, of many of its inhabitants, for it offered them
a better chance of security against foreign attack and of
predictable legality and honest administration, some educational opportunity, and long-term economic growth. At
the same time, however, the austerity and authoritarian
discipline of Prussia repelled many Germans, particularly
those outside its borders. They saw it as a vast barracks
yard, ruled by a royal drill sergeant. (12)

Jean Edward Smith places the two traditions in a comparative
perspective when he suggests that the East German "government
relies on the traditional form of the administrative state; the
Rechtstaat of Bismarck and the Emperor. And in this way, Socialism
in East Germany merges into the traditional pattern of Prussia.
The citizen obeys, but he does so freely. And growing economic
prosperity -- plus a genuine beliefe in many of the new norms --
makes the graft seem permanent." (13)

2) *Marxism-Leninism in the GDR*. Traditional German values obviously play contemporary roles in the present East German political system, but the direct influence of Marxism-Leninism provides
a more precide focus for an appreciation of foreign policy behavior. Looking at this tradition in relation to the GDR's legitimacy
problem is necessary.

East Germany provides an interesting, if not sad, historical
paradox for students of political legitimacy. It is true, on the
one hand, that the GDR cannot lay claim to an inclusive national
boundary; it can only speak for seventeen out of seventy-six
million Germans. Unlike post-war socialist regimes in Czechoslovakia, Poland, Hungary, Romania, and Bulgaria, East German political leaders have been placed in the uneviable situation of having
to undertake not only wide-ranging social, economic, and ideological programs of "socialist construction", but problems of nation-

building as well. This dilemma has been made especially difficult
in light of the ability of Western Germany to successfully out-
compete the GDR in social and economic attractiveness. The decision to build the Berlin Wall eloquently speaks for itself. On
the other hand, the GDR can boast a national tradition of Marxism,
a claim no other bloc-state can make. Indeed, East German elites
are not only in the position of claiming the author of *das Kapital*
as one of their own, but of a philosophical tradition which includes Friedrich Engels, Rosa Luxemburg, and Karl Liebknecht. Jean
Edward Smith touches this aspect of East German historical-cultural traditions with appropriate care:

... (It) would be naive to assume that the Communist government in Pankow is the result simply of Russian force majeure.
To begin with, communism is not an alien ideology of Germany
Marx and Engels were nothing if not German, and the entire
logical structure of Marxist thought rests on the imposing
edifice of 19th Century German philosophy -- and especially
the works of Hegel and Feuerbach. In many respects, if
there was a Marxist movement in the late 19th Century, it
was German. With the exception of Lenin, most early interpretations of Marx were German; and it was in German along
in the Europe of 1912 where the Marxists constituted the
largest single party in the Parliament ... And the Left
Marxists -- under Karl Liebknecht and Rosa Luxemburg -- were
fully as significant in the *International* as Lenin and
Trotsky. (14)

3) *World War II and the Occupation*. A third important historical-
cultural factor in East German history has a more immediate bearing on the domestic-foreign policy relationship. In simplest terms,
the German Communists' years of exile and oppresion during the
Third Reich, and the immediate post-war Soviet Occupation period
have played substantive parts in current elite definitions of
foreign policy alternatives. (15) Whereas the first period, 1933-
1945, has provided the current leadership with an image of martyr-
dom and sacrifice on behalf of a "future German socialist nation",
the second period, 1946-1949, has been used as a means of providing
a viable alternative framework for national development. (16) Of
crucial importance has been the impact of Soviet values and norms
within the reality worlds of elites and masses in the GDR.

East German definitions of political reality and strategic
feasibility have been colored by the Soviet occupation experience.
Conceptions of state and party rule, the nature of its social
institutions, and the broad definition of external "socialist
friends and capitalist enemies", represent the visible areas in
which Soviet influence has made the GDR a "penetrated system". (17)

4) *Competition and Non-Recognition*. A fourth item provides a
direct look at roles of historical-cultural factors in the GDR;
since the end of World War II, East Germany has been engaged in a
never-ending competition with its West German relative. From political ideology to comparative living standards, the two German

states have attempted to measure and evaluate their relative sense of legitimacy in relation to the successes and failures of their post-war rival. With some exceptions, the GDR has come out on the short end of the competition.

Because of its relative importance in U.S. strategic planning, West Germany has been able to combine its natural economic and geographical superiority with the claim that it is the sole representative of the German nation. Once again, the GDR was forced to supply an answer to the West German claim, though in contrast with "material" competition between two economic systems, the challenge was symbolic in this instance. From 1949 through the late 1960s, the GDR countered this argument by defining itself as the "progressive alternative" within all-German history, a claim it emphasized by disavowing any responsibility for Nazi crimes against humanity. With the coming to power of Erich Honecker, however, greater attention has been given to making East Germany more "differentiated" from its West German rival.

5) *The GDR's Survival Relationship with the USSR*. The final, and in many ways the most significant, historical-cultural determinant of East German domestic and foreign policies -- especially their linkage -- lies in the special relationship it enjoys with the Soviet Union. From the beginning of East Germany's political existence in the immediate post-war era, East German elites have necessarily been forced to coordinate their domestic political, economic, and social goals, with the requirements of a Soviet influenced, if not dominated, foreign policy.

Regularities within the GDR's relationship with the Soviet Union should not, of course, be allowed to blur important nuances which have developed within it, especially since the construction of the Berlin Wall. Though East German domestic politics is inevitably influenced by Soviet foreign policy initiatives, as recent detente policies of the West Germans have once again illustrated. the GDR has become "more equal" partner of the number one socialist state in Europe, if not the world. Nonetheless, a recent statement by the new GDR political leader, Erich Honecker, underlines, once again, the intensity and depth of East Germany's survival relationship with the USSR. Responding to an "on-the-record" question posed by an interviewer of the SED newspaper, *Neuesdeutschland*, the linkage between domestic and external politics in the GDR could not have been made clearer:

Question: During the VIIIth Partyday Congress of the SED, the importance of cooperation with the Soviet Union was underlined. How would you characterize the situation and perspectives on the development of relations between our parties: the CPSU and the SED?

Answer: For many years our party has viewed the relationship with the CPSU as the crucial axis of our policies. In this spirit communists are educated and they behave accordingly in the GDR. At the present time it is becoming increasingly evident that this relationship will have fruitful conse-

quences for GDR domestic and external policies. Let me once
more underline the following: The Socialist Unity Party of
Germany and the German Democratic Republic are for all time
closely and irrevocably bound with the Soviet Union. This
friendship is not only an important living foundation; in
equal measure it is an existence-need. "Our way" -- those
events and experiences -- strengthen the historically-justi-
fied thesis that relations with the USSR and the CPSU represent the test of proletarian internationalism. Our party,
indeed, the whole working class of our republic, feel ourselves bound with Pride and Joy to the Leninist Avantgarde. (18)

Socio-Economic Factors

If East German elites had enjoyed the relatively favorable
occupational climate greeting West German political leaders in the
late 1940s, their legitimacy problem might have been resolved with
less pain. Without downplaying the importance of politics, especially the denial of civil liberties, East Germany's basic source
of systemic instability, it can easily be argued, stems from
socio-economic dilemmas. On the one hand, it was subjected to
crippling reparations by the Soviet Union during the formative
stages of its development; instead of receiving generous recon-
structed aid, the GDR was left holding a thirteen billion dollar
bill. On the other hand, it lost roughly three million citizens
between 1949 and 1961. (19) With little exaggeration, few systems
have experienced less auspicious beginnings.
Two basic themes have been generated from initial socio-economic
difficulties. One, social integration and economic modernization
have proceeded simultaneously in the GDR. Beginning with the New
Economic System in early 1963, the GDR has been able to achieve
an impressive rate of industrial growth up to the early 1970s, a
phenomenon accompanied by a visible increase in personal mobility
and living standards, Baylis and Ludz have dealt with the domestic
ramifications of economic modernization -- some attention is given
to how these domestic events have contributed toward an understanding of the GDR's foreign policy "image". (20) Two, East Germany's
foreign policy role is linked with a variety of institutional
obligations which have evolved from its membership in the Soviet-
bloc. In pure economic terms, the GDR occupies a key role within
the "socialist world system" as a supplier of industrial products.
An understanding of foreign policy making in East Germany must
include an appreciation of this factor.
1) *Performance and Legitimacy*. In early 1963, Walter Ulbricht
announced a wide-reaching plan of administrative and economic
modernization. Following in the footsteps of Soviet developments,
the GDR attempted to revamp the nature of its economic system.
Comparing past practices with future planning goals, Ludz touches
on the main elements of proposed change:

Compared to the unrealistic goal expressed in 1958, which
had been to catch up to or even surpass the Federal Republic
in per capita consumption within several years, the economic
goals of 1963 were far more carefully formulated. The concepts of profit, cost, price, profit-earning capacity,
economic cost accounting were finally accepted as principles
of industrial management in the GDR. Wages and bonuses were
raised, and therefore the situation of the working population was considerably improved. Even more important was the
first hesitant recognition of the principle of performance
(Leistungsprinzip) ... (The) Leistungsprinzip meant that
wages in industry, etc. were to be set according to the
worker's performance. (21)
    As the "NES" later called the "developing system of socialism"
became a permanent aspect of East German society, it increasingly
began to perform functions of system legitimization. In a narrow
sense, an East German sense of "national-identity" was fostered
through appeals to traditional German values of industriousness
and efficiency. From this vantagepoint the SED strove to link its
rule with more enduring patterns of behavior within the mass population. In a somewhat broader sense, "socialist concerns". or
factories became focal points for the transmission of pro-regime
values and norms. Linking performance in the work place with individual citizenship, the "NES" became a favorite means of creating
patterns of diffuse indentification within the workforce. By the
late 1960s regime theorist were even arguing that the NES was the
vital "hub" around which other institutions, including political
one, revolved. (22)
    Changes at work in the East German economic system began to
alter the GDR's foreign policy image, especially in the Soviet-bloc.
From a chronically unstable system, the GDR began to exhibit signs
of political influence and economic prowess by the early 1960s.
Under the banner of the "NES", Walter Ulbricht proudly advertised
the GDR's vital and increasingly co-equal relationship with the
Soviet Union. Indeed, he even began to assert that East German
economic success was a sine qua non for the pursuit of socialist
goals in the international system. With obvious satisfaction, if
not blatant smugness, he maintained that, "Ultimately it contributes to the well-being of the GDR's working class and the strengthening of world socialism. It consolidates the economic foundations
and external "image" of our Republic, thereby strengthening the
political, moral, military, and cultural potential of our worker's
and peasant's state in its struggle for European security and the
maintenance of peace." (23)
    With the successful introduction of economic reforms in the GDR,
a number of visible foreign policy impacts began to make themselves
evident by the middle 19602. As the GDR moved into a partnership
status with the Soviet Union, its international image rose accordingly. Thus, Ulbricht was able to simultaneously carry on renewed
competition with West Germany on the basis of the GDR's "own econom-

ic miracle", while making a number of successful diplomatic forays
into the Third World. Linking diplomatic activity with increased
economic stability, the GDR was able to persuasively make its case
for recognition by making its appeal turn on the promise of financial aid. (24)

The recent change in SED leadership has brought a certain moderation in the GDR's external image. Though the now "developed
social system of socialism" is still the most obvious means through
which East German elites attempt to communicate the GDR's sense of
legitimacy, Erich Honecker's regime has clearly tried to develop a
lower international profile. In this vein, the policy of "demarca-
tion" (Abgrenzung) mirrors an attempt to stabilize the GDR's foreign policy image in line with Soviet strategic and political
goals. Though hard conclusions come with difficulty -- if they
come at all -- one result of this power transfer, from Ulbricht to
Honecker, might be a gradual abandonment of the attempt to link
foreign policy visibility with "pure" economic prowess. (25)

2) *The GDR in the "Socialist State Community" (Sozialistische
Staatsgemeinschaft)*. In the wake of Hitler's defeat, the Soviet
Union was able to create a system of quasi-dependent "socialist"
regimes in the eastern part of Europe. Though economic and political coordination has been an integral part of these relationships
since the late 1940s, most Eastern European regimes have been
able, with varying degrees of success, to arrive at workable compromises with their number one patron, the USSR. Thus, Hungary
has gained a relatively high degree of cultural freedom while
hewing a strict Soviet line in external affairs; Romania has re-
versed the bargain, opting for relative external independence and
domestic (i.e. conservative Soviet) retrenchment; Poland has
gained something from both worlds -- occasional foreign policy
independence, combined with a degree of domestic pluralism,
especially in the performing arts. The GDR has been unable to and
perhaps incapable of exercising these dual alternatives. Its
"survival relationship" with the Soviet Union may not explain
particular nuances within East Germany's domestic and foreign
policy behavior; the relative absence of independence in either
area, however, can be traced to this crucial relationship. (26)
The nature of its membership in what is now referred to as the
"socialist state-community" provides another insight into socio-
economic determinants of GDR foreign policy while simultaneously
shedding light on its special dependency status.

The GDR's role within the socialist state community suggests
an obvious anomaly. On the one hand, it has been able to reach an
enviable, at least from an East European perspective, level of
economic development: it boasts the highest living standard in the
Soviet-bloc. On the other hand, the GDR is heavily dependent on
its socialist neighbors for a variety of economic resources which
it cannot provide for itself. Joachim Krüger, an East German economist, provides an explanation of this problem:

(At the end of World War II ... (T)he manufacturing industry

in Germany was separated from its traditional raw materials
area ... In 1945 the area within the GDR possessed a mere
1.3% of raw iron products, 7% of the steel-producing industry,
2% of the bituminous coal production, and 16% of all-German
manufactured products in the metallurgical and foundry industry. In 1949 there were one hundred and twenty-one blast
furnaces (mostly new) in West Germany, there were our old
ones in the East.)
Blaming the Western powers for creating such unfavorable "take-
off" conditions in the economic sector, Krüger concludes, "As an
advanced industrial state within a constricted land area and a
small population, the GDR is faced by the very nature of its situation with the ongoing task of furthering intensive external
trade (Aussenhandel) and external economic relations in pursuit
of raw materials and sales markets".(27) These considerations
throw light on dominant challenges facing the GDR economy.
    On the societal level, East Germany faces a population dilemma.
Ludz deals with this side of the problem:
    In 1946 approximately 18.5 million people lived in what is
    now the GDR. At the end of 1968, the population came to
    only 17.1 million ... From 1946 to 1961 about 0.5% of the
    population of 17.1 million, about 7.8 million were males
    and about 9.3 million females. (28)
In a parallel vein, the English journalist, David Childs, throws
light on another aspect of population difficulties in the GDR:
    East Germany suffers not only from having too few people,
    it also has the wrong kind. Out of every hundred Germans
    in 1939, 67.5% were of working age. By 1965 this percentage
    had dropped to 58.2. And although the percentage of children
    under 15 years old had increased since 1939 -- 23.2 as
    against 21.4 -- so has the percentage of old people -- 18.6
    as against 11.1. (29)
The growth of the "young innovator" movement, for example, represents an attempt to stretch a static labor supply by encouraging
newly arrived job holders to devise novel ways to "rationalize"
the production process. Further, the existing labor supply is
encouraged to enthusiastically participate in the "production
process" by the reward of top executive posts to young technocrats.
Beyond these immediate efforts, the regime does supply parents
with financial and social-service premiums for raising large
families. (30)
    Shifting attention to East Germany's membership in a socialist
economic community, its role in the Soviet-controlled "Council For
Mutual Economic Aid" is of special interest (Rat für Gegenseitige
Wirtschaftshilfe, or RGW). Founded in 1949, the RGW is organized
around the goal of perfecting "economic and scientific-economic"
cooperation between socialist countries. As the primary means
through which bloc-members conduct economic business, the RGW has
been of special importance for the GDR. As Krüger notes, "next to
the USSR, the GDR is the main deliverer of machines and equipment

to RGW members" Thus, "30% of all machine imports for member
states come from the GDR". (31) On the other hand, East Germany's
raw material needs (coal, steel, oil) are met, if only imperfectly,
by membership in the RGW. (32)
    Strictly speaking, the GDR's economic situation is inseparable
from political considerations: National division, and the development of competing political structures in both parts of the country, accent the influence of political variables over socio-
economic ones. In the immediate, or "operational", world within
the GDR is called upon to operate, however, its levels of industrial performance, the age and occupational make-up of its population, and the on-going conduct of East German foreign policy
within the socialist "economic" community, revolve in large degree
around socio-economic questions.
    If foreign-policy making involves decision-making in coordina-
tive planning, and consultative, activities, there is little argument that East Germany's external policies are strongly reflected
in socio-economic issues. Beginning with 1945, with the onset of
crippling reparations and dismantling schedules, and ending with
the use of economic reforms as a means of engendering political
legitimacy (and hence stability), the GDR's foreign policy identity
has been linked with socio-economic variables: population losses,
social mobilization, changes in living standards, and involvement
in the RGW, persuasively underline the importance of linking
foreign policy behavior with these factors.

Institutional Factors

    One of the few systematic studies dealing specifically with the
foreign policy of a single communist country -- the Soviet Union
-- provides a useful model for assessing the significant factor of
institutional input. By using the concept of foreign policy
decision-making as a process, Triska and Finley arrive at a model
involving the phases of 1) information selection and collection,
2) formulation of purpose, 3) information interpretation, 4) formulation of alternatives, 5) commitment to action, 6) elaboration,
explanation, interpretation, 7) reiteration, confirmation, ratification, 8) dissemination and implementation. (33) In a study making
use of this phase-model, it was found that major institutional
inputs of GDR foreign policy emanate primarily from 1) the Party,
2) the State, 3) organizations, and 4) interest groups. (34)
    1) *Party*. The major institutional input into GDR foreign policy
decision-making comes from the Politburo and the Secretariat of
the Central Committee of the SED. (35) Although decision-making is
a collective responsibility of the Politburo, there is a division
of labor among its present 16 full and 10 candidate members. Each
is assigned a resort, or area of specialization, but the assign-
ments are not permanent.
    The areas of specialization are most clearly identifiable among

Politburo members who also serve in the Secretariat of the Central
Committee, the administers departments and sections, controls
personnel, and makes up Politburo meeting agendas. For instance,
regarding foreign affairs specialization, Politburo member
Hermann Axen is Secretary for International Affairs in the Secretariat -- thus, he is responsible for coordination of foreign
policy for the Party, maintaining contracts with other Communist
Parties, and keeping abreast of developments in the international
communist movement. Paul Verner, as Secretary for Security, is
believed to be primarily concerned with domestic security, but
probably also is involved in foreign aspects. Additionally, Albert
Norden is Secretary for Propaganda, Werner Jarowinsky for Foreign
Trade and Supply, and Werner Krolikowski is believed to be Secretary for Economics (replacing Günther Mittag, who relinquished
this position in October, 1973). Honecker, as 1st Secretary, in
addition to heading the Secretariat, is believed to have special
responsibility for foreign policy and personnel. Other Politburo
members who do not have resorts in foreign affairs, nevertheless
have top-level contracts abroad or with foreigners visiting East
Berlin and so are logical recipients of highly relevant foreign
policy information. Thus, all Politburo members have significant
roles in the decision-making phase of information selection and
collection, formulation of policy purposes, and commitment to
foreign policy actions.

Additionally, those decision-makers in the Secretariat can request their staffs on occasion to interpret long-range trends
relevant to the action-commitment phase. Thus, the Secretariat is
important in the purpose-formulation phase, formulation of alternatives, the elaboration, -explanation, -interpretation phase, as
well as the reiteration, -confirmation, -and-ratification phase
-- in short, the supervision and implementation of Politburo
foreign policy decisions.

Aside from its Secretariat, the Central Committee's apparat
plays an additional institutional role in nearly all phases of
the foreign policy decision-making process. Its Departments may
be called upon for technical interpretation of foreign affairs
information, as in the information-interpretation phase, the formulation-of-alternatives, and the elaboration, -explanation, -and-
interpretation phase. Departments tapped for such assistance could
include International Relations, Foreign Information, Trade,
Supplies and Foreign Trade, Propaganda, State and Legal Questions,
and the West Department. Similarly, the specialist Sections of
the Central Committee Departments are active in the information-
interpretation phase.

Academic units related to the Central Committee, too, are influential in foreign policy input, especially for information
interpretation. These units include the Institute for Social
Sciences, a research as well as training institute. Many of its
members, for instance, contribute foreign policy articles to the
SED's theoretical journal *Einheit* -- it is interesting to note that

in recent years Institute authors have been especially concerned with West Germany. (36) The Central Committee's Institute for Marxism-Leninism, too, turns out foreign-oriented research (international workers' movements), as does its Institute for Socialist Economic Research. The new Institute for International Politics and Economics (growing out of a merger of the former DIZ and DWI institutes), now is the major center for research concerning the West. (37) It is believed to be closely related to the Party's Central Committee.

The Party's involvement in foreign affairs is further intensified in that it appears to have its own apparat which has direct contracts to Communist Parties abroad.

2) *State*. While the Party's input clearly dominates the foreign policy decision-making process, in recent years the GDR's state apparat also has won considerable acceptance.

During the period of Ulbricht's leadership, the major state institutional foreign policy input came from the State Council (Staatsrat). Organized in September 1960 and chaired by former 1st Secretary Ulbricht, it met frequently and served as a collective state executive. (38) Honecker, however, after his assumption of SED leadership has not used the Staatsrat in the same way. (Willi Stoph now is Chairman.) Instead, it now rarely meets and no longer is the state power and decision-making center of the GDR.

The downgrading of the State Council was achieved by upgrading the Council of Ministers (Ministerrat), a kind of super cabinet made up of Ministry heads. This process has been a gradual one. It may be said to have begun with the 1968 Constitution in which Article 78 declared that the Council of Ministers organizes the execution of the social tasks of the socialist state on behalf of the Peoples Chamber (Volkskammer). Thus the old law of April 17, 1963 stipulating that the Ministerrat was the executive organ of both the Volkskammer and the Staatsrat (39) was rendered invalid. The upgrading of the Ministerrat continued when a new law was passed on October 16, 1972 making the Ministerrat the government of the GDR. (40) Now it no longer is responsible to the Staatsrat, but only to the Volkskammer. Wile Willi Stoph was its chairman he made clear that the Ministerrat would work collectively and that its role now was legally fixed ("staatsrechtlich fixiert"). (41) Further, it is to carry out, as the 1968 Constitution says, "political, economic, cultural and social ... and defense tasks." According to the old law, the Ministerrat's emphasis was confined to economic matters.

As the leading state body, the Ministerrat, now chaired by Horst Sindermann, is believed to contribute significantly to charting foreign policy by channeling views (especially from the Ministries for Foreign Affairs, Defense, and Foreign Trade) directly to the Politburo or indirectly through its Chairman, who is a Politburo member. Apparently the views represented by the Ministerrat are entertained in all phases of the decision-making process, except perhaps the crucial phase of commitment to action. (42)

Further, the various Ministries have close connections to corresponding Central Committee departments and make their influence felt via these routes.

Obviously another important area of foreign policy input of the Ministerrat is its involvement in the GDR's foreign economic aid activities. Because it is the coordinator for developmental aid it has, for instance, set up a High School for Economics which includes an Institute for the Economy of the Developing Countries. Another source of important Ministerial input is the Academy for State and Legal Science (DASR), where foreign affairs personnel are trained.

In addition to the Ministerrat, another important state institution relating to foreign affairs is the National Defense Council. Organized in October 1960, the Council is considered an "emergency government", or cabinet. Headed by Honecker, the Council's Chairman is considered by some specialists to be "the second most important position in the GDR power structure". (43) According to the Constitution (Article 73), the Council's members are appointed by the Staatsrat, and the Council "is responsible to the People's Chamber and the Council of State for its activities". (Its relationship to the State Council, now, however, is largely formal.) Those activities are described as being the making of fundamental decisions about the organizing of the country's national defense and security. Thus the Council is given responsibility to organize and coordinate the defense-related activities of the various Ministries, as well as to articulate "prognostic concepts". (44) Although it is not known with certainty, it is believed that in addition to 1st Secretary Honecker, the Defense Council includes the Central Committee Secretary for Security Questions (Paul Verner), the Minister for Defense (Heinz Hoffman) and his deputy, the Minister for Security (Erich Mielke), and the Minister of the Interior (Friedrich Dickel). (The Prime Minister may also be a member.) It is not clear at what phase of the decision-making process the National Defense Council operates. A logical assumption, however, is that it would be influential during phases where security interests are most pressing, i.e. the information-selection-and-collection phase, the formulation-of-alternatives, the elaboration, -explanation, -interpretation phase, and perhaps even the crucial commitment-to-action period.

Much less important but worthy of mention is the Peoples Chamber (Volkskammer), or Parliament, and its foreign policy related groups. These would include the Foreign Policy Committee and the Committee for National Defense. Although the Foreign Policy Committee plays a relatively insignificant role in formulating foreign policy, it sometimes has indirect importance because of the prestige and positions in other policy organs of some of the committee members, such as its Chairman. Similarly, the Committee for National Defense usually is headed by a Volkskammer member who also is a member of the Politburo. Finally, state agencies for international propaganda obviously also have a significant foreign policy input in the dissemination-and-implementation stage. Such agencies would include Radio Berlin International (whose new director, Erich Jungmann, is a personal acquaintance of Honecker) and the radio stations Deutschlandsender, directed at West Germany, the Berliner Welle, broadcasting to West Berlin. (The coordination bodies for the electronic media of the DDR are the State Committees for Radio and Television.) In addition, the DDR's press agency, ADN, is a significant in foreign policy dissemination -- it is responsible to the Press Office of the Ministerial Council.

3) *Organizations: Mass, Professional, International*. In all communist states mass organizations play a key role in social mobilization and implementation of policy lines. Thus, the international departments of GDR mass organizations of which they are members.

A more unique foreign policy role has been filled by the GDR's international organization, i.e. helping pave the way for diplomatic recognition. For instance, it is reported that there are 53 bilateral West German friendship societies in existence in non-socialist states, 172 committees for the recognition of the GDR, and cultural relations with 70 nations. (45) Such activities are under the control of the Foreign Ministry, according to a February 1970 statute defining the role of the Ministry, and are coordinated by the League for Peoples Friendship. (46)

4) *Interest Groups*. The policy input role of interest groups in communist systems has been given increased attention in recent years. Skilling, for instance, has suggested that in addition to the Party and state interests, managers, agriculture, the military, and cultural, professional, and scientific intelligentsia have emerged as interest groups affecting public policy. (47) Since their intention is to influence policy rather than seek power, this obviously means access to the top levels of the Party, especially in the formulation-of-purpose phase of the decision-making process. In the specific case of foreign policy in the GDR, at least three such interest groups appear to be significant. They are:

a) Military/Security, including elites from the Defense Ministry, Ministry of Interior, and Ministry of Security. Their primary concern, locally, is continued military alertness in foreign affairs matters.

b) Economic/Technical/Scientific, including elites from the State Planning Commission, directors of research institutes, and members of the Academy of Sciences. Under Honecker's leadership, the influence of the Academy has become especially significant. At the 4th Central Committee plenum session in mid-December 1971, for instance, Honecker made clear that science would continue to play an increasingly important role in modernizing the society and economy.

Regarding foreign affairs generally, the influence of this interest group would be for broadening international contacts which could mean access to advanced technology and information exchange. (It is interesting, therefore, to note that new measures for in-

creasing scientific and technical cooperation with Czechoslovakia
and Hungary recently have been taken.) Another logical interest
issue would be that of resource allocation, as for economic modernization and research.

c) Cultural/Intellectual, including officers of intellectual
groups with foreign contacts, such as the Union of German Writers,
the Society for Cultural Relations, the German Academy of Art, as
well as University presidents, especially those whose institutions
specialize in area foreign affairs training. Here the logical interest input would be for increased international contacts.

Elites in the Policy Process

In considering elite linkages with policy-making, the analyst
has more systematic background material to draw on than in the
case with other input factors. For instance, in the case of the
GDR, the pioneering work of Peter C. Ludz is well known. (48)

According to Ludz, there are two major elite groups in the GDR.
One is what he describes as the "strategic clique". These are
veteran party leaders (apparatchiki) with long experience in organizational work of the Party, but limited education. The other
group, the "institutionalized counterelite" (technocrats) have
specialized educations, are influenced by more differentiated
philosophical and ideological views, and appear to be more open
to change. The interaction of these two groups within the Party
organization has led to what Ludz calls "consultative authoritar-
ianism" which acknowledges "quasi-pluralistic" forces.

Both groups remain committed to maintaining the essentials of
the "Developed Social System of Socialism". However, Ludz feels
the influence of the technocrat group is seen in the Party's acknowledgement of social conflicts, improvement in communications,
and concentration on economic and social policy. He argues, for
instance, that the Central Committee, with its increased number
of educated, specialized members, has become a kind of "consultative assembly". Additionally, interchangeability between the
governmental party, economic, and educational bureaucracies, a
conscious SED policy, has contributed to the modification of the
SED's leadership, organization, and style of ruling.

Later studies, however, have some reservations to the Ludz
thesis. While accepting his concept of elite-influenced change in
the GDR, some specialists see the divergences between elites as
being more "issue-oriented". Baylis, for instance, points out that
within the "counterelite", or technocrats, there are differing
perspectives on the issue of the means for achieving the goal of
economic growth. Some, for instance, favor market-line devices and
greater autonomy at lower level of decision-making. Others support
sophisticated mechanisms of central planning and control. (49)

1) *Foreign Policy Decision-Makers*. Regarding specifically foreign policy elites in the GDR, the previous section on institutional

inputs suggests who might be included. Even more specifically, a
recent study hypothesized that among those elites the following
Party and state leaders hold key foreign policy decision-making
positions : (50)

Politburo members Erich Honecker (1st Secretary), Paul Verner
(Secretariat Secretary for Security), Hermann Axen (Secretariat
Secretary for International Relations), Willi Stoph (Prime Min-
ister), Günther Mittag (Secretariat Secretary for Economics).
(At the time of the study, before the downgrading of the State
Council, Ulbricht, too, was included as a key decision-maker be-
cause of his position as Chairman of the State Council.)

Central Committee apparat member Paul Markowski (head of the
Central Committee Department for International Relations).

State leaders Otto Winzer (Minister of Foreign Affairs), Peter
Florin (1st Deputy Minister and State Secretary in the Foreign
Ministry), and Horst Sölle (Minister for Foreign Trade).

In examining these foreign policy decision-makers, several aspects of their background were suggested as significant to their
foreign policy input:

a) *Shared Ideological Belief System*: (51) The mental filter
through which decisions pass is what some specialists call a "belief system" (or belief-disbelief system). It consists of specific
opinion, habitual opinions, attitudes, and ideological beliefs.
Within the last portion are socio-political values, i.e. general
directions toward which actions should be directed. Those goals
for the domestic society, in turn, condition the goals to be
achieved abroad. In the case of the GDR, both the values and goals
grow out of Marxist-Leninist philosophy. They form part of the
mental context within which the decision-makers make their choices.

Systematic analysis suggests that the official version of that
context concerning foreign policy include the concepts that
a) Socialism calls for a new, a socialist, foreign policy (foreign
policy which promotes the interests of the working masses),
b) Foreign policy reflects domestic policy, c) Socialist foreign
policy must promote democracy and oppose counterrevolution (necessity to destroy the power of the international ruling class and
put power in the hands of the masses), and d) Socialist foreign
policy must end war and keep peace.

Against this philosophical background, the GDR Constitution
incorporated its political view of foreign policy in Article 6. (52)
According to Foreign Minister Winzer, "An important peculiarity of
the socialist Constitution of the GDR, in contrast to every bourgeois constitution, is precisely that it does not seek to conceal
the goals, principles, and rudiments of our foreign policy, but
rather formulates them clear and simply". (53)

The generalized Marxist principles and Constitutional articula-
tions, in turn, are clearly visible in specific theoretical enu-
merations of the GDR's present foreign policy goals. Those general
goals, intended naturally to promote national interests, are articulated ideologically by the SED in this way:

a) To create international conditions favorable to the development of socialism.
b) To strengthen the socialist alliance.
c) To support the cause of freedom of developing countries.
d) To promote peace and detente, especially in Europe.
A crucial dimension of the last goal is the GDR's concept of its
role as keeper of the peace, i.e. its position vis-à-vis the FRG.
The GDR feels it has a national and European responsibility to
hinder the renewed outbreak of a war from German soil. According
to its logic, the GDR has taken care of this problem on its own
territory by erecting a socialist economic system which elemenates
the profit motive which drove previous German societies to war.
Thus, the GDR sees its goal as preventing the FRG from following
the way of revanchism, atomic armament, and warlike foreign
policy. (54)
    b) *Roles Within the System*: (55) Studying roles as a factor
influencing elite input into foreign policy decision-making is
significant because the conflict between roles and the ambiguity
of roles may account for important aspects of social and organizational behavior. Common role dilemmas, for example, are the
choices political decision-makers must make between their superi-
or's orders and loyalty to a friend, or the ambiguity which results
when a decision-maker does not know how far his responsibilities
in a given position extend.
    In an authoritarian and hierarchical political system such as
the GDR's, the functions of Party leaders are relatively clearly
defined by the Party. Deviations from defined roles may result in
purges, reprimands, expulsion, reassignment, etc. Clearly, then,
those leaders who do rise to the top -- and stay there -- are
those who best fit the expectations of the Party, as defined at
a given time by the Politburo's then most influential members.
What the Party expects of its decision-makers can be gleaned from
Party documents and actions, as well as the decision-makers' statements plus their behavior. By analyzing the key decision-makers'
roles in this way, one may form some idea of the political motivations underlying constancy and continuity of foreign policy elite
political behavior. This, in turn, provides clues as to what political behavior one may reasonably expect from the key decision-
makers.
    Regarding general Politburo roles, some of the Party's expecta-
tions were found to include a) responsibility (collective and
personal), b) "scientificness" (to plan, emphasize prognosis, see
social development as a process, see democratic centralism, among
other things, as a pragmatic necessity, think broadly, overcome
"departmental work methods", overcome past separation of political-
ideological and organizational work in Party organizations),
c) maintaining contact with workers, d) use of persuasion and
education, and e) leading a model, stable personal life. Additionally, constraints imposed are those of democratic centralism,
Party discipline, criticism and self-criticism, collective leader-

ship, and Soviet confidence.

The score for the GDR's Politburo's role fulfillment is relatively good -- since 1949 ten Politburo members have been expelled
by the SED (1 in 1950, 6 in 1953, 2 in 1956, 1 in 1963) and 4 of
those have been "rehabilitated". Some specialists point out that
this constancy indicates the power the 1st Secretary has to per-
suade majority support in the Politburo. Others believe it reflects
the inherently homogenous view of the GDR Politburo -- the members
have much in common, for a number were acquainted during World War
II exile and most worked together to found the GDR. Such shared
experiences extending over years and reinforced by continuing
personal contacts are not easily set aside.

Concerning general state roles the major expectation seems to
be that of subordination to Party rulings. Additionally, as in
the case of Politburo members, scientificness and service to people
are expected.

Applying these expectations, plus the specific ones dictated by
the position held, it is suggested that the foreign policy role
expectations of the key decision-makers are:

First Secretary -- exercising foreign policy control; continuing statesman image of 1st Secretaryship;
integrating Party into society.

Secretary for Security -- maintaining national security, as
through modern personnel policies.

Secretary for International Relations -- maintaining contact
and securing support for GDR policies among
other Communist Parties.

Secretary for Economy -- achieving national economic growth
via approved Party means to support foreign
policy goals.

Central Committee Department Head for International Relations
-- obtaining and preparing foreign policy
information.

Chairman, Council of Ministers -- projecting effective national
representation for Party and people; achiev-
ing efficiency in state implementation of
Party decisions.

Foreign Minister -- achieving national foreign policy goals
set by Party.

1st Deputy, Ministry of Foreign Affairs -- achieving national
foreign policy goals; meeting daily foreign
policy operational problems.

Minister for Foreign Trade -- winning friends and support for
GDR foreign policy through economic means
capitalizing on foreign economic relations
to aid in realizing GDR economic goals.

c) *Social Background*: (56) In examining further the political
elites suggested above as being the key foreign policy decision-
makers, five aspects of social background were suggestive for
their potential effect on foreign policy input:

1) Family Background: Most were sons of workers. Unfortunately the biographic material offers almost no clues concerning the role of their mothers and their backgrounds.

2) Communist Party Entry: Four were sons of active KPD fathers, and thus undoubtedly were influenced toward communism in childhood. It is speculated that others, because of their worker background, joined the Party out of adult convictions. Younger men are believed to have been intellectually influenced toward SED membership by experiences as a Soviet POW or postwar membership in the FDJ.

3) World War II Experience: Backgrounds vary as to experience in concentration camps, prison, exile in the West, exile in Moscow, or service in the Hitler army.

4) Education and Expertise: Excluding Party training, the variations in education include Volksschule (grammer school) only, Volksschule plus some additional trade training, Mittelschule (equivalent to high school), or University education.

A good number have had top-level management/administration experience. Many have expertise in conspirative work or methods, mostly because of their pre-World War II experience while the Party was underground or hounded by the Nazis. Communications in another area of expertise shared by a number, and similarly, youth work was part of their background.

Nearly all have had Party organization experience, while some have experience in making the state apparat work. Additionally, there is experience in industrial affairs. The relatively limited amount of "scientific" expertise available in areas crucial to modern states becomes unusually significant in contemporary decision-making at a time when industrial and economic perspectives assume great importance in foreign affairs.

5) Personalities: People who have known the decision-makers personally and worked with them during the first decade of the GDR's existence, and those who have observed them from a less personal vantage point since then, are in agreement that they represent a very energetic leadership. They are seen as optimistic, deliberate, rational. Along with leaders of other modern nations, the GDR's decision-makers are viewed as tense. The fact that they also are judged as relatively suspicious and possessing significant frustration tolerance may be a factor distinguishing them from leadership groups who have not come to power through circumstances such as conspirative work and postwar chaos. Furthermore, they are seen as intellectually alert and organized.

2) *Diplomatic Personnel*. Despite the GDR's present need to reach out for non-professional diplomats to fill the many new posts created by the so-called "wave" of diplomatic recognition, its diplomatic elites increasingly are being specifically trained in foreign affairs. They, thus, can be relied upon for sophisticated reporting from their host countries. This is especially true of the newest generation of diplomats who have been educated at the German Academy for State and Legal Sciences 'Walter Ulbricht'

in Potsdam/Babelsberg. (Thus the GDR follows the trend throughout Eastern Europe to professionalize the diplomatic service.) The diplomats presently trained at the Potsdam/Babelsberg Institute received a five-year training course, sometimes supplemented by studies at the Moscow High School for Diplomacy or the Moscow Institute for International Relations. These younger men contrast sharply with the oldest generation of diplomatic personnel sent abroad by the GDR in the beginning years of its existence. As Foreign Minister Winzer explains:

"Proved anti-fascists ... worked in the diplomatic missions we had at first. They had absolved their studies in the high school of proletarian internationalism in the resistance struggle against the Hitler regime, in the international workers movement, in emigration and had already learned well to see the world from the perspective of the class struggle. They were sons of the working class as well as progressive intellectuals ... in the state apparat entirely new people had to be brought in; for the "former ones" were disqualified as Nazi activists." (57)

Between the young and old diplomats is a group of middle-aged men who represent a transitional phase in East German diplomatic development. They are individuals who in the early years of the GDR were selected by the SED from among young students, workers, or returned prisoners of war, especially from FDJ ranks, to study social sciences. After some years of practical professional performance they then were selected to enter foreign affairs work.

Since the diplomatic apparat now is seen as a merger of state and Party apparats, it is pointed out that ambassadors and Foreign Ministry employees face special challenges -- they usually are Central Committee members at home and in their host country must maintain Party as well as state contacts. Thus, loyalty to the Party line, high professional knowledge, comprehensive understanding of Marxism-Leninism, cultural development, intellectual balance, and initiative are all required characteristics.

3) *Economic Elite*. Largely responsible for the GDR's high standard of living, the highest in Eastern Europe, the economic elites' foreign policy input obviously is significant -- they are concerned about creating conditions which enable the GDR to maintain the economic status which is important to its international image, as well as domestic stability. Thus, for example, Politburo decisions regarding resource allocation is a primary interest.

But as already has been noted, the technocratic representation among the foreign policy specialists in the Politburo is limited. The situation within the Politburo as a whole is not different. In fact, one specialist sees the post-Ulbricht developments as a "substantial dilution" of technocratic influence in the Politburo. (58) The new Honecker appointments of 3 new full members (Lamberz, Krolikowski, Hoffmann) did not represent a plus for technocratic interests at the top of the Party where foreign policy decisions are made. (Lamberz's background is primarily agitation and press;

Krolokowski, too, has agitation experience and regional Party administration; Hoffmann is Minister of Defense.) Of the 7 candidate members appointed, however, one (Tisch) has had experience as a regional economic secretary, and Schürer heads the State Planning Commission. (The other new candidate members include Mielke, Minister for State Security; Hermann, editor of *Neues Deutschland*; Lange, women's affairs; Felfe and Naumann, regional Party administrators.)

The situation in the Secretariat is similar. Technocratic interests have not been strengthened by new appointments. (Lange has been named Secretary for Women's Affairs; Krolikowski, with Party administration background, replaces Mittag, who had a University education in economics, as Secretary for Economic Affairs; Mückenberger, who heads the Party Control Commission, is specialized in agricultural affairs, and Dohlus, named "member" of the Secretariat rather than "Secretary", had his experience in Party organization, or personnel, work.) Thus, tendencies within the Secretariat to give Party organization considerations priority over pragmatic economic considerations relating to foreign policy may have been reinforced.

On the state side of the GDR's dual governmental system, however, to a study of the Ministerrat through 1969, there has been a steady increase of economically trained experts and young peoples (59) If this trend has continued, it could be seen as significant to foreign policy considerations, especially in light of the Ministerrat's responsibility for economic leadership, according to the new 1972 law .

Among the state's economic elite, Ministry of Foreign Trade personnel may be assumed to have increased importance as the GDR expands its economic relations with the West, within Eastern Europe, and with the Third World. The Ministry for Foreign Trade traditionally has had an unusually significant foreign policy input influence because the GDR, during its years of non-recognition, frequently utilized its trade missions as substitutes for the embassies and consulates it did not have. Thus, the Foreign Ministry worked closely with the Ministry of Foreign Affairs. The Foreign Trade Ministry operates enterprises and institutions to carry out the state's foreign trade monopoly -- such as the Foreign Trade Enterprises, the Customs Administration, the German Foreign and Reinsurance Office. It also is responsible for the Chamber of Foreign Trade (founded in 1952 to establish contacts with trade and economic circles in the West), the international Leipzig Fair, and the Interwerbung GmbH (advertising corporation). Additionally, it supervises the Office for Foreign Economic Relations formed in April 1970 to contribute to the development of foreign trade and other relations in the area of foreign economics.

In summary, in considering elite linkages, the nature of elite groupings, as well as their varied reactions to issues, belief systems vis-à-vis foreign policy, specialized foreign policy roles, social background, etc. are significant. Especially important with-

in the GDR context, are Party, diplomatic, and economic elites.
Precisely when and how they contributes to the foreign policy
process remains the tantilizing question.

Conclusion: A Pre-Theory of GDR Foreign Policy? (60)

The argument behind examining linkages between domestic and
foreign policy is cogently outlined by Hanrieder:
> It has been widely recognized that contemporary historical
> circumstances throw serious doubt on the value of retain-
> ing the traditional and comfortably neat separation between
> international and domestic policies and the corollary dis-
> tinction between external and internal dimensions of for-
> eign policy projects. Although the nation-state may still
> be regarded as the major actor in world politics, both the
> nature of the nation-state and that of the political pro-
> cesses of the international system have changed to such an
> extent that the analytical formulation of these transforma-
> tions is a question of immediate concern. (61)

If these theoretical considerations help one to understand the
national behavior determinants of foreign policy making in the
contemporary global environment, they hold special meaning for
students of divided nations whose operational political identities
have been shaped by the conscious intervention of external elite
value systems. The recently concluded Soviet-East Germany Treaty
on "Friendship, cooperation, and mutual assistance" is only the
most recent example of how external elite stewardship by a major
foreign power has been able to once again verify the empirical
strength of Hanrieder's argument. (62)

From the outset, East Germany has conducted a foreign policy
effectively precluding distinctions between domestic and external
politics. The first section of this chapter has attempted to show
the ways in which historical-cultural traditions have contributed
to this reality. The impact economic factors has, if anything,
tended to reinforce the degree to which the GDR's foreign policy
concept simultaneously involves external and internal concerns.
As a final analytical focus, the behavior of various governmental
and political institutions in the foreign policy process was discussed in relation to the external-internal dimension within which
East German foreign policy establishment is expected to operate.
Elite values and perceptions are seen as crucially important within this institutional matrix.

As the GDR begins to exercise increasing degrees of influence
within the non-communist international community. Traditional ways
of defining relationships between external and internal variables
will gradually be eliminated, if only because East Germany has
finally been able to carve out a distinct foreign policy role for
itself with the Soviet bloc. Nonetheless, the overall pattern of
external (Soviet) domination within the East German foreign policy-
making process should continue over the foreseeable future. (63)

NOTES

1. See Henry A. Kissinger, "Domestic Structure & Foreign Policy", *Daedalus*, XCV (Spring 1966), p. 503.

2. See R. Barry Farrell (ed.), *Approaches to Comparative and International Politics* (Evanston, Il.: Northwestern University Press, 1966), For an outstanding discussion which deals with domestic-external determinants of foreign policy behavior over time, see Richard N. Rosecrance, *Action & Reaction In World Politics* (Boston: Little, Brown & Company, 1963).

3. See Paul Y. Hammond, "The Political Order and the Burden of External Relations", *World Politics* (April, 1967), pp. 443-464; Wolfram R. Hanrieder, *West German Foreign Policy* (Standford University Press, 1967), and "Compatability & Consensus: A Proposal for the Conceptual Linkage of External and Internal Dimensions of Foreign Policy", in *APSR* LXI (December, 1967), pp. 971-982; Herbert Kelman, "Patterns of Personal Involvement in the National System: A Social-Psychological Analysis of Political Legitimacy", in James N. Rosenau (ed.) *International Politics & Foreign Policy* (2nd edition) (New York: The Free Press, 1969), pp. 276-288; James N. Rosenau, "Comparative Foreign Policy: Fad, Fantasy, or Field?", *International Quarterly*, Vol. 12, No. 3 (September, 1968), pp. 296-329, "Moral Fervor, Systematic Analysis, and Scientific Consciousness in Foreign Policy Research", in Austin Ranney, *Political Science & Public Policy* (Chicago: Markham Publishing Co., 1969), pp. 197-236, and, finally, *Linkage Politics* (New York: The Free Press, 1969).

4. See James N. Rosenau, "Political Science in a Shrinking World", in *Linkage Politics* (New York: The Free Press, 1969), p. 7.

5. One "case-study" attempt has been made to link the foreign-policy behavior of East and West German elites. See Kurl L. Shell's excellent study of the Berlin crisis of August 1961, *Bedrohung und Bewährung: Führung und Bevölkerung in der Berlin-Krise* (Köln und Opladen Westdeutscher Verlag, 1965).

6. Two important contributions which integrate domestic and external factors in studies of West and East German foreign policy-making respectively are found in: Karl K. Kaiser, *German Foreign Policy in Transition* (New York London Oxford: Oxford University Press, 1968), and Anita Dasbach Mallinckrodt, *Wer macht die Aussenpolitik der DDR?* (Düsseldorf: Droste Verlag, 1972).

7. Several West German writers have dealt with this subject. For a glimpse at the early period of East German economic reconstruction, see John P. Nettl, *The Eastern Zone and Soviet*

Policy in Germany: 1945-50 (London New York Toronto: Oxford University Press, 1951); for contemporary analyses of East German economic growth and performance, see Karl W. Kahrs, *The Economic System of Socialism in East Germany* (University of California, 1970), a dissertation; Peter Christian Ludz, *The German Democratic Republic from the 60's-70's* (Harvard University: Center for International Affairs, No. 26, November, 1970), esp. pp. 65-78; and, finally, Konstin Pritzel, *Die Wirtschafts-integration Mitteldeutschlands* (Köln: Verlag Wissenschaft und Politik, 1969).

8. Knowledge about the GDR, as Jean Edward Smith several years ago, "comes hard". In light of contemporary research on the GDR, however, the most crying need clearly is in the area of institutional, or governmental, behavior -- as distinguished from "party" developments. For an all-too-brief official (East German) description of "state" functions, see *Handbuch Der Deutschen Demokratischen Republik* (Staatsverlag der DDR, no date given), Pt. III, "Die DDR-Der Sozialistische Staat der Werktätigen", 181-314; for West German treatment of state organs, see Ernst Richert, *Macht Ohne Mandat* (Köln und Opladen: Westdeutscher Verlag, 1963), and a good discussion of how state institutions perform economic-planning functions in the GDR in Peter Christian Ludz, *Parteielite Im Wandel* (Köln und Opladen: Westdeutscher Verlag, 1968), pp. 103-151; for some discussion of state functions in the GDR in English, see Donald D. Dalgleish, "Walter Ulbricht's German Democratic Republic", in Peter A. Toma, *The Changing Face of Communism in Eastern Europe* (Tucson, Arizona: University of Arizona Press, 1970).

9. For a fine, though somewhat short, look at the historical background of elite development in the pre-WW II German Communist Party, see Hermann Weber, *Von Rosa Luxemburg Zu Walter Ulbricht* (Hannover: Verlag für Literatur und Zeitgeschehen, 1970). More contemporary glimpses into the social-psychology of elite settings are provided by Heinz Lippmann, *Honecker: Porträt eines Nachfolgers* (Köln Verlag Wissenschaft und Politik, 1971); Peter Christian Ludz, "Wandlungs- und Beharrungstendenzen im ideologischen System", in *Parteielite Im Wandel*, ibid., pp. 259-323; Anita Dasbach Mallinckrodt, "Lebenslauf und Entwicklungsweg", in *Wer macht die Aussenpolitik der DDR?*, ibid., pp. 129-178; Ernst Richert, *Die DDR-Elite* (Hamburg: Rowohlt Verlag, 1968); Carola Stern, *Ulbricht: A Political Biography* (New York: Praeger, 1865).

10. For a thoughtful account on the contemporary meaning's applied to the German national character, see Ralf Dahrendorf, *Society & Democracy in Germany* (New York: Doubleday & Co., Inc., 1969).

11. Peter C. Ludz, *The German Democratic Republic from the 60's-70's*

ibid., pp. 2-3.

12. See Karl Wolfgang Deutsch, "The German Federal Republic: The German Political Heritage", in Roy C. Macridis & Robert E. Ward (eds.) *Modern Political Systems: Europe* (New Jersey: Prentice Hall, Inc., 3rd edition, 1972), p. 326.

13. See Jean Edward Smith, "Limitations of Political Persuasion: The German Democratic Republic and Soviet Policy in Central Europe", a paper presented at the annual conventional of the American Political Science Association, (September 10, 1966: New York Hilton Hotel), p. 12.

14. See Smith, ibid., p. 5.

15. See Hermann Weber's discussion in *Von Rosa Luxemburg Zu Walter Ulbricht* (Mannheim Verlag Für Literatur Und Zeitgeschehen, 1970), esp. Chapter II, "Die Stalinisierung der KPD", pp. 47-75.

16. This is an especially interesting as well as complex theme involving the interrelated subjects of elite development in the GDR and the creation of an East German "national-German" tradition. For slightly contrasting views on this subject see Henry Krisch, "Official Nationalism in the German Democratic Republic", a paper given at the March, 1973 meeting of the American Association for the Advancement of Slavic Studies (Dallas, Texas), pp. 1-23, and Klaus Montag, "The Problem of Evolution of the German Democratic Republic as a Socialist Nationstate", a private paper.

17. See Wolfram F. Hanrieder, "Compatability & Consensus", *APSR* (December, 1967), p. 979.

18. See Erich Honecker, "Antwort auf aktuelle Fragen: Zwei Interviews" (Berlin: Dietz Verlag, 1971), p. 13.

19. See Peter Christian Ludz, *The German Democratic Republic from the 60's to the 70's* (Harvard University: Center for International Affairs, 1970), pp. 1-10 provide some insights into background issues surrounding the GDR's development. For a brief discussion of socio-economic problems, see David Childs, Chapter 6, "The Other German Economic Miracle?", pp. 136-159, in *East Germany* (New York & Washington: Praeger, 1971).

20. See Thomas A. Baylis, "In Quest of Legitimacy", *Problems of Communism*, March-April, 1972, and Peter Christian Ludz, "Continuity and Change Since Ulbricht", in *Problems of Communism*, March-April, 1972.

21. See Ludz, *The GDR* ....., p. 7.

104

22. See Rolf Sieber and Günther Söder, *Politik Und Ökonomie Im Sozialistischen Gesellschafts System* (Berlin: Dietz Verlag, 1970), p. 39.

23. See Walter Ulbricht, "Die gesellschaftliche Entwicklung in der Deutschen Demokratischen Republik bis zur Vollendung des Sozialismus", p. 437 in *An die Jugend* (Verlag Neues Leben).

24. See Anita Mallinckrodt, "Internationale politische Kommunikation-Lebens-wichtiges Instrument der Aussenpolitik der DDR", *Deutschland Archiv*, Sonderheft, November, 1971, pp. 13-30.

25. This is a difficult argument to prove, though there is little question that "pure" economic explanations of political legitimacy have been downplayed in the GDR since Honecker's takeover. Since mid-1971, regime spokesmen have stressed the formative role of political-ideology and individual participation. See Alexander Abusch's veiled critique of the Ulbricht "legitimacy formula" in "Kunst, Kultur und Lebensweise in unserem sozialistischen deutschen Nationstaat", pp. 728-729, in *Einheit*, June, 1971; see Kurt Hager "Die entwickelte sozialistische Gesellschaft", *Referat auf der Tagung der Gesellschafts-wissenschaftler am 14. Oktober 1971 in Berlin* (Berlin: Dietz Verlag, 1972), p. 26.

26. For a recent statement on the all-inclusive nature of this relationship, see Erich Honecker, "Antwort auf aktuelle Fragen: Zwei Interviews", (Berlin: Dietz Verlag, 1971)p. 13.

27. See Joachim Krüger, "Die DDR-fest und untrennbarer Bestandteil der sozialistischen Staatengemeinschaft - die Entwicklung der Beziehungen der DDR zu den anderen sozialistischen Staaten", pp. 283-284, in Quilitsch und Krüger *Sozialistische Staatengemeinschaft* (Berlin: Staatsverlag der Deutschen Demokratischen Republik, 1972).

28. See Ludz, *The GDR* ....., p. 3.

29. See Childs, *East Germany* ....., p. 142.

30. See Herbert Wolf, "Erwartungen und Einstellungen Junger Produktionsarbeiter In Sozialistischen Industriebetrieben", in *Jugendforschung*, May 1968, pp. 35-52. For a recent comparison of socio-economic and political differences between East and West Germany see H. Jung, et. al., *BRD-DDR: Vergleich der Gesellschafts-systeme* (Cologne: Pahl-Rugenstein Verlag, 1971).

31. See "Die DDR-fester und untrennbarer Bestandteil ....", p. 317.

32. See "Die beiden deutschen Staaten in der Welt und ihr Verhältnis

zu einander - Aspekte und Tendenzen", p. 11 in *Materialien zum Bericht zur Lage der Nation 1971* (Bonn: Hans Heger Verlag, 1971).

33. See Jan F. Triska and David D. Finley, *Soviet Foreign Policy* (New York, 1968).

34. See Anita Dasbach Mallinckrodt, *Wer macht die Aussenpolitik der DDR?* (Düsseldorf: Droste Verlag, 1972), pp. 35-42, 185-222.

35. Decision-makers are defined in this chapter as persons who hold official foreign policy positions, that is, have authority plus power or influence and are the selectors of courses of actions from among alternatives.

36. Mallinckrodt, op. cit., pp. 208-213.

37. *Neues Deutschland*, July 13, 1971.

38. Before the Staatsrat was organized, the President was the top state job.

39. *GBl.* 1, No. 6/1963, April 17, 1963.

40. "Gesetz über den Ministerrat der Deutschen Demokratischen Republik - vom 16 Oktober 1972", *GBl.* 1, No. 1/1963.

41. Willi Stoph, "Die Lösung der Hauptaufgabe bestimmt Arbeit der Regierung", *Neues Deutschland*, 17 Oktober, 1972.

42. Mallinckrodt, op. cit., Chapter VI.

43. Peter C. Ludz, "Continuity and Change Since Ulbricht", *Problems of Communism*, March-April 1972, p. 66.

44. *Der Parteiarbeiter*, October 1967.

45. Department of State New Release, Bureau of Public Affairs, December 8, 1972.

46. *GBl.* II, No. 23, March 14, 1970, pp. 173-175.

47. H. Gordon Skilling, "Interest Groups and Communist Politics", *Communist Studies and the Social Sciences*, ed. by Frederic J. Fleron, Jr. (Chicago: Rand McNally & Co., 1969), pp. 281-197.

48. Peter C. Ludz, *The Changing Party Elite in East Germany* (Cambridge: The MIT Press, 1972).

49. Thomas A. Baylis, "Political Change in East Germany", *Problems*

of Communism, November-December 1972, p. 74.

50. That study, Mallinckrodt, <u>op.</u> <u>cit.</u>, is the basis for this section.

51. Mallinckrodt, <u>op.</u> <u>cit.</u>, Chapter III.

52. "Article 6: 1) The German Democratic Republic, faithful to the interests of the German people and the international obligations of all Germans, has eradicated German militarism and nazism on its territory, and pursues a foreign policy serving peace and socialism, international friendship and security. 2) The German Democratic Republic fosters and develops allround cooperation and friendship with the Union of Soviet Socialist Repub'.ics and other socialist states on the basis of socialist internationalism. 3) The German Democratic Republic supports the aspirations of the peoples for freedom and independence, and fosters relations of cooperation with all states on the basis of equality and mutual respect. 4) The German Democratic Republic strives for a system of collective security in Europe and a stable order of peace in the world. It supports general disarmament. 5) Militarist and revanchist propaganda in all forms, war-mongering and the manifestation of hatred against creeds, races and nations are punished as crimes."

53. Otto Winzer, *Deutsche Aussenpolitik* (Berlin: Staatsverlag, 1969), p. 54.

54. Werner Hänisch, "Problems der Internationalen Stellung der DDR", *Deutsche Aussenpolitik*, No. 2, März-April 1970, pp. 188-192.

55. Mallinckrodt, <u>op.</u> <u>cit.</u>, Chapter IV.

56. Mallinckrodt, <u>op.</u> <u>cit.</u>, Chapter V.

57. "Diplomaten der DDR-Kader der Arbeiterklasse", *Horizont*, 27/1971, pp. 3-4.

58. Ludz, <u>op.</u> <u>cit.</u>, "Continuity and Change Since Ulbricht", p. 72.

59. Ursula Hoffmann, *Die Veränderung in der Sozialstruktur des Ministerrates der DDR 1949 bis 1969* (Düsseldorf: Droste Verlag, 1971).

60. See James N. Rosenau, "Pre-Theories & Theories of Foreign Policy", in R. Barry Farrell (ed.) *Approaches to Comparative & International Politics* (Evanston, Il.: Northwestern University Press, 1966), pp. 27-92.

61. See Wolfram F. Hanrieder, "Compatability & Consensus", *ASPR* (December 1967), pp. 972-973.

62. For a short treatment of this recent event, see Dusco Doder, "Yugoslavs Fear Soviets Revive Intervention", *Washington Post*, October 12, 1975, p. A8.

63. For a discussion on current East German foreign policy prospects, see John Starrels/Anita Mallinckrodt, "International Relations", in *Politics in the German Democratic Republic* (New York: Praeger, 1975), pp. 362-375.

Chapter V

THE FOREIGN POLICY OF HUNGARY

Ferenc A. Váli

Prior to 1948

With the dissolution of the Austro-Hungarian Monarchy at the
end of World War I, Hungary, after 400 years, regained her independence in foreign affairs. (1) 1918-19 were years of several re-
volutions in Hungary. The Republic was declared in November 1918.
In March 1919, under the trauma of having lost two-thirds of her
territory and more than half of her population (including nearly
three million ethnic Hungarians), the country fell prey to a tiny
number of Communists, mostly former prisoners-of-war returned from
Russia under the leadership of Béla Kun. The first Communist dic-
tatorship lasted less than three months and was succeeded by the
official restoration of the monarchy. But because it was impossible
under the existing international situation to fill the throne,
Admiral Horthym the last Commander-in-Chief of the Austro-Hungarian Navy, was elected Regent.

The amputation of Hungary was legalized by the Peace Treaty of
Trianon in 1920 and 1921. As a result of all these developments,
Hungary's interwar foreign policy was essentially determined by
two predominant goals: the partial or complete restitution of her
former territorial status quo, and fight against the threat of
Communism. Until 1938 the first objective was frustrated by the
pressure of the Little Entente (Czechoslovakia, Romania, and
Yugoslavia) which comprised the Eastern tier of the French alliance system. The second objective was defeated in two stages. The
first involved the folly of Hitlerite Germany which, under the
Stalin-Hitler Pact, helped to destroy the cordon sanitaire of
small states along the western borders of the Soviet Union. In the
second stage the German invasion of Russia rendered inevitable the
wartime alliance between the West and the Soviet State which en-

abled the latter to establish itself in East-Central Europe.

In 1938-39 German and Italian pressures disintegrated the Little Entente, and Hungary was able to recover temporarily some parts of her lost territories. The fact that the Axis promoted Hungarian territorial gains largely influenced Hungary's stand in the war, although the foreign-policy leadership foresaw the eventual collapse of the German effort. (2) When the fortune of war turned against Germany, the then Prime Minister Miklos Kállay concluded a secret agreement with the Allies. But Hitler forestalled the plan by occupying Hungary in March 1944. (3) In October 1944 Soviet forces penetrated into Hungary. Regent Horthy offered to surrender but was again prevented from doing so by the Germans and their Hungarian Nazi allies. A Hungarian government was formed in Debrecen in December 1944, under the auspices of the Soviet Army. This government concluded an armistice with the major Allies in Moscow on January 20, 1945 and the Hungarian government was moved to Budapest soon thereafter. But it was a government which was operating under the supervision of the Armistice Control Commission, headed and dominated be generals of the Red Army.

Although during the armistice period Hungary's coalition government and foreign-policy experts tried to establish meaningful contacts (especially before and during the Peace Conference in Paris) with countries other than the Soviet Union, such attempts were thwarted partly by the Soviet authorities, partly by the Communist elements already very powerful in the government. During the peace negotiations Hungary failed to achieve a revision of her borders vis-à-vis Romania or to prevent an "exchange" of Hungarians in Czechoslovakia against Slovaks in Hungary. In fact, the Hungarian Communist Party, blindly obedient to Soviet instruments, even supported such plans harmful to national interest. (4) The expulsion of Hungarians from Czechoslovakia was only discontinued when, after 1949, both countries had full-fledged Communist governments.

The Stalinist Period

With the advance of full Communist control, even the modest attempts to pursue an independent Hungarian policy line disappeared. The Hungarian foreign service not only developed into an instrument of Soviet power, it had to sacrifice the interests of its own country whenever Soviet interests became involved. There were endless diplomatic protests and requests for compensation submitted to Hungary by Western chancelleries for damages suffered as a result of Soviet occupation in Hungary. It had become imperative never to indicate or admit actions of the Soviet Army which resulted in the damage; thus, Western governments were prevented from raising the matter in Moscow. (5)

Despite the coming into force of the Peace Treaty in 1948, Soviet forces continued to be stationed in Hungary. Even when the State Treaty with Austria was concluded in 1955 under which Soviet

forces were withdrawn from that country, contrary to the Peace
Treaty with Hungary they were never withdrawn from Hungary and
participated in crushing the Hungarian uprising of 1956.
    During the Stalinist period and thereafter, Hungarian policies,
primarily foreign policy, remained completely streamlines to that
of Moscow. Every ministerial pronouncement or newspaper article
on foreign-policy issues was mostly verbatim replica of similar
pronouncements by Moscow. The "leadership" exercised by the Communist Party of the Soviet Union over all other Communist parties
(in other words, the control of other Communist-ruled governments)
was most noticeable in the management of foreign affairs. Among
the Communist states of East-Central Europe only Yugoslavia succeeded in extricating herself from Soviet domination during
Stalin's lifetime.
    During the Stalinist and post-Stalinist periods, Hungarian in-
dependent statehood remained purely fictional. Hungary, although
a member of the United Nations since 1955 (6) and officially
treated as a sovereign state, was in every respect and, especially,
in the management of foreign affairs, a satellite of Soviet power.
Thus, when Moscow turned most vehemently against recalcitrant
Yugoslavia, official Hungary's echo was indistinguishable from
the dominant Soviet voice. When again, under Khrushchev, Moscow
practiced rapprochement with Belgrade, Hungary attempted to
follow. Actually, Rákosi's inability to imitate his master in
Moscow (because of Tito's adamant hostility) was instrumental in
bringing about the fall of the "Hungarian Stalin" in July 1956.

1956 and After

    During the successful days of the Hungarian Revolution of 1956,
the multi-party government of Imre Nagy, for a short while, regained a precarious control over domestic and foreign affairs. One
of the difficulties the government of Imre Nagy had to face was
the direction of the Hungarian Foreign Service which was permeated
more than any other Hungarian agency (except, of course, the Security Police) with stooges of Moscow and even Soviet citizens
(often disguised as Hungarians). (7) The Ministry of Foreign
Affairs, during the revolutionary days, was split between those
favoring the Revolution and those "muscovites" who feared retribu-
tion. Similarly, Hungarian missions abroad were divided in their
allegiance and hard-core Stalinists often had to seek asylum from
the host country against members of their own staff. In consequence, Imre Nagy had to bypass the unreliable Foreign Ministry
when sending his appeals abroad.
    The story of the first Soviet military intervention is particu-
larly revelatory with regard to the true character of Hungarian-
Soviet relations. Supposedly, the Soviet forces stationed in
Hungary which intervened in the early morning hours of October 24,
1956, were invited to do so by the Hungarian Government.

But not even the United Nations Special Committee on the Problem of Hungary was able to ascertain who had issued the alleged "invitation" and doubted whether such an invitation really had been extended. This writer believes that there has been no formal invitation; it was the result of some informal contracts (as existed almost permanently) between the Hungarian Party Headquarters and its Soviet advisers, possibly Soviet Ambassador Andropov and his military advisers. This is, of course, not the manner in which international relations on such an important matter are conducted between independent and sovereign states. (8)

The second, decisive, and massive armed intervention which ended the Revolution was equally characteristic of how the alleged independence of Hungary was respected by her Muscovite superlords. A group of Communist leaders, headed by János Kádár, was installed as Hungarian Government by Khrushchev in the Soviet town of Uzhgorod and, after the occupation of Budapest by Soviet forces, brought to the capital of Hungary. Subsequently, it was alleged that the Kádár Government (still on Soviet territory and without evident Hungarian support) had asked for the very military intervention which helped it to move to Budapest. (9)

The action by the Hungarian Government during the revolutionary period which marked its regained independence was the declaration of withdrawal from the Warsaw Pact Organization and announcement of Hungary's neutral status. Contrary to the accusations that this action was contrary to international law and provoked the second Soviet intervention it should be stated that Imre Nagy's cabinet resorted to this act of despair only after Moscow poured division after division into Hungary with the evident aim of suppressing the revolutionary achievements and removing the multiparty government. But, as it is well known, Imre Nagy's hopes that this action would induce the United Nations to protect Hungary were sadly dissipated by inaction and delay, and by the tragically inopportune Anglo-French invasion of Suez.

For a few months after the occupation of Hungary by Soviet troops in November 1956, the Kádár Government remained a complete puppet of its Soviet master. Only gradually was it able to pursue first a definite domestic and, to a much more restricted extent, certain foreign-policy activity -- but both and in particular the latter -- under the close supervision of the Kremlin. By the late 1950s and early 1960s a pattern of Soviet guidance was applied to Hungary which was similar to that practiced vis-à-vis Gomulka's Poland: domestic affairs were left in large measure to the discretionary management of the Hungarian Party and Government, provided that Party rule and other "achievements of Socialism" were not endangered. On the other hand, in the realm of foreign policy and defense, Moscow retained the main lines of its directing and controling jurisdiction.

The control maintained by the Soviet Union in foreign and defense matters is carried out through different channels: the line of command between the Soviet Communist Party and its Hungar-

ian affiliate; through the Soviet diplomatic representation in
Budapest (Soviet ambassadors at times acted as "proconsuls" in
Hungary); the Soviet Military Command; and -- last but not least
-- the Soviet Security Police in its contact with the Hungarian
counterpart.

The Hungarian Foreign Service

Hungarian diplomatic missions abroad are expected to follow
and support the attitude and actions taken by the respective
Soviet missions. Thus the Hungarian delegation to the United
Nations almost blindly obeys, parrots Soviet policies and official announcements. There is not one instance to be registered
when the Hungarian representative has cast a vote different from
that of his Soviet colleague.
Members of Hungarian diplomatic missions abroad report not only
to their Ministry of Foreign Affairs, they also are instructed to
inform the leaders of the Soviet mission in the same country of
everything important which they may know. But this is a one-way
channel: the Soviet embassies refrain from giving out information
often much needed to their Hungarian counterparts. For instance,
at the time of the Cuban missile crisis, the Hungarian Embassy in
Washington was instructed by the Soviet Embassy to start burning
their papers, but they were not told of the conversation which
the Soviet Ambassador held with the White House. (10)
Despite this client relationship to the Soviet Union, Hungary
and other countries of the Soviet bloc behave and are internation-
ally treated as if they were fully independent states (they are
members of the United Nations, maintain diplomatic relations,
sign and ratify treaties, etc.). The dependence on the Soviet
policy line is successfully concealed by the apparent machinery
which deals with foreign relations. The organization of the concerning the withdrawal of these forces, such hopes were twice dissipated: first, after the collapse of the Hungarian Revolution in
1956, and then after the invasion of Czechoslovakia in 1968.
Hungarians are fully conscious of the fact that the presence of
Soviet troops, unlike that of foreign forces in NATO countries,
does not serve the protection of their country against an outside
enemy, but rather the preservation of Soviet control and Communist
rule. It is formally the Warsaw Pact, concluded in 1955, which
provides the legal basis for the presence of Soviet forces as well
as an Agreement for the Temporary Stationing of such troops,
forced upon Hungary in 1957. The Warsaw Pact organization imitated
NATO in the sense that it established a Joint Command (which is,
in fact, a Soviet Command) and directs joint military maneuvers in
one or another of the member countries.
In view of Hungary's subservience to Soviet control, it was
natural that she (unlike Romania) participated in the invasion of
Czechoslovakia in August 1968. It was equally natural that the

Hungarian regime openly welcomed the so-called Brezhnev Doctrine, the principle of "limited sovereignty" for members of the Socialist Commonwealth. Under this Doctrine, Moscow assumed the right to defend Socialism (in other words, to intervene militarily) if it should be threatened. Actually, the same principle had already been applied to Hungary in 1956 and the Kádár Government owes its existence to its application.

Relations with Neighboring Countries

Although it is self-evident that Hungary's interests cannot be Hungarian foreign service is modeled on that of the Soviet "big brother" but naturally on a much more modest scale.

The Hungarian Ministry of Foreign Affairs is led by a Minister (who since 1961 has been János Péter, a former Calvinist minister), by a First Deputy Minister, and four Deputy Ministers. There are in the Ministry, eleven area sections: section I for relations with the USSR; section II for those with Czechoslovakia, Poland, and the German Democratic Republic; and section III for relations with Albania, Bulgaria, Romania; and the Danube River Commission. Other sections deal with Asian Socialist countries; with the United States, Canada, Britain, and the Federal Republic of Germany; with Austria, the Benelux, Scandinavian countries and Switzerland; with Latin America; with Sub-Saharan Africa; with the Arab countries; with the Asian "capitalist" countries; and. finally, with France, Italy, Spain, Portugal, Greece, Turkey, Cyprus, and San Marino.

Hungary officially maintains seventy embassies (a large number for such a small state) but in some cases the accredited ambassador combines more than one post. (11)

Hungary also maintains permanent missions to the United Nations, to the European Office of the United Nations in Geneva, and the UNESCO in Paris. She also runs a number of consulates and permanent trade missions, such as that maintained in West Germany.

The main guarantee of Hungary's subservience to Soviet interests (in addition to the acceptance by the Hungarian Communist Party of the Soviet "leading role") is the contingent of Soviet forces (four to five divisions) in Hungary. If anybody cherished hopes always identical with that of the USSR, the policy which the Kremlin considers essential is being slavishly followed by Hungary and other loyal members of the Warsaw Pact. Nevertheless, since Hungary, as every other nation, must have individual interests and policy aims, she may still pursue some limited individual objectives within the limits of Soviet tolerance. Sometimes the Hungarian regime must find it difficult to support a Soviet thesis which clashes with the national interests of Hungary. Thus, Kádár and his associates were little successful in invoking the German danger which is being so successfully employed by Gomulka of Poland in order to defend the necessity of Soviet "friendship".

While temporarily after the end of World War II, Germans were
feared and hated, the more deeply felt antagonism against the
Soviets, the present oppressor, eliminated previous phobias.
Hungary, except for the official pronouncement in this respect,
is really not interested in whether Germany is reunified or not.
On the other hand, mainly for reasons of commercial and tourist
relations, she is eminently interested in strengthening her ties
with West Germany.

Similarly to the official "fraternal" relations with the Soviet
Union, relations between Hungary and Romania, Czechoslovakia,
Poland, and Bulgaria are very friendly. Popular sentiment only
partly supports these official attitudes. With Poland genuine historically proven sympathies exist; there are no reasons for discord between Hungary and Bulgaria. The contacts with Czechoslovakia and Romania are, however, influenced by the existence of a
large Hungarian ethnic minority in both these countries.

As mentioned before, immediately after World War II, Czechoslovakia attempted to expel the Hungarians (as she did with her
German minority) but this attempt was only partly successful;
more than half a million Hungarians still inhabit Slovakia. Since
the 1950s the treatment of this minority has considerably improved
and complaints are little in evidence. It is in the interest of
the Soviet overlord to eliminate disputes between countries under
his protective umbrella; there it is assumed that Soviet influence
also contributed toward the improvement of the fate of the Hungarians in Czechoslovakia. (12)

In Romania the number of Hungarians is considerably higher;
they number 1.8 million. Until about 1958 the treatment of this
ethnic group was satisfactory; in that part of Transylvania where
Hungarians were predominant, a Hungarian Autonomous Province was
established under the Constitution. After 1958, when Romania began
to pursue a more independent policy line and when her government
became desirous to rely on the strong national sentiment of the
people, the soft handling of national minorities ended. In 1962
even the Hungarian Autonomous Province was dismantled. The impression in Hungary is that the Romanian Government aimed at de-
nationalizing the Hungarian ethnic element and to absorb them into
the Romanian national community. (13)

The Hungarian Government undertook to assist these Hungarians
not so much by diplomatic steps as by using the good offices of
the Soviet union, and through the channel of communication existing between the Hungarian and Romanian Communist parties. But
these steps proved to rather sterile: Moscow was reluctant to
deteriorate even further its relations with Bucharest by intervening on behalf of another Communist country. If the Soviet Union
will bring pressure on Romania, the fate of the Hungarians in
Transylvania will have no priority over other grievances which
Moscow may harbor against the Romanians.

The relations between Hungary and Yugoslavia, a country whose
population includes half a million Hungarians, have undergone many

changes during the past twenty years. These changes were not so much prompted by Hungarian or Yugoslav policy objectives but followed slavishly the attitudes taken by Moscow against Belgrade. After the open hostility during the Stalinist years, an improvement has set in. Tito's Yugoslavia was sympathetic toward the Hungarian ferment prior to the Revolution of 1956 and also, with certain reservations, toward the revolutionary effort itself. As relations between the Soviet Union and Yugoslavia worsened in the years 1957-1959, so did those between Budapest and Belgrade. After Khrushchev's ouster, these relations again improved and at present they are amicable. These contacts are not as close as those between Hungary and other members of the Soviet bloc, but there is really no cause for any friction. Hungarians in Yugoslavia are treated better than in any other successor state of the Austro-Hungarian Monarchy, save Austria herself.

Hungary's western neighbor is Austria, a country with which memories of former union are cherished and ancient prejudices forgotten. But Austria is the only non-Communist neighbor of Hungary and the Iron Curtain (manifested by minefields and barbedwire fences along the border) separates Hungary from her. Over the past six years, however, relations between the two countries have significantly improved but, naturally, only to the extent that ideological differences permitted. Hungarian and Austrian heads of government exchange visits, and commercial and cultural contacts have been widened. Austria is a neutralized country and there the Communist government of Hungary must have felt that restraints are less called for than in its relations with members of the North Atlantic Treaty Organization.

Relations with the West

Hungary's cultural and economic needs make closer relations with Western Europe a necessity. She has belonged to the cultural circle of the countries west of her borders for ten centuries. An exchange of goods with the highly industrialized countries of the West is indispensable for her economic development and modernization. Her relations with the principle European NATO countries, France, Britain, and Italy, have developed normally during the past ten years but were far from cordial. The contacts with the nearest NATO member, the Federal Republic of Germany, have remained limited because of the lack of normal diplomatic relations.

Trade relations between Hungary and West Germany are recognized by the former as the main reason for the deepening of contacts. Because Hungary, as other Communist countries, maintains full diplomatic relations with the German Democratic Republic, the Hallstein Doctrine (the policy pursues by Bonn until 1967 that no diplomatic relations be established with governments recognizing East Germany) prevented the establishment of normal diplomatic exchanges between the two countries. In 1967, however, West Germany restored full diplomatic ties with Romania despite the continued presence of an East German ambassador in Bucharest. Hungary was impeded in following that lead because of Soviet displeasure about Romania's independent action. Recognition by the Federal Republic of East Germany, of the Oder-Neisse Border, and other conditions were mentioned as the prerequisite to the establishment of normal diplomatic contacts. (14) Only permanent trade missions (later with the right of consular privileges) have existed between Hungary and West Germany since 1963.

While earlier Hungary had parroted Soviet accusations of revanchism and militarism against West Germany, she modified its tone, similar to the attitude of Moscow after the elections of 1969 in the Federal Republic. (15) It became evident that Hungary was highly interested in the resumption of full diplomatic relations with West Germany. In March 1970 the Hungarian Minister for Foreign Trade, Jozsef Biro, traveled to Bonn and conducted prolonged negotiations with West German economic leaders and also with Foreign Minister Walter Scheel. However, it may be assumed that any decision had to be postponed until the negotiations with Moscow and Warsaw, more important for West Germany, have been completed. With the Treaty of August 12, 1970, between the Soviet Union and Federal Germany, the road appears to have been opened for the normalization of diplomatic contacts between Bonn and Budapest.

Relations between Hungary and the United States were unfavorably affected by the character of Soviet occupation during the armistice period. The American, similarly to the British, member of the Allied Control Commission exercised hardly any authority vis-à-vis the Soviet chairman and the Soviet occupation force. As a gesture of goodwill, Washington resumed diplomatic relations with Hungary even before the signature of the Peace Treaty and a Hungarian diplomatic Minister was received in January 1946. Relations between the two countries became strained after the Communist takeover in 1947-48. Not only was American property, together with the confiscation of all industrial enterprises, nationalized but American citizens and members of the United States Legation were subjected to harrassments and restrictions. Normal diplomatic relations were suspended after the suppression of the Revolution of 1956 by Soviet forces and the installation by them of the Kádár regime. From 1956 to 1966 the American Legation in Budapest and that of Hungary in Washington were headed by chargés d'affaires.

This uneasy situation which coincided with the restricted admission of Hungarian representatives in the United Nations were eased in 1963 when a political amnesty was declared in Hungary. Only in 1966 was the resumption of full diplomatic contacts agreed upon with the simultaneous raising of the Budapest and Washington legations to the Embassy level. Discussions on outstanding questions were resumed in 1964. Such questions are: indemnity for war damages and nationalized American property, the operation of the embassy (travel restrictions, limitations of personnel, etc.) and the intensification of cultural and commercial ties. Some questions have, in the meantime, been settled by agreement. The most delicate questions still unsolved are the presence of Cardinal Mindszenty at the American Embassy in Budapest and the return of the Holy Crown of Saint Stephen to Hungary. Both are problems loaded with religious and national siginificance.

Cardinal Mindszenty, the Hungarian Catholic Primate, was given a life sentence in 1949 after a rigged trial on charges of treason and conspiracy. During the Revolution of 1956 he was freed and resumed his post as Archbishop and Primate of the Hungarian Catholic Church. When the Russians moved into Budapest, the Cardinal took refuge in the American Legation. The Kádár Government never asked for his surrender (which might have been embarrassing for then because they would have had to imprison him again) and so he has lived in the building ever since. He refused to go to Rome (as would have been permitted by the Hungarian authorities) unless the Pope would order him to do so. He insisted that he should be rehabilitated and allowed to return to his Archbishopric. The amnesty which was proclaimed in 1963 did not extend to the "crime" he was supposed to have committed; the Hungarian regime does not want him to exercise ecclesiastical authority. The Cardinal is now 78 years old.

The Crown of Saint Stephen was given to the first king of Hungary by the Pope around 1000 A.D. and it has served for more than 900 years to crown the kings of Hungary. It thus acquired both religious and historical meaning and was regarded as the symbol of Hungarian nationhood. The Crown was taken to Germany in 1944 before the arrival of the Red Army in Hungary and there the United States Army took possession of it. It has remained in the custody of the United States ever since and is being kept in a secret place in Washington. The Hungarian Government demanded its return to Hungary while Hungarian exiles and Catholic circles opposed its surrender to an atheistic regime. Washington wishes to hold this invaluable treasure "in trust" for the people of Hungary. (16)

Some of the unsolved issues between the United States and Hungary were settled in a four-point accord in August 1969 which included such items as the following: the establishment of a Hungarian Trade Office in New York, payment for the surplus-property debt to the United States, increased staffing of the American Embassy in Budapest and the Hungarian one in Washington. and social security payments to Hungarian beneficiaries. Other outstanding questions have been left still pending.

Among the international relations of the Hungarian Government those with the Vatican deserve attention. After the Communist takeover the persecution of all churches was noticeable. But the first among those was that of the Catholic Church which appeared least prepared to subordinate itself to the demands of the regime. The Communist government considered the Catholic Church, whose Head resides abroad, as a potential danger to its power. After initial resistance (which resulted in the arrest of many bishops and

priests, including Cardinal Mindszenty), the Catholic hierarchy
reluctantly consented to cooperate by taking an oath of allegiance
to the Government and accepting additional conditions. In the
early 1960s the Kádár Government realized that without coming to
an understanding with the Vatikan, questions relative to the appointment of bishops, the maintenance of seminaries and other
related issues could not be satisfactorily settled. An agreement
concluded in 1964 partially regulated some questions and most of
the vacant bishoprics were filled with common consent. Budapest
insisted that only persons it approved could be appointed to
ecclesiastical offices. In January 1969 an additional agreement
provided for the appointment of other vacancies; still, a number
of dioceses are still administered by apostolic administrators
(auxiliary bishops) but their person also must be unobjectionable
to the Government. It seems clear, however, that the Hungarian
Government now attributes importance to its contacts with the Holy
See although there is no question yet of appointing a permanent
diplomatic representative to the Vatican.

Hungary has not only been a member of the United Nations since
1955, she is also a member of many other international organizations such as the International Labor Organization, UNESCO (the
U.N. Educational, Scientific and Cultural Organization), the World
Health Organization, the Food and Agricultural Organization, the
International Atomic Energy Agency, and others. The Kádár Government together with the Soviet Union have been censured by the
General Assembly of the United Nations for their attitude during
and after the Revolution of 1956 but none of the demands made to
them by the United Nations have been complied with (to restore
freedom of the Hungarian people, allow for free self-determination,
and to withdraw Soviet forces from Hungary). In 1963 the credentials of the Hungarian Delegation were accepted by the United
Nations General Assembly (previously they were neither rejected
nor accepted). The Hungarian desire to regain respectability after
the loss of prestige before and during 1956, without, however,
making meaningful concessions, proved successful in the face of
indifference and acquiescence in the World Organization. When Hungary was elected to a nonpermanent seat on the Security Council (a
seat rotating between the East-Central European member states), it
was acclaimed as a great success for the Hungarian regime.

Foreign Trade and Tourism

Hungary maintains diplomatic relations not only with the European Powers (excluding Spain and Portugal) but also with most
countries in the Americas, in Asia and Africa. It may be questioned
why such a relatively small country requires such an extensive
diplomatic network. The answer is partly to be found in the Soviet
need for diplomatic support (when launching protests and for obtaining additional information) and partly in the Hungarian need

for trade relations wherever possible. (17)

As a small and relatively overpopulated country, Hungary is poor in raw materials and therefore is vitally dependent on foreign trade. The exchange of goods with the Soviet Union and other Communist countries (about 70 percent of her foreign trade) (18) does not by any means satisfy her basic needs. In her international contacts, she must take note of economic requirements to a much larger extent than other Communist countries (except East Germany and Czechoslovakia) which may practice some measure of self-sufficiency. To raise the standard of living of the people of Hungary, and thus popularize itself, the regime wishes to extend its foreign trade into every part of the world. The chronic lack of convertible currency also pushes Hungary to seek a trade surplus woth countries outside the Soviet bloc.

About 18 percent of Hungary's foreign trade is with the countries of the European Economic Community (Common Market), among them mainly with the Federal Republic of Germany and Italy. About 13 percent of her foreign trade is with the countries of the European Free Trade Association (EFTA), among them mainly with Britain, Austria, and Switzerland. Whereas Hungary was able to export more to the Socialist countries than she imports from them, her trade balance showed a constant deficit in the exchange of goods with developed non-Communist states. The all-important trade relation with the Common Market countries remained especially unsatisfactory in this respect. Hungary, similarly to other Communist countries, is affected by the common policies and tariff of the EEC and she is endeavouring to come to terms with Brussels.

Partly to counteract the detrimental influence on her international trade relations, Hungary is one of the members of the CMEA (Council for Mutual Economic Assistance), the organization for economic cooperation between the Soviet bloc countries, which would like to see its activity more intensified and rationalized. For instance, Hungary had supported the plan of a clearing-system together with the convertability between the currencies of the CMEA members. However, she was opposed by both the Soviet Union which wishes to uphold bilateral trade relations between itself and the individual bloc countries, and by Romania which country is unwilling to submit to a division of labor and other restrictions impairing her financial and economic sovereignty. It seems thus fairly certain that CMEA cannot be a counterforce which could compete with the Common Market. Therefore, Hungary feels compelled to seek rapprochement with the essentially Western institutions promoting international trade, such as the GATT (General Agreement on Trade and Tariffs). In early 1970, Budapest requested admission to GATT (only Czechoslovakia, among the Soviet bloc countries, is a member) which event will force her to alter many of her trading habits and assimilate them to those current among non-Communist states.

The Hungarian eargerness to open up economic ties with the West and even to resort to schemes -- fantastic when considering the limitations of Hungarian efforts -- was revealed by the planned Canadian potassium deal. Under this project Hungarian workers were to be sent to Canada to exploit potash mines near Dundurn, Saskatchewan. Hungary would also have sent mining equipment and would have been paid in potash, while the savings of the Hungarian miners would have increased dollar-holdings of the Hungarian National Bank. However, the plan was turned down by the Canadian Ministry of Manpower and Immigration. (19)

The interest in increasing earnings of convertible currency has led Hungary to foster by all possible means tourist travel from the West. There is no doubt that a major task of Hungarian foreign agencies, whether IBUSZ, the State Travel Agency, or consular offices issuing visas, is to promote visits to Hungary which may also be considered as one of the foreign-policy goals of that Hungary, one which is barely political and thus outside the interference of Moscow.

The number of foreign tourists increased from 153,000 in 1953 to 3 million in 1969. But 85 percent of these visitors came from other Socialist countries and only about half-a-million from non-socialist countries (147,000 from Austria, 106,000 from West Germany, 36,500 from the United States, 33,000 from Italy, 14,500 from Britain, and 16,000 from France). The relative importance of dollar tourists is well realized and extensive preparations are being made to provide high-quality accommodations to these valuable guests. (20)

The Hungarian regime also wishes to exploit for touristic and propaganda purposes the fact that out of 15 million Hungarians living outside the borders of Hungary is as follows:

TABLE 5.1

Hungarians Living Outside Hungary (21)	
Czechoslovakia	730,000
Romania	1,850,000
Yugoslavia	550,000
Soviet Union	170,000
Total in Socialist countries	3,300,000
Federal Republic of Germany	50,000
Austria	50,000
France	50,000
Great Britain	25,000
Other European countries	60,000
Total in Europe	235,000
	Continued...

122

Table 5.1 continued

United States	800,000
Canada	100,000
Brazil	60,000
Other American countries	30,000
Total in Western Hemisphere	990,000
Australia	35,000
Africa and Asia	25,000
Total in other countries	60,000
Total in non-Socialist countries	1,285,000

Budapest is making great efforts to pursuade Hungarians living particularly in Western countries to return home, at least for a visit. Even those who have left illegally (that is, without passports, such as in the years after 1945 and again after the collapse of the Revolution of 1956) are constantly assured that they will not be harmed. But the Hungarian authorities ambiguously still consider the post-World War II and post-Revolution refugees to be Hungarian citizens (even if in the meantime they have acquired citizenship in their country of residence) unless they have been granted formal release from Hungarian citizenship. According to Hungarian reports, 85,000 West European and Western Hemisphere Hungarian residents visited their homeland as tourists in 1969.

The regime has considerably eased conditions for the issuance of entry visas to Hungary. This is in marked contrast to the slow and difficult procedures of some ten years ago. Simultaneously, Budapest also eased the issuance of passports and exit visas to its own citizens. But the great majority of the latter may only travel to other Socialist countries. The restrictions on the purchase of convertible currencies not only reduce the numbers of those who are able to travel but also limit the time which they can spend in the West. But persons considered unreliable or those whose relatives abroad have left the country illegally are barred from obtaining passports. (22)

Major Policy Issues

In the great issues which divide the world, Hungary naturally sided with the positions taken by Moscow. Although she would have liked to follow the Romanian line of neutrality in the Sino-Soviet conflict, on every possible occasion she fully endorsed the condemnation of Peking and Maoism in general. When Moscow recalled

its ambassador from Peking, so did Hungary. When, in the spring
of 1970, a new Soviet ambassador was dispatched to the Chinese
capital, also a Hungarian was soon to follow. There is even appre-
hension in Budapest that, similarly to the invasion of Czechoslovakia, Moscow may require Hungarians to send troops to Asia to
participate in an eventual clash with the Chinese. Under the
Warsaw Pact only "aggression in Europe" is mentioned but the
latest Soviet-Czechoslovak Friendship Treaty is so generally
phrased that assistance in a Far Eastern conflict might also include the dispatch of Czechoslovak troops to that part of the
world. In Hungarian circles, even Party circles, it is being
feared that Moscow might force upon Hungary a new treaty similar
to that concluded with Prague, one that not only endorses the
Brezhnev Doctrine but also military assistance in any part of the
world.

The Hungarian regime, of course, fully supported the Soviet
Union in its policy toward the Indochinese War. There were frequent visits between Hungarian leaders and those of Hanoi. The
Hungarian Foreign Minister, János Péter, once even made a tragi-
comic act of mediating in favor of a peaceful solution which proved
to lack seriousness. Hungary promptly recognized the Vietnamese
National Liberation Movement when Moscow gave the signal. On the
other hand, Hungary failed, like Moscow, to recognize the exile
government of Prince Sihanouk and maintained here diplomatic relations with the government Lon Nol of Cambodia.

The subordination of Hungarian foreign policy to the will of
Moscow was also manifested in the approach of Budapest to the
Arab-Israeli conflict. Unlike Romania, Hungary withdrew her ambassador from Tel Aviv in 1967 and severed diplomatic ties with
Israel, following the footsteps of Moscow, Hungary maintained relatively important trade contacts with Israel which were negatively
affected by this step. The action of the Government was clearly
inconsistent with the attitude of the Hungarian public which (if
only to oppose Moscow's stand) sympathized with the Israelis and
rejoiced over the Arab defeat in 1967 -- an event considered to
be a defeat for the Soviets. In the wake of the official anti-
Israel attitude even limited anti-Semitism reappeared in the circles of official Hungary though not to the extent practiced in
Poland, Czechoslovakia, or the Soviet Union.

Stalinist terrorism and uniformism had stirred up the uprisings
in East Berlin, in Poland, and Hungary in the 1950s. Soviet fear
of losing Czechoslovakia prompted the intervention of 1968. The
relatively greater liberalism in some East-Central European Communist countries strengthened the self-confidence of these peoples
and induced even their Communist leadership to evaluate the real
interests of their states. It is being more and more clearly
realized that the Soviet superpower's selfish interests are by no
means identical with those of its smaller "allies". This is, in
particular, the case with Hungary. (23)

The restrictions on individual liberty and discontent at economic hardships are sorely felt in Hungary as in other countries in the area. But, as history has proven, hurt national feelings can provide an even more virulent material for dissatisfaction. While Soviet support and the presence of Soviet forces in Hungary protect the regime, they simultaneously are counterproductive because they underline what everybody appears to realize; namely, that Hungary is really not an independent country. She has no foreign policy which is geared to safeguard her genuine interests. While NATO is felt to be a shield for its members, the Warsaw Pact nations, other than Russia, dread invasion from their principal ally, the Soviet Union.

Hungarians, already frustrated by their helplessness to provide assistance to their conationals threatened with denationalization in Romania, are following with jealous eyes the relative success of Romanian autonomy. They would like to imitate these maverick moves but their leadership is in no position to act in such a manner. The participation of Hungarian divisions in the invasion of Czechoslovakia was generally considered humiliating. While Hungary thus exposed herself as a willing tool of Soviet imperialism, Romania welcomed the visit of General de Gaulle and, subsequently, that of President Nixon. The impotence of the Hungarian desire for free national determination is matched by a sense of inferiority which emphasizes the futility of acting against the realities of geography and military power. "Still" -- people say in Budapest -- "the Romanians did it".

The lack of independent Hungarian foreign policy concerning the essentials of national life remains the Achilles-heel of the regime. Despite the improvement which has taken place in many fields during the past ten years, the dependence on Soviet decision-making has remained unchanged. If nothing else, such a historic and human anomaly, which surrounds the Soviet Empire in East and West and North and South may have, at a time of crisis or by slow erosion, cataclysmic effect on the continued survival of the Marxist superpower.

NOTES

1. Prior to 1867, foreign affairs of the Habsburg Empire were directed from Vienna. With the Ausgleich of 1967, Hungary gained equal partnership with Austria but foreign affairs (together with defense) remained a matter of "common concern" and were handled by the Austro-Hungarian Ministry of Foreign Affairs.

2. In 1940 and 1941, the Hungarian Prime Minister Count Teleki endeavored to maintain the neutrality of his country. When German armies marched through Hungary against Yugoslavia, the Prime Minister committed suicide. Ference A. Váli, *Rift and Revolt in Hungary* (Cambridge, Mass.: Harvard University Press, 1961), p. 26.

3. See C.A. Macartney, *October Fifteenth: A History of Modern Hungary, 1920-1943* (Edinburgh: Edinburgh University Press, 1957), Vol. II, pp. 139-148.

4. For the difficulties encountered by Hungary in her foreign-policy endeavors in that period, see Stephen D. Kertesz, *Diplomacy in a Whirlpool: Hungary Between Nazi Germany and Soviet Russia* (Notre Dame, IN: University of Notre Dame Press, 1953).

5. Personal recollection of this writer.

6. The Security Council of the United Nations had blocked the admission of Hungary (and that of Bulgaria and Romania) because of their violation of human rights guaranteed by the Paris Peace Treaty. In 1955, by a "package" agreement, Moscow caused to veto the admission of new members, the Geneva Summit Conference agreed to lift the ban of Hungary's membership in the United Nations.

7. One conspicuous case was that of the Hungarian Permanent Representative to the United Nations, one Péter Kos, who on October 28 opposed the consideration by the Security Council of the Hungarian Question. As it was subsequently revealed, he was a Soviet citizen by the name of Leo Konduktorov. See Ferenc A. Váli, *Rift and Revolt in Hungary*, p. 329.

8. See United Nations, *Report of the Special Committee on the Problem of Hungary*. General Assembly, Eleventh Session, Supplement No. 18 (A/3592), New York, 1957, p. 37. See also Ferenc A. Váli, "The Hungarian Revolution and International Law", *The Fletcher Review*, Summer 1959, p. 13.

9. For description and analysis of these events, see Ferenc A.

126

Váli, *Rift and Revolt in Hungary*, pp. 369-380.

10. Private information given to this writer.

11. For instance, the ambassador to India, residing in New Delhi, is also accredited to Ceylon and Nepal.

12. See Research Institute for Minority Studies on Hungarians, *Hungarians in Czechoslovakia* (New York, 1959).

13. See Ferenc A. Váli, "Transylvania and the Hungarian Minority", *Journal of International Affairs*, XX, No. 1, 1966, pp. 32-44.

14. See Ferenc A. Váli, *The Quest for a United Germany* (Baltimore: Johns Hopkins Press, 1967), pp. 155-156, 238-244.

15. See the interview with János Kádár in which he stated that no "progressive initiative" by the Bonn Government will be rejected, *Népszabadság* November 30, 1969.

16. See the article in the *New York Times*, April 19, 1970.

17. With Spain, Hungary lately established consular relations in addition to already operating trade mission.

18. In 1968 the share of the Soviet Union was 35.7 percent in Hungary's imports and 38.1 percent in her exports.

19. *Magyar Hirlap*, July 5, 1969; *New York Times*, July 27, 1969.

20. With American funds, two luxury hotels have been built in Budapest -- the Duna-Intercontinental and a Hilton Hotel. Budapest is at present the most popular showplace among cities in Communist countries and is being geared to serve as a place of attraction to Western "capitalist" tourists.

21. *Magyar Hirek*, April 19, 1969. Most of these data are evidently based on estimates.

22. On March 3, 1970, a new Decree-Law and Executive Order regulated the conditions of obtaining passports for travel abroad. Under these new rules no passport can be issues to persons: a) whose stay abroad impairs or endangers the internal or external security of the state; b) who wish to visit agencies or persons engaged in hostile activity against a Socialist State; c) against whom legal proceedings are pending, or who are serving a penal sentence; d) who are subject to police surveillance or are banned from their domiciles; e) who wish to visit people abroad illegally, or whose parents, children, husband, brother, or sister are illegal abroad; or f) who do

not possess the economic resources necessary to finance a trip abroad. *Magyar Közlöny* (Hungarian Official Gazette), March 3, 1970.

23. See Henry Tanner's article, "Eastern Europe Displays Nationalist Tendencies Under the Soviet Aegis", *New York Times*, August 16, 1970.

Chapter VI

THE FOREIGN POLICY OF POLAND

James F. Morrison

The study of post-World War II Polish foreign policy, like the study of the foreign policies of the other communist-ruled states of Eastern Europe, has been largely neglected by professional scholars. (1) Poland, of course, frequently has been treated indirectly by scholars writing about the communist international system, Soviet foreign policy, or the policies of the NATO states toward the communist world. In these instances, however, Poland usually has been viewed as a target of the policy of other states -- most notably of the USSR -- and not as a policy generating state. It is rare to find anything at all written about how Polish foreign policy is made and executed, what the interests, objectives, and perceptions of Polish policy-makers really are, or what constitute the major internal and external foreign policy determinants. The limitations imposed by the USSR are about the only determinants ever discussed.

The only substantive aspect of Polish foreign policy that has been treated in any detail or with any frequency is the problem of the Oder-Neisse (2) boundary and the Polish Western territories -- and then usually from a western perspective or by a Polish writer trying to justify the status quo. (3) Even in these cases the policy-making process has almost always been ignored. Another place in the literature on polycentrism. (4) While the Polish position has not been ignored completely by writers in this field, the focus of the discussion has been relatively narrow, treating for the most part only Polish relations with the USSR, and has been less concerned with explaining the objectives and policies of Poland and the other Eastern European states than with discussing the consequences for the international communist system of the erosion of Soviet dominance in the area. In any case, it is clear that the study of post-World War II Polish foreign policy is far

130

from adequate or complete.

This neglect can be attributed both to the general tendency of scholars to ignore the foreign policy of smaller and medium sized states and to the fact that Poland has obviously been in the political and military shadow of the Soviet Union since 1944 and has clearly had severe restrictions placed upon it. (5) Under these conditions it has been easy to assume that no significant policy-making has occured in the Polish People's Republic and that its foreign policy is made in Moscow for all practical purposes. A closer examination of the facts, however, suggests that the situation is more complicated and that Poland, does, indeed, have a foreign policy -- one that provides a very interesting example of the complex interrelationships of internal and external foreign policy determinants. Reliable hard data about the details of the Polish foreign policy-making process are difficult to obtain, of course, but enough material is available for us to discern with a fair degree of accuracy at least the general outlines of Polish foreign policy-making. Hopefully this chapter will contribute something to an understanding of the complexity of the factors involved and will help point the direction for future research.

Popular Assumptions About Polish Foreign Policy

Despite the lack of good scholarly work on the subject, there seem to be two major and apparently conflicting interpretations of Polish foreign policy underlying most of the popular journalism about Poland as well as many of the more scholarly works on Poland-Soviet foreign policy, the communist international system, and western policies toward the communist world. The first of these views, still widespread in emigre circles, is the "obedient satellite" or "Soviet puppet" theory, which argues that Poland is still almost totally subservient to the USSR in foreign affairs, has almost no latitude in making independent decisions, and always follow the Soviet lead in foreign policy because it has no other choice. The second interpretation, most popular during the late 1950s and early 1960s, is the "independent satellite" theory, which argues that Poland achieved a large measure of independence from the USSR during the October, 1956 crisis in Polish-Soviet relations and has subsequently pursued a course in both foreign and domestic policy that deviates significantly from Soviet preferences. Both of these views are, in the author's opinion, inaccurate and misleading oversimplifications that have fortunately been discarded by leading scholars in the Eastern European field. (6) The point of view of this chapter is that within certain absolute Soviet-imposed limits the Polish United Workers' Party elite has had considerable room for initiating its own deviant policies since 1956 and that following the development of the Sino-Soviet split it has had even more room for maneuver and experimentation in both domestic and foreign policy -- far more latitude for deviation, in fact, than it has attempted. This chapter also argues that internal determinants are at least as important as external ones in explaining the failure to deviate more from the Soviet line.

The wide discrepancy between the two popular views outlined above -- the "obedient satellite" and "independent satellite" theories -- is probably explained not so much by ignorance of the available data or the lack of sufficient data, though this is also a factor, as much as it is by the superficial approach of their adherents, selective emphasis on different issues and policies stemming from different political perspectives, and differing interpretations as to how much deviation from the Soviet position is necessary before it is "significant".

It is worth noting that these two theories have one thing in common: both seem to have been derived from an approach to the study of Polish foreign policy that begins with the question of how much control the USSR exercises over the latitude of Polish policy-making and arrives at its conclusions by trying to determine how often and in what ways Polish policy deviates from Soviet policy. This approach of comparing official Soviet and Polish policy output, however, has its weaknesses and may be very misleading if one really wants to understand Polish foreign policy. Such an approach assumes that Polish interests and foreign policy objectives are greatly different from those of the USSR and that the greater the degree of deviation from Soviet policy, the greater Polish independence. Such assumptions ignore the very real possibility that there may be a large area of foreign policy where there is a coincidence of Polish and Soviet interests, or at least a coincidence of the interests of the Polish and Soviet ruling elites. In such a case, the measuring stick of deviation from Soviet policy would be inaccurate as a measure of independence because Polish policies might be independently made, yet very similar to those of the USSR. On the other hand, they might also differ from Soviet policy, yet reflect the approval of the USSR. In some cases the policies may differ because of a Soviet desire to create a misleading perception of disagreement of diversity with the socialist camp or the need to send up a trial balloon to test the reaction of other states. In other instances it might be politically indelicate for the Soviet Union to initiate certain contacts or negotiations or to voice certain views that were really an accurate reflection of the desires direction of its policies. Moreover, identical official foreign policies may reflect not the dominance of one state over another, but rather the result of lengthy negotiations of initial differences and mutual compromise. While the USSR is clearly in a more powerful bargaining position than Poland, the latter is large enough and important enough to force some compromise on the part of the USSR, especially since the Sino-Soviet dispute.

Rather than concentrating on the degree of difference between Soviet and Polish foreign policy, it would seem to make much more sense first to attempt to discover what the Polish perceptions of their interests really are, what limitations stand in the way of the realization of those interests, and what foreign policy objectives and strategies are likely to follow from the given combination of interests and limitations. Then there is some meaningful basis on which to compare Soviet and Polish foreign policy and assess the degree of Polish independence. In general, it seems clear that we are likely to learn less about Polish foreign policy be approaching it from the perspective of the USSR or the West than if we study the subject out of a genuine concern for understanding Polish foreign policy itself. Western and Soviet objectives and pressures, then, become not the purpose of the inquiry, but external variables that play a part in influencing the making and execution of Polish foreign policy and can be evaluated as such. (7)

The purpose of this chapter is to attempt a rough and tentative outline of such a direct and objective approach to the study of Polish foreign policy. It is impossible to cover adequately such a broad and complex topic in a single chapter, but hopefully some of the major domestic and external variables determining Polish foreign policy and the complex relationship between them can be more clearly outlined here than they have been heretofore. Most of the chapter will be devoted to a presentation of general background determinants of Polish foreign policy, but the second part will include a discussion of Polish policies toward the Federal German Republic, the USSR, and CMEA.

Analytic Assumptions About Polish Foreign Policy

Given the variety of approaches to foreign policy it seems useful at this point to note a few of the assumptions that underlie this chapter and to set forth the basic framework used by the author. (8)

1) A foreign policy consists of the goals or objectives of a given state in relation to other states and a set of strategies and tactics for overcoming the obstacles perceived as lying in the way of the realization of those goals.

2) When we speak of Polish foreign policy herein, we mean the official policy that has agreed to by the formal representatives of the Polish state and of the ruling Polish United Workers' Party (hereafter referred to as the PZPR after its initials in Polish). It is important to note, however, that there are several levels of official policy and that what is publicly announced or communicated in private to other states as official policy does not necessarily reflect all policy levels. All states sometimes find it convenient to hide their real goals and strategy by announcing something quite different. Objectives and strategies may be overstated for bargaining purposes or to intimidate opponents. Some goals may be emphasized while others are never announced in order

to avoid threatening other states (both friends and foe) and prevent reactions that would reduce the probability of achieving
long run goals. In other cases, the preferred policies of a state
may have to be altered as a result of pressure from powerful
neighbors or coalition partners. Such compromise in effect means
altering the tactics or even the strategy that would otherwise be
adopted, but not necessarily abandoning the agreed upon long-range
goals. The PZPR, for example, may have certain foreign policy objectives in relation to the USSR or relations with the West, yet
its announced policy may differ considerably because of the limitations imposed by the USSR or because of a compromise negotiated
in the interest of presenting a united front to the west. The fact
that the preferred policies are not published, however, does not
mean they have been abandoned as legitimate alternatives.

3) It is important to distinguish between the foreign policy
preferences of the politically relevant elite and the foreign
policy preferences of the population as a whole -- to the extent
that they have any clear preferences -- especially in countries
such as Poland where the public at large has even less influence
on foreign policy-making than in more democratic systems. In this
chapter it is the preferences of the elite that will receive the
greatest attention, as they are more important for understanding
Polish foreign policy. The conflict between elite and mass foreign
policy preferences is often greater than the conflict between the
policy preferences of the Polish elite and those of the USSR. In
fact, the beliefs and survival interests of the Polish elite
(especially of those in the highest state and Party posts) are
frequently more important than Soviet pressure in creating a
Polish-Soviet alignment in foreign policy. Most westerners tend
to look at Eastern Europe foreign policy from the point of view
of the whole population -- as if they had clear and well-articu-
lated alternative foreign policies in mind -- and jump to the conclusion that it is the USSR that makes Eastern European foreign
policy, ignoring the mediating role and interests of the Eastern
European elites.

4) There is frequently considerable disagreement among the
politically relevant elites (even within the PZPR) on foreign
policy objectives and strategies -- disagreement that arises from
differing experiences, perceptions of the world, expected consequences of a given course of action, values and priorities. (This
disagreement among domestic elites, incidentally, provides one
important lever for the Soviet Union to use in influencing Polish
foreign policy.)

5) It is more useful to think of states as having not a single
foreign policy, but rather a set of foreign policies -- by no
means completely rational or necessarily consistent with one
another. This inconsistency has several sources. First of all, no
one agency in complex modern states has a complete monopoly on the
making and execution of foreign policy. Separate agencies have
specialized tasks to perform in the making and execution of diplo-

matic, economic, military propaganda, and intelligence gathering policies. (9) Despite efforts by the Party to integrate the efforts of these different agencies, there are almost inevitably contradictions arising from their various specialized task orientations. Second, policies must be applied to more than one country, giving rise to policy inconsistencies stemming from differing sets of issues, relative bargaining power, and levels of urgency in a state's relation to various other states.

6) When studying the foreign policies of Poland or other communist-ruled states, it is often helpful to distinguish between two separate but related levels of foreign policy: namely, foreign policy concerned primarily with relations between communist parties. On the level of state relationships there are two major kinds of interactions: first, routine exchanges or negotiations handled exclusively by representatives of state institutions and, second, more complicated negotiations requiring top level policy making decisions. In the latter case, both Party and state institutions may be involved in the negotiations. The Party leadership in any case will be consulted about policy positions. Often, however, the Party leadership itself will take an active part in the negotiations with direct communication with their counterparts in the ruling parties in the other states involved. Contacts between party leaders, in fact, are often more important than the negotiations between formal state representatives. (10) Such interaction between communist party leaders often establishes basic inter-state agreements that are later formalized through agreements signed by representatives of the respective countries at the state level. The various Eastern European ruling party central committees have their own foreign affairs committees and the party secretaries have their foreign affairs departments and staff that are responsible both for general foreign policy questions and personnel assignment and for relations with other Communist Parties -- both ruling and non-ruling.

Interactions may occur at meetings of top party leaders or of more specialized party sub-committees, at party congresses between the fraternal delegations sent by each major party, and at special multi-lateral party meetings called to discuss major policy issues affecting the international communist movement. While many of these inter-party contacts are directly related to inter-state relations, others have only an indirect hearing and are concerned primarily with general ideological questions or questions of the organizations and activities of the international communist movement. These contacts may also involve attempts to influence a given party's general domestic policy (e.g., the case of Czechoslovakia in 1968) or a more specific domestic policy (e.g., the case of the attempt by the SED of the German Democratic Republic to force the PZPR into accepting a policy of full agricultural collectivization in the late 1950s and early 1960s). In the case of contacts between ruling communist parties and non-ruling communist parties, relations between the states are even less directly involved. (Polish United Workers' Party relations with the French Communist Party, for example, have been particularly intense in recent years.) It is also worth noting that the issues that are involved in inter-party relations are often quite different from those that occupy the attention of the formal state representatives. While trade and scientific and cultural exchange agreements have been the preoccupation of the latter, inter-party issues have been of a much more ideological nature, often revolving around the Sino-Soviet rift, and the proper attitude toward Yugoslavia, the West and the third world.

7) Despite certain continuities in the interests and objectives of states, a foreign policy is seldom a static set of goals and strategies. Policies obviously must change to take into account new developments affecting the domestic and external limitations on policy and successes and failures of past policies. Moreover, as internal and external circumstances change, not only the issues but also the relative importance of the foreign policy determinants are likely to change -- a fact that makes it very difficult to generalize about a state's foreign policy over a very long period of time.

8) There is a very close interrelationship between foreign and domestic policy. Each area of policy making has significant consequences for the other. Decisions about the rate of economic growth and the type of investments to be made, for example, have an important effect on the long-range capabilities of the state. In fact, post-World War II Polish economic development has probably been one of the most important factors in strengthening the bargaining position of the Polish United Workers' Party in relation to the USSR. Likewise, a decision to pursue a particular foreign policy objective or to use a given strategy will make greater or lesser demands on the resources of the country and affect the kind of domestic policies that can be adopted. Polish participation in the Korean War (by providing support for North Korea) and cold war rearmament policies, for example, had a disastrous effect on Poland's first five year plan.

9) The power of a state to effect its foreign policies is relative and not absolute. A state's power depends not only on how its resources (or capabilities) compare with those of the other states that have to be persuaded to accept the foreign policy objectives in question, but also on the objective itself. The objective is important for two reasons: first, because it determines how many of its capabilities each of the states involved in likely to commit to promoting or opposing the objective in question, and, second, because different objectives and in different circumstances. The Polish geographic position, for example, makes its foreign policy objectives in relation to German Democratic Republic more important than its objectives in relation to Japan. Consequently, the Poles presumably would be willing to commit more of their resources to influencing Soviet policy toward the GDR than they would to influencing Soviet policy toward Japan. This willingness

to commit resources, plus Poland strategic location between the GDR and the USSR presumably gives Poland more influence (power) over Soviet policy toward the GDR than over Soviet policy toward Japan.

10) Although most of the discussion in this chapter deals with the objectives, strategies, and relative capabilities of Poland, the USSR, and the Federal German Republic it is important to keep in mind that Polish foreign policy making and the political inter-action with the USSR and Germany takes place within a larger con-text of the communist international sub-system with its own set of institutions (e.g., CMEA, the Warsaw Treaty Organization, ad hoc multilateral party meetings, and the tradition of CPSU leader-ship) and norms and its own political problems. In addition, of course, Polish policy is made and executed within the context of the still larger world-wide international system with its insti-tutions (e.g., the U.N.) and norms and other regional sub-systems in conflict with the communist sub-system (e.g., the United States and NATO, the EEC and EFTA). These larger systems of institutions and norms, as well as the foreign policy objectives, strategies, and capabilities of other individual state units all provide op-portunities for and impose limitations on Polish foreign policy making.

Dominant Themes in Polish Foreign Policy

There are three major themes running through the analysis of Polish foreign policy that follows. It seems useful to state them briefly at this point:

1) There has been a certain continuity in the dominant theme of Polish foreign policy since the period before the partitioning of Poland in the late 18th century: namely, the overriding and ever-present concern of a relatively weak state for the protection of its territory and the preservation of its independence in the face of pressures from stronger and potentially expansionist neigh-bors, whether Germans, Mongols, Tartars, Lithuanians, Turks, Swedes, Bohemians, Austrians, or Russians. Following the Polish experience of over 100 years of partition and occupation by Prussia, Russia, and Austria beginning in the late 18th century, and the even more devastating experience of partition by the USSR and Nazi Germany during World War II, this theme has become even more dom-inant than before.

2) While Polish foreign policy has been closely intertwined with Soviet foreign policy ever since World War II, there have been significant developments since 1955, both in Poland and in the communist international system as a whole, that have signifi-cantly altered the nature of the relationship between Soviet and Polish foreign policy makers. In brief, the relevant changes in Poland included a) rapid economic development and increased Polish economic and military capabilities, b) more complete domestic con-

solidation of power in the hands of the PZPR leadership, and greater self-confidence in their ability to define their own objectives and strategies, c) more popular domestic policies after 1955 and the elimination of most of the grievances that divided the PZPR leadership from the CPSU, thereby contributing to d) greater legitimacy of the PZPR-dominated Polish government and greater Polish national unity, and e) greater popular acceptance of official foreign policy objectives and strategy. The relevant system level changes include a) the erosion of the dominant position of the Soviet Union and the system, b) more opportunities for individual parties to deal pragmatically with domestic problems rather than having to follow a rigid Soviet model, and c) more decentralization of decision-making in the system (with collective political, economic, and military decisions being made less by the USSR unilaterally in pursuit of its own interests and more through bargaining with the Eastern European states with consideration for their interests). These changes in the system had the effect of making Polish relations with the USSR and the rest of the communist system less costly and also allowed the above-mentioned domestic reforms to be carried out, thereby helping to increase the legitimacy and popularity of the PZPR and the Polish government -- a fact that further strengthened the bargaining position of the PZPR and the Polish government vis-à-vis the USSR.

3) While there are still very important limitations placed on the range of Polish foreign policy alternatives by the USSR, it would be a great oversimplification to argue that these limitations are always the major determinant of Polish policy. There are many instances in which there is a fairly extensive coincidence of interests between the leadership of the USSR and that of the PZPR, especially where relations with Germany are concerned. It is also fair to add that much Polish foreign policy -- especially that relating to the Federal Republic of Germany -- even seems consistent with the perceptions and policy preferences of what is probably a majority of the politically tuned in Polish population. Even where it does not reflect such majority preferences, the Polish ruling Party has sufficient capabilities at its disposal to carry on its policies without Soviet intervention. In other words, one need not point to Soviet domination as the only relevant explanation of most Polish foreign policy. Moreover, there is another important area of Polish foreign policy that cannot be explained by the notion of Soviet domination: namely, the demands made against the USSR by the Polish political leadership in the many instances where there are conflicts of interest between the two.

This is not to maintain that there are no instances where the USSR forces Poland to adopt a foreign policy position against its will but only to argue that it is a gross oversimplification to attempt an explanation of Polish policy by continuing to insist that the Soviet Union dictates everything. The main outlines of Polish foreign policy -- especially toward the West -- can be largely explained by Polish domestic determinants plus external influences beyond the borders of the communist international system (most notably the perceived threat posed by the policies of the Federal Republic of Germany without considering the reinforcing elements of the limitations that the USSR obviously places on Poland (just as it places certain limits on the behavior of Finland and Austria). A more complete explanation of Polish foreign policy, of course, requires a consideration of Soviet objectives, capabilities, and strategies. This is especially true for understanding Polish policy toward the communist world, but the existence of the USSR is also clearly a factor that profoundly affects Polish policy toward the West. We are used to thinking of Soviet influence in terms of the limitations it may impose on Poland, but in some instances Soviet foreign policy may actually support and strengthen Polish foreign policy objectives and make possible what the Poles would find difficult to achieve by themselves, e.g., persuading the GDR and eventually the FRG to recognize the Oder-Neisse boundary. Other Soviet diplomatic initiatives, such as disarmament efforts or initiatives aimed at achieving a detente with the West, also affect the context within which Polish foreign policy operates.

Before exploring these three propositions in greater detail it would seem useful to outline the major institutions involved in the formulation and execution of Polish foreign policy and to list briefly what seem to be the major domestic and external determinants involved. This will provide a more systematic overview of the major institutions and variables for the more detailed discussion later.

The Institutions Involved in Polish Foreign Policy Formulation

The highest organ of Polish government is the unicameral parliament, the Sejm. Each of its two annual sessions, one in the autumn and the other in the spring, lasts several months. Most of the work of the Sejm is done in sub-committees known as commissions. For our purposes the most relevant commissions are those for Foreign Affairs, National Defense, and Foreign Trade. Although the Sejm and its Commissions are more active than is typical for parliaments in the communist world, their role in foreign policy making is very limited according to the standards of the U.S. and Western Europe. The Sejm Foreign Affairs Commission apparently meets as regularly as the other Sejm commissions but presumably plays a less active role in suggesting policy modifications. Sejm deputies have exercised their right to question government ministers fairly frequently since 1956, but foreign affairs are not often a subject of controversy within the Sejm.

Somewhat more important is the Council of State, one of two collective executive organs elected by the Sejm. The Council of State not only performs certain executive functions, but also carries on a number of legislative functions when the Sejm is not in session, including declaration of war and issuance of decrees with the force of law. The Council of State is also normally responsible for the appointment and recall of Polish representatives to other states, the accreditation of foreign representatives to Poland, and the ratification of treaties and agreements with other states. The Chairman of the Council of State is also the ceremonial head of state.

The Sejm also officially appoints and recalls the Government of the Polish People's Republic, who constitute the membership of the Council of Ministers, the chief executive and administrative organ of the state. The Chairman of the Council of Ministers acts as Prime Minister and head of the government. In matters relating to foreign policy the Council of Ministers is responsible for the general direction of relations with other states, national defense, and economic affairs, including foreign trade. Under the Council of Ministers are the Ministries of Foreign Affairs, Foreign Trade, National Defense, and Interior (responsible, among other things, for intelligence and internal security), as well as the State Planning Commission, which is concerned with foreign trade in addition to purely domestic economic development. A Vice-Premier from the Presidium of the Council of Ministers has also served as Poland's representative to CMEA and Chairman of the Polish State Committee for Foreign Economic Relations.

The Ministry of Foreign Affairs, however, is clearly the locus of foreign policy making expertise in the government and for the Party as well. Although the PZPR leadership and some of its sub-organs, to be discussed below, establish the general guidelines and limits to Polish foreign policy, they depend on the much larger and more experienced staff of the Foreign Ministry and its Institute for International Affairs for both technical guidance and ideas. There is considerable evidence that the Polish Ministry of Foreign Affairs has played a considerably more active role in shaping the development of foreign policy than is generally true in Eastern Europe. Reports to this effect are confirmed by the fact that since July, 1956 the Polish Foreign Minister, unlike the foreign ministers of almost all other Eastern European countries, has been a member of the PZPR Politburo. (11)

The organization of the Ministry of Foreign Affairs need by outlined only briefly here. The chief decision-making body is the Collegium, which consists of the Minister, the two Deputy Ministers, Directors of major groups of departments in the ministry, Head of the Press and Information Department, Head of the Personnel Department, key specialists, and special staff assistants. There are also the usual departments specializing in geographic areas: The USSR and Eastern Europe; Communist Asia, The British Commonwealth, the USA, Scandinavia; Other Western Europe, Greece, Turkey; Other Asia, Africa; and Latin America. In addition, there are specialized departments for Protocol, Legal Affairs and Treaties, International Organizations, Cultural and Scientific Affairs, Consular Affairs, Administration, Press and Information, Communications, Archives, and the Institute for International Affairs. (12)

The Ministry of Foreign Affairs also supervises the work of the major institutions involved in the execution of Polish foreign policy abroad: namely, the Polish mission to the United Nations and 55 Polish embassies and 25 separate consular offices around the world that handle relations with the 90 states with which Poland has diplomatic relations. (13) In terms of diplomatic activity, Poland ranks with the USSR, Czechoslovakia, and Yugoslavia as among the most active states in the communist world.

Turning to the Party institutions involved in foreign policy formulation, it is not necessary to spend any time discussing the Party Congress, which is theoretically the highest Party organ but in practice serves primarily as a legitimazing body. It hears and approves reports from the PZPR leadership in the area of Party foreign affairs policy, but clearly plays no active role in policy formulation. The Central Committee, formally elected by the Party Congress, plays a somewhat more active role through its Committee on Foreign Affairs. This committee works with the support of the modest staff of the Department of Foreign Affairs in the Party Secretariat. The Director of the Department of Foreign Affairs reports to one of the Central Committee Secretaries, who supervises and directs the work of the Department. Although the CC Committee on Foreign Affairs undoubtedly contributes to the formulation of the general outline of Polish foreign policy and the ideological justification for it, it is the Party Politburo and the First Secretary who certainly have the most important voice in determining its final shape. The policy making interaction between the various specialized Party and state organs becomes quite complex, of course. There is always at least one Politburo member who specializes in foreign policy, and he is a part of the Central Committee's Committee on Foreign Affairs. The Committee will in the course of its work call on the Department of Foreign Affairs staff for assistance -- as will the First Secretary and Politburo directly when important foreign policy decisions are being considered. The Department of Foreign Affairs staff, in turn, will call on the Ministry of Foreign Affairs and Institute for International Affairs specialists for technical information and guidance. In addition, there is overlap between the membership of the Politburo and Secretariat and that of the Council of Ministers and Council of State. There is also usually one Party Central Committee member on the Foreign Affairs Commission of the Sejm. Further coordination is achieved because of overlap between the memberships of the Politburo, the specialized committee of the Central Committee, the Council of State, and the other major ministries involved in foreign affairs.

In addition to participating in the development of guidelines for Polish foreign policy, and concerning themselves with personnel matters, it is worth noting that the CC Foreign Affairs Committee and the Department of Foreign Affairs of the Secretariat also have some responsibility for PZPR relations with other commu-

nist parties, both ruling and non-ruling ones, and with various
"progressive" movements and individuals around the world, especially in the developing countries.

Domestic Determinants

   Although domestic determinants are listed separately here for
analytical purposes, it is important to keep in mind that there
is constant interaction between domestic and external determinants
and that many of the domestic determinants discussed here are themselves a product of external determinants operating in the past.
   I. Socio-economic and military determinants
   1) Geography, demography, natural resources, and level of
economic development -- the underlying determinants of state capabilities:
   a) Poland is located on a relatively flat, defenseless
plan, exposed to the USSR on the east and Germany (now the GDR)
on the west. The Carpathian mountains provide a relatively good
natural boundary with Czechoslovakia on the south. On the north
Poland has 694 kilometers of Baltic coastline, including the three
developed ports of Szczecin (Stettin), Gdansk (Danzig), and Gdynia
and the three smaller ports of Kolobrzeg (Kolberg), Darlowo
(Rugenwalde), and Ustka (Stolpmunde). (The five-fold increase in
Poland's coastline, plus the incorporation into Poland of the
southwestern half of former East Prussia and a sizable strip of
German territory along Poland's western border seem to have been
net gains from the post-war boundary adjustments that moved Poland
roughly 130 miles to the west, despite a reduction in territory
from 388.6 to 311.7 thousand square kilometers.)
   b) The Polish population ranks third in the communist
world after China and the USSR and numbers a little more than 32
million people, nearly all of them ethnically Polish and in the
Catholic religious tradition. (This homogeneity is in sharp contrast to pre-war Poland and is a result of Hitler's extermination
of more than three million Polish Jews and of the post-war boundary
settlement that left former Ukranians and White Russians behind in
the USSR and expelled the Germans from the "recovered" territories
in the west and north.) The Polish population, thanks to the war,
is also relatively young and characterized by one of the highest
birth rates in Europe. The level of education and skill of the
population is above average for Eastern Europe. The urbanization
level now exceed 50%.
   c) Poland has moderately good natural resources. It is
exceptionally well endowed with coal and sulphur, but most import
almost all of its oil and iron ore. Its agricultural land is only
fair. There is much sandy soil and a moderately cold climate with
a relatively short growing season. There are significant forest
reserves, however, and the land is sufficiently fertile to make
Poland self-sufficient in most agricultural commodities with surplus

left over for export. Despite improved agricultural techniques, the growing population and a much improved standard of living have begun to put a strain on Polish agriculture, however.

    d) Poland's level of economic development places it behind, Czechoslovakia, the GDR, and the USSR, but ahead of the other communist-rules states. In terms of total production Poland ranks third behind the USSR and China. Like the other Eastern European states Poland has made impressive industrial progress since 1939, but like the rest of the communist world is falling technologically farther behind the west and finding it increasingly difficult to compete in western markets despite the rapid shift from a basically agricultural to basically industrial economy since before the war. A major impact of Poland's technological lag is to create a strong set of domestic pressure for increased trade with the west. Increasing problems with the supply of raw materials are beginning to develop as industrial production mushrooms. There is also great need for economic reform, but the Poles have lagged behind Czechoslovakia, Hungary, and the GDR in this area.

    2) Military capabilities:

    a) Although Poland ranks third in population in the communist world (far ahead of any other Eastern European communist state in this category) and perceived considerable long range threat to its territories from the FRG, the size of the Polish armed forces do not reflect this situation. While the Polish military is obviously dwarfed in comparison to that of the USSR and China, Romania (with less than 20 million people) has military forces approximately those of Poland (with 32 million people). Several other East European states also have proportionately larger armed forces.

    b) Though not as well equipped or as heavily armored as the Soviet military, the Polish military is relatively well equipped and trained, though the Polish "temperament" shows little enthusiasm for military discipline.

    c) There is no reason to believe that the Polish forces would not fight loyally under any circumstances in which they might be used. They would be loyal to Polish leadership in any conflict with the USSR or other communist states, and they would fight with the USSR in any engagement with western forces, particularly if the FRG were directly involved in the military action.

    d) Poland, however, obviously does not have adequate military capabilities to engage in any serious foreign adventures and even with full mobilization would clearly find it impossible to defend itself against either the USSR or Germany with its own resources.

    II. Historical and cultural determinants

    1) Polish traditions, culture, and "national character": (Although "national character" is difficult to pin down or measure and is of questionable value as a variable in any serious study of foreign policy determinants, it may be argued that certain personality traits, behavior patterns, beliefs, norms, and values are

common enough among Poles -- especially those who tend to occupy positions relevant to foreign policy decision-making -- that some mention to them should be made, at last.)

a) It is difficult to spend any time in Poland without coming away with the impression that Poles tend to be highly individualistic, suspicious of authority, skeptical, sensitive to any limits placed on their individual or collective freedom, difficult to organize for any but the most pressing common purpose and surprisingly resistant to the imposition of any rigid ideology.

b) Poles -- especially educated, urban, and young Poles -- also tend to be warm, open, tolerant, talkative, fun-loving, and capable of laughing at themselves. They tend to be this worldly and oriented toward finding ways of making the present enjoyable. Among older Poles there is a tendency to reminisce about earlier times. The future is not ignored completely, but when it is discussed it is often with an aim of resignation or even of fatalism.

c) There is a strong Western orientation in art, music, literature, language, fashion, architecture, religion and style of behavior. They see themselves as an integral part of western civilization and wish to maintain close ties with the West.

d) Poles tend to be highly nationalistic in almost all of their thinking and cultural pursuits. This is especially true for those with at least a high school education. These attitudes and the high degree to which personal identity seems to be intertwined with the nation have undoubtedly been intensified as a result of the Poles' historical experience during the 19th century occupation of their country by the Prussians, Russians, and Austrians, their national rebirth after World War I, and the near national annihilation during World War II. The Poles tend to have both a certain sense of inferiority toward the West and a fierce pride in their own cultural achievements and a strong feeling of cultural and moral superiority toward their neighbors, especially toward the Russians. (They admire the technical and organization competence of the Germans and Czechs, but look down on their styles of life, their materialism, and their conformism, and tend to feel morally superior to them.)

e) The post-war attempt to introduce a Marxist worldview into Poland and to create a Polish version of the new socialist man has been only partially successful at best. There has been considerable success at selling the ideas of nationalization of industry, greater economic equality, and the necessity of maintaining friendly relations with the USSR, but the ideas of proletarian internationalism, the leading role of the USSR, the necessity of hard work, collective efforts, and serious-mindedness about building socialism have met stiff resistance. The Marxist-Leninist world-view is much more prevalent among the Party elite than among the masses -- and there are certainly some ideological zealots -- but it is hard to avoid being struck by the extent to which a high proposition of Party members are apparently indifferent to the official ideology.

2) Polish memories and perceptions of the world:
a) The Poles have intense memories of the honnor of
World War II and a continuing fear of war that is often almost
obsessive. It is clear that there is no desire for war for any
purpose, even on the part of those who would like to see Poland
"liberated" from communist rule.

b) Poles tend to have very intense memories of what the
Germans did to Poland and her people during the last war. They
also remember the earlier German moves toward the east at their
ancestors' expense and particularly the period of the partition
and occupation when the Germans tried to stamp out Polish culture
and identity. They see the Germans as almost incurably cruel,
militaristic, and expansionist as a nation, though individually
they are usually willing to acknowledge the possibility of meaningful relationship with them. There is as a consequence of the
above a deep-seated fear and distrust of Germany (including the
GDR) and a strong bias toward viewing Germany as an everpresent
future threat. Such deep-seated attitudes make it very difficult
to adjust to the more recent realities of developments in the FRG
and to deal with the Bonn government in a realistic way. (While
the Polish policy-making elites may take a more realistic view of
the FRG and the Bonn government, the fact remains that they have
a vested interest in perpetuating the German threat and the popular
Polish perception of an armed and "revisionist" capitalist FRG.
Although there have been some reasonably objective newspaper and
TV documentaries on the FRG in recent years, the Polish press,
radio, TV, cinemas, and bookstores are still filled with material
about the war, German rearmament and militarism, and the strength
of the neo-Nazi movement and "revisionist" sentiment in the FRG.
Whether this has been a deliberate move on the part of the Polish
political elite or not, the resulting Polish obsession with the
war and Germany more than 25 years after VE day has certainly
served the interests of the PZPR leadership well.)

c) The Poles have less intense, but still strong memories
of their suffering under the Russians during the 19th century
occupation, the abortive uprisings and Siberian exile, the Molotov-
Ribbentrop Pact and the Soviet role in the fourth partition of
Poland, the Katyn massacre of over 10,000 Polish officers, the
failure to aid more effectively the Warsaw uprising of 1944, and
the role of the USSR in imposing a communist government on the
country in 1944-1945 not to mention the more recent excesses of
the Stalinist period, the unfavorable terms of trade, the attempts
to Sovietize Polish culture and society, etc. In addition, the
Party members also remember Stalin's dissolution of the Polish
Communist Party in 1938 and the execution of many of its leaders
in the purges, as well as the Stalinist excesses affecting the
PZPR until 1956. Nevertheless, for whatever reason -- official
silence about the past grievances against the USSR, objective perceptions that the honnor of the German occupation was worse, gratitude for liberation from the German and defense of the recovered

territories, or simply rationalization of the inevitable -- it is clear that the Polish feelings toward the Germans are far more negative and intense than toward the Russians. The relationship with the Russians might best be described as a business partner- ship to which there is an inescapable commitment. For only a few Poles is it a genuine friendship.

d) At the same time there is the perception of the USSR as an enormous and almost invincible colossus against which any resistance is futile. Immediately after World War II -- and even into the 1950s -- there was still some fairly widespread hope for liberation from the communist camp on the part of a great many Poles. The advent of nuclear weapons and missiles, sputnik, the crushing of the Hungarian uprising, the American failure in the Bay of Pigs and Vietnam, and the more recent invasion of Czecho- slovakia have further strengthened the perception of the invinci- bility of the USSR -- at least as far as Europe is concerned. There also seems to have been a growing acceptance of the inevita- bility and permanence of communism in Poland and even an increas- ing tendency to see the rest of the world as inevitably falling under communist control -- though not necessarily Soviet control, as there is also a tendency to perceive China as a rising star in the long run. Poles may prefer the west, but they are pessimistic about its future.

e) The Poles increasingly perceive that there can be no realistic expectation of any defense of their interests on the part of the West, good intensions and mutual interests and common heritage notwithstanding. The clear perception of the disastrous results of the interwar attempt to go it alone and rely on alli- ances with France, Britain and other central European states has been enough to convince most Poles that an accommodation with the USSR or Germany is the only realistic position for Poland. The fact that the USSR and World War II spared the Poles the need for an agonizing debate over the question of with which side to make an accommodation is accepted by most Poles as one of the unpleasant but very real facts of life that has to be accepted. The same post- war events (noted above) that strengthened the Poles' perception of the USSR as a colossus have also served to reinforce the Polish view that they can expect no help from the West.

f) The Polish perception of the rest of communist-ruled Eastern Europe is mixed and in the process of change. The Poles have not felt as strong ties with the rest of Eastern Europe as they have with France, for example, in the West, but there have been some considerable feelings of warmth toward Hungary and more recently toward Romania (e.g., the inter-war alliance) and Yugo- slavia (especially since the break with Stalin and the Polish October). As suggested earlier in the paper, Polish attitudes to- ward Czechoslovakia have been generally negative (not only for cultural reasons, but also because of the interwar boundary dis- pute). Attitudes toward the GDR in some ways are more negative than toward the FRG. Paradoxically, the GDR provides no real threat to Poland, yet a number of facts seem to lead to a negative reaction to it. First of all, it is under the Soviet thumb and has shown no independence. Second, the East Germans have seemed to the Poles to be models of docile Stalinists and have, moreover, applied traditional German diligence and thoroughness to building the kind of system that most Poles dislike. Third, the GDR has been among the states that have put most pressure on Poland to conform to the Soviet model and has also gone out of its way to put obstacles in the way of closer Polish ties with the FRG. On the whole, however, there seems to be a gradual realization on the part of most educated Poles that it is not sufficient to fream of reunification with the West and that reality and self interest dictate closer ties with the other states of Eastern Europe. The economic development and urbanization of these countries, plus closer diplomatic and economic relations with them--and more tourism -- have helped overcome the more traditional attitudes and the isolation of the Stalinist period.

3) Changes in Polish society relevant to Polish foreign policy:

a) Developments in Poland since World War II have had the cumulative effect of increasing rapidly the number of people who have a definite stake in the Polish system. Many have been coopted into positions of authority, but more important the growth of government authority and industrial expansion have created large numbers of new jobs for which the PZPR takes much of the credit in the minds of most Poles. The PZPR likewise takes credit for the reconstruction of the country, the defense of the recovered territories, and virtually all technological innovation and development that would have normally gone on no matter what government was in power. (Such are the advantages of being the incumbent in any system.) In addition, the specific policies of the communist regime in Poland have clearly broadened the opportunities for upward mobility for the sons and daughters of the workers and peasants through new schools, jobs and special preferences for those of working class background in school admission and hiring. Likewise, there have been significant advances for the workers and peasants in the fields of welfare, most notably in the expansion of medical care, day care facilities, on the job cafeterias, and cultural events and mass media for the general populace.

b) The reforms that followed the Polish October in 1956 further reduced the domestic opposition to the system. In addition, the 1956 events in Hungary, the March 1968 student riots in Poland, and the invasion of Czechoslovakia in August 1968 have eliminated most Polish hopes for any significant change in the system in the near future. The reforms following the December 1970 strikes and riots have also helped decrease dissatisfaction with the system at least temporarily.

c) The Party's control of the mass media also undoubtedly helped shape popular attitudes more favorably toward the new system, as did the Party control over the content of the educational process and over the mass organizations of Polish society (such as the trade unions, youth organizations, veterans groups, etc.). The control over the media was undoubtedly particularly effective in shaping popular attitudes toward foreign affairs because of the limited personal experience that most people had with events outside their own country.

d) In any case, it is clear that the cumulative result of the changes in Polish society and the passing of time has been a much greater tendency for people in Poland to identify with the new system and to accept the basic legitimacy of the government and Party, and to decrease the distance that separated the foreign policy preferences of the PZPR elites and the general population in the late 1940s. The Party's ability to mobilize new and formerly politically indifferent segments and the young has been a major factor in reducing the elitemass gap.

III. Institutional determinants

1) Politics and the organization of collective decision-making:

a) Decision-making in Poland -- especially in the foreign policy area -- is concentrated in the hands of the PZPR leadership. This fact increases the relative importance of elite values and goals in foreign policy making. These elite goals certainly include elite survival (i.e. staying in power), the avoidance of war, territorial security, Polish economic development, increasing Party legitimacy, minimizing pressure from other communist-ruled states (especially from the USSR), increased trade with the West and improvement in terms of trade (e.g. more favorable credit terms, lower tariffs and eliminations of quotas, fewer embargoed goods), and increasing the prestige of Poland and the PZPR.

b) The increased popular identification with the socialist system and the increased legitimacy of the government and the PZPR noted above have reduced the dependency of the Party and government on the USSR and have consequently increased their bargaining power vis-à-vis the USSR and the rest of the communist system.

c) The Polish elites have been able to make skillful use of a number of external events and popular perceptions of the outside world to strengthen their position within the country and to gain popular sympathy for their foreign policy position. First, there is the Polish fear of Germany, noted above, which the PZPR has exploited to justify close ties with the socialist camp and to strengthen national unity and the legitimacy of the PZPR rule. Second, there is some reason to believe that the PZPR leadership encouraged the circulation of stories about its tough stand against the USSR in 1956 to create a more nationalist and popular image for itself. (Planned or not, this was the result and had the effect of further strengthening the bargaining position of the Polish government and the PZPR vis-à-vis the USSR.) Another 1956 event that the PZPR used with some skill was the Soviet invasion of Hungary, stressing the fate that awaited Poland if the Polish people did not moderate their demands and accept the leadership of

148

Gomulka as the best they could get under the circumstances. The
Polish fear of war has also to some extent been utilized effectively by the PZPR through its support for disarmament, and especially its sponsorship of the Rapacki and Gomulka Plans discussed
below.

d) The Polish Communist Party was dissolved by Stalin in
1938 and most of its top leaders executed or imprisoned. The
reasons are obscure (presumably to avoid complications with the
USSR and Nazi Germany at Polish expense), but the consequences are
not. First of all, the Polish Party after it was revived in 1943
under the Polish Workers' Party (PPR) label has remained suspicious
of the USSR and has tended to see the world more through Polish
eyes than through Soviet eyes. Second, when Stalin made the decision to revive the Polish Party after the break with the London
government over Katyn, it was necessary to build the Party prac-
tically from scratch. This meant that recruitment into the Party
had to be rapid and almost indiscriminate if the Party was to have
the strength to transform Poland into a socialist state after the
war. This rapid recruitment, however, meant that those within the
Party were more likely to reflect the general Polish attitudes of
nationalism, liberalism, tolerance, and preference for western
culture. It also meant that they would be more likely to approach
the problem of governing and transforming from a pragmatic point
of view rather than an ideological one, given the obviously pragmatic (or opportunistic) motives that most recruits had for joining
the Party. The fact that the initial recruitment took place in the
USSR behind the front line, plus the fact that so many of the early
recruits were Jewish, sowed the seeds of later conflict with the
Party. The Poles who had spend the war working in the communist
underground in Poland never quite trusted those recruited and
trained in Moscow, particularly the Jews whom they suspected of
being a little too oriented toward the Marxist norm of socialist
internationalism (in this case, too oriented toward Soviet interests). There was also the related problem of the Polish-Jewish
cultural gap, jealously that so many of the top and middle-range
Party jobs were held by Jews, and traditional antisemitism. Some
of the most notorious Stalinist Jews (e.g., Berman and Minc) were
purged in the 1955-56 period, but the basic conflict was unresolved
until the aftermath of the 6 days war in the Middle East in 1967
when many Jews in the Party and military expressed admiration of
Israel and found it difficult to support the Soviet and Polish
foreign policy toward the Middle East. This combined with the involvement of a number of children of Jewish Party leaders in student protests in March 1968 was apparently sufficient to trigger
an antisemitistic purger of the Party and of the country generally
in 1968 and 1969. (It should also be pointed out that many of the
Jews who were Moscow trained and Stalinists before 1956 had become
good "liberal", reform-minded in the years following, and in still
another way came into conflict with the so-called partisans, who
tended to want tough, no-nonsense policies domestically.)

e) A further consequence of the Party's basically weak starting position in Poland has been to make the Party sensitive to the need for external support. Although this dependency on direct support from Moscow and the threat of intervention if necessary has become less important with time, it is still clear that that PZPR (or at least those currently occupying leadership posts) would run considerable risk if there should be any disintegration within the bloc. Such disintegration would erode the popular impression of the inevitability of communism and the basic unity of the communist camp. The Polish Party must also have seen the greater risk in such a situation -- or in the event of war -- that the FRG might be tempered to reunite Germany and attempt to recover the German territories lost to Poland. In any case, it seems clear that the PZPR leadership perceives that it is very much in its interest to preserve the basic unity of the communist system, to avoid open conflict between the USSR and China, and to avoid war anywhere in the world that might involve the USSR or Eastern Europe.

External Determinants

In very brief outline form the major external determinants of Polish foreign policy are as follows:
1) At the level of the international system:
a) The basic bi-polar structure of the system and the conflict between the US and the states of Western Europe on the one hand and the USSR, Eastern Europe, and China on the other. Although the Sino-Soviet dispute increases Poland's room for maneuver in some ways, the continuing Soviet perception of an American and German threat means that the USSR is almost certain to object to any Polish moves that would increase American or Polish moves that would increase American or German influence in Poland, especially given Poland's strategic location between Germany and the USSR.
b) The ever present danger of nuclear war and the inevitable consequences this would have for Poland. In light of Polish experience in World War II, this threat of war has made peace and security a very high priority in Polish foreign policy objectives.
c) The absence of a well-developed set of norms that could mediate the east-west conflict or provide any real protection for Polish interests independently of an alliance with a major power.
d) The growing east-west detente, which makes it easier for the Poles to expand their trade and cultural exchange programs with the West in pursuit of technology and economic advantage as well as greater political independency from the USSR.
2) At the level of the communist international system:
a) The growing economic needs of the CMEA states for more sophisticated technology, management, and organization and for more raw materials, creating the need for closer ties with the West, for domestic economic reform, and for a further development in CMEA organization.

b) The contined development of CMEA as a semiautonomous institution and the attempt at economic specialization among the
CMEA membership.

c) The development of the Warsaw Treaty Organization as a
viable mechanism for integrating the armed forces of Eastern Europe
with those of the USSR under an effective Soviet-dominated command
structure.

d) The continued Soviet leading role in the Eastern European
part of the communist international system, underlined by the
August 1968 invasion of Czechoslovakia to reverse its course of
domestic development and the attempted justification by the Brezhnev
Doctrine, claiming the right of the USSR and other socialist states
to intervene when any existing socialist state is threatened in any
way. Also the attempt to give the doctrine treaty status.

e) The Sino-Soviet split and the subsequent intensification
of the quarrel between the two major communist powers, thereby improving the Polish bargaining position vis-à-vis the USSR.

f) The post-1956 acknowledgement of the sovereignty of the
East European states, the decentralization of decision-making in
the Eastern European sub-system and the greater Soviet attention
to the needs of the individual Eastern European states. This decentralization both increased the value and legitimacy of CMEA
thereby increasing the incentive to participate voluntarily, and
made it easier for member states to express their grievances by
opting out of active participation.

g) The continued erosion of Soviet authority in the Eastern
European sub-system, symbolized by the successful departure from
the integrated system of Yugoslavia, Albania, and in part, Romania.
The Czech case also suggests the inability of the USSR to exercise
its authority there short of military invasion.

h) The renewed emphasis on the idea of many roads to socialism (within limits) and the elimination of the norm of strict ad-
herence to the Soviet model, with the consequent reduction in the
rate of accumulation and the increase in the production of consumer goods.

i) The overwhelming military and economic capabilities of
the Soviet Union in relation to the other states of Eastern Europe.

3) At the level of the individual states:

a) The growing economic and military power of both Germanies.

b) The growing economic power and technological accomplish-
ments of Western Europe as a whole.

c) The growing economic and military power in Poland in relation to the USSR, especially after the diversion of Soviet capabilities to its eastern frontier following the Sino-Soviet split.

d) The development of the Western European common markets
and their effect on Polish opportunities for trade with Western
Europe.

e) The objectives of the Federal Republic of Germany; the
degree to which it rearms; its policies toward Poland and the USSR;
opportunities for trade and economic cooperation; the end of the

Hallstein doctrine.

f) The state of Soviet relations with the FRG.

g) Events in other parts of the world that involve the USSR, China, the Eastern European states or threaten the peace, e.g., Vietnam and the Mid-East War (1967).

h) Policies of the US and other western states toward Poland and the rest of Eastern Europe; opportunities for trade. In the case of both the US and Western Europe, the greater the trade opportunities, the greater the temptation to help solve technology problems through closer relations with the West.

Polish Relations with the West

Now let us turn to a more specific examination of one aspect of Polish policy -- namely Poland's relationship with the Federal Republic of Germany.

Poles almost invariably point to their "unfortunate geographical position" as the most important fact of their collective existence. By their geographical position, of course, they mean not their absolute physical position as much as they mean their relative position between two much stronger states (i.e., Germany and Russia) that have traditionally had territorial ambitions in their direction. Although Poland in the 15th and 16th centuries was one of the most powerful states in Europe, the problem of defending her borders against the Germanic tribes and states went back as far as the origins of the Polish state in the 10th century. Although more successful against the Russians to the West during the first several centuries as a state, Poland has had to worry about the defense of its territory against the Russians ever since the early part of the 17th century following the abortive attempts by the Poles to further expand their territory to the west at Russian expense. The three successively devastating partitions of Poland between the Prussians, Russians, and Austrians in the late 18th century were followed by over a century of occupation and systematic attempts to assimilate the Poles into the respective occupying empires. (The Germans and to a somewhat lesser degree the Russians placed great stress on Polish assimilation.) The humiliation of the partitions and the shock of the occupation had a lasting effect on the Poles, as already noted above, and heightened their determination following the rebirth of Poland after World War I to preserve their independence at all costs. When faced again with the simultaneous threat from more powerful neighbors on both sides -- the Bolshevik Russians on the east and the Nazi Germans on the west -- the Poles found it impossible to think of an independence-limiting accommodation with either side and chose instead to ally themselves with relatively weak Romanians and with the distant French and British, who proved incapable of preventing still another partition of Poland in 1939 -- this time by Stalin's Russian and Hitler's Germany.

The second rebirth of Poland, though formally under the auspices of the four allied powers, was in effect administered by the
USSR in the wake of the westward advance of the Red Army. A minority government dominated by communists and dependent on the USSR
was easily established in the war-ravaged country. The new government and its supporters had a number of reasons for being sympathetic to close ties with the Soviet Union -- reasons of ideology,
dependence on the USSR for their political power, gratitude for
liberation from the Nazis, or reluctant acceptance of the inevitable shift in the balance of power in central Europe to the USSR
and the equally inevitable need for reaching some sort of accommodation with the USSR. There was an additional reason, as well --
one that in the long run was probably most important for winning
popular Polish acceptance of close ties with the USSR: namely, the
need to develop and defend the "recovered" territories.

One of the provisions of the allied wartime agreements was the
incorporation into the USSR of about one third of the pre-war Polish territory in the east. (With the exception of the major Polish cities of Vilno and Lwow, this land was inhabited primarily
by Ukranians and White Russians and had been originally offered to
the Soviet Union by the allies after the First World War, but the
Poles had managed to win it back on the battlefield.) In return,
and as compensation for their wartime losses, the Poles were to
receive about half of East Prussia and that portion of Germany
proper that lay east of the Oder-Neisse (14) rivers. The land was
to be administered by Poland until a Peace Treaty formalized the
disposition of the territory. To facilitate the transfer of the
new territory to Poland, the allied wartime agreements also called
for the expulsion of the remaining German population from the new
Polish territories, freeing them for occupation by the Polish population expelled from the land taken over by the USSR and by emi-
grants from central Poland. As there was obviously no opportunity
to recover the territory lost to the USSR, because there were considerable advantages to the new territories (e.g., the greater
coastline and ports, a well-developed if badly damaged industrial
infrastructure in lower Silesia), and because these were lands
that for the most part had been part of Poland centuries ago, the
Poles clearly had a strong incentive to hold on to these "recovered"
territories. To hold, develop, and defend these territories was
one of the few things that almost all Poles could agree upon.

At the same time, there were strong Polish long-range fears
about the Germans and doubts about whether the Germans would in
the long run accept this transfer of territory to Poland, particularly in light of the fact that several million German expellees
from the territories were in the western zone of Germany and would
help keep the issue alive for years to come. The development of
the cold war, the failure to finalize the boundary settlement in a
peace treaty, and the establishment of a rearmed West German state
associated with NATO further reinforced the Polish fears for the
future of their recovered territories. In short, the recovered

territories, combines with the Polish mistrust and fear of a rearmed Germany made close ties with the Soviet Union seem desirable,
or at least tolerable, particularly in light of the historically
demonstrated inability of potential allies to the west or elsewhere in Eastern Europe to offer any effective defense of Polish
interests in the event of war. Moreover, the realities of the
Soviet presence in and of the western absence from Eastern Europe
was increasingly apparent. The net effect of the war had been to
make the Soviet Union the dominant power in Europe. There seemed
to be no viable alternative to living with the USSR. The Korean
War, West German rearmament, the vigorous activities of the expellees and right wing extremists in West Germany, and the failure
of the US and the FRG to recognize the permanence of the Oder-
Neisse boundary further strengthened the increasingly widespread
Polish conviction that the only viable defense of the recovered
territories -- in which much economic and psychological investment
had been made since the war -- lay in close ties with the USSR.

The strategy for securing recognition of the borders from other
states has involved a number of separate approaches : first, a
campaign to establish the historically Polish character of the
territory through heavy emphasis on archeological exploration,
scholarly research and publication of any material that points to
the early Slavic settlements or Polish activity in the area.
Second, a propaganda campaign to establish sympathy for the Polish
moral and legal claim to the new territories, including publication of materials and the making of films stressing the theme of
the terrible Polish wartime losses and suffering at the hands of
the Germans and emphasizing the collective guilt of the Germans
and the justice of turning these lands over to Poland as compensation. Another theme has stressed the continued danger to Poland
and the peace of the world from the FRG and the neo-Nazi and revisionist elements there. It has also been necessary to reassert the
allied intent at Potsdam that the Polish administration of the
territories be a transition stage toward permanent incorporation
of the territories into Poland and not merely a temporary occupation pending a different settlement following the signing by the
allies of a peace treaty with Germany. There has also been a serious attempt to establish the justice of the Polish claim to continued and permanent occupation of the territories by stressing the
heavy investment that Poland has made in the land, Polish economic
dependence on the territories, and the fact that as time passes an
increasing proportion of those living in the recovered territories
were in fact born there and that to change the status of the territories once more in the name of justice to the individuals who were

uprooted in the name of collective guilt would make no sense at
all in view of the suffering inevitable for those presently living
there.

Much of this propaganda has been directed toward internal consumption to strengthen the Polish determination to hold on to the
territories and to foster national unity, but the same type of
material has been heavily stressed in foreign radio broadcasts
and propaganda publications: POLAND ILLUSTRATED, POLISH PERSPEC-
TIVES, THE POLISH WEEKLY, CONTEMPORARY POLAND, POLISH WESTERN
AFFAIRS, and in countless books and news releases and speeches by
Poles at home and abroad. Special efforts have also been made to
reach the Polish emigree population living in the West.

The Polish government has also tried to achieve greater recognition for the recovered territories through pressure applied to
the Catholic Church in Poland. The pressures, however, have been
largely unsuccessful in moving the Vatican to revise its traditional policy of not adjusting its administrative boundaries to conform with political realities until they have been finalized in
the form of a formal treaty. (The failure of the Church to give
full recognition to the new boundaries has incidentally also
served as an effective weapon in the hands of the PZPR in its campaign to undermine the authority of the Church in Poland.)

A further part of the strategy for recognition of the present
boundaries has been on the diplomatic front. Here the Soviet Union
was undoubtedly of considerable help to Poland in securing the
formal recognition of the Oder-Neisse boundary by the German Democratic Republic in the Zgorzelec Treaty signed in 1950. The Poles
received many private assurances from western diplomats to the
effect that their government indeed looked upon the present boundaries as permanent and that they would oppose vigorously any attempt
by the FRG to alter the borders by force, but that formal recognition had to await the signing of a peace treaty. Such assurances,
however, were of little interest to the Poles. More important were
the statements made in 1959 by President Charles de Gaulle of
France, in effect accepting the present boundaries as proper ones.

The problem of securing American and West German recognition of
the boundaries proved more difficult. The West German goals were
trade and eventual unification of the two Germanies, and were
presumably using non-recognition of the Oder-Neisse boundary primarily as a lever to exert pressure on the Poles to get them to
provide some support for eventual unification of Germany, or at
least to get them to make some concessions on the border issue or
make possible some sort of compromise involving the return of some
German settlers. In any case, domestic political pressures in West
Germany were such that, pending an agreement for reunification,
the government could only lose votes by recognizing of Oder-Neisse
line.

As much as the Poles were interested in expanded trade with the
FRG, they know that this was also what the West German government
wanted -- perhaps more so in fact than they really wanted reunifi-

cation. Although the Poles seemed willing to discuss trade and
closer ties with Bonn separately from the border issue between
the fall of 1956 and the fall of 1958 -- a period when Bonn seemed
cool to the idea -- after the Berlin crisis of 1958 the Poles began tying the issue of border recognition to that of trade and
closer political ties. (15) In other words, recognition of the
Oder-Neisse boundary became a pre-condition to closer ties and
expanded trade. Although this was also a period of a harder Soviet
line toward the GDR, the Poles also seemed to be willing to sacrifice trade advantage in hopes of winning boundary recognition by
playing on the obvious desire of the FRG to expand its markets and
influence in the east. A West German trade mission was eventually
established in Warsaw and a series of mutually advantageous trade
arrangements were worked out between Polish firms and western
private enterprises (especially after 1965), but it was clear that
the main structural support for building bridges to the east would
have to be final recognition by the FRG and the US of the Oder-
Neisse frontier. Despite considerable pressure from the US on
Germany to in fact adopt a more flexible policy toward the east
and to extend recognition of the Oder-Neisse frontier and some
important overtures to the Poles in this direction by the FRG
Kiessinger government, it was not until the victory of Brandt in
the FRG that real progress was made and West German recognition
of the Oder-Neisse frontier finally extended through the Bonn-
Moscow renunciation of force agreement signed in August 1970 and
in the Bonn-Warsaw agreement of November 1970. (16) (Gomulka had
proposed to Brandt a treaty recognizing the Oder-Neisse frontier
again in May, 1969, but as Brandt was interested in getting recognition for eventual German reunification rights from the USSR and
since Moscow also had a considerable interest in security recognition for the Oder-Neisse frontier to stabilize the situation in
Europe, it obviously made more sense for the first discussion of
the question to take place between Moscow and Bonn. Although the
Poles at times in that past may have worried privately about the
prospects of a Soviet-West German agreement at their expense,
this time there cannot have been too much concern, as the Soviets
clearly had a vested interest in stabilizing the European front
and, moreover, could not afford to alienate Poland in a period
when it clearly need allies in its struggle to prevent the disintegration of the East European sub-system and in its relations
with China.)
     It is worth noting again that a solution to the Oder-Neisse
boundary question is by no means an unmixed blessing to the Polish
leadership, which has some interest in maintaining the German
threat, as noted above. From the western perspective, of course,
one of the most significant ways of weakening the Soviet influence
over Poland and of strengthening the hand of the liberals within
the PZPR would have been to recognize and formalize the present
borders long ago -- but the peculiar internal political problems
of the FRG and the NATO reliance on German troops made it difficult

for the US to bring much pressure to bear on Bonn. The fact that
the Polish elite, in spite of the apparent self-interest in keeping
the issue alive, chose to continu to push for recognition of the
Oder-Neisse line is another indicator of the overriding importance
that preservation of the recovered territories has for all Poles
and of the need for expanded trade with the West. Moreover, it
seems likely that the Polish leadership calculated that the German
threat, or at least the Polish perception of it, would not disappear for a long time in any event, that they were in a strong
enough position to continue their control over Poland even without
the German revisionist threat, and that the formalization of the
boundary would give Poland even more bargaining power vis-à-vis
the USSR, not to mention the advantages of more secure basis for
expanded trade ties with the FRG.

At this point let us turn to a consideration of Polish attempts
to neutralize potential German military power -- the second major
strategic objective of the Poles. The Polish government, of course,
has consistently joined in support of all Soviet and communist
front efforts to secure disarmament and the weakening of the relative power of the US and NATO. In addition, they have proposed
several disarmament plans of their own. Before outlining these
plans it seems worth spending a little time exploring the relationship between disarmament and Polish interest. One might argue that
support for disarmament is in effect support for the status quo in
Eastern Europe, which most Poles probably do not prefer, thereby
negating one of the theses of this chapter that most Polish foreign
policy reflects the commonality of Soviet and Polish interests.
While it is possible to make a case for this point of view, it
must rest on the premise that most Poles want western liberation
from communism and the USSR, and that a strong NATO and an east-
west arms race makes this liberation more likely, and that the
liberation can take place without destroying or at least doing ir-
reparable harm to Poland and risking the restoration of the recovered territories to Germany. Although most Poles certainly have
dreamed about liberation and the disappearance of the USSR -- and
some probably still do -- the realities of Soviet power make such
dreams totally unrealistic without a horribly destructive war.
Once the realities of Soviet power and the realistic possibilities
of international politics in the present, then it seems fair to
assume that the weakening of western power in general and of German
power in particular is perceived by most Poles as being in their
interests. Also any lessening of tensions between east and west
seems likely to increase the degree of Polish freedom from Moscow's
control rather than decreasing it, as the excuse for Soviet intervention disappears along with the relaxation of tension. Increased
tension created by an arms race or western political moves can do
nothing to help the position of the Polish people or increase the
bargaining power of those in the Party who favor reform, liberalization, and independence.

Some of Polish disarmament plans deserve mention here. The best

known of these, the Rapacki Plan, is actually several related
plans, each one a revised version of the previous one and designed
to meet western objections. The original plan (as prescribed in
the spring of 1957) called basically for a nuclear free zone in
central Europe, encompassing Poland, the two Germanies, Holland,
Czechoslovakia, and Hungary. (Later versions of the plan included
fewer states.) The basic objection of the west to the plan was
that it would leave them at a disadvantage because it did not take
into account the superior Soviet position in conventional weapons.
The major aim of the plan from the Polish point of view was to
prevent nuclear weapons from falling into the hands of the Germans,
but it was also emphasized that the plan would serve as a limited
experiment in disarmament and could serve to build mutual confidence and trust between east and west and might serve as a stepping
stone to much more extensive disarmament and an east-west detente.
The plan also had the additional advantage of increasing Poland's
relative security in the event of a nuclear war. Although Rapacki
denied it was intended to get Poland out of the Warsaw Pact, the
adoption of the plan would almost certainly have loosened the ties
that bound Poland to Moscow. Although the USSR and the other relevant Eastern European states had been persuaded to accept the plan
by the end of 1957, Bonn's lack of interest in the plan (even
after it had been revised to take its objections into account),
plus the Berlin crisis of 1958 and Khrushchev's worldwide disarmament plan of 1959 had the effect of killing the plan for the time-
being. It was revived once more, however, by Gomulka in his UN
speech in September 1960. Although the new Kennedy administration
showed some interest in it and though it was submitted in still
another revised version to the Geneva Disarmament Conference in
March 1962, it was never really the basis of any serious negotiations.

In December 1963 a second major Polish initiative -- the Gomulka
Plan -- was introduced. It called for a freeze on national armaments
and all states were to agree not to allow local troops access to
nuclear weapons (stationed on their soil by another country). Once
again, the Polish plan was aimed at reducing the potential threat
of Germany. And once more the Polish plan came to naught, though
it may be argued that the discussion that the two plans generated
may have generally increased international sympathy for disarmament
and may have contributed to the support eventually necessary for
the negotiations and ratification of the nuclear non-proliferation
treaty in the late 1960s.

There were, of course, many other Polish attempts to reduce the
potential power of Germany through the use of diplomatic channels
and propaganda. The sharp attacks on the American proposal for a
multi-lateral nuclear force at sea is one such example.

A related Polish foreign policy effort that deserves mention
here was the campaign for an all-European security conference to
negotiate some sort of European security agreement to stabilize
the status quo, replace NATO and the Warsaw Pact, neutralize

Germany, and reduce American influence in Europe. Here again, it can be argued that there is a considerable coincidence of Polish and Soviet interests -- in reducing the German threat, significantly lowering the level of American involvement in Europe and especially of American support for the FRG, diminishing the level of tension in Europe, and creating an atmosphere for expanded trade needed to hasten the development of the communist economies. It can also be argued that there is an additional advantage of the CSCE for the Poles: namely, that implementation of the principles outlined in the CSCE Final Act of 1975 could create the pre-conditions for increased Polish flexibility in further expanding trade and other economic relations with western Europe. It should also have the effect of strengthening the position of the Polish intellectuals and PZPR members who favor greater political and economic liberalization by reducing significantly the major external threats used as arguments against liberalization.

Poland and the Communist International System

The second major post-World War II Polish foreign policy concern -- both at the state level and at the party level -- has clearly been maximizing its independence in relation to the USSR and the rest of international communist movement. (Note that maximizing independence is not the same thing as minimizing contact or interaction but rather means creating a situation in which interaction can be a maximum benefit and minimum cost, i.e., a situation in which there are the fewest possible restrictions on one's behavior.)

As already noted in the section above, at the end of World War II, the Polish people found themselves being absorbed into the Soviet-dominated communist international system without any realistic choice to the contrary. Resistance under such circumstances would have been fruitless and suicidal. In addition, many Poles saw considerable hope in the new system (which, for tactical reasons had advertised itself not as a communist regime, but as a broadbased, nationalist coalition). Still others saw the change as a mixed blessing with some advantages. While enthusiastic proponents of the system were certainly a minority, the overwhelming Soviet presence, the obvious need to reconstruct the country and get it moving again, the promise of democratic reforms and welfare, and the determination to protect Polish interests from Germany in the future were sufficient to provide the basic support needed by the new government to maintain itself in power. Over the years the cooptation of significant numbers of new citizens into the new centralized politico-economic-social mobility, broadening opportunities for education and welfare, plus media control and indoctrination and the Polish government, which was also able to take credit for all the reconstruction and post-war reforms inevitable under any system. Although there was much disagreement with govern-

ment policies -- particularly during the Stalinist period from
1948-1956 -- the terror and the Soviet presence made any alternative seem out of the question. There was also strong opposition
to the isolation of Poland from the West, to the increasing Russian
influence in cultural matters, and to the inequitable economic
treatment of Poland by the USSR. (Some of the agreements were particularly costly, such as the coal agreement, which forced Poland
to sell most of its coal production to the USSR at a fraction of
the world market price when there was a large potential demand for
Polish coal in the West.) The Soviet veto of the Polish desire to
participate in the Marshall Plan was also a source of grievance.
    Even within the Party there was considerable opposition to
Soviet policies toward Poland and to the Russification of the
country. Gomulka, for example, had fought with moderate success
against the Soviet practice of stripping German factories in the
Polish western territories, but was unsuccessful in his struggle
against Soviet pressure for agricultural collectivization and in
his defense of a separate Polish road to socialism. Because of the
overpowering Soviet presence -- psychologically and through the
influence of the secret police and loyal Soviet supporters within
the party -- and because of economic, military, and political dependence of the Polish communists on the USSR, those in the Party
had little choice but to follow the lead of the Soviet Union and
of the Poles in the Party who believed in the correctness of Soviet
leadership or who had so little imagination of their own that they
were at a loss about what to do. It seems clear that everyone in
the Polish Party was not entirely pleased with the post 1948 turn
of events. Some, like Gomulka, were purged and arrested. Others,
less exposed and vulnerable, quietly went along with the new direction from Moscow. It should be emphasized, however, that the major
source of unhappiness within the Party during this period was almost certainly with Soviet interference in domestic Polish policies
and less concern over the Soviet line in foreign policy toward the
West. There was also undoubtedly some concern with the degree of
Soviet influence within the Party, army, and secret police, but
these facts were probably less well known at the lower levels of
the Party and among the public at large. The period of intensive
economic development and demands made on Poland economically by
the USSR during the Korean War had very serious consequences for
the Polish economy, and by 1953 and the death of Stalin there was
widespread economic chaos and political crisis brewing throughout
Eastern Europe. Relaxation of the intensity of economic accumulation and expansion and easing up in the drive to collectivization
in 1953 and 1955 did not solve the problem. Growing disillusionment with the system clearly called for more fundamental action,
especially after the demoralizing impact of Khrushchev's February
1956 destalinization speech. The political uncertainty in Moscow,
destalinization, the call for a new course in the USSR and Eastern
Europe, the widespread discontent in Eastern Europe, and the precarious position of the EE leadership created a further dilemma:

160

to reform and risk losing control, or to tighten up the controls
even further and risk an even greater explosion later. The emergence of communist China, the first great power able to challenge
the USSR within the framework of the communist system -- and one
with a different revolutionary tradition -- was also an important
factor in changing the institutions and norms of the communist
system.

The details of the thaw in Poland are well known and are beyond
the scope of this paper, but the significant developments of the
period for purposes of foreign policy analysis can be briefly
summarized: following the June 1956 riots in Poznan, Poland, the
PZPR, after much internal debate and political struggle, opted for
the return of Gomulka to power and the adoption of his ideas for a
Polish road to socialism -- but only after serious and sharp discussion with the Soviet leadership. Nevertheless, the Polish communists under Gomulka succeeded in introducing a number of reforms
without losing control of the country. The October, 1956 showdown
with the USSR (in the light of the increased anti-Soviet feeling
in the country following the revelation of the worst of the Soviet
economic exploitation and political control of Poland) further
increased the popularity of the new Polish communist leadership
and added to their bargaining power in relation to Moscow.

It is worth noting here that Polish position has always been
strongest where interference in its domestic policies has been
involved. This has probably been the case because of the Polish
perception that it has limited capabilities to act independently
in foreign policy, that its interests are roughly similar to those
of the USSR in the area that really matters (namely Germany), and
that in other areas its bargaining position has been strong enough
to win concessions where necessary. (17)

In this connection it is important to add that the Polish position to China, Yugoslavia, and Romania have borne a close relationship to this concern for maintaining independence in domestic
policy. It seems clear that the Polish leaders must calculate that
it is not in its interests to see either China or Yugoslavia ex-
cluded from the communist camp on the grounds that diversity --
especially of domestic policy -- within the socialist camp provides the perfect precedent and justification for its own deviations from the Soviet model, and Poland more than any other East
European country except Yugoslavia has found domestic deviation
from the Soviet model desirable. Moreover, the diversity of intellectual viewpoint within such an international system is more com-
patible with the Polish intellectual tradition than is the more
monolithic and orthodox conformity necessary during the Stalinist
period. It should also be emphasized that it is very much in the
interests of the Polish elite to preserve the communist camp
against Germany, but also against the possibility of -- however
remote -- domestic revolt. The appearance of permanence of the
communist system is good insurance against any growing unrest at
home.

The Polish position on CMEA must also be mentioned at least briefly here. The Polish leadership has come to the conclusion that whatever the advantages of expanded trade with the West, there are also additional advantages to be gained from a rational division of labor in East Europe. This advantage is dictated not only by the political inevitability (and desirability from the point of view of the elites) of continued close ties with the USSR and the other socialist states, but also by the backward technological level of Eastern Europe that makes exports to the West difficult, not to mention the additional threat that the Western European common market poses to the export of goods to Poland's traditional Western European markets. Here again, Polish and Soviet interests (as well as those of the GDR, Czechoslovakia, and Hungary) have to a great extent coincided.

While it might be argued that from the point of view of many Polish citizens, trade with the West would be more desirable and would more quickly narrow the technological gap that separates Poland from the West, the fact remains that 25 years of communist rule and trade with other communist-ruled states has significantly altered the nature of the Eastern European economies and made trade with the West relatively less profitable and more difficult than before. Some kind of increased integration -- or at least rationalization of trade relations with the other East European states seems clearly in the interests of the Polish people -- at least as long as it is not at the expense of maximizing Western trade and aid ties.

There is the question, of course, of why the Poles agreed to participate in the invasion of Czechoslovakia in August, 1968. We must speculate at this point, but it is possible that some of the Polish leadership, like some of the Soviet leaders, were genuinely concerned about developments in Czechoslovakia and felt personally threatened by the consequences of what was going on there. The Polish people were obviously interested in what was going on in Czechoslovakia, as were the younger and more liberal members of the PZPR. They could see all too well the very real possibility of a revolt within the PZPR that would dump the present leadership and institute the kind of reforms that the PZPR leadership had been opposing for years.

Moreover like the Russians, the Poles probably also sensed the consequences for the GDR if the Czech liberalization should prove successful. Similar liberalization in the GDR would almost certainly eliminate all barriers to German reunification in the long run, and the Polish western territories would be endangered. Or, before the move toward reunification got too far, there was the danger of Soviet intervention that could trigger off World War III and all the risks for Poland that this entailed.

Certainly the invasion of Czechoslovakia was not widely perceived in Poland by the population at large as necessary or desirable. Moreover, there was particular guilt in Poland because it so totally contradicted all the Poles had been saying for years about

the sovereignty and equality of socialist states, the sanctity of
the principle of non-intervention and so forth. In any case, whatever the reasons or rationalizations for Polish participation may
have been, it is also clear that the Polish leadership must have
felt it had little choice but to go along with the rest of its
Warsaw Treaty Organization partners.

It is, of course, impossible to provide a complete or adequate
picture of any state's foreign policy in such a short space. In
addition, limitations as to the amount of hard data available
about the private thinking and policy preferences of the PZPR
leadership have made speculation necessary. Hopefully, however,
the general background discussion at the beginning of the chapter
and the two case studies at the end have at least provided some
insight for the reader as to the kind of variables that are involved
in Polish foreign policy-making and as to the nature of the complex
relationship between domestic and external factors. Such a study,
though, is only a beginning and even with the present level of
available data, much work can still profitably be done on Polish
and East European foreign policies.

NOTES

1. There have been a number of fairly objective and comprehensive
    studies of Polish foreign policy in the interwar period, in-
    cluding Euzebiusz Basinski, ed., *Stosunki Polsko-Radzieckie w
    Latach, 1917-1945* (Warsaw, 1967); Bohdan B. Budurowycz, *Polish-
    Soviet Relations, 1932-1939* (New York: Columbia University
    Press, 1963); Raymond L. Buell, *The Foreign Policy of Poland*
    (New York: Foreign Policy Association, 1938); Roman Debicki,
    The Foreign Policy of Poland, 1919-1939 (New York: Praeger
    Publishers, Inc., 1962); *Dokumenty i Materialy Do Historii
    Stosunkow Polsko-Radzieckich* (Warsaw, undated), Volumes 1
    through 6; Stephan Horak, *Poland's International Affairs,
    1919-1960, A Calendar* (Bloomington, Indiana: Indiana University
    Press, 1964); Josef Korbel, *Poland Between East and West:
    Soviet-German Diplomacy Toward Poland, 1919-1933* (Princeton,
    New Jersey: Princeton University Press, 1963); Piotr S. Wandych,
    Soviet-Polish Relations, 1917-1921 (Cambridge, Mass.: Harvard
    University Press, 1969); and *France and Her Eastern Allies,
    1919-1925* (Minneapolis, Minnesota: University of Minnesota
    Press, 1962).
    There also have been some interesting studies of wartime and
    pre-war diplomacy relating to Poland, including Anna M. Cienciala,
    Poland and the Western Powers, 1938-1939 (London: Routledge &
    Kegan Paul, 1968); *Documents on Polish-Soviet Relations, 1939-
    1945* (Warsaw, 1966); Edward J. Rozek, *Allied Wartime Diplomacy:
    A Pattern in Poland* (New York: John Wiley & Sons, Inc., 1958).
    Concerning Polish foreign policy since the Second World War,
    there has been virtually nothing written of any significant

scope. In general see the volumes by Charles Gati, ed., *The International Politics of Eastern Europe* (New York: Praeger Publishers, Inc., 1976) and James F. Morrison, *The Polish People's Republic* (Baltimore: Johns Hopkins Press, 1968), as well as the standard work done by Zbigniew K. Brzezinski, *The Soviet Bloc: Unity and Conflict* (Cambridge, Mass.: Harvard University Press, revised and enlarged edition, 1967). See also the journal of the Polish Institute of International Affairs *Studies on International Relations* beginning bi-annually in 1974.
For a limited treatment in comparative perspective see Robert W. Dean, "Foreign Policy Perspectives and European Security: Poland and Czechoslovakia" in Robert R. King and Robert W. Dean, eds., *East European Perspectives on European Security and Cooperation* (New York: Praeger Publishers, Inc., 1974), pp. 118-151.

2. Note that the Polish names for the Oder and Neisse are Odra and Nysa.

3. A small sampling of the hundreds of books written on the border question includes Z. Anthony Kruszewski, *The Oder-Neisse Boundary and Poland's Modernization, The Socioeconomic and Political Impact* (New York: Praeger Publishers, Inc., 1972); Manfred Lachs, *The Polish-German Frontier* (Warsaw, 1964); Wolfgang Wagner, *The Genesis of the Oder-Neisse Line: A Study in the Diplomatic Negotiations during World War II* (Stuttgart: Bretano-Verlag, 1957); and Hansjakob Stehle, *The Independent Satellite* (New York: Praeger Publishers, Inc., 1965).

4. The polycentrism literature is extensive, but see in particular Paul Zinner, ed., *National Communism and Popular Revolt in Eastern Europe* (New York: Columbia University Press, 1956); Kurt London, ed., *Eastern Europe in Transition* (Baltimore: Johns Hopkins Press, 1966); Stephen Fischer-Galati, ed., *Eastern Europe in the Sixties* (New York: Praeger Publishers, Inc., 1963); Adam Bromke, ed., *The Communist States at the Crossroads* (New York: Praeger Publishers, Inc., 1965); Richard Lowenthal, *World Communism: The Disintegration of a Secular Faith* (New York: Oxford University Press, 1966); and the two special issues of *Survey* titled "Polycentrism" (42, June, 1962) and "International Communism: The End of an Epoch" (54, January, 1965).

5. It should be noted, however, that it has not only been communist-ruled states that have had their foreign policy alternatives restricted by the USSR. Finland, and to some extent, Austria have also had to take into account Soviet sensitivities and demands.

6. Brzezinski and Stehle, both of whose works are included in note 1 above, are among the more sophisticated writers treating Polish foreign policy. (Brzezinski is a well-known Columbia University professor and Director of the Research Institute on Communist Affairs and Stehle is a noted journalist who spent five years in Poland writing for the *Frankfurter Allgemeine Zeitung*.)

7. This does not mean that the question of the degree of deviation is of no importance -- only that it needs to be evaluated in light of Polish interests and objectives.

8. See Keith R. Legg and James F. Morrison, *Politics and the International System* (New York: Harper & Row, 1971) for a more detailed presentation of the author's framework for the comparative analysis of foreign policy.

9. It would also be interesting and useful to consider the semi-independent relationship between Polish intelligence gathering agencies, military organizations, economic enterprises, and scientific, trade union, professional, and cultural organizations and those of other states. This, however, is beyond the scope of this chapter.

10. Even in such cases, however, the Party may call upon the expertise of the Ministry of Foreign Affairs or specialized intelligence gathering and evaluation units of the Ministry of Internal Affairs and Ministry of Foreign Trade.

11. Poland's best known Minister of Foreign Affairs was undoubtedly the late Adam Rapacki, a member of the Polish Socialist Party before its December, 1948 merger with the Polish Workers' Party to form the PZPR. Rapacki became a member of the Politburo but was downgraded to candidate member during the Stalinist period that followed, though he continued to hold a number of important government posts until he took over as Foreign Minister from Skrzeszewski in April 1956. In July of that year Rapacki again became a PZPR Politburo member. (See Stehle, op. cit., pp. 230-234, for a more detailed biography of Rapacki.) Rapacki was succeeded by Stefan Jedrychowski in December 1968 after the former was forced to resign as a result of ill health and political complications. Jedrychowski, in turn, was replaced by Stefan Olszowski in 1971. Both Jedrychowski and Olszowski were full Politburo members during their service as Foreign Minister.

12. See R. Barry Farrell, "Foreign Policy Formation in the Communist Countries of Eastern Europe", *East European Quarterly*, 1, 1 (March, 1967), pp. 39-74. An organization chart of the Ministry of Foreign Affairs appears on page 61. See also his "East

European Foreign Policy Leadership, 1964-1970", *Studies in Comparative Communism*, 4, 1 (January, 1971), pp. 80-96.

13. See *Rocznik Polityczne I Gospodarcze 1970* (Warsaw: Panstwowe Wydawnictwo Ekonomiczne, 1971), pp. 777-788 for a detailed listing of Polish embassies and consulates.

14. For discussion of recent FRG foreign policy see Wolfram F. Hanrieder, *The Stable Crisis: Two Decades of German Foreign Policy* (New York, Harper & Row, 1970); and Lawrence L. Whetten, *Germany's Ostpolitik: Relations Between the Federal Republic and the Warsaw Pact Countries* (New York: Oxford University Press, 1971), and Karl E. Birnbaum, *Peace in Europe: East-West Relations 1966-1968 and the Prospects for a European Settlement* (New York: Oxford University Press, 1970).

15. For a detailed discussion of Polish-FRG relations in the late fifties and early sixties, see Stehle, <u>op. cit.</u>

16. For a discussion of the Warsaw-Bonn agreement see Adam Bromke and Harold Von Riekhoff, "The Polish-West German Treaty", *East Europe*, 20, 2 (February, 1971), pp. 2-9.

17. Some writers -- notably Hansjakob Stehle -- have argued that Gomulka, in effect, agreed to support Soviet foreign policy in exchange for Soviet support for domestic deviation from the Soviet model.

Chapter VII

THE FOREIGN POLICY OF ROMANIA IN THE SIXTIES

Horia Socianu

A decade ago, the policies and attitudes of Communist Romania were highly praised for their correctness and loyalty by Soviet and East European leaders, and criticized by American and West European leaders. Western scholars whose field of research was East European politics could not avoid discussing the Romanian case, but there was no challenge or excitement attached to such work. To the Western observers the Romanian leaders conveyed the image of Koestler's moronic "politruks", incapable of more complex mental operations other than sheer memorization and faithful reproduction of their masters' thoughts. Carola Stern's description of the people who took over the leadership in East Germany -- those automatons reacting with a sort of *Kadavergehorsam* or corpselike obedience, after being doubly brainwashed by Nazi and Soviet bosses -- fitted the Pankow leaders no less than the Romanian chiefs implementing in Bucharest the Soviet dictates.

Since 1947, the Romanian party and government had been carefully avoiding the slightest deviation from the Soviet line. No lesser an authority than Professor Skilling was describing Romania in the fall of 1962 as an "orthodox satellite", incapable of serious resistance to Soviet pressure. According to the Canadian scholar, the Romanian leaders were unconditionally supporting the Soviet views against Peking, Yugoslavia, and Albania, while Romania's economy was "closely integrated" through CMEA with the economies of the Soviet Union and Eastern bloc. (1)

One year later, however, the "orthodox satellite" was rejecting the Soviet plans for economic integration of the bloc countries. Romania's opposition to the establishment of a supranational planning body was officially announced in a communiqué published at the end of the Central Committee Plenum held in March 1963. Romania's "new course", launched by Gheorghiu-Dej for economic reasons, was consolidated and expanded by his successor Nicolae Ceausescu to military integration and foreign policy areas. Independent attitudes -- assumed by the Romanian Workers' Party*, later the Romanian Communist Party** -- in interparty affairs, as well as the autonomous decisions on foreign issues made in opposition to Soviet requests and interests, have gradually turned Romania into a virtually nonaligned member of a hierarchical bloc.

After a series of Soviet-Romanian disputes and party encounters, a climactic point was reached in August 1968 when the RCP adopted a defiant posture in the wake of Czechoslovakia's invasion and occupation by Soviet-led forces of the Warsaw Treaty Organization. For a while, it seemed as of the Soviet leaders were hesitating between a similar operation against Romania and a more lenient attitude towards Bucharest. But the spirit of moderation prevailed at Kremlin, and Romania was spared Czechoslovakia's ordeal. The Ceausescu regime survived, and 1969 and 1970 have been years of consolidation and expansion of foreign, interparty and trade policies.

In analyzing the foreign policy of Romania in the sixties, an attempt will be made to find answers to two questions of great significance for the Soviet bloc: 1) Why did two conservative communist leaders like Gheorghe Gheorghiu-Dej and Nicolae Ceausescu initiate and expand foreign and interparty policies consonant with Romania's national interests but opposed to Soviet interests?; and 2) Why did the Soviet leaders tolerate the Romanian insubordination?

For the needs of our analysis, we propose to use a framework focusing on six determinant factors of Romanian foreign policies: the international situation; the significance of the country's geographic location; the power interests of the decision-making elite; and the specific nature of Romania, as a small, nonaligned, and developing nation. The first three factors will be mainly considered in the following section which is an issue-minded historical periodization. The impact of smallness, economic underdevelopment and nonalignment position on Romania's foreign policy will form the subject of separate sections.

First Stage, 1960-65: Departure

In 1954, the Soviet Union agreed to dissolve the Soviet-Romanian joint-stock companies. In 1957, the Soviet troops were withdrawn from Romania. These two steps enabled Gheorghe Gheorghiu-Dej, the First Secretary of the RWP, to launch a new policy of economic modernization. Khrushchev's concessions were probably motivated primarily by a sincere desire to make possible the process of destalinization in Romania by eliminating the most blatant elements of stalinist exploitation of that country. There was, also in the Soviet gestures a sign of confidence in Gheorghiu-Dej's leadership and the RWP's loyalty to the Soviet interests.

Under Khrushchev's leadership, the Soviet government evidenced a marked preference for institutionalization of the Eastern bloc ties by means of Soviet-controlled organizations. By activating the dormant CMEA, for example, the Soviet leaders might hope to a- chieve a better control of the East European economies without resorting to Stalin's repressive measures.

In June 1962, the governments of the Soviet Union and East European allies announced their agreement on the future of economic cooperation within the framework of CMEA. A joint statement -- *The Basic Principles of International Division of Labor* (2) -- elabo- rated the concepts intended to speed up the economic integration of Eastern Europe -- coordination of national foreign-trade plans; production of goods with foreign-trade profitability; regional division of labor based on national industrial specialization; and development in each CMEA countries of those industrial branches for which there was domestic availability of raw materials.

Similar views were advocated later in the year by Khrushchev in an article he published in the Soviet journal *Kommunist*. The Soviet leader called for coordination of production and foreign trade plans of the participating nations, intrabloc specialization, and the establishment of a supranational planning agency.

At the end of the 17th Plenary Session of the Council for Mutual Economic Aid, TASS announced that the Council had discussed the coordination of national plans for the period 1965 to 1980 and agreed to extend the Communist divisions of labor. (3)

Actually, the Romanians, who have decided to launch a very ambi- tious plan of industrialization, have already started a process of economic rapprochement with the West. Between the integrative objec- tives formulated in the CMEA communiqué, and the practical steps undertaken by the Romanians, the contradiction was obvious.

On November 26, 1962, a Franco-British consortium signed a con- tract with Romania for the building of a $ 36 million steelplate mill at the projected Galati metals combine. In December 1962, Romania and Great Britain agreed to increase the volume of their trade exchanges, and in February 1963 France and Romania concluded a three-year agreement providing for a 50 percent increase in their economic exchanges.

The new course was formalized in March 1963. A communiqué which was issued at the end of a meeting of the RWP Central Committee, refrained from rejecting the socialist division of labor but stressed that relations among socialist countries must be based on respect for the national independence and sovereignty, full equality of rights, and mutuality of advantages. There was so much emphasis on national interests in the RWP's statement, that it became ob- vious what the Romanians thought about Khrushchev's "economic multilateralism". They preferred bilateral deal to bloc integration, and the Iron Gates Agreement, concluded with Yugoslavia in June 1963, was additional evidence of Romania's new approach to regional issues. (4)

Three additional steps of a political nature underlined Romania's resolution to pursue an independent course. In April 1963, Romania

became the first East European country to resume full diplomatic
relations with Albania. (5) In June 1963, the RWP published the
summary of a Communist Chinese letter addressed to the Soviet leadership. The Soviets had labeled the message as "groundless and slan-
derous", and refused to make it public. In July 1963, Austria and
Romania settled outstanding financial issues. This was the first of
a series of agreements whereby Romania consented to pay compensation for foreign properties nationalized after World War II.

Finally, in July 1963, the integration dispute between Bucharest
and Moscow was settled in Romania's favor. The CMEA Council met in
Moscow and it was agreed that the "socialist division of labor" be
carried on in accordance with the principles of national sovereignty, equality and mutual advantages. Bilateral consultations between
CMEA countries were acknowledged as a means for achieving agreements on mutual economic development. Khrushchev's concept of a
central planning agency -- a supranational body governing the
economies of the East European countries -- was abandoned.

Gheorghiu-Dej's foreign policies were inspired by three major
principles, consistently applied by the Romanian decision-maker until his death in March 1965 -- peaceful relations with all states,
regardless of their social and political systems; autonomous decision-making at party and state levels; and neutrality in the
Sino-Soviet dispute. (6)

During the last years of Gheorghiu-Dej's tenure Romania concluded or renewed trade agreements with Western countries. Of major
significance for the economic development of Romania were the
agreements reached with West Germany, Italy, France and Great
Britain. To demonstrate their independence, the Romanian leaders
also increased the volume of foreign trade with both Communist
China and Albania, even though those two countries had been ostra-
cised by the Soviet bloc.

The Romanian new course was not marked by any changes in the
party's autocratic style of government. Professor Fischer-Galati's
work on the new Romania attempts to present Gheorghiu-Dej's rejection of Khrushchev's integration schemes as motivated by feelings
of ardent nationalism. Throughout the book, the late Romanian leader is presented as totally committed to the execution of so-called
"anti-Russian plans". (7) According to Professor Fischer-Galati,
Gheorghiu-Dej's "anti-Soviet revolt was obvious from the beginning".
(8) However, a careful assessment of Gheorghiu-Dej's past might
lead to different conclusions. It is worth mentioning that for
thirteen years "Gheorghiu-Dej patronized the criminal activities
against the party and state aktivs". These were the words addressed
by Secretary-General Ceausescu to the Party Aktiv of Bucharest in
April 1968. (9) Tortures, staged trials, summary executions, illegal interventions in the judiciary process, destruction of docu-
mentary evidence, unjustified purges of party activists -- all
these and many other illegalities have been perpetrated by
Gheorghiu-Dej and his collaborators. (10) The Bucharest Aktiv was
told by Ceausescu that it was Gheorghiu-Dej who ordered the arrest

of Minister of Justice Lucretiu Patrascanu and "His vile assasin-
ation at the end of a staged trial and prolonged tortures". (11)
Why was it necessary to order Patrascanu's execution in 1954, "at
a time when other socialist countries and the Soviet Union had
made public similar unlawful acts and initiated the process of
rehabilitation of the victims?" (12) Ceausescu avoided to give an
unequivocal answer but his clever formulation of the issue at
stake made clear Gheorghiu-Dej's motives in perpetrating his supreme villainy.

Patrascanu had to be "liquidated" in 1954 because Gheorghiu-Dej
was afraid that his jailed rival might take his place in the event
of a change of the stalinist guard in Romania. In the Soviet Union,
as Ceausescu told his audience, the process of destalinization had
begun. But Gheorghiu-Dej, who was responsible for the implementation in Romania of Stalin's policies, could not demote himself!
It was logical for Gheorghiu-Dej to reject Khrushchev's plea for
destalinization of the Romanian regime, and the Polish and Hungarian events of 1956 justified his domestic position.

Khrushchev's second plea was made in the early sixties. He
wanted to institutionalize the Soviet political and economic control of Eastern Europe by means of a supranational planning agency.
The Soviet call for integration of East European economies was
rejected by Gheorghiu-Dej who decided to complete the process of
destalinization in Romania. The new doctrine of national independence, state sovereignty and party autonomy, formulated by
Gheorghiu-Dej in his Statement on Interparty Relations by April
1964, was the logical outcome of the struggle of a stalinist leader who refused to yield power either domestically or externally.

Had Gheorghiu-Dej agreed to subject Romania's economy to the
dictates of a so-called supranational agency, he would have sur-
rendered the substance of his political power to the Soviet bureaucrats. It is true that the policy of total surrender to foreign
dictates was the rule when Stalin was in command. At least, however,
Stalin guaranteed the survival of satellite governments against the
will of their own peoples. Khrushchev's new course had set free
disruptive forces which threatened the survival of stalinist
governments. In Hungary, Rakosi had been ousted under popular pressure, and in Poland Gomulka had reemerged and replaced stalinist
leaders with his followers. It was obvious that the Romanian leader could not accept Khrushchev's requests and abandon his fate in
the hands of a man whose policies had caused the erosion of the
bloc unity. Moreover, what guarantees did Gheorghiu-Dej possess
that after he foolishly agreed to erode the foundations of his
power position through internal destalinization and bloc integration of Romania's economy, he would not be thrown to the wolves by
a volatile and unstable Khrushchev during a crisis similar to the
Polish October or the 1956 Hungarian revolt?

As known today, Gheorghiu-Dej's choice was a risky one, but his
calculations were correct. At a time when Soviet policies were de-
stablizing authority within the Soviet bloc, the Romanian leader

and his team were able to survive by dissociating themselves from Moscow's lines.

On March 19, 1965, Gheorghiu-Dej died. The new First Secretary of the RWP, Nicolae Ceausescu, decided to continue and expand the foreign policy of national independence. Under Ceausescu's leadership, the Romanian party became one of the most dogmatic and authoritarian in Eastern Europe. The fusion of the party and state activities, announced by Ceausescu in December 1967, reflected a strong taste for absolute power and centralized control. (13) Even by Soviet standards, the organization of the party machinery and enforcement of party discipline are very rigid in Romania. Party unity and domestic consensus are maintained by that party leadership with an iron hand whose grip never relaxes. Thus the Romanian leaders were able to maintain an independent and neutral posture in interparty affairs the limits of which are dictated by geography and political realities.

The Ninth Congress of the RCP was held in July 1965. In his report to the Congress. the First Secretary Ceausescu announced the Party's desire to speed up the industrialization of Romania as the "decisive factor in guaranteeing independence and national sovereignty". (14)

The major objectives of Ceausescu's foreign policy became soon evident. They were a) political and economic rapprochement with the Western countries; b) economic and military disengagement from the Soviet bloc, while formally maintaining membership in CMEA and the WTO; autonomy in interparty relations.

High-ranking Romanian delegations increasingly visited the Western countries, and Western officials came to Romania on state visits. Special attention was given to improvement of relations with France, West Germany, Italy and Britain. Trade agreements were concluded or expanded, and important West European firms agreed to play their part in the industrialization of Romania. West Germany, Italy and France became the most important trading partners of Romania outside the Eastern bloc.

President Charles de Gaulle's visit to Romania in May 1968 underlined the similarities and differences between the foreign policy approaches of the two latin countries. Both practised a policy of independence and nonalignment within regional groupings. But France had already withdrawn from the Western military alliance, while Romania preferred to stay in the Eastern bloc and to reject its military and economic commitments.

Romania-West German relations followed a rapidly ascending course. Between these two countries there was no territorial dispute or historical anagonism. Romania was the only East European country where massive German minorites were allowed to live after World War II. Traditionally, economic relations have always been beneficial to both nations. In October 1963, permanent trade missions were established in Bonn and Bucharest. In 1965, Krupp Company, Gutehoffnungshuette Corporation, and other industrial firms of West Germany started supplying equipment for the Galati Metallurgical Combine at generous credit terms.

On January 31, 1967, Romania resumed diplomatic relations with West Germany in the teeth of fierce Soviet, East German and Polish opposition. *Neues Deutschland*, the press organ of the East German Communist Party, deplored Romania's gesture and criticized the Romanian government for having failed to deny the West German claim to speak for all Germany. In an unprecedented move in the history of Communist interparty relations, *Scinteia* rejected *Neues Deutschland*'s criticism as "inadmissible interference in Romania's internal affairs". (15) The Romanian party newspaper also stated that "foreign policy decision-making is one of the inalienable attributes of Romania's national sovereignty". (16)

The exchange of ambassadors between West Germany and Romania took place in the summer of 1967, and was followed in August 1967 by an agreement for cooperation in technical and scientific domains, highly beneficial to a developing country like Romania. Both events were the first successes of the new West German policy towards Eastern Europe. Chancellor Willy Brandt, under whose guidance the "Ostpolitik" became an important factor in European relations, described the West German-Romanian rapprochement as "an example of a realistic kind of cooperation that pushes solid bridges far beyond the difference of political conceptions." (17)

Romanian Disengagement from the Soviet Bloc: Rejection of Economic Integration

Romanian political leaders and researchers refuse to see an advantage in integrating their country's economy for the sake of a regional balanced system. (18) The Romanian economists have argued that economic integration, based on labor division and narrow specialization, might condemn developing countries to a state of permanent backwardness. Economic integration, therefore, might be possible only when the countries of the socialist bloc will be at the same economic level. (19) Romania has rejected the Soviet, East German, Czech and Polish arguments that the criterion of foreign trade profitability should govern the industrialization policy of the profitability criterion, since "what is not profitable today might become so tomorrow." (20)

Furthermore, Romania has not only rejected the integration of production plans, but refused to participate in a coordination of foreign trade plans. As a leading Romania economist put it, "each socialist country must first elaborate its own plans of production and foreign trade with a view to national needs and characteristics." (21)

Ceausescu himself has frequently expressed his opposition to "any conceptions or proposals urging the integration of CMEA countries or endowing CMEA with supranational attributes." (22) Romania has also persistently rejected the concept of jointly-owned enterprise, as incompatible with CMEA's statutes. (23)

According to unofficial sources, the leaders of the CMEA countries signed in April 1969, at the end of the 23rd session of the Council, a secret document establishing that supranational agencies may be created under the auspices of CMEA. "Romania's agreement to the secret arrangement was given with two reservations: 1) Romania should not be pressed to become a member of any supranational agency, and 2) newly-created supranational agencies will not be allowed to interfere in Romania's internal economic affairs." (24)

Under Ceausescu's leadership Romanian attitudes became increasingly critical and non-cooperative on issues of military integration. Here are some of the attitudes asserted by Romania in the strategic field:

1) *Opposition to military blocs and alliances.*

Romanian leaders have frequently stated that the rivalry between military blocs creates the danger of a new world conflict. Romania sees no need for the preservation of rigid blocs; it militates for the dismantling of military alliances. Even though the party, government, and mass media take good care to denounce the Atlantic Pact, Romania has maintained a constant record in advocating the simultaneous dissolution of both NATO and WTO. (25)

2) *Need for a strong national army.*

A stand which goes against the very essence of military integration is symmetrical within the need for "strong, monolithic national parties". On June 19, 1967, Ceausescu stated that "as long as the WTO exists, Romania will continue to cooperate in the joint training of our armies". He added, however, "Of course, we shall proceed from the principles which govern the relations between socialist countries, from the fact that each country, each army must be well organized, must be powerful in all respects and have its own national command capable of meeting all the requirements." (26) On November 14, 1968, speaking to the Artillery Units of the Romanian Army, Ceausescu stressed the concept of individual preparedness when stating that "Romania is a member of the Warsaw Pact but she also must strengthen its own military power. Thus, Romania will increase the force of the whole Pact." (27)

3) *Opposition to the organizational structures of the WTO.*

According to frequent press reports, the Romanian leadership is dissatisfied with the present setup of the bloc military organization. Among other suggestions, Romania would like to see the position of WTO Commander-in-Chief rotated between officers belonging to different state members of the alliance. It also seems that the Romanians have repeatedly insisted on an internationalization of the military leadership by involving more East European officers in the command structure. (28) The Czech General Prchli advocated similar changes in a radio interview of July 15, 1968, and the angry Soviet reactions revealed the Kremlin's sensitivity on matters related to the strategic control of Eastern Europe.

4) *Need for an independent production of arms.*

In order to keep the East European armies under control, Moscow has made them dependent on Soviet deliveries of arms and component parts. According to a UPI report, during the March 1968 meeting of the Warsaw Pact Political Consultative Committee, the Romanian delegate expressed "dissatisfaction with the outmoded e-quipment furnished by the Soviet Union to her allies." (29) On July 26, 1967, the Romanian Minister of Defense, General Ion Ionita, stated that "Romania should produce new types of military techno-logy and reduce expensive imports." (30)

5) *Denunciation of the use of the WTO forces in the invasion of Czechoslovakia.*

Romania refused to associate herself with the other members of the Warsaw Pact and participate in the invasion of Czechoslo-vakia. "If a country belongs to a military bloc." said Ceausescu, "that does not mean she is free to disregard the norms of inter-national law or ignore her responsibility to the international community." (31)

Ceausescu's independent line in foreign affairs is the logical consequence of the Romanian stand on interparty relations. The 1964 *Statement on the Stand of the RWP* had reaffirmed the princi-ples of independence, equality, and non-interference, and called on every communist party to refrain from criticisms or attacks against other parties. The document also stated that "no party is allowed to bypass the party leadership in one country or another, and so much the less, to launch appeals for the removal or change of the leadership of a party." (32)

Since April 1964, these principles have been consistently en-forced by the Romanian leadership in interparty relations. Only a strong and monolithic party leadership could remain an autonomous decision-making center and be able to maintain its neutral atti-tude in interparty affairs. (33)

Under Ceausescu's leadership, the RCP refused to participate in collective denunciations of the Chinese Communist Party; obstructed the convening of preparatory meetings of the world communist con-ference; rejected the bloc "party line" towards West Germany and opted for rapprochement with the latter; adopted a neutral stand in the Arab-Israeli conflict and declined to sign the bloc denun-ciation of the Israeli "aggression"; criticized East European in-terference in the internal affairs of the Czechoslovak Communist Party; and refused to attend the Soviet-inspired meetings between the Czechoslovak and East European leaders.

Ever since they appointed themselves mediators of the Sino-Soviet dispute, the Romanian leaders were careful to maintain a neutral position between Moscow and Peking. In June 1966, Chou En-lai's state visit to Romania ended in discord between guest and hosts. A Bucharest rally was delayed for more than two hours, apparently because the Romanians had refused to let the Chinese Premier deliver one of his violet anti-Soviet diatribes. Chou's visit ended

176

without the customary joint communiqué, and the Romanians published only a unilateral statement.

The Romanian stand on party independence has been frequently
reasserted in recent years in connection with Soviet attempts at
convening an international conference of the communist parties.
There is a long list of communist meetings held without Romanian
participation. On April 24, 1967, the RCP refused to send a delegation to the Karlovy Vary Conference, and Radio Bucharest stated
that "the Romanian Communist Party does not attend because in the
course of consultations no agreement could be reached in advance
on the character, purpose and proceedings of the conference". On
February 28, 1968, the independent note was struck even harder
than usual, as the Romanian delegation walked out from the Budapest
Consultative Meeting after the Syrian delegate had denounced the
RCP's neutral stand in intraparty affairs. The Syrian spokesman
described the Romanian party's attitude during the Arab-Israeli
war as "destructive", and went so far as to state that the Romanians were "putting themselves outside the Communist Movement."
The Romanian delegate Paul Niculescu-Mizil asked for immediate re-
tractation by the Syrian delegate of his anti-Romanian remarks and
threatened to withdraw the Romanian delegation from the Conference.
It is interesting to note that later in the day the Conference
organizers yielded to Niculescu-Mizil's ultimatum, and Khaled
Bagdash, the Syrian offender, officially retracted his injurious
remarks. Even though the RCP had thus obtained a significant
success, Ceausescu ordered his representatives to leave Budapest.
On March 1, the Permanent Presidium of the RCP released a communiqué that fully endorsed the attitude adopted by the Romanian
delegation at the Budapest Conference and reaffirmed in very strong
terms the "RCP's decision to reject any interference in its internal affairs." (34)

The Middle East conflict of June 1967, between Israel and the
Arab states, occasioned one of the gravest disputes at party and
state levels between Romania and the rest of the bloc parties and
governments. From the beginning of the new crisis, Romania refused
to associate herself with the Soviet bloc policy of condemning
Israel as the aggressor. In addition, Romania refused to break off
diplomatic relations with Israel, as all the countries of the bloc
did. At the Moscow meeting of June 10, 1967, Romania did not sign
the bloc Declaration denouncing the Israeli aggression, and issued
a separate statement recommending to contending parties to initiate
negotiations for the settlement of the dispute. (35) Furthermore,
later in the year, the Romanian Minister for Foreign Trade visited
Israel and renewed the trade agreement between the two countries.
Adding insult to injury, the expanded trade agreement was signed
in Jerusalem -- a city whose complete occupation by the Israeli
forces was one of the results of the June War. (36)

Tensions between the RCP and the bloc parties reached a dangerous peak before, during and after the Czechoslovak crisis of summer
1968. For several months, the Romanian leadership maintained an

unbroken record in defending the right to autonomous decision-making of the Czechoslovak Communist Party.

As the gravity of the Soviet-Czechoslovak crisis steadily increased, it appeared that the more exposed the Romanian position was becoming, the more provocative the Romanian actions and statements were. The chronology of the Romanian activities during the pre-invasion period reveals astonishing boldness and an unexpected propensity to gambling the future of the RCP. (37)

After the invasion and occupation of Czechoslovakia by Soviet-led troops of the WTO states took place, Ceausescu spoke at a mass rally in Bucharest. He called the invasion "an infamous moment in the history of the revolutionary moment, a flagrant violation of the national sovereignty of a free and independent state." A statement of the RCP denounced the event and declared that the use of the WTO forces "violated the treaty's provisions". The Romanian Grand National Assembly held on August 22 an emergency session and adopted a resolution condemning the "reprehensible interference in the internal affairs of a socialist state" and calling for the immediate withdrawal from Czechoslovakia of the WTO forces.

Tito and Ceausescu, the leaders of the two East European parties and countries threatened by Soviet aggressiveness, met on August 24 at Vrsac, presumably to coordinate plans for the common defense in the event of a Soviet-led attack. The Yugoslav-Romanian meeting was noticed by *Izvestia* which accused both leaders of actively aiding Czechoslovak "counterrevolutionaries".

The defeat of the Dubcek regime demonstrated the Soviet firmness in reasserting their dominance in Eastern Europe. According to a West German jurist, the invasion and occupation of Czechoslovakia proved that the nature of the Soviet bloc as "closer to a de facto protectorate relationship with a tendency towards vassality". (38) But, if Dr. Schweisfurth's thesis was useful for describing the legal status of both the Czechoslovak victim, and the Bulgarian, East German, Hungarian, and Polish assistant-executioners, it obviously could not apply to the Romanian case. Even though Romania continued to change their course from independence to vassality.

Third Stage, 1968-1970: Survival

On November 12, 1968, speaking at the Polish United Workers' Party Congress, the Soviet First Secretary Leonid Brezhnev expounded the doctrine of limited sovereignty of socialist countries. According to the "Brezhnev Doctrine", each socialist country must take into account not only her national interests but also the interests of the entire community of socialist nations. In effect, the doctrine states that one of several socialist countries may intervene in the internal affairs of another "to protect socialism".

The Romanians have denounced the Soviet theory as contrary to the principles of socialist internationalism, national sovereignty and independence, and party autonomy. In 1969 and 1970, Ceausescu and other Romanian leaders have spoken out sharply on numerous occasions against foreign domination and violation of such basic principles of international life as sovereignty, equality among states, and non-interference in other states' or parties' internal affairs. (39)

The Romanian Chief Party Ideologist, Paul Niculescu-Mizil, reiterated the Romanian position at the 12th Congress of the Italian Communist Party where he led the RCP delegation. "Internationalism", said Niculescu-Mizil, "is linked with the principle of party autonomy (and) in the Communist Movement cannot exist ruling and ruled parties." (40)

The Romanian leadership also refused to alter what has become Romania's traditional attitude towards CMEA activities and bloc economic integration. On the occasion of the 20th anniversary of CMEA, A *Scinteia* editorial pointed out that "the establishment of supranational planning bodies is contradicting the principles of equality of states and the CMEA statutes." (41)

In spite of Soviet and Polish pressures, Romania continued to oppose any scheme for integration or creation of jointly-owned enterprises on Romanian soil. Late in April 1969, a special session of the CMEA Council was held in Moscow, and the vagueness of the final communiqué proved that no progress has been made in integration issues. (42)

The April 1969 session of CMEA was accompanied by renewed Soviet-Romanian polemics. In answering *Pravda*'s criticism of "nationalistic attitudes", the Romanian magazine *Lumea* published the strongest indictment of the Brezhnev Doctrine that emanated from a Romanian source since the Soviet invasion of Czechoslovakia. The author of the indictment was Nicolae Corbu, a well-known Romanian journalist. He wrote that the "limited-sovereignty doctrine is a narrow and unscientific conception, a pseudo-theory... that violates the norms of socialism." (43) According to Corbu, "sovereignty means liberty, and a socialist country with limited sovereignty would be an anomaly, a paradox as well as a tragedy." (44)

In June 1969, Moscow hosted the long-awaited Conference of Communist and Workers' Parties. Ceausescu made a statement announcing that "the Romanian delegation will not walk out of the conference despite the rejection by the Soviet and other delegations of the Romanian plea to put a stop to the anti-Chinese attacks." Finally, the Romanians signed the Conference document with reservations. (45) It seems that the Romanian leader did not look upon his participation in the Moscow Congress as a renewed pledge of loyalty towards the Soviet Union. Less than two weeks after the signing of the Conference document, Ceausescu granted an interview to the Argentine newspaper *Panorama* and used the occasion for a reaffirmation of his foreign policy principles. Ceausescu also stated that Romanian views on the invasion of Czechoslovakia by Soviet-led forces "have not changed one millimeter." (46)

Early in August 1969, President Nixon paid a 36-hour visit to

Bucharest where his presence was interpreted as a gesture intended
to underline America's interest in the fate of a small country and
her leadership whose independence was threatened by a powerful
neighbor. (47)

A few days after President Nixon's departure from Romania, the
RCP held its Tenth Congress. The bloc countries sent secondrank
teams, and Communist China did not attend at all, after being
warned that interparty polemics would be forbidden. Even though
the chief of the Soviet delegation Katushev attacked the Eastern
policy of the West, the Romanian Congress was not troubled by any
dramatic ideological encounter. (48)

On August 17, Romania and Israel announced their agreement to
raise their diplomatic relations to full ambassadorial status. The
Arab reaction was swift and angry. The first to retaliate, was the
Iraqi government which withdrew its chargé d'affaires from Buch-
rest. Two days later, Sudan broke off diplomatic relations with
Bucharest, and on August 23 and 24 Egypt and Syria followed suit.
Short notes of the Romanian Foreign Ministry answered tersely each
of the four Arab countries and stated that the raising of the
status of diplomatic relations is an inalienable attribute of
national sovereignty. Arab allegations were rejected by Romania as
"unwarranted interference in the internal affairs of a sovereign
country." (49)

The Romanian gesture towards Israel, and Ceausescu's firmness
in accepting the consequences of his diplomatic willfulness served
as a reminder that Romania's nonaligned attitude vis-à-vis the
pro-Arab policy of the Soviet change has not changed since June
1967. This was the first time since Ceausescu had assumed power
that the foreign policies of Romania and Yugoslavia followed different courses. As a friend of the Arab countries, Yugoslavia's
attitude towards the Middle East conflict was similar to the Soviet
view. But, as Tito recently put it, "if we can convince one another,
so much the better; if not, why should we get angry? Let each of us
follow his course, and see who will advance faster." (50)

It seems that in the economic field Romania enjoys now the same
advantages as Yugoslavia in the late forties and early fifties. In
1969 and 1970 long-term trade agreements were concluded by Romania
with West Germany and France. In only three years, from 1966 to
1969, the annual volume of West German exports to Romania has increased from $ 140 million to $ 185 million, while the Romanian
exports to West Germany jumped from $ 74 million to $ 110 million.(51)

As the political and economic rapprochement with the West became
a permanent fixture of Ceausescu's foreign policy, Romania maintained her aloofness towards CMEA and the WTO. On January 25, 1969,
CMEA commemorated twenty years of existence at a solemn session in
East Berlin. The Romanians employed their customary tactic, and a
series of editorials warned the Soviets before the conference that
Bucharest was not interested in any type of bloc integration. The
Romanian maneuver was shrewdly based on two approaches. On the one
hand, the Romanians reaffirmed their principles of economic cooper-

ation: 1) autonomous decision-making based on national needs and interests; 2) a marked preference for bilateral arrangements; 3) absolute rejection of joint ownership on Romanian territory and 4) economic exchanges with all states, regardless of their social and political systems. (52) On the other hand, instead of the frontal approach against CMEA, the Romanian press developed a type of oblique attack against Eastern integration. Romanian economists and development researchers started a campaign of denigration against the evils of the Western model of economic integration -- the Common Market. (53) The Romanian anti-integration campaign also includes attacks against Scandinavian (54), Latin-American (55), and African (56) attempts to find a solution of economic difficulties through integration. Actually these criticisms, even though seemingly call attention to non-communist attempts at economic integration, are but thinly-veiled denunciations of similar CMEA endeavours. Under the guise of scientific investigations of Western failures, the Romanian economists are censuring the Soviet pressures for integration of East European economies. The mot d'ordre given by the Romanian Communist leadership to Romanian scholars and researchers is to demonstrate that the policy of economic integration contradicts the national interest of small nations, enables the great powers to establish their domination over regional groups, and perpetuates the technological gap between industrialized and underdeveloped countries.

By rejecting both economic integration and participation in jointly-owned enterprises, Romania has become a sort of "permanent observer" rather than a full-fledged member of CMEA. In 1970, the CMEA Council was held in Warsaw; the final communiqué revealed that Romania has refused to be a member of the newly established Investment Bank that would make decisions by majority vote. (57) It seems that the bloc-integration had become a "dead issue" when on August 14, 1970, Radio Moscow reopened the old controversy with a commentary that stressed the role of the Investment Bank in integrating the East European economies. The Soviet commentator brought up a highly sensitive issue, by stating that "industrial specialization is accompanied by the liquidation of non-profitable enterprises in some countries (and) the building of large profitable units in others." (58) The Soviet arguments were promptly rejected by Bucharest. An article published by the Romanian magazine *Viata Economica* reminded the Soviet leaders that the concept of country specialization within the framework of regional division of labor might cause economic stagnation and deepening of economic disparities. In short, the Romanians reiterated their view that economic integration is not "consistent" with the requirements of national interests. (59)

Similar arguments are used by the Romanians against military integration in Eastern Europe. Romania refuses to allow WTO maneuvers on her territory or to give up national command of the armed forces. (60) When the Warsaw Treaty Organization announced in April 1969 that joint maneuvers had been held in Bulgaria with the participation of Soviet, Romanian and Bulgarian units, it was reported that Romanian sources have indicated that "Romanian staff officers have participated not in military maneuvers but in 'extended staff exercises'." (61)

According to Romanian viewpoints, the three major instruments of foreign policy -- diplomacy, economic policies and military power -- must remain national, which means that they can be used only by a national decision-making center. This autonomous center is the leadership of the Romanian Communist Party and Government.

Romania's unwillingness to participate in the new integrated WTO forces was reaffirmed in spring 1970, when Ceausescu referred to the Romanian Army as a national army "under the sole command of the party, government and military leaders. These are the only (agencies) who can give orders to our army, and in the Socialist Republic of Romania only their orders can be carried through." (62)

After Ceausescu's categorical rejection of military integration, the Romanian Embassy in Paris denied rumors concerning acceptance of WTO maneuvers on Romanian territory. (63) In October 1970, the WTO High Command announced that the "Brotherhood of Arms" maneuvers had been held in East Germany with Soviet, East German, Polish, Bulgarian and Romanian participation. (64) But the Romanian Embassy in Paris again denied that Romanian military units had participated in the maneuvers held in East Germany. "As in the preceding exercises," the Romanian denial went on, "Romania was represented by a team of staff officers." (65)

The Romanian needs for East-West rapprochement and an international guarantee of the status quo shaped Ceausescu's foreign policies in 1970. In June, he paid a state visit to France; in September, he went to Austria; and in October, the Romanian President came to the United States where he addressed the UN General Assembly and conferred with President Nixon in Washington. On all occasions, joint communiqué acknowledged Romanian views on national sovereignty, peaceful settlement of international disputes, equality of rights, and non-interference in other countries' internal affairs. As long as the Soviet leaders also abide by such principles in their intraparty and foreign relations with Romania, the Romanian leadership will be able to continue its complex act of balancing between East and West, between Moscow and Paking, and to keep under control the diplomatic, economic, and military policies of Romania.

It is significant for understanding the foreign policy perceptions and motivations of the Romanian leaders, that when General de Gaulle resigned in April 1969 from the French presidency a *Scinteia* praised him for his foreign policy in support of *"a Europe without an iron curtain, a Europe in which all states, all nations will be the masters of their destiny, a Europe which will cooperate in her entirety for progress and peace."* (66)

Because of Soviet threats and pressures, Romania seeks a loosening of the world blocs. In this respect, there is a strong similarity between French and Romanian foreign policy objectives. But demo-

graphic, geographic, economic and political differences between
France and Romania rule out a total identity of foreign policy
means. A prerequisite of French and Romanian nonaligned foreign
policies is the East-West detente. This common need might explain
why the signing of the Soviet-West German Treaty of Nonaggression
was warmly greeted by French and Romanian leaders.

Every international act that moderates the Soviet expantionism
by committing the Soviet Union to a policy of restraint and peaceful settlement of disputes serves the Romanian interests. According to a Western correspondent who visited Eastern Europe after
the signing of the Soviet-West German Treaty, "many Yugoslavs and
Romanians are certain that the Moscow-Bonn Agreement will restrain
Soviet adventurous policies in the Balkans. They also hope to enjoy a longer breathing space in their confrontation with the
Russian colossus." (67)

One final issue, dealing with intrabloc relations, will close
our survey of the foreign policy of contemporary Romania. On
February 3, 1968, the Soviet-Romanian Treaty of Friendship and
Mutual Assistance expired. Even though the draft of the new treaty
was already prepared by spring 1968, it took more than two years
to sign it. Tensions created by the invasion of Czechoslovakia,
Soviet irritations caused by Ceausescu's constant obstructionism
of foreign policy and intraparty matters, and Romanian dissatisfaction with specific draft formulations might have been among the
most important causes of delayed signing. At least, the new treaty,
signed by Kosygin and Ceausescu in August 1970, contains no reference to the Soviet doctrine of limited sovereignty of socialist
countries. Romania signed similar treaties with Poland, on November
12, and Bulgaria on November 20.

Formally 1970 was ending on a note of relaxation of intrabloc
tensions. Its seems that the Soviet Union and her closest East
European allies have accepted Romania's independent position on
foreign policy issues, intraparty affairs and bloc integration as
a permanent feature of the Soviet bloc. Acquiescence is the word
best describing Kosygin's, Gomulka's, and Zhivkov's decisions to
sign their treaties with Romania. After all, one does not renew a
formal partnership unless one in convinced of the need for such
action. By signing the new treaties, the Soviet, Polish, and Bulgarian leaders have formally acknowledged to Ceausescu's Romania
that "special relationship" which was brutally refused to Dubcek's
Czechoslovakia. Even though reluctantly, the Romanian deviation
has been incorporated in the Eastern bloc in an attempt to keep
under control the impact of a disrupting force. In the long run,
this uneasy solution, made possible by Soviet resilience and
Romanian firmness and resolution to "obstruct within the system",
might prove to be beneficial to all the parties to the deal.

NOTES

1. H. Gordon Skilling, *Communism, National and International: Eastern Europe After Stalin* (Toronto: University of Toronto Press, 1964), pp. 52, 62, 66.

* (Hereafter RWP).

** (Hereafter RPC).

2. See Robert McNeal (ed.), *International Relations Among Communists* (Englewood Cliffs, N.J.: Prentice-Hall, 1967), pp. 125-127.

3. The Session was held in Bucharest from December 14 to 20, 1962.

4. Romania and Yugoslavia agreed to build a joint hydroelectric power and navigation project on the Danube with an annual output of 10.7 billion kw hours.

5. The East European countries had broken off diplomatic relations with Albania in 1961.

6. See the "Statement on the Stand of the Rumanian Workers' Party Concerning the Problems of the World Communist and Working Class Movement", April 22, 1964. Reprinted in McNeal (ed.), op. cit., Part I, pp. 127-129; Part II, pp. 165-166.

7. Stephen Fischer-Galati, *The New Rumania, From People's Democracy to Socialist Republic* (Cambridge, Mass.: The M.I.T. Press, 1967), esp. Chapter 4.

8. Ibid., p. vii.

9. *Scinteia*, April 28, 1968.

10. Ibid.

11. Ibid.

12. Ibid.

13. Speaking at the National Conference of the RCP, Ceausescu criticized overlapping and duplication of party and government functions and asked that only one individual should deal with issues at both party and state local level. On December 7, 1967, Chivu Stoica proposed elimination of duplication between the highest state and party organs. After two days, the Romanian Grand National Assembly elected Party Secretary-General Ceausescu as President of the Council of State.

184

14. *Scinteia*, July 20, 1967. The Congress also approved a new Constitution which proclaimed Romania a Socialist Republic.

15. *Scinteia*, February 4, 1967.

16. Ibid.

17. Willy Brandt, *A Peace Policy for Europe* (New York: Holt, Rinehart and Winston, 1968), p. 108.

18. O. Ciulea, "Rolul Industrializarii in Ocuparea si Utilizarea Rationala a Fortei de Munca in unele Tari Socialiste din Europa" (The Role of Industrialization in the Hiring and Rational Utilization of Manpower in some of the Socialist European Countries), *Probleme Economice*, Vol. 19, No. 11 (November 1966), pp. 92-105.

19. Dana Vionea and Nicolae Belli, "Cu privire la egalizarea nivelurilor economice ale tarilor membre ale C.A.E.R. (On the Equalization of Economic Levels of CMEA States), *Lupta de Clasa*, Series V, Vol. 45, No. 1 (January, 1965), pp. 70-76.

20. C. Gavrilescu, "Principii si forme ale cooperarii economice internationale" (Principles and Forms of International Economic Cooperation), *Probleme Economice*, Vol. 20, No. 4 (April, 1967), p. 137.

21. See Professor I. Rachmuth's Statement at the Proceedings of a 1964 Economic Conference in Michael C. Naser, *Economic Development for Eastern Europe, Proceedings of a Conference Held in 1964 at Sofia by the International Economic Association* (London: MacMillan, 1968), pp. 152-153.

22. N. Ceausescu, "Speech at the Grand National Assembly", *Scinteia*, November 30, 1968.

23. N. Ceausescu, "Speech at Lupeni", *Scinteia*, August 11, 1968.

24. "Geheimabsprache an der Comecon-Konferenz, Unterziehung eines Dokuments (Secret Agreement at the CMEA Conference, Signing of a Document), *Neue Zürcher Zeitung*, May 1, 1969.

25. N. Ceausescu, "Speech to the Brasov Party Aktiv", *Scinteia*, June 20, 1967. See also N. Ceausescu, "Speech in Belgrade", *Scinteia*, May 28, 1968.

26. *Scinteia*, June 20, 1967.

27. Ibid., November 15, 1968.

28. Paul Wohl, "Romania Asks Change in Warsaw Pact", *Christian Science Monitor*, July 26, 1967.

29. See RFE, *Rumanian Situation Report*, March 6, 1968.

30. General Ion Ionita, "Speech at the Grand National Assembly", *Scinteia*, July 27, 1967.

31. N. Ceausescu, "Speech at the Grand National Assembly", *Scinteia*, November 30, 1968. For an authoritative restatement of the Romanian position in international and interparty affairs see Nicolae Corbu, "Pentru ca forta socialismului sa se manifeste din plin" (For a Full Development of Socialism), *Lumea*, No. 18, April 24, 1969, pp. 9-11.

32. McNeal (ed.) op. cit., pp. 165-166.

33. Professor Kenneth Jowitt referred to the same issue when he wrote that the "Romanian elite's redefinition of bloc unity has been its belief in and assertation of the Romanian party's political maturity." See Kenneth Jowitt, "The Romanian Communist Party and the World Socialist System, a Redefinition of Unity", *World Politics*, Vol. 23, No. 1 (October, 1970), p. 44.

34. *Scinteia*, March 1, 1968.

35. For a comprehensive presentation of the Romanian leaders' stand see editorial "Pentru Pace si Securitate in Orientul Mijlociu" (For Peace and Security in the Middle East), *Scinteia*, June 13, 1967.

36. Cf. Leo Heiman, "Politics or Economics? Romania's Trade Agreement with Israel", *East Europe*, Vol. 17, No. 2 (February, 1968), pp. 9-13.

37. On July 15, 1968, Ceausescu spoke before the Galati Aktiv and said that interference in the internal affairs of the Czechoslovak Communist Party was unwarranted, since "nobody can claim to possess a method in socialist construction of universal application." On the same occasion, the Romanian President told the Czechoslovak leaders and people that, "Romanians wish them from the bottom of their hearts the fulfillment of their plans." (*Scinteia*, July 16, 1968). On August 1, 1968, the Romanian delegate at the Disarmament Conference spoke against outside interference in the internal affairs of other states, and declared that "European security can be based only on respect of sovereignty and national independence." (*Scinteia*, August 2, 1968). On August 7, 1968, *Scinteia* expressed dissatisfaction with the exclusion of Romania from the Communist summit conference held at Bratislava on August 3. On August 14, speaking before the

graduating class of the Romanian Military Academy, Ceausescu declared that the forces of the WTO "cannot be used for interfering in the internal affairs of any member-state." (*Scinteia*, August 15, 1968). But the most serious provocation occured during the state visit to Prague of the Romanian President Ceausescu and Prime Minister Maurer, from August 15-17. A new treaty of friendship between Romania and Czechoslovakia was signed by Ceausescu and Svoboda, even though the expired treaties with the Soviet Union, Hungary, Poland and Bulgaria had not yet been renewed by Bucharest. It is possible that, aware of the Soviet decision to settle the Czechoslovak crisis by invasion, the Romanians wished to launch a supreme warning against a military intervention. A formal mutual-assistance commitment between Romania and Czechoslovakia, the Romanians hoped, might create a state of uncertainty in Moscow and induce the Soviet leaders to abandon their military plans. The Romanian calculations were invalidated by subsequent events. Barely five days after the signing of the Romanian-Czechoslovak Treaty of Friendship and Mutual Assistance, Soviet military forces led units from other WTO countries in the invasion of Czechoslovakia. Obviously, either the Soviet policy-makers ruled out the possibility of Romanian counter-measures, or they ridiculed the impact of a Romanian military involvement and decided to proceed with their plans.

38. Theodor Schweisfurth, "Moskauer Doktrin und sozialistischer Internationalismus" (The Moscow Doctrine and Socialist Internationalism), *Aussenpolitik*, Vol. 19, No. 12 (December, 1968), p. 719.

39. See N. Ceausescu, "Speech on the Harvest Day", *Scinteia*, October 7, 1968); "Speech at the National Conference of Teachers", *Scinteia*, February 8, 1969; "Speech at the International Conference of Communist and Workers' Parties", *Scinteia*, June 10, 1969; "Interview with *Corriere della Sera*", *Scinteia*, May 12, 1969; "Report of the Secretary-General of the RCP Central Committee at the 10th Congress of the Party", *Scinteia*, August 12, 1969; "Speech on the 25th Democratic Government Anniversary", *Scinteia*, March 7, 1970; "Interview with *La Figaro*, May 22, 1970; "Interview with American Diplomatic Correspondent John P. Wallach", *Scinteia*, October 7, 1970.

40. Paul Niculescu-Mizil, "Congresul Partidului Communist Italian -- un remarcabil eveniment politic (The Congress of the Italian Communist Party -- A Remarkable Political Event), *Scinteia*, March 31, 1969.

41. *Scinteia*, January 25, 1969.

42. "Rumänische Selbstbehauptung", *Neue Zürcher Zeitung*, May 9, 1969.

43. Nicolae Corbu, "Pentru ca forta socialismului sa se manifeste din plin" (For a Full Development of Socialism), *Lumae*, No. 18, (April 24, 1969), p. 9.

44. Ibid., p. 10.

45. "Declaration of the RCP Delegation to the Conference of the Communist and Workers' Parties", *Scinteia*, June 17, 1969.

46. "Rumäniens unabhängiger Kurs" (Romania's Independent Course), *Neue Zürcher Zeitung*, June 29, 1969.

47. At the peak of the Soviet-Romanian crisis after the invasion of Czechoslovakia, President Lyndon Johnson made also e gesture in support of Romania by warning the Soviet leaders "not to unleash the dogs of war".

48. Katushev stated that the "perfidious tactic of bridgebuilding by Western governments is undermining the cohesion of the socialist countries." *Scinteia*, August 8, 1969. On the Soviet angry reaction against Nixon's visit to Bucharest, see also "Moskaus Reaction zum Rumänienbesuch Nixons" (Moscow's Reaction Against Nixon's Visit to Romania), *Neue Zürcher Zeitung*, July 1, 1969. And Ryszard Wojnam deputy-editor of the Polish paper *Zycie Warszawy*, asked the President this question: "What would be the U.S. reaction if Brezhnev visited Peru?" See "Neue Töne in der polnischen Aussenpolitik" (New Tones in the Polish Foreign Policy), *Neue Zürcher Zeitung*, July 19, 1969.

49. See "Despre Relatiile Diplomatice dintre Romania si unele tari arabe" (On Diplomatic Relations Between Romania and Several Arab States), *Romania Libera*, August 26, 1969.

50. "Presedintele Tito despre unele probleme internationale" (President Tito on some international Problems), *Scinteia*, May 3, 1969.

51. *Frankfurter Allgemeine Zeitung*, December 23, 1969.

52. E. Hutira and C. Moisiuc, "Diviziunea internationale a muncii si eficienta participarii active la circuitul economic mondial" (The International Labor Division and the Efficiency of Active Participation in the World Economic Circuit), *Probleme Economice*, Vol. 21, No. 6 (June, 1968), pp. 3-12. See also I. Radulescu, "Raportul national-international si colaborarea economica intre state" (The National-International Relationship and Economic Collaboration Among States), *Probleme Economice*, Vol. 21, No. 9 (September, 1968), pp. 70-87. For a presentation of Romanian "conditions" for economic cooperation, see Ion Fintinaru, "Cadrul principial al politicii de cooperare a tarii noastre"

188

(The Basic Framework of the Cooperation-Policy of Our Country),
Scinteia, January 19, 1969. See also Mihail Levente, "Bazele
economice ale colaborarii economice a Romaniei cu tarile
sistemului socialist mondial" (Economic Bases of Romania's
Economic Collaboration with the Countries of the World Socialist
System), *Probleme Economice*, Vol. 22, No. 9 (September, 1969),
pp. 40-45. For an explanation of Romanian preference for bilateral economic relations, see Radu Negru, "Contributii la
problema bilateralismului si multilateralismului in relatiile
economice internationale" (Contributions to the Issue of Bi-
lateralism Versus Multilateralism in International Economic
Relations), *Probleme Economice*, Vol. 22, No. 2 (February, 1969),
pp. 60-68. For direct criticisms of the "socialist integration",
see N.S. Stanescu, "Integrarea in contradictie cu cerintele
dezvoltarii relatiilor economice internationale" (Integration
Contradicts the Requirements of the Development of International
Economic Relations), *Scinteia*, January 24, 1969. See also
V. Iliescu, "20 de ani de la infiintarea C.A.E.R." (Twenty Years
of CMEA Existence), *Scinteia*, January 26, 1969.

53. For Romanian criticisms of the Common Market arrangements, see
Eugen Prahoveanu, "In corsetul Pietii Comune" (In the Strait-
jacket of the Common Market), *Scinteia*, October 30, 1968;
"Franta si alti membri ai Pietii Comune nu doresc sa remita
atributii nationale unui organism supranational" (France and
Other Members of the Common Market Do Not Wish to Transfer
National Attributes to a Supranational Agency), *Scinteia*,
January 14, 1969; "Integrarea economica vest-europeana in deza-
cord cu suveranitatea nationala" (West European Economic Integration Contradicts National Sovereignty), *Scinteia*, January
21, 1969; L. Stroja, "Economistii britanici contesta mitul
integrarii Angliei in C.E.E. (British Economists Dispute the
Myth of England's Integration in the European Economic Community), *Romania Libera*, January 22, 1969; Ilie Serbanescu,
"Europa comunitara -- prinicipii si fapte" (The European Community -- Principles and Facts), *Lupta de Clasa*, Vol. 50, 5th
Series (February, 1970), pp. 76-85.

54. Cf. Serban Berindei, "Dezacorduri majore in jurul integrarii
nordice" (Major Disputes Over the Northern Integration),
Scinteia, January 23, 1969.

55. Cf. Eugen Pop, "Scara fara tepte a integrarii latino-americane"
(The Ladder Without Steps of Latin-American Integration),
Romania Libera, January 14, 1969.

56. George Nicolescu, "Gustul amar al asocierii africane de Piata
Comuna" (The Bitter Taste of African Association With the
Common Market), *Romania Libera*, January 15, 1969.

57. "Comunicat cu privire la cea de-a 24-a sesiune a Consiliului de Ajutor Economic Reciproc" (Communiqué of the 24th Session of the Council for Economic Mutual Assistance), *Scinteia*, May 15, 1970.

58. RFE Research, *Rumanian Situation Report*, September 2, 1970.

59. N.S. Stanescu, "O politica de comert exterior coerenta si consistenta" (A Coherent and Consistent Foreign Economic Policy) *Viata Economica*, No. 34 (August 21, 1970).

60. After the Soviet-led invasion of Czechoslovakia, the Romanians stiffened their opposition to WTO maneuvers on Romanian territory. In order to complicate the issue, it was decided that any approval by the Council of State of joint maneuvers on Romanian soil must be ratified by the Grand National Assembly.

61. "Die Warschaupaktmanöver in Bulgarien. Rumänische Präzisierungen" (The Warsaw Pact Maneuvers in Bulgarien. Romanian Clarification) *Neue Zürcher Zeitung*, April 12, 1969. See also "Manöver in Rumänien verhindert?" (Forbidden Maneuvers in Romania?), *Frankfurter Allgemeine Zeitung*, February 27, 1969.

62. "Die Hegemonieansprüche Moskaus" (Moscow's Claims to Hegemony), *Neue Zürcher Zeitung*, March 19, 1970.

63. Ibid.

64. "Die Warschaupacktmanöver in der DDR" (The Warsaw-Pact Maneuvers in the German Democratic Republic), *Neue Zürcher Zeitung*, October 14, 1970.

65. "Les manoeuvres du Pacte de Varsovie" (Maneuvers of the Warsaw Pact), *Le Monde*, October 13, 1970.

66. Quotation from de Gaulle's speech delivered in the Romanian city of Craiova during the 1968 state visit to Romania of the late French President. Italics are *Scinteia's*. Cf. Ion Fintinaru "Generalul Charles de Gaulle, personalitate remarcabila a politicii de intelegere si colborare internationala" (General de Gaulle, Remarkable Personality of the Policy of International Understanding and Collaborative), *Scinteia*, April 30, 1969.

67. "Auswirkungen des deutsch-sowjetischen Vertrages auf Osteuropa" (Repercussions of the German-Soviet Treaty in Eastern Europe), *Neue Zürcher Zeitung*, October 23, 1970.

Chapter VIII

ROMANIA AND THE POLICY OF PARTIAL ALIGNMENT

Robert L. Farlow

It has been almost twenty years since the Romanian Communist
Party (RCP) initiated the construction of an independent foreign
policy. In the course of that construction, Romania had performed
the paradoxical feat of remaining within the constellation of
party-state institutions and commitments which constitutes the
Soviet-East European alignment system or bloc while at the same
time engaging in numerous policies directly opposed by the other
members of the bloc, particularly by the leading member, the Soviet
Union. Romania had carved out a position of independence and yet
avoided a major sanction from the Soviet Union.
Romanian foreign policy is, then, the most important in Eastern
Europe, with the exception of Yugoslavia's non-alignment policy.
First under the leadership of Gheorghe Gheorghiu-Dej and since
1965, Nicolae Ceausescu, the RCP has opposed and deviated from many
Soviet-inspired bloc policies. In terms of ideology, the Romanians
have revised traditional perspectives on the international communist
movement in such a way as to eliminate all possible bases for
hegemony or stratification therein, arguing instead for pluraling
and diversity based upon respect for the principles of party-state
independence, equalities and sovereignty. (1) In the economic realm,
the RCP has pursued a policy of multilateral industrialization,
undertaken against its allies wishes, and in the process has reduced the nation's linkages with and dependence upon Soviet-East
European markets, while concomitantly expanding trade with the West,
developing countries, and such non-conformist socialist states as
China, Albania and Yugoslavia. (2) With regard to particular political policies in international affairs, the Romanians have con-
flicted with their formal allies on a wide range of issues. Thus,
in the period since 1958, Romania has among other things: successfully opposed Soviet plans for the supranational economic integra-

tion of Eastern Europe, resisted proposals for greater military integration of the Warsaw Pact and limited its participation therein, revitalized its economic, political, and cultural contacts with the West, initiated a rapprochement with China, Albania and Yugoslavia, maintained a diplomatic relation with Israel, asserted a position of neutrality in the Sino-Soviet dispute, supported Dubcek's policy of socialist humanism in Czechoslovakia, condemned the invasion of Czechoslovakia, refused to participate in various multi-lateral communist party meetings and generally criticized Soviet leadership of the alignment system. (3)

Despite the obvious importance of Romanian foreign policy, it has been subject to limited analysis. If the existing literature on Romanian foreign policy were to be examined, one would find that it is heavily weighted toward historical description and that it is weak in terms of systematic explanation. There have been few attempts to apply recent frameworks and theories of foreign policy to the subject matter or to generate hypotheses that might serve more adequately to explain Romanian behavior. (4)

With these deficiencies in view, the present study has two objectives. First, it seeks to conceptualize the nature of Romanian policy in such a way that it might be seen as a particular manifestation of a more general behavioral phenomenon, what will be called herein the foreign policy behavior of partial alignment. Second, it attempts to explore systematically the sources or determinents of Romanian policy. These will be examined in terms of four sets of variables, as suggested in the work of James N. Rosenau: idiosyncratic, systemic, governmental, and societal. (5) Thus, the general purpose of the analysis is explanatory rather than descriptive.

Romanian foreign policy may be conceived as one of partial alignment. A state pursuing a policy of partial alignment stresses the primacy of national interests and goals, as defined by its political elite, over any collective or general interests articulated by the other members of its respective alignment systems. Consequently, a state's cooperation with its formal allies is premised on the degree of congruence between its own interests and those collective interests and policies agreed upon by the other members as being essential to the advancement of the collectivity. A policy of partial alignment is premised on the argument that the system will advance only to the extent that the individual members are left free to follow their proclivities and assumes that these individual tendencies will often find a basis for mutual cooperation and assistance. Should, however, the policies of the individual state be significantly opposed to allied policy, the state will not inevitably abandon its stance. Partial alignment, then, leads to a pattern of conflict and cooperation.

The conflict resulting from a policy of partial alignment is most prominent between the deviant state and the leading member of the system, since it is the superpower which has the most influence in setting forth the system's policies. Deviance or non-cooperation ultimately becomes a challenge to the pre-eminence of the leading member. The leading state, however, is unwilling to employ force and yet is not ready to accept the policy of the non-leading state. On the other hand, the non-conforming state, not wishing to overly provoke its more powerful ally, is unwilling to disengage from the system.

While the non-leading state may create some dysfunction in the subgroupings of the system, it is not powerful enough to incapacitate them. The only actor which could restore conformity, the superpower, will not use its full economic and/or military power since it calculates that the gains of such an action would not outweigh the risks and probable losses. If this force were ever applied against a non-conforming state, partial alignment would be terminated, particularly in the case of a military sanction. The continuation of a policy of partial alignment represents a loss of prestige for the leading state, a weakening of the international collective influence of the alignment system, and an increase in the international prestige of the deviant state, especially among those states most hostile to the alignment system.

Partial alignment is a relatively recent development, associated with the loosening of the Atlantic and Soviet bloc systems. Romania and France are the most visible, durable and important examples of such behavior. Poland and Hungary in 1956, as well as Czechoslovakia in 1968, were brief manifestations. More recently, Greece, Turkey and, to a lesser extent, Canada, have been asserting partial alignment within the Atlantic bloc. Thus, it is a pervasive phenomenon which has an important bearing on the nature of the international system, since it involves the relationship between the superpowers and their allies. Partial alignment affects the prestige and capabilities of the leading powers and, as a result, provides certain limits and opportunities for the behavior of other states.

Romania: Internal-External Linkages

The explanation of partial alignment, when using the nation-state, rather than the interaction patterns of the international system, as the main level of analysis, involves a complex of internal and external variables. (6) This, of course, is not peculiar to explaining partial alignment, but in so far as a state pursuing such a policy is involved in an alignment system, the impingement of the external environment on the internal setting tends to be more pervasive, particularly in the early stages of non-conformity, than were it not so involved. Consequently, the linkages between the internal-external settings become crucial for explaining this type of foreign policy. Indeed, the "nexus between the domestic and external aspects of state affairs", is what David Vital has called the "central mystery" of international politics. (7)

Several frameworks, centering on this nexus, have been presented.

Among them is one by David O. Wilkinson and another by James N. Rosenau. Both scholars believe in the efficacy of internal-external conceptualizations as a prelude to the development of middle-range foreign policy theory. Both suggest that foreign policy can be explained in terms of five major variables:

Wilkinson (8)	Rosenau (9)
1. Power (capability)	1. Idiosyncratic
2. Will and Prescription	2. Societal
3. Political Culture	3. Role
4. Political Institutions	4. Governmental
5. Political Processes	5. Systemic

Rosenau states that "all foreign policy analysts either explain the external behavior of societies in terms of five sets of variables, or they proceed in such a way that their explanations can recast in terms of five sets." (10) The five sets of variables which Rosenau suggests are conceived as follows: Idiosyncratic refers to the personal characteristics and psychological predispositions of decision-makers; societal refers to all non-governmental factors influencing policy; role refers to the bureaucratic constraints on a decision-maker which emanate from the particular position which he holds; governmental encompasses the general structure of the political decision-making center and its distribution of power; and systemic includes all events and conditions in the environment of a state. (11)

The Wilkinson variables, which are not as analytically comprehensive as the Rosenau variables, could be contained within the Rosenau framework. Thus, power and political culture are elements of the societal variable. Will, a somewhat vague concept which connotes decisive action on the part of a decision-maker, would be part of the idiosyncratic variable. Prescription, which is Wilkinson's term for bureaucratic routine and tradition, is the equivalent of the role variable. Political institutions and processes are obviously governmental variables. Wilkinson does not employ a specific category for external developments.

The variables suggested by Rosenau will be applied with some modification, in this study. They have certain analytical advantages. First, the variables provide general guidelines for the collection of data. Second, if applied as Rosenau has advocated, by ranking the variables in terms of their causal potency for the foreign policy under analysis, a foundation for the construction of foreign policy theory will be advanced -- provided others also adopt the approach.

In applying this framework, a modification will be made. The distinction between role and governmental variables is too fine for data available. Moreover, it can be argued that any complex structure, governmental or otherwise, is a multiplicity of roles based upon some division of labor. Since governments are, in one

sense, a collection of roles, the two sets of variables will be
considered as one. (12) With this revision, it is now possible to
apply the framework to an analysis of the Romanian policy of partial alignment.

It will be argued herein that the primary determinants of Romanian foreign policy have been the idiosyncratic and systemic
variables and that the secondary determinants have been the societal and governmental variables. To assert the idiosyncratic and
systematic as primary means that the qualitative changes in the
international system conjoined with the Romanian elite's images
and predispositions resulting from their experiences with the
Soviet Union were of such a nature as to prompt the initiation and
continuation of an independent foreign policy. To assert the societal and governmental as secondary is to suggest that the nature
and pact of partial alignment were influenced by these factors,
but that neither separately nor together were they of sufficient
potency to promote a major revision of external behavior. The reconstruction of Romanian policy was and is a product of elite origins, grounded in the values and images of the elite, and forged
in the favorable context provided by a changing international
system. The societal and governmental variables helped to shape
the content of the elite initiative and contributed to its success.
Each set of variables and their inter-relation will now be analyzed.

Idiosyncratic Variables

It is extremely difficult to operationalize the concept of idiosyncratic characteristics or to relate, even in an impressionatic
manner, the idiosyncratic nature of a political elite to policy
outcomes. The task is especially difficult in the East European
context where information on the background of the political elite
is rather limited and access to their values and views also constrained. Recent studies on East European political elites have
operationalized in terms of the educational backgrounds of the
leaders (13) or in terms of the various career channels which they
followed in their rise to top political power. (14) These are interesting analyses, but no clear pattern emerges which could relate
these idiosyncratic characteristics to policy decisions. (15)

In another vein, the idiosyncratic aspect of foreign policy has
been approached from the perspective of delineating the images
which decision-makers hold, an image being "the organized representation of an object in an individual's cognitive system." (16)
Images evoke positive, negative or neutral feelings on the part of
the person who holds them and are thus associated with attitudes.
It has been asserted that the "link between image and decisions is
indeed the master key to a valuable framework of foreign policy
analysis". (17)

Decision-makers' images can usually be approached only in a
rather indirect manner -- by examining their background experiences,

their actions, and their public statements. The risks involved are many. However, a thorough immersion in the available data may suggest some tentative understanding of a decision-maker's images.

In the context of Romania it is important to find the image of the political elite (members of the Politburo) with reference to the Soviet Union. Since Romanian foreign policy has centered around the relationship between the Romanian party-state and the Soviet party-state, information on the nature of the Romanian elite's image of the Soviet Union may provide a partial clue to the explanation of their foreign policy.

The new Romanian foreign policy is essentially the creation of that elite faction of the RCP which gained complete control of the party in 1957, although this group had been predominant in the party from 1952 and had been active in the party prior to 1945. (18) The undisputed leader of this group was Gheorghe Gheorghiu-Dej. Associated with him and holding positions in the Politburo, as of 1960, were: Gheorghe Apostol, Nicolae Ceausescu, Alexandru Draghici, Ion Gheorge Maurer, Alexandru Moghioros, and Chivu Stocia. Two other Politburo members -- Petre Borila and Emil Bodnaras -- had extensive backgrounds in the Soviet Union and the closeness of their relationship to Dej is not clear, especially in the case of Borila.

The emergence of Dej and his associates as the victors in the intraparty struggles for leadership brought to the top a relatively homogeneous elite in terms of ethnicity, education, political experiences, personal relationships, and political values. (19) Except for Bodnaras, Borila and Moghioros, all were native Romanians. Most of them had worked together in the early revolutionary activities of the RCP and had spent most of their lives in Romania. Primarily of proletarian and peasant backgrounds their socialization experience was within Romania. In this they differed from many of their opponents within the party who had non-Romanian ethnic backgrounds and long tenure in the Soviet Union, from which they came to see themselves as representatives of Soviet interests within Romania.

The Dej faction had collaborated together prior to the communist seizure of power and was prominent in various aspects of party-state administration after the establishment of the Romanian People's Republic. The group thus had long and detailed experience with the Soviet union and its policies toward Romania. One of the major features of the CPSU-RCP relationship, whether in the years that the RCP was declared illegal or in the post-World War II period when it emerged victorious, was the consistent subordination of Romanian interests by the Soviet Union for the benefit of the latter's interests.

In the pre-war period the RCP was forced to adopt policies which undermined its popularity within the country, policies which sacrificed Romanian interests for the benefit of the Soviet Union. The most notable of these was the RCP advocacy that Romania cede large positions of its territory to the Soviet Union. In addition to interference with policy, the Soviet Union constantly intervened

in party affairs by changing the RCP's leadership. In the post-war
period this subordination was coupled with a blantant exploitation
of Romania that was manifest in the onerous war reparations which
were paid to the Soviet Union, the control of the Romanian economy
by the Soviets, under joint Soviet-Romanian companies or Sovroms,
the equitable prices paid by the Soviets for Romanian goods, and
the penetration of the Romanian apparat with Soviet agents. Paul
Marer has calculated that between 1945-60 the Soviets extracted,
on balance, approximately $ 14 billion from Eastern Europe. The
bulk came from East Germany, but "significant amounts" also came
from Romania and Hungary. (20) Even in the period of communist rule,
the RCP was forced to sacrifice legitimacy and popularity with its
own citizens for the sake of satisfying the economic and political
demands made by Moscow.

The crucial point that emerges from this is that while the RCP
leaders were willing to submit to these policies in order to preserve their own political positions, it can now be seen that their
national sensitivities and their concern for the efficacy of
Romanian Communism were violated by Soviet behavior. As a result
Dej and his associates developed a very negative image of the
Soviet Union. When the time appeared more opportune to shed the
politically expedient praise of the Soviet Union, this negative
orientation was publicly articulated and became a primary determinant in the construction of an independent foreign policy. The
image operated as a determinant in that it predisposed the elite
to question the motives behind Soviet policies, to distrust and
ultimately reject policies put forth as being in the "general"
interest of the Soviet bloc.

Although the origins of an independent Romanian foreign policy
can be traced back to 1958, it was not until the RCP had won its
first major confrontation with the Soviet Union that the anti-
Soviet inclination of the elite became a subject of direct public
articulation. It was not until after Romania had successfully
thwarted Khrushchev's plans for the economic integration of
Eastern Europe under a proposed supranational CMEA that the Romanian leadership felt it could begin to express its true inclinations,
taking into account, of course, the other internal and external
factors which were fortuitously combining to protect the Romanian
position of partial alignment.

The elite's negative image of the Soviet Union was first articulated in the now-famous 1964 Statement of the then-called Romanian
Workers' Party. In that document the Romanian party criticized the
Soviet controlled Comintern for its interference in various parties'
affairs and asserted:

> In that period our Party too underwent hard trials.
> Interference in its internal affairs was most detri-
> mental to the Party line, to its cadres policy and
> organizational work, to the Party's links with the
> masses. (21)

Moreover, the Statement went on to say that "after the emergence of the socialist world system, those practices were also extended to inter-state relations, and this rendered their consequences the more serious." (22)

The Dej regime saw a continuity between the pre-communist and post-communist periods in that the Soviet Union continously refused to recognize the independence of the RCP or its right to set national policy. Instead of reducing the Romanians' negative image of the Soviet Union, Soviet post-war policies reinforced it. This negative image extended to the various sub-structures of the bloc (CMEA and the Warsaw Pact) which were seen as instruments of Soviet control.

Ceausescu, who was part of Dej's inner circle and succeeded Dej in power, has articulated a similar orientation toward the Soviet Union. In one of his most important speeches to date, Ceausescu, on May 7, 1966, elaborated the history of the Romanian communist movement and carried further the criticisms found in the Statement. In some detail he linked the weakness of the Romanian party in the pre-communist period to the policies imposed on the party from without. (23) The conclusion which he drew from these experiences is particularly important:

> The negative effects of these practices and methods
> applied in that period in the working-class movement
> of our country demonstrate the tremendous importance
> for the revolutionary struggle of the strict obser-
> vance of the right of each Party to independently
> shape its own policy, since it is only the respective
> Party that is in a position to know the realities in
> its country, to objectively assess the political tasks
> of each stage. (24)

The RCP, under Ceausescu, has also stated that the type of actions associated with this earlier period have not been abandoned, that:

> the old practices of immixture in the internal affairs
> of other parties and socialist states, the tendencies
> of imposing points of view from the outside, of label-
> ling and resorting to accusations and condemnations
> have not been given up. (25)

Taken together the Romanian political elite's sense of national identity and long experience with the policies of the Soviet Union produced on their part a negative image of that country and a concomitant predisposition to resist all Soviet policies which were seen as a continuation of the exploitation and subordinate pattern that had characterized Soviet-Romanian relations for decades. In order to comprehend the Romanian deviation, this focus on the elite level is extremely important for, unlike Hungary in 1956 and Czechoslovakia in 1968, there was no significant pressure from sub-groups within the population for radical change. The desire of the masses for change was latent and, of course, easily actuated once the decision to challenge the Soviet Union had been made. It was, however, only when other conditions were beneficial that this

basic predisposition of the elite became an active, primary determinant of the policy of partial alignment.

Systemic Variables

This set of variables deals with those conditions and events
external to a state which have an impact on the nature of its
foreign policy. Until approximately 1958 the sources of Romanian
foreign policy were for all practical purposes mainly systemic in
that Romania abided by the dictates of the Soviet Union is formulating its foreign policy.

The consolidation of political power by Dej and his associates
in the late 1950s corresponded with fundamental changes in Romania's
external environment, changes which fortuitously assisted the
creation of an independent policy and without which that policy
might never have evolved to the extent that it has today. These
changes include the following: 1) Soviet attempts to integrate
Eastern Europe, economically and militarily, at the time when the
Moscow leadership was seeking to promote a policy of "peaceful coexistence" with the West, 2) the general fragmentation of international communism, most notably the Sino-Soviet dispute, and
3) the greater receptiveness of the West, particularly Europe, to
exchanges with Romania.

The Soviet doctrine of peaceful coexistence provided the Romanians with a much needed ideological justification for seeking a
rapprochement with the West. While the Romanian decision to expand
diplomatic and economic contracts with the West occured in 1958,
(26) the process of disengagement from excessive dependence upon
the bloc was accelerated by the Soviet attempts to bring about
economic integration and, later, military integration of Eastern
Europe. In this context, the Romanian leadership, fearing Soviet
policies, speeded up the process of detente with the West under
the umbrella of peaceful coexistence. Inadvertantly the Soviets
provided the Romanians with an impetus for disengagement and, although not intended as such, a doctrine to justify alternative
sources of external support, most notably in terms of trade. Thus,
Dej stated in 1960 that "peaceful coexistence and international
trade are closely linked and are conditioning each other." (27)

This approach by the RCP, however, would have failed had not
the advanced Western states agreed to engage in trade with Romania
and thereby provided the concrete economic bases needed for a
policy of partial alignment. The Western share in total Romanian
trade rose from around 17% in 1958 to 35% after 1968, although
this has been at the expense of a rather large deficit with the
West. (28) As de Gaulle's 1968 visit and Nixon's 1969 visit to
Bucharest symbolized, the RCP leaders have found in the West
economic and political leverage against the Soviet Union and its
allies.

In a similar vein both Dej and Ceausescu have cultivated Romania's ties with socialist states which are in disfavor with the Soviet Union and have thus skillfully used the fragmentation of international communism as a means of securing additional external support. Of all the conflict within internal communism, that between the Soviet Union and China has been most conducive to the development of Romanian independence. As a factor explaining Romanian foreign policy, the Sino-Soviet conflict is very important, but it is not the major factor as some analysts have suggested. For example, Adam Ulam states that the Romanians "cannot fail to realize that it is precisely the quarrel between Russia and China which has enabled that small Balkan country to put on such airs." (29) Such an argument fails to take cognizance of the other determinants of Romanian policy.

The Sino-Soviet dispute has been beneficial to the unfolding of Romanian foreign policy because it has provided the RCP with the option of taking a position closer to the Chinese than the Russians in certain areas of foreign policy and thereby further eroding Soviet prestige within the bloc and throughout the world. The position of neutrality taken by the Romanians indicates their willingness to exploit the issue for their own political gains. In order to forestall greater Romanian cooperation with the Chinese, the Russians have had to be very restrained in the face of Romanian deviance.

In addition, the Soviet leadership realized that the Romanians would probably fight a Soviet military intervention. the result of which would be a disrupted country with no significant section of the Romanian party willing to be the Soviet lackeys who would restore order. On the other hand, major economic sanctions would only prompt a more rapid turn to non-CMEA markets. It is a fortuitous combination of factors, not just the Sino-Soviet dispute, which has given rise to partial alignment.

Collectively these external changes were of primary importance to the initiation and implementation of the Romanian policy of partial alignment. As the Dej and Ceausescu regimes disengaged Romania from many aspects of bloc policy, other external bases of support were cultivated. Romania's isolation within the system was balanced by contacts outside which have constrained the Soviet Union in its attempt to bring Romania back into line. Ceausescu has made reference to this fact:

> We can thus say that both as a result of the home policy and of international activity, Romania has won friends on all meridians of the globe, that she has today such friends as she never had before. Precisely this policy which has brought her so many friends is a guarantee of the continuous development and progress of independent and sovereign Romania, of her contribution to the cause of cooperation and peace in the world. (30)

Societal Variables

The societal variables include non-governmental internal factors which impinge upon the shaping of foreign policy. Certain societal elements seem relevant for the present analysis: the level and potential of the economy, social stratification and its relation to economic development, and the mass political culture.
The societal determinant has been accorded a secondary ranking in terms of Romanian foreign policy because the pressure and direction for change came primarily from within the upper levels of the party. Particularly in the beginning of the revision there was no groundswell of pressure from the masses. And, if there was direct influence from the intelligentsia, it was not openly manifested. Despite this lack of overt pressure from sub-groups, there were certain conditions and developments within Romanian society which encouraged the leaders of the RCP to stake out an independent path and which helped to shape the nature of partial alignment. These were: 1) the rapid growth of the economy; 2) the concomitant changes within the social stratification pattern, especially the emergence of the intelligentsia; and 3) the anti-Russian bias of the general population.
Since 1945 the RCP's program for the development of Romania has been centered around the primacy of the industrial sector. It is an irony of communist history that at the very time when the Romanian economy was reaching the point of take-off in industrial development, the Soviet Union proposed to relegate Romania to a raw materials-agricultural producing country within an integrated Eastern Europe. This would have undermined the party's efforts since coming to power, further eroded its popularity with the masses and strengthened Soviet control over the state. The revision of Romanian foreign policy was clearly intended, in part, to protect and further the on-going economic program. In turn, the success of that program served to validate the new Romanian policy. During the 1960-65 Plan period Romania's average rate of industrial growth was 14.4 percent; during the 1966-70 Plan period this growth was 11.7 percent.
The industrialization process initiated fundamental changes in the social structure of Romania, creating in a short time an industrial working class, a gradually diminishing peasant class, and a middle class or intelligentsia which provides the skills needed for the RCP's socio-economic policies. The development of an independent foreign policy was intended also to protect from outside intervention the party-determined priorities and policies for which the intelligentsia had been brought into existence and upon which their privileged position in society rested. Resistance to Soviet hegemony brought the intelligentsia into closer cooperation with the regime. (31) Thus, the new foreign policy prevented the alienation of the most advanced segment of Romanian society.
Another important societal factor is the mass political culture. A dominant feature of that culture, which has been noted by most

students of Romanian politics, is the traditional anti-Russian bias of the population. (32) In challenging Soviet control and Russian cultural influence, the Romanian leadership knew full well that it was reintegrating elite policy with the basic values of the mass political culture. This had the effect of creating mass support for the new foreign policy and for the regime.

Illie Verdet, one of the men Ceausescu raised to power within the party, has lucidly described the link between the societal context and foreign policy:

> The foreign policy has never been and can nowhere be an isolated compartment in the life of a country. It is closely connected to the national realities -- to the condition of the economy, to the moral and political cohesion of the people, to the societal evolution as a whole. Without a sound foundation in the life of the entire country, an independent, clearly outlined and principled foreign policy is inconceivable. And we can say... that Romania has such a foundation. (33)

Governmental Variables

The relationship of the governmental determinant to foreign policy has most often been approached under the open vs. closed dichotomy. (34) It is, however, very difficult to relate open and closed governmental structures to specific kinds of foreign policy. The suggestion of the present analysis would be to concentrate on the essential bureaucratic nature of all governmental structures from the perspective of elite cohesion and concentration of authority. It is suggested that in those political systems which are relatively free from direct, external control or where that control is being resisted, and where policy-making power is concentrated in a small, unified elite, governing over a relatively unified bureaucracy, the chances that a foreign policy will undergo significant change are enhanced. Conversely, to the extent that foreign policy behavior is the product of an elite which is divided and/or must bargain with competing factions in the bureaucracy, the chances of a foreign policy being innovative and changing are lessened.

The governmental variable is a secondary determinant in that it facilitated the initiation, development and success of a radically different Romanian foreign policy. While the pressure of the idiosyncratic and systemic variables was probably strong enough to bring about a change in foreign policy, the existence of societal conditions, as discussed above, and the nature of the governmental variables were such as to further encourage and define the nature and pace of Romanian independent action. The extent and intensity of partial alignment would no doubt have been limited by a divided elite and bureaucracy.

The removal of Soviet troops from Romania in 1958 and the earlier dismantling of the joint Soviet-Romanian economic companies (Sovroms) coincided with emergence of the Dej faction as the leaders of the Romanian party-state. The victory of Dej indicated that his opponents had either been removed from the party or were so weak as to no longer constitute a threat. The unificiation of the political elite was followed by an extensive purge of the lower-level rungs of the bureaucracy. Between 1955 and 1960 over 30,000 persons were removed from the party-state apparat. (35) Most of these were individuals whom Dej could not rely upon -- either because of their training in the Soviet Union or because of their previous connections with his opponents.

At the time of Dej's death in 1965 the RCP leadership was more unified than any other ruling elite in the bloc. In addition, the apparat had been streamlined to ensure that there would be no serious opposition to the implementation of the policy. The RCP constituted a unified structure with significant control over the society. It was thus not very susceptible to manipulation from outside sources.

This unity and control has been heightened under Ceausescu. As was to be expected, he has removed most of the old guard members of the Politburo who were close to Dej and replaced them with younger, more educated Romanians loyal to the party and to its new leader. Eventually the upper levels of the party-state apparat were completely dominated by Ceausescu's handpicked men.

Just as Dej had purged the apparat of lower-level bureaucrats who had been trained in Moscow or whose loyalties were doubtful, Ceausescu initiated an administrative restructuring in 1967 which had the effect of increasing party control over the apparat by removing thousands from their positions. On the national level Ceausescu criticized the over-lapping functions and responsibilities between party and state officials which led to duplication and confusion. He thus announced that "with a view to the unitary solving of problems by the Party and State bodies... it is necessary that, both along the Party channel and the State channel, one single comrade, belonging to the leadership, deal with one and the same field of activity." (36) This decision integrated the party and state levels to a greater extent than before, making it easier for the party leadership to assign duties and assure personal responsibility.

In another move, Ceausescu restructered the system of local government by abolishing the two administrative divisions within the country -- 16 regions and 150 districts -- and replacing them with 39 countries. The creation of one local level made that level more accessible to the central authorities. Ceausescu also announced that the leadership of local government -- the people's councils -- would be headed by leaders from local party organizations, thereby abolishing the distinction between party and government at the local level. (37)

These decisions were so far reaching in their impact that over 30 percent of the apparat personnel lost their jobs in the early

part of 1968. (38) While the regime pledged to find them other
positions, many would not be relocated within the apparat.
While in the 1970's Ceausescu's administrative changes have
become somewhat arbitrary, the unit of the RCP was more impressive
and concentrated than any other bloc party. This provided
Ceausescu with the requisite structural base on which to further
Romania's drive for independence.

Conclusion

This analysis has suggested that in terms of explaining the
Romanian policy of partial alignment, the idiosyncratic variables
-- conceived in terms of the Romanian political elite's experiences,
national identity and images -- shared a position of primacy, along
with the systemic variables. The systemic variables take on full
explanatory significance only when seen in linkage with the idiosyncratic nature of the Romanian leadership.
The secondary variables -- societal and governmental -- contributed to shaping the content or nature of the leadership's response.
The societal variables were not potent enough to forment a major
transformation of Romanian foreign policy, but in conjunction with
the elite predisposition and external change, they guided the
shaping of that policy to meet national needs and goals. The governmental variables, viewed in terms of elite cohesion and concentration of authority, facilitated the internal ease with which policy
was changed and served as a barrier to external manipulation of
the decision-making apparat, thereby contributing to the policy's
success.

NOTES

1. For an analysis of the elements in the Romanian ideological
    revision see Kenneth Jowitt, *Revolutionary Breakthroughs and
    National Development: The Case of Romania, 1944-65* (Berkeley:
    University of California Press, 1971), pp. 198-294; and Robert
    L. Farlow, "Romanian Foreign Policy: A Case of Partial Align-
    ments", *Problems of Communism*, XX, No. 6 (November-December,
    1971), pp. 55-58.

2. A brillant analysis of Romania's economic policies may be found
    in John Michael Montias, *Economic Development in Communist
    Rumania* (Cambridge: M.I.T. Press, 1967).

3. A comprehensive analysis of the development of Romanian foreign
    policy is contained in Jacques Levesque, *Le Conflit Sino-
    Sovietique et l'Europe de l'Est* (Montreal: Les Presses de
    l'Université de Montreal), pp. 99-255. In addition, see Farlow,
    op. cit., pp. 54-63. For the most recent developments, see

Robert R. King, "Autonomy and Detente: The Problems of Rumanian Foreign Policy", *Survey*, XX (1974), pp. 105-120.

4. An exception is Jowitt, op. cit., although his theoretical
emphasis is more on internal political dynamics than foreign
policy per se.

5. James N. Rosenau, "Pre-theories and Theories of Foreign Policy",
in R. Barry Farrell, ed., *Approaches to Comparative and International Politics* (Evanston: Northwestern University Press,
1966), pp. 27-92. Also, see his more recent *The Adaption of
National Societies: A Theory of Political System Behavior and
Transformation* (New York: McCaleb-Seiler, 1970). For a recent
analytical review of Rosenau's theory see Patrick J. McGowan,
"Problems in the Construction of Positibe Foreign Policy
Theory"; in James N. Rosenau, ed., *Comparing Foreign Policies:
Theories, Findings, and Methods* (New York: Halsted Press, 1974),
pp, 25-44.

6. J. David Singer, "The Level of Analysis Problem in International Relations", *World Politics*, XIV, No. 1 (October, 1961),
pp. 77-92.

7. David Vital, "On Approaches to the Study of International Relations, Or, Back to Machiavelli", *World Politics*, XIX, No. 4
(July, 1967), pp. 551-562.

8. David O. Wilkinson, *Comparative Foreign Relation: Framework
and Methods* (Belmont, California: Dickenson Publishing Co.,
1969).

9. Rosenau, "Pre-theories and Theories of Foreign Policy".

10. Ibid., p. 42.

11. Ibid., p. 43.

12. Rosenau, in his more recent work, has himself dropped the
"role" variable. See *The Adaptation of National Societies*.

13. R. Barry Farrell, "Top Political Leadership in Eastern Europe",
in R. Barry Farrell, ed., *Political Leadership in Eastern
Europe and the Soviet Union* (Chicago: Aldine Publishing Co.,
1970), pp. 88-107.

14. Carl Beck, "Career Characteristics of East European Leadership",
in R. Barry Farrell, ed., *Political Leadership*, pp. 157-194.

15. For a more recent and somewhat broader operationalization of
elite characteristics see Carl Beck, et al., *Comparative*

206

Communist Political Leadership (New York: David McKay Co., 1973), especially the introductory chapter by William Welsh, pp. 1-42.

16. Herbert C. Kelman, "Social-Psychological Approaches to the Study of International Relations", in Herbert C. Kelman, ed., *International Behavior* (New York: Holt, Rinehart and Winston, 1965), p. 24.

17. Michael Brechner, et al., "A Framework for Research on Foreign Policy Behavior", *Journal of Conflict Resolution*, XIII, No. 1 (March, 1969), p. 81.

18. An account of the factional conflicts is found in Ghita Ionescu, *Communism in Rumania, 1944-1962* (London: Oxford University Press, 1964). In addition, see Jowitt, op. cit., pp. 73-173.

19. See the excellent analysis by D.A. Tomasic, "The Rumanian Communist Party Leadership", *Slavic Review*, XX (October, 1961), pp. 477-494.

20. Paul Marer, "Soviet Economic Policy in Eastern Europe", in Joint Economic Committee, *Reorientation and Commercial Relations of the Economies of Eastern Europe*, 93rd Congress, 2nd Session, (Washington, D.C.: U.S. Government Printing Office, 1974), p. 145.

21. Romanian Workers' Party, *Statement of the Stand of the Romanian Workers' Party Concerning the Problems of the World Communist and Working-Class Movement*, April, 1964 (Bucharest: Agerpres, 1964), pp. 44-45.

22. Ibid.

23. Nicolae Ceausescu, *The Romanian Communist Party -- Continuer of the Romanian People's Revolutionary and Democratic Struggle, of the Traditions of the Working-Class and Socialist Movement in Romania* (Bucharest: Agerpres, 1966), pp. 28, 33-38, and pp. 49-53.

24. Ibid., pp. 37-38 (Italics added.)

25. "Strengthening the Unity of the Communist and Working-Class Movement -- A Supreme Duty", in *Documents, Articles and Information on Romania* (Bucharest), Supplement (February 28, 1967), p. 14.

26. This decision was first announced in "Interview of the Chairman of the RPR Council of Ministers, Chivu Stoica", *Agerpres Information Bulletin*, IX, No. 23 (November 30, 1958), Supplement.

207

27. Gheorghe Gheorghiu-Dej, "International Situation of the People's Republic", August 30, 1960 in *Agerpres Information Bulletin*, XI, No. 17 (September 5, 1960), p. 6.

28. For a detailed analysis of the interaction between political and economic factors in Romanian foreign policy see Cal Clark and Robert L. Farlow, *Comparative Patterns of Foreign Policy and Foreign Trade: The Communist Balkans in International Politics* (Bloomington: International Development Research Center, Indiana University, forthcoming).

29. Adam B. Ulam, *Expansion and Coexistence: The History of Soviet Foreign Policy, 1917-1967* (New York: Praeger, 1968), p. 713.

30. Nicolae Ceausescu, "Speech at the Working Meeting of the Party Active in the Sphere of Ideology and Political and Cultural-Educational Activity", July 9, 1971, *Romania: Documents-Events* (Bucharest), I, No. 40 (1971), p. 9.

31. An interesting analysis of the relationship between the new intelligentsia and the political elite is found in Jowitt, op. cit., esp. pp. 184-197.

32. Stephen Fischer-Galati, *The New Rumania* (Cambridge: M.I.T. Press, 1967), pp. 1-3.

33. Illie Verdet, "Speech", Session of the Grand National Assembly, 1967 (Bucharest: Agerpres, 1967), p. 96.

34. R. Barry Farrell, "Politics of Open and Closed Political Systems", in R. Barry Farrell, ed., *Approaches to Comparative and International Politics*, pp. 167-208.

35. *Statistical Pocket Book of the Socialist Republic of Romania, 1968* (Bucharest: Central Statistical Board), p. 46.

36. Nicolae Ceausescu, *Report Concerning Measures for Perfecting the Management and Planning of the National Economy and for Improving the Administrative-Territorial Organization of Romania*, December, 1967 (Bucharest: Agerpres, 1967), p. 116.

37. Ibid.

38. Nicolae Ceausescu, "Speech at the Meeting of the CC of the RCP", March 22, 1968 in *Documents, Articles and Information on Romania*, XIX, No. 6 (March 30, 1968), p. 2.

Chapter IX

YUGOSLAV FOREIGN POLICY

Richard P. Farkas

The substance and direction of Yugoslav foreign policy are acknowledged to be "interesting" and relatively satisfying to the
Western observer. But these attributes have caused some analysts
to retreat to a set of classic "area studies" explanations emphasizing the "uniqueness", peculiarities, and singularity of Yugoslav
policy. From this indictment, it must be clear that the priorities
in this analysis focus on Yugoslav foreign policy -- its development and its impact -- for the purpose of verifying the usefulness
of a systematic and comparative format (concepts and variables)
and to illustrate how those methods can help us to take a fresh
look at the determinants, process, and output of a dynamic political system.

In the course of my research and travels in Yugoslavia, it has
become increasingly clear that there is little or nothing in either
the Yugoslav political system or in the society which should be
uncommon to the political scientist. The deceptive factor, however,
which seems to mislead scholars, novices and initiated alike, is
the unusual mixture or combination of components which cast an
aura of individuality over the society, polity and economy of
Socialist Yugoslavia. At the heart of this proposition is a premise
that is nothing short of the id of every comparative political
analyst. In fact, one would do well to hypothesize and examine the
degree to which this aura of uniqueness is a conscious product of
the internal and external determinants of foreign policy. If this
speculation can be supported it follows that this "special attribute" is a functionally valuable factor in the "game plan" of
current Yugoslav policy.

The objective then is clear: to search out a rigorous and more
system-oriented framework with which to understand Yugoslav politics. The following pages are some preliminary notions on one way

this might be accomplished. Foreign policy is but one of the areas, one of the policy processes, at which a study might be levelled. It offers much raw data from which to work and is a relatively high visibility policy area. It is also an area, equalled only by political decisions about economic development, which has universally penetrating impact on the system as a whole. To understand the substance of foreign policy is but one of the objectives, sharing its place in this analyst's curiosity with questions like: what systemic attributes seem to condition or restrict policy, and is it possible to consider foreign policy an independent variable which conditions or affects systemic development over time? By raising such questions, one is vulnerable when such "answers" are not yet crystallized. However, this chapter should present some propositions which might serve as the keys to hunting for a more complete understanding of such political dynamics.

Analysis of Capability

The format for this investigation is structured around the conceptual "factors" enumerated in Wilkinson's *Comparative Foreign Relations: Framework and Methods*. (1) While hardly an ideal framework, it offers a thoughtful and partially operationalized pattern for our analysis. In essence, its foci are 1) capability factors; 2) leadership factors; 3) "residuals"; and 4) output. Wilkinson's description of the components of his framework create some problems. However, on balance a good case can be made for his penetrating, inclusive and general construct. In all, a preliminary attempt is being made via the Wilkinson framework to present a universe of variables (or types of variables) which affect the tone, nature and place of foreign policy in the over-all political system of modern Yugoslavia. The first of the four units to be presented in this chapter corresponds to Wilkinson's *capabilities*.

Considered collectively the Wilkinson variables and the hypothesized relationship among them do suggest a Yugoslav pattern of foreign policy development and conduct. This pattern can be productively contrasted with the policy experience of other Communist systems. A discussion of Yugoslav foreign policy or Yugoslav politics for that matter would be remiss if it did not cite and pursue this significance.

Validity of method, data, and theory is the goal, especially if it can be tempered and enhanced by a sufficiently constant concern for arriving at a level of generalization which provides fertile ground for other political researchers. To some, such an effort is quixotic, to others it is full of truisms -- in essence, the dilemma of our times.

Capability has certainly be one of the key traditional concepts in analyzing foreign policy. Often correlated intuitively with "power", the classical hypothesis prescribes (although not in this language) that capabilities are the independent variable, output (policy) is the dependent variable, and leadership, culture, style, institutions and process are intervening variables. Further the corollary is that the independent and dependent variables are directly related. Thus, the weighting and relationship of those components in the broad conduct of foreign relations has, for many, lingered an unchallenged and untested "given". While basic to most of our training and thought, this premise is disturbing. Through cross-national investigation guided by a relatively neutral paradigm a penetrating test may be possible.

The framework lists the following capability factors: 1) Geo-demographic base; 2) Military-economic-political means; and 3) Capacity for collective action. (2)

Seeking the data necessary to so describe the capabilities of Yugoslavia or any other communist state is not a routine task. Methodological problems, numerical discrepancies and statistical idiosyncrasies among them, abound. That having been said, the Yugoslav case enables one to rely more heavily on such criteria than does any other communist society. Two conditions account for this: 1) the eagerness with which the Yugoslavs have participated in United Nations and OECD programs including information gathering and disseminating; and 2) the relatively sophisticated and annually published *Yugoslav Statistical Yearbook (Statistical Godisnjak Jugoslavije)* produced by the Federal Institute for Statistics in Belgrade. From these and selected other sources it is possible to make use of most of Wilkinson's variables.

All of Wilkinson's variables do not lend themselves to quantification and others remain difficult to code. As these problems are confronted, a subjective evaluation of the capability level has been offered. Such "soft" assessments are temporary concessions to the difficulties at hand. Future efforts can speak to the problem of re-conceptualizing, sophisticating or replacing such stubborn variables.

The first set of variables are those collectively labelled "Geo-demographic base". Divided along spatial, material, and populational lines, a brief assessment of the variables follows leaning heavily on both the statistical data available and Pounds' geographic study, *Eastern Europe*. (3) Of particular relevance to Yugoslav foreign relations are three spatial factors: facility for access to external areas, factors pertaining to neighboring states, and distance from area-dominant super-power. Yugoslavia enjoys the most accessible geographic location in Eastern Europe. Three of its neighbors are non-communist states while four others are communist party-states. It is at no point contiguous with the Soviet Union. Three of the four communist systems are Warsaw Pact members while two of the three non-communist neighbors are NATO members. None of these five are, however, central states (in a "power" sense) in their respective groups. In all, Yugoslavia holds a relatively positive and enviable geographic position which affords both access and a measure of political insulation.

Materially, indicators of arable land, energy resources, and

raw mineral wealth are readily available. The Yugoslav state reports 14.6 million hectares under cultivation with a population
per square mile of arable land of approximately 600. Essentially
this reflects the relatively high ratio (for Eastern Europe) of
population to productive land which is a consequence of Yugoslavia's
varied landforms and a large naturally forested countryside. The
agricultural sector produces one-fifth of the social product,
employs nearly 50% of the labor force and, most significantly,
accounts for more than 15% of Yugoslavia's commodity exports. The
World Bank reported in 1975 that "... the surplus in foreign trade
which originates in the agricultural sector has more than doubled
in the past decade." Energy production (hydro-electric) is moderately impressive with 19 billion kilowatt hours being produced
annually supplying the average Yugoslav consumer with 753 kwh per
year. Generally assessed, basic raw materials exist in quantities
abundant enough to have kept pace with domestic industrial demands.
    Population figures found in the capability tables indicate both
raw size and projected growth by 1984. Ethnic homogeneity is an
illusive variable. The multiplicity of nationalities might be
sufficient to indicate the degree of heterogeneity. However, it
can be clearly demonstrated that socialization has produced significant trends toward homogeneity. It is nontheless true that
Yugoslavia has the lowest percentage of population who speak the
dominant language among all Communist states. Cultural and educational levels are discernible from a set of variables including
percentage of population literate, number of institutions of
higher learning, and school pupils as a percentage of the population segment between five and nineteen years of age. While regis-
tering only moderate levels in the first and last of those categories, Yugoslavia is second only to the Soviet Union in institutions, enrollments, and graduates of higher education. Distribution of technical and organizational skills remain in one of those
illusive measures which will have to be deferred for future investigations.
    Wilkinson's "military-economic-political means" grouping of
factors is largely self-explanatory. The syndrome of variables
focusing on the state's economic condition is hardly innovative.
In fact, most of those variables listed by Wilkinson are those
which Rummel's "Dimensionality of Nations" and aggregate projects
have strongly correlated to GNP-related measures. Thus, in an
effort to distill Wilkinson's shotgun approach to a representation
of economic power, a few of those GNP-associated variables of particular interest are presented in the summary table. Annual revenue
and expenditure figures also appear. Before moving on to military
capability variables, one economic aspect of the Yugoslav system
remains hidden in the thicket of mathematical and econometric indicators. I refer here to the level of development (social development if you like) of the industrial, commercial, financial, and
trade sectors of the de-centralized Yugoslav enterprise system.
The collective leadership and direction of the managerial elite

TABLE 9.1

YUGOSLAV CAPABILITY DATA

Basic Resources

Area	255,804 sq. km
Population	20,522,000
Population Projection-1984	23,053,000
Inhabitants per km	80
Persons per household	3.8
Persons per dwelling	3.9
Dwellings constructed	
public	44,693
private	90,126
Mean age	31

Economic Performance

Average annual inflation (since '70)	17%
Federal budget	$1,885 million
National income	$15,746 million
Defense expenditure as % of gross receipts	24%
GNP	$20,089 million
GNP per capita	$926
GNP average annual change	+11%
Agric. population as % of economic active population	47.3%
Average no. workers in ag. firm	255,466
Average no. workers in industrial firm	1,696,124
Average annual increase in industrial production (since '70)	10%

214

Figure 9.1 continued

Internationalism

Vessels in merchant fleet	387
Passenger aircraft	43
Annual commercial arrivals & departures	1,600
Foreign tourists	5.5 million
Percentage of books published by foreign authors	10%
Primary EXPORTS: bauxite, wood, steel products, ships	
Primary IMPORTS: wheat, coal, fertilizers, iron, petroleum, raw steel, and machines	
No. of countries with diplomatic relations	90

Education

Percentage of population illiterate	15.1%
Scholars	62,207 (15% social scientists)
Universities "peoples"	190
"workers"	226

All data is for 1973 and is from the Yugoslav Federal Institute
for Statistics.

working in a semi-independent environment have stimulated a growth
and development with significantly complements the political leadership's pursuits in foreign policy. (4)

The *World Outlook 1970*, a reputable product of the *Economist's*
Intelligence Unit summarizes those dominant, current features of
the Yugoslav economy,

"Although it is expected that the very high growth
rate in the economy will slow down towards the end of
the next year... consumption will continue to run
ahead of production. Consequently, inflation is certain to continue. The trade gap is likely to widen
but the effects of this will have been mitigated
by a record inflow from tourism, and by renewed efforts to get Yugoslavs working abroad to repatriate
their foreign earnings. The inflow of foreign capital
will increase as a result of the foundation of the
International Investment Corporation for Yugoslavia,
but... until further inducements are created and confidence in the economy built up, the benefits to
Yugoslavia will be slow to develop." (5)

Apart from the equivocation, one can see in this assessment both
the remnants of programs uncommon and unprecedented in a communist
state, and a distinct external or outlooking orientation for the
economy. The World Bank in its 1975 Country Report on Yugoslavia
makes the following economic observations:

1) Rapid increase in production has been sustained over the
past decade. The growth of industrial output averaged over 10%
per year;

2) Inflationary pressures reflect excess demand as well as cost
push factors;

3) Decentralization has weakened fiscal policy making. Major
legislative reform may impose more financial discipline;

4) An incomes policy is being formulated which could significantly strengthen management effectiveness;

5) Measures have been imposed which strengthen the financial
discipline of enterprises;

6) The balance of payments situation has been a major constraint
to accelerated development;

7) Liberalization of trade and payments has been achieved;

8) The total external debt is up but greatest concern stems
from the debt service ratio which is also up to 24% and has been
increasing on the average more than 1% per year. Credit management
is an area to which the Yugoslavs will have to commit more energies.

Research suggests that the Yugoslav managerial elite working
with, but not for, the political elite are responsible for this
current. External orientation will be mentioned briefly at the
conclusion of this section as a critical input into the development of a state's foreign policy.

The military posture and military emphasis of the state constitute another determinant of capability. Total defense expenditure

as a percentage of GNP, number of men in armed forces as a percentage of total population, and some notion of the dependence of the state on the supply of arms from external sources seem adequate to represent the military factor in Yugoslav policy formulation. Military personnel as a percentage of total population has decreased from 2.17% in 1959 to 1.35% in 1967. In 1970 there were just under 300,000 men in the Yugoslav armed service most of which have a one year commitment. Defense expenditure as a percentage of GNP was 7.3% in 1959 and in 1973 was 24% of total gross receipts. Thus, one may generalize that this percentage has gone up significantly. Yugoslavia is currently using weapon systems and equipment produced by no less than five different nations. It is worthy of note as well that they are making a concerted effort to manufacture their own military equipment especially in the areas of tactical aircraft including helicopters. During the first six months of 1969 the government purchased "Firearms of war and ammunition" valued at approximately $10,000 entirely from non-communist nations (Table 9.2). Since the thorough-going economic and social reforms of 1965, some groups have found the latitude to actively pressure for a de-centralized military with independent regional commands. The federal government has to date effectively avoided the issue.

In terms of political capabilities narrowly defined, two factors are included. First, is the degree of government commitment in personnel and revenue to foreign representation, and second, the impact of foreign identity and penetration into domestic political affairs. Yugoslavia currently has diplomatic relations with ninety countries, seventy-five of which are full-status embassadorial relations. This represents an official set of external political linkages which, in the Communist World, is second only to the Soviet Union. These provide tangible informational and communicative resources. The degree of foreign political penetration into political affairs is negligible. However, it is clear that a group does exist within the LCY, although diminishing in size as a result of pointed assualts by the Tito forces, that might be characterized as "conservative and Stalinist". It is likely that those who remain in the system have so compromised themselves that their manifest collective political effect is quite modest. Their latent political potential is a subject about which speculation is very difficult. Consequently, it is untenable in contemporary Yugoslav politics to hold that any foreign power has significant political influence over the affairs of state or any group which might influence such affairs.

The last of Wilkinson's categories is "Capacity for Collective Action". Under this heading are subsumed social, psychological, and political facets. The search for meaningful and concrete indicators which reflect the "degree" of social integration, cohesion unity, discipline. and organization" is difficult. One is forced to respond with an equally disjointed set of variables which are basically *stability* and *communication* focused. If one is to

TABLE 9.2

TRADE AND BALANCE OF TRADE

SELECTED IMPORTS-EXPORTS for 6 month period January-June 1969 in U.S. $*

	Imports	Exports
World totals	1,036,917,000	641,234,000
Totals with Communist States**	254,139,000	190,824,000
Total Electrical Energy	908,000	54,000
Total Electrical Energy with Communist States	730,000	none
Total Iron & Steel	71,045,000	19,327,000
Total Iron & Steel with Communist States	29,781,000	9,550,000
Total Firearms of war & Ammunition	10,000	none
Total Firearms of war & Ammunition Communist States	none	none

* Yearly *projections* may be attained by doubling figures.
**"Communist States" include USSR, East Germany, Poland, Czechoslovakia, Hungary, Romania, Bulgaria, Albania, China, N. Korea, N. Vietnam.

TOTAL IMPORTS/EXPORTS TO COMMUNIST STATES

Breakdown: By country in declining order (Volume in U.S. $)

	Imports	Exports
USSR	87,417,000	92,367,000
Czechoslovakia	60,919,000	22,918,000
East Germany	38,931,000	17,408,000
Poland	24,417,000	19,559,000
Hungary	20,178,000	19,147,000
Romania	11,269,000	8,787,000
Bulgaria	9,660,000	9,050,000
Albania	745,000	1,266,000

218

Table 9.2 continued

Source: OECD Statistics of Foreign Trade, Series C
        Trade by Commodities, Jan-June 1969

BALANCE

Year	Balance in dinars	Exports as % of imports
1961	-5802	62.5
1962	-3353	77.8
1963	-4327	74.8
1964	-7310	67.5
1965	-3339	84.7
1966	-6041	77.4
1967	-7746	73.3
1968	-9063	70.3
1969	-11208	69.1
1970	-20313	58.4
1971	-24439	55.8
1972	-16924	69.2
1973	-28195	63.2
1974	-63431	50.4

Source: Yugoslav Federal Institute of Statistics-reported in
        January 1975.

accept the validity of these variables vis-à-vis social integration, etc., it will be necessary to accept that intra-societal
communication promotes, that is, is positively related to organization and integration, and that stability engenders unity and
solidarity if not consent. These propositions deserve much closer
independent examination, but for the moment they will remain a
priori assumptions. When one attempts to use stability as an indicator of social discipline and institutional flexibility, we
are, it seems, on much firmer ground.

There is an average of one radio for every six Yugoslavs. That
number is up from one in ten in 1967. The ratio for television
sets is 1:10. In 1967 there was one telephone for every fifty
persons. By 1971 the increase was impressive rising to one for
every twenty persons. On each of these variables Yugoslavia does
not fare well in relation to the other contemporary communist
states. However, on the selected measures of stability it far exceeds the other cases. Two measures are employed: an "Executive
Stability Index" computed by dividing number of years independent
(since WWII) by number of chiefs of state who have held power,
and total deaths from domestic group violence. Statistics for
suicides may also have been interesting and valuable but it appears that most communist states including Yugoslavia have not
reported such figures. On the Executive Stability Index, the state
shows a perfect, maximum score as a function of Josef Broz Tito's
"permanent presidency". As for total deaths from domestic group
violence (1950-1962) a figure of zero was reported. Therefore, if
these are minimally adequate variables bearing the hypothesized
relationship to discipline and flexibility on the one hand, and
cohesion, solidarity, and "popular unity" on the other, then one
can take refuge in the intuitively apparent political and personal
popularity of the Yugoslav leader and of the system he directs.

Moral of psychological factors can be divided into two sets:
a) morale, spirit, perserverance; and b) inventiveness, flexibility, and adaptability. "National character" is a meaningful term
only when carefully operationalized to include all of these and
other concepts. Subjective evaluations are inherently disturbing
and justifiably vulnerable. Yet one cannot ignore the moral and
psychological complexion of the society. Clearly, those observations which follow are of a highly conditional nature. With reference to category "a" the Yugoslavs could hold their own if some
measures of cross-national comparison were available. National and
ethnic identifications within the state reflecting sometimes sharp
cultural diversity could be used to call this proposition to question. Precisely this element thwarts efforts to make a generalization about the "b" unit. An inclusive assessment of Yugoslav inventiveness, flexibility and adaptability would paint a very dim
picture indeed. Exceptions exist, Slovenians, some Croats, and
fewer Serbs have shown themselves, in both their occupational and
personal lives, to be remarkably adaptable and innovative. On the
balance sheet though one would be challenged to produce a measure

or index which could be used to compare Yugoslavia favorably on these variables with most other Eastern European states if the emphasis were on technical inventiveness, etc. By emphasizing political inventiveness and adaptability Yugoslavia would certainly be in the upper echelon of East European nations.

The remaining phase of Wilkinson's framework, "Capacity for Collective Action" is the least explicit. This may reflect the fact that it seems improperly placed in a discussion of broad societal factors which are pertinent to the development and conduct of foreign policy. To be sure "quality of command, diplomacy, bureaucracy, policy, or rule" are essentially valuable concerns if we are to explain and predict policy. Yet unless we discuss here either the ability of the society to provide quality leadership or popular perceptions of systemic "quality", we will have shifted gears in the middle of our analysis and pre-empted the specific discussions of leadership, residuals, and output which follow in subsequent units. The political "capability", the specific concern of this segment, *is* the totality of the variables introduced above.

Quantification of the capability variables for any single state is of little value to the comparative analyst without some parallel data on the states within the same international sub-system or within some other general frame of reference. For this reason, Table 9.3 which follows represents an *initial* effort at collecting such comparative indicators for communist states. Certainly one eventually would want to be able to evaluate Yugoslavia's capabilities in other than this context and indeed such an effort may be rewarding. The limitations of this chapter prevent consideration of such comparison.

For heuristic purposes one might find it useful to settle on a single value, an index, for a state's capability. (6) From this a ranking within the frame of reference (supra-system) would be possible which in turn could be compared with (and conceivably challenge) rankings more classically devised.

On the subject of capability rankings and policy, Wilkinson, reflecting his concern for a valid, systematic ranking, nonetheless acknowledges the need for such an index when he writes,

> "Even with all the qualifications that must be introduced into specific rankings, any measurement or estimate of material capabilities will eventually confer upon an actor certain relative international capability ranks or power statuses -- one in the world systems at large, another in the smaller regional and local subsystems of which the state is a member, and another in its relations with each other state with whom its ties are strong and close." (7)

One will notice in the above passage a retreat into the standard interpretation of equating "capability" and "power". Coupled with the following hypotheses Wilkinson's position becomes clearer.

1) The higher the capability rank of a state, the larger is its chance of success in the pursuit of any given policy.

TABLE 9.3
BASIC CAPABILITY DATA: EAST EUROPE

	POPULATION				PRODUCTION/CONSUMPTION				COMMUNICATIONS			
	Population (millions) *	Pop. per sq.mi. Arable Land	% pop. in cities over 20,000	% pop. in cities (100,000 & over)	GNP per capita *	Tot. consump. of energy per capita	passenger cars per 1,000	Arable Land in cultivation (million hectares)	TV's per 1,000 inhabs.	Radios per 1,000 inhabs.	Telephones per 1,000 inhabs.	Daily newspaper circulation per 1,000 inhabs.
Yugoslavia	21.0 (3)	600 (4)	18.6 (6)	9% (8)	926 (8)	1610 (8)	7 (2)	10.2 (3)	113 (7)	171 (7)	44 (7)	72 (8)
USSR	249.8	250	35.5	27%	1627	4767	6	545.0	162	404	53	216
GDR	17.0	880	36.2	22%	NA	5996	6	4.7	283	355	130	426
Czechoslovakia	14.6	720	25.3	14%	1941	6843	6	4.3	228	263	154	272
Poland	33.4	510	31.9	21%	1311	4556	7	19.9	157	175	63	146
Romania	20.8	470	18.0	17%	1197	3145	NA	9.8	94	150	39	169
Hungary	10.4	470	37.0	25%	1140	3279	9	5.9	201	245	89	167
Bulgaria	8.6	460	15.3	16%	1134	4130	6	5.8	150	268	68	146
Albania	2.4	900	NA	9%	355	NA	6	.55	5	70	NA	49

All data is from UN sources for the years '72 or '73. Exceptions where data from the Sixties is presented are marked with an asterisk. Figure in parenthesis is Yugoslavia's rank in East Europe on the given variable.

222

Table 9.3 continued

	DEFENSE		SERVICES		EDUCATION			
	Military Personnel as % of total pop. *	Men in Armed Forces *	Pop. per hospital bed	Physicians per 10,000	Literacy (15 yrs. & over) *	# Institutions of Higher Learning	# grads per annun of institution learning per 10,000	Students per 1,000 inhabs.
Yugoslavia	2.17^2	$270,000^3$	190^9	13.5^7	$76\%^8$	260^2	9^2	157^2
USSR	1.72	2,425,000	110	24.6	98%	742	15	186
GDR	.62	126,000	80	16.8	99%	44	8	90
Czechoslovakia	1.62	220,000	100	21.8	98%	48	8	88
Poland	1.04	275,000	130	16.0	95%	74	6	110
Romania	1.18	176,000	130	13.2	89%	171	6	69
Hungary	.75	103,000	140	20.7	97%	90	7	87
Bulgaria	2.04	152,000	140	19.3	85%	46	7	122
Albania	2.25	20,500	180	NA	71%	8	4	NA

2) The higher the capability rank of a state, the larger is
the scale of the objectives it can pursue with a given change of
success.

3) The higher the rank, the more active the policy -- that is,
the larger the number of situations in which decisions to take
action are made by the state.

4) The higher the rank, the greater the adaptability, coherence,
stability, and flexibility of policy. (8)

These projections of political behavior may be valid for a segment of the state actors in the internal community, but their
application to the communist system is hardly satisfying especially
if one tries to confront and understand intra-system relations.
As a guide to anticipating the nature, range, and effectiveness --
in Wilkinson's words, "success, scale, activity, assertiveness,
status quo orientation, stability, and flexibility" -- of a communist state's foreign relations these hypotheses can be dangerously
misleading. Yugoslavia as well as Albania, Romania, Cuba, North
Vietnam are examples of surpassing their "capabilities" as ranked
either by the D.O.N. data or by other formulae. Czechoslovakia and
East Germany represent at least two cases of higher relative "capability" and generally lower policy output in the terms prescribed
above. To area specialists two immediate retreats are available:
1) that the Soviet Union is willing to permit greater latitude to
those less capable states on the calculation that they have not
the strength to "break away" from Soviet tutelage, or 2) that
those more "independent" states are geo-politically more distant
from Moscow and therefore find it possible to flex in some foreign
policy matters. In spite of their prevalence, neither of these are
minimally satisfying.

The conclusion is evident, either we are using the wrong indicators of capability (9), or other critical factors are playing a
part in the development of policy, thus undermining the afore-
mentioned hypotheses. The general measure of "success" in Yugoslav
foreign policy can be and has been, in the normal course of events,
out of proportions with relevant capabilities.

One possible explanation of this imbalance which is central to
appraisals of Yugoslav policy is the state's "external orientation".
Basically this involves a mix of capability factors (societal inputs) and leadership factors (motivational inputs). Such a group-
ing of variables can go a long way toward explaining contemporary
foreign policy -- its impact and its momentum.

The variables listed below with the available data for Yugoslavia and the subsequent rank within the communist international
system will serve to indicate a strong Yugoslav external orientation. This thrust could be either a contributing and shaping factor in the conduct of Yugoslav affairs or it could be a product or
an impact of policy centrally directed from Belgrade. There appears
to be adequate foundation to suggest that both effects are operative. Nevertheless, since we are interested more in the essentially
noninduced, non-governmental determinants of foreign relations, the

TABLE 9.4

YUGOSLAV EXTERNAL ORIENTATION VARIABLES:
RANK AMONG EAST EUROPEAN STATES

Variable	Rank
Items of Foreign Mail Sent per capita	2nd (behind E. Germany)
Immigrants per thousand population	2nd (behind Poland)
Emmigrants per thousand population	2nd (behind Poland)
Radios per thousand population	7th
Passenger cars per thousand pop.	2nd (behind Hungary)
Tourism--Total Foreign Visitors	1st
Import/Export of long films	1st
--	
Military personnel as % of pop.	3rd
Expenditure on defense as % of GNP	2nd
No. of nations from which military equip.	1st
--	
Foreign trade (imports-exports) as % of GNP	1st
Diplomatic Relations (# states with)	2nd (behind Soviet Union)

Data is generally from late '60s or early '70s -- selected to accommodate comparisons.
See also Table 9.2-Trade and Balance of Trade
Transport and Communications variables reflect substantial activity. Among those examined but not presented are: Foreign exchange receipts of enterprises of public transport, transshipment, and communications; International passenger railway transport; Exports and imports of goods by railway; International sea-borne goods traffic; Vessels entered seaports; Passenger traffic at seaports; and Number of entries of foreign motor vehicles and passengers.

reader will find the emphasis on broadly societal indicators of external orientation.

This discussion of capabilities is meant to schematically represent the "capability" of Yugoslavia and to identify an initial challenge to the Wilkinson format's hypotheses regarding the basic relationship of capabilities to policy. Only through mingling with a full range of measures of national capability, processed if possible in a comparative way to enhance at least ordinal ranking, can one challenge the classical concept of the relationship between power and policy. That in itself is one justification, but the primary purpose in this chapter is to establish a firm base upon which to move on to an examination of the system's leadership, residuals, and output.

Analysis of Leadership

Leadership and all of its aspects -- style, tone, security, longevity, prestige, viability, and legitimacy -- certainly warrant ranking as one of the key determinants of a state's foreign policy. This said, one might hasten to point out that this apparently sound proposition often lures analysts to dwell in normative and subjective terms about a particular national leadership. The case of Yugoslavia is one that would lend itself to such romanticism. However, recent scholarship in the area of Eastern European elites and their behavior has responded to such ills (if only in a preliminary way) and produced a rather more firm foundation upon which to make our assessments. (10) Broad scale comparative leadership studies of East Europe have been published elsewhere. (11) This chapter will concern itself centrally with the features of the leadership which seem most critical to the creation and conduct of foreign policy. The objective is to better understand the impact and control of Yugoslav elite behavior on foreign relations.

The framework for this section. like the others, is borrowed liberally from Wilkinson, emphasizing that this is done not on the basis of his construct's overall strength but on the benefits for comparative analysis of an established model. Wilkinson presents another set of determinants he calls "*will, prescription, and volition*". Both in tone and substance one might choose to label these concepts, albeit imperfectly, as "leadership" or "motivational" determinants.

The linkage between Yugoslav capabilities and leadership is most apparently reflected in the state's general external orientation. It is here that the set of decisions and calculations are made, conditioned by capabilities (positive and negative) and commensurate with leadership objectives and interests. In discussing the leadership we are essentially looking at the drive forces behind foreign relations which are certainly relevant to how successfully the final policy product overcomes challenges or resistance.

It will be increasingly apparent, if it is not already, that none
of the determinants presented are either independent (in a functional sense) or mutually exclusive. Foreign policy is the product
of a maze of social inputs processed in so many ways at different
points in time that our conclusions must always be tempered. However, no one should interpret that to mean that we cannot make
real progress toward better understanding patterns of policy determination through systematic investigation.

    Prescription is the first of the leadership factors from Wilkin-
son's model. Drawing on the framework's description,

    Prescription is the label for the common element in a set
    of widely varied and otherwise ill-assorted political pro-
    cesses: it is the living presence of the past in current
    policy-making; it is that santification of tradition, that
    bureaucratic inertia, that permits us to explain a decision
    of today by referring to the policy of yesterday... (12)

one will recognize this concept as a central and traditional one.
Political scientists and historians have dwelled on this input
and have generated an impressive literature if kept in perspective.
(13) The fortunate tendency is to imply uni-dimensional or single
factor explanation and to casually posit causal relationships.

    In the case of Yugoslavia, the utility of the concept of pre-
scription is largely dependent upon the period that one is examining. For example, the sharp and deliberate break with the past
(the socialist revolution if you like) following World War II,
markedly reduced the impact of pre-war policy relevant routines
and perspectives. Prescription vis-à-vis pre-war tradition was
negligible. But that is not to suggest that traditional problems
and issues did not linger most pronounced in the affairs of state
and foreign policy.

    The years immediately following World War II might well be very
fertile for a study of foreign policy formation given that it was
a time of new leadership, new institutions, and rapid societal
change. It is, however, a very difficult period to study because
of these basic changes. For the moment, we will pass over this
period, simply qualifying the proposition above (prescription was
lacking as a determinant in post-war Yugoslav policy) to suggest
that the tradition, the bureaucratic pattern that was influential
in this period was that of the Soviet Union and was therefore
exogenous to Yugoslav politics.

    After '48 and the famous "split" the Tito clique embarked upon
what has become to date a thirty year program to gradually (if
unevenly) eliminate Soviet prescriptive influences from policy
formation. As this was accomplished, elements of the Yugoslav
socialist pattern of organization and policy formation inevitably
developed their own norms and tradition. The qualitative differences should not be underestimated. The post-'48 tradition is distinctly Yugoslav in the sense that it is the product of Yugoslav
leadership and it is wholly "modern" tradition. By this I mean
that the prescriptive factors are disjointed from the pre-war po-

litical culture and still benefit from the image of reform, newness, and experimentation. Functionally this makes such "modern
traditions" relatively impotent when the leadership wishes to em-
bark upon a new policy course, an apparently enviable situation
from the leadership's perspective. This takes on even more meaning
and validity as long as a single leadership circle is in power;
still the case in Yugoslavia. A major question remains, whether,
after Tito's departure from leadership, the subsequent leaders
will be able or choose to oscillate from the distinct, central
themes of contemporary Yugoslav foreign policy. The proposition
here is that only after a leadership change will it be possible to
disect the impetus of modern prescriptive determinants on foreign
policy from the system-continuity promoted by the in-power group.
From observing and interviewing a small segment of the Yugoslav
political elite (14) it appears reasonable to put forth the following proposition: Yugoslav leadership is increasingly influenced
by and committed to prescriptive factors in foreign policy decision-making. Verification for this proposition can be and was
illicited by seeking responses on such subjects as foreign policy
goals, central themes of policy, and role expectations. The influence of the on-going system and the confidence in its successes
have created both confidence and commitment to relatively new organizational and policy patterns. In essence, this precipitates a
notion of the institutionalization of the system, which, as it
becomes more differentiated and de-centralized, has also broadened
its base of support. Without a sample of the size which would
enable one to be conclusive, one can nonetheless make the observation that as one ventures downward through the various leadership
strata an increasingly prescriptive orientation is evident. The
only exception to this general observation exists among some of
the more dynamic enterprise "Direktors" whose sense of innovation,
while hardly adventuristic or irresponsible, was impressively and
increasingly entrepreneurial. This increase in prescription orientation as one examines lower strata may constitute an exception
to "normal" organizational development and behavior.

Effort has been exerted to avoid any qualitative judgements
about the measure and direction of prescriptive forces in Yugoslavia. It is certainly true that stability can be drawn from such
forces as well as stagnation. Clearly, though, one of the present
dangers (and that which lurks for the post-Tito leadership) is the
imbalance of prescriptive versus innovative orientations and the
possibility that this schism parallels the varied perspectives and
influences of the upper versus the lower elite strata. The balance
between prescription and will is critical to the development of
the political system and it is to this subject that we now turn.

Some operational definitions of *will* and *volition* are needed.
Wilkinson writes,

"Will is... an objective political phenomenon, where we
find in combination independence, demand, action, and
resolve... associated with certain particular individuals

in a political leadership." (15)
    Volition or, as Wilkinson prefers, the "V phenomenon" is a
"special manifestation of will in the political life of a state,
... injecting special kinds of leadership, ideas, rhetoric, centralization, drama, and conflict." (16)
    From the definition given and a few scant phrases about the
relationships among them -- "... will and V both contrast with
prescription... (they) also both override (whether by harnessing
or extirpating) old prescription and create new prescription." --
one is left with the task of molding the concepts into a meaningful construct for inquiry. A brief effort along these lines may
prove helpful. An illustration (Figure 9.1) follows which should
help explain the dynamic relationship among prescription, will,
volition, and the development of "modern" tradition ("modern" prescription). Most simply put, there are conflicting strains in
every political system between tradition and change or between
routine and innovation. In our model these are labelled "prescription" and "will" and are spurred by bureaucratic leadership and
revolutionary leadership respectfully. To be sure the clash is not
of the "zero sum" type although it may, given certain manifestations of conflict, be perceived as such. A functioning system than
has some mix of prescriptive and initiating forces playing a role
in the creation of policy. The two leadership propensities can of
course erupt from the very same persons responding to different
stimuli or varied goals at specific points in time. It could also
be the case that the two types represent two amorphous, anomic
groups which opt into the two types on specific issues or issue
sets. Finally, there could be two (or more) clearly differentiated
and formal alignments whose interests and inclinations are readily
identified. This typology while useful for analysis (especially if
developmental hypotheses are added) would not alter the representation in Figure 9.1A.
    Given that the relationship between will and prescription (based
upon an equilibrium of political forces) settles into a pattern,
and the innovative leadership through some special power or impetus
presses the prescription to shrink from its "normal" dimensions,
volition has become a policy-relevant input. This may create a
qualitative change in the tone, substance, or immediacy of policy.
Seldom can such "special" thrusts be sustained if indeed it were
in the interest of the leadership to sustain them. Therefore,
volition will subside, leaving in the void not the old prescription
which it supplanted but instead a new set of policies, organizations,
or precedents which become part of a "modern" tradition (prescription). Represented in Figures 9.1B and 9.1C, the concept of a
"tidal V" can be found, if in very sketchy form, in Wilkinson's
framework, "When V existed in the past, it may have occured in
bursts or tides." (17)
    Making use of the model developed above, one might observe a
distinct pattern of development in post-war Yugoslav foreign policy.
This pattern may also provide insight for the analysis of Yugoslav

FIGURE 9.1

PRESCRIPTION, WILL, AND VOLITION

IN FOREIGN POLICY FORMATION

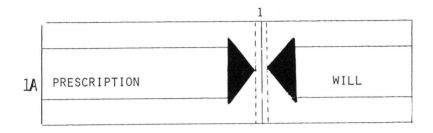

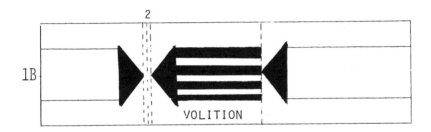

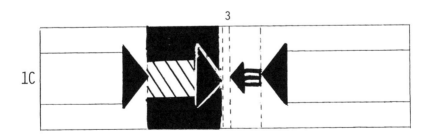

MODERN

TRADITION

domestic policy. The essence of this pattern has already been introduced in this chapter. While a strong influence of *will* and a facility for injecting *volition* had been characteristics of Yugoslav politics since the advent of Tito, after '48 the system realigned its priorities toward pushing back, dissolving, and replacing the prescriptive influences of the Soviet model which had so effectively grasped the other Eastern European states. Even in the early days, this foreign/domestic policy was met with rather substantial support in the Yugoslav leadership. (18)

Prescription based upon the Soviet system became a policy issue in and of itself. The tension between traditional and innovative leadership was of a special type. It had, built into it, the dimension of Soviet versus Yugoslav determination of policy. Naturally, this made rallying the forces easier even among the Party members whose allegiance or inclination may have to the former. Given that the primary political conflict of the entire system took this form, foreign and domestic issues were often fused, and Tito's personal leadership institutionalized out of necessity. The measure of will that the Tito elite managed to bring to bear on the formation and execution of policy was always significant. After '48 it became predominant. Some of the factors which contributed to it have been mentioned but it would be unfair to the leader and the role he developed to neglect to mention that he accrued a broad base of support (mass and elite) primarily through respect and faith (personal as much as political) growing out of cautious but enlightened domestic policy and prestigious and innovative foreign policy. For the system, I would suggest that the enduring significance of the way that Tito has developed the pattern of politics has been to formly establish the place of *will* in leadership and policy formation in Yugoslavia.

Volition is a different matter. Although Tito himself has found it useful and effective to call up a measure of drama, centralization, rhetoric, conflict, etc., a case can be made that he is trying to develop a political system which thwarts or defuses the future use of such "V" elements. His efforts to de-centralize the system in many respects and his recent overtures to creating a structure for governmental succession are the best indicators of this. As mentioned, we can easily find instances of volition in Yugoslav foreign policy. Among these the '48 Break, the '55 Soviet-Yugoslav Reconciliation, leadership among the Non-aligned and the Belgrade Conference of '61, the Economic Reforms of '65 with their pronounced foreign policy implications, and the dismissal of Rankovic in '66 stand as historic examples. Each of these established or accentuated central policy themes which in turn sired new organizations, routines, and policies having, in time, their own prescriptive influences. Such determinants have been labelled "modern" tradition of which there are huge quantities in contemporary Yugoslavia. The Yugoslavs recognize both the potential and the dangers of such a political situation. (19)

Figure 9.2 may be helpful in illustrating one interpretive pat-

tern in the development of leadership influences in Yugoslav foreign policy, and indeed in the system as a whole. Relying on the
scheme and data presented, one can draw some tentative conclusions
about the form and dynamics of the leadership factor in the determination of foreign policy. It is suggested that "modern tradition"
is growing vis-à-vis a gradual ebbing of volition. Will remains an
essential and (for the moment) unchallenged feature of the system.

If the yardsticks ("objective indicators") of the Wilkinson
framework are accepted, we can review the existence and impact of
the various leadership factors.
PRESCRIPTIVE INFLUENCES on foreign policy:
    a. the psychocultural dispositions and habit patterns of
       mass publics and of long-established conventionally
       selected elites, i.e. the expectations of mass and
       elite
    b. restrictive and conservative institutional structures
    c. legitimate and customary decision-making routines.

The central proposition of this chapter with regard to contemporary Yugoslav prescriptive forces is that they have been molded
by the contemporary elite themselves ("modern" traditions) and are
therefore generally consistent with leadership designs. However,
it is evident that the leadership remains wary of such influences
and in some cases has forged policy to inhibit their effectiveness.
The rotation policy can be viewed in this light to stunt the growth
of a "long-established, conventionally selected elite". Yugoslavs
have shown themselves increasingly to be "output-oriented" (20) in
the sense that their newly found economic well-being and their international prestige cause them to identify and support an innovative political regime. Their "system-orientation", while a growing
factor with the passage of time and development of modern tradition,
is still a secondary phenomenon. Today in Yugoslavia the organization which is most often spoken of in terms of "conservative"
structures is the LCY (League of Communists of Yugoslavia) itself.
Of course, the term is relative and one would not be hard pressed
to make a case for the LCY's progressive and flexible position.
Decision-making routines do not seem to present a critical challenge to innovation -- organizational or substantive. The potential
is real, however, since the state has reallocated political responsibility for particular policy areas to various sub-structures
-- the Federal Executive Committee, the National Assembly, the
republican governments, and the enterprise among them. On the
balance sheet, prescriptive influences in Yugoslav foreign policy
are limited, but bear substantial potential if viewed as an emerging set of "modern" traditions. A responsible analysis suggests
that these will grow and become central to the political system
because the political leadership (Tito) see them as stability nur-
turing and beneficial to system maintenance. It must be noted
though, that once developed, prescriptive forces can become very
entrenched as any Yugoslav will underline when discussing nationalism in his country.

FIGURE 9.2

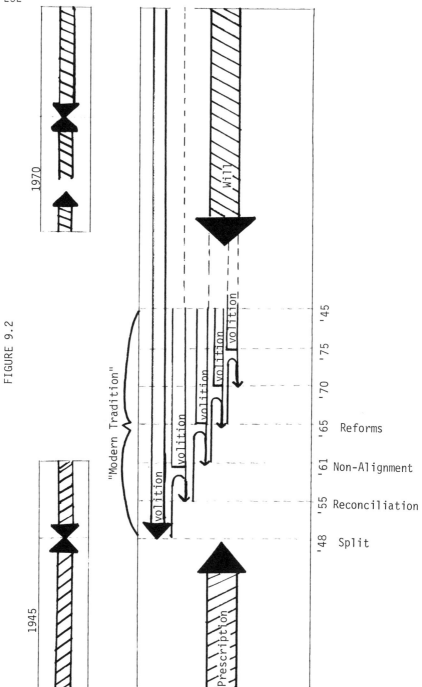

WILL in foreign policy:
  a. lack of external penetration and internal paralysis
     of the decisional structure (autonomy, self-direction,
     self-determination)
  b. clear and strong demands in the political talk of
     the governors
  c. evidence of deliberate decisions in behavior designed
     to procure these demands
  d. evidence of substantial resistance to these demands
     and of behavior persistently directed at overcoming
     resistance and obtaining goals.

Tito and those with whom he has filled leadership roles in
Yugoslavia are the enduring embodiment of the characteristics listed.
They, the national leadership, have thwarted direct external influence in decision-making, a very real threat for the Yugoslavs
from both East and West, and have wages a struggle against "internal paralysis" especially that coming from nationalities within
Yugoslavia. The strength of the leadership is a matter of historical record, and in most cases the direction of Yugoslav foreign
policy has been crystal clear to all affected. (21) To be sure,
such formidability is without precedent in that state's history.
The Western social scientist is pressed to acknowledge that the
"vanguard" function of Tito and the rest of the elite has been
impressive, enlightened, and more than relatively successful.
Phyllis Auty's biography is fitting testimony to an effective
statesman. (22)

VOLITION in foreign policy:
  a. the preeminent influence of new men of a special character
  b. an increased centralization of state resources and of
     the decision-making process (with increased speed,
     volume, scope, and co-ordination of decision)
  c. a rise in the political saliency of personalities (as
     opposed to prescription or institutions)
  d. a sharpening of statements or positions accentuating
     activism, novelty, or hostility.

Two tasks present themselves when applying this concept to the
Yugoslav case. First, to determine what measure of volition we
find in foreign policy, and second, to come to some conclusion
about the relationship among "V", policy formation, and policy
substance.

It has already been suggested that volition does seem to be
present in the most recent period of foreign policy. Further the
point is made that, especially in the earlier periods, there was a
high degree of volition even relative to the other Eastern European
states whose systems accommodate such leadership machinations. The
recent development of the political system seems directed at
limiting this leadership option. If this proposition is correct
then there is good cause to look favorably upon the political
future of the Yugoslav state. There is a subtle pitfall in the
above assessment. It explicitly suggests that the decline of

volition in the situations in which the Tito leadership utilized
"V" brought negative or even less than optimal foreign policy
results. In fact, the most substantial challenge which one might
level at this reasoning is that the Yugoslav society, torn as it
has been by economic inequality and continued subsystem nationality clashes (essentially domestic ills), may not yet be cohesive
enough to survive without volition-type leadership.

The foreign policy realm may be a somewhat different matter.
If the international situation is critical or threatening and if
the risks have already been imposed. then volition can be a calculated and defensible method. For the present at least Yugoslavia
does not find itself in such foreign policy dilemmas. It is
established in the internal community and in the leadership of the
Non-aligned World (whatever its constituency); it has active
trading relations which constitute a predominant vested interest
in international "normalcy". In essence, it is basking in the
place that it risked so much to establish. The leadership's character, in response, has been to reduce *volition*, maintain a strong
will, all the while working to create a formidable set of "modern
traditions".

The question was raised earlier of the relationship of volition
to policy. Wilkinson's posture on this relationship is depicted in
the following two passages:

> "The presence or absence of the V complex, and of will
> within it, is the most important factor, after capability,
> in accounting for foreign policy."

> "To the degree that V is present, it deflects all these
> prescriptive influences and, conjointly with capability,
> virtually suffices to account for the content, quality,
> objectives, and success of policy." (23)

Will and volition in Yugoslav policy, that is, the guidance and
dynamism, have certainly keynoted the development and success of
decisions. It seems reasonable to suggest that without the stability of will and the prodding barbs of volition, the quality and
success of Yugoslav foreign policy would have been markedly different. To the extent that objectives develop from a rational
assessment of policy options vis-à-vis both the dilemma and the
level of domestic support, they too will be reflective of volition.
But we have not yet confronted the encompassing nature of Wilkinson's propositions. The conclusiveness and scope of those statements is disturbing because they sharply minimize the impact of
the "residuals" -- political culture, institutions, and processes
-- on the substance of policy and upon the decision-makers themselves. To be sure a leader exercising high volition is, by the
nature of his act, pressing residual influences into the background
but it is equally true that he is not operating in a vacuum and
that his actions and perceptions have been conditioned by those
elements making up the formal political environment. In short,
they (the leadership) are themselves socialized and limited in
their actions regardless of the measure of volition. This is evi-

235

dent especially in the conduct, as opposed to the formation, of
Yugoslav foreign policy. The third section of this chapter will
examine the residual influences on foreign policy. On the basis of
the Yugoslav case, one can ascribe to the essence if not the proportions of Wilkinson's assessment of leadership factors in foreign policy determination.

If the system evolves along the lines suggested earlier in this
chapter to the point where volition is institutionally and pre-
scriptively limited -- a reasonable operationalization of political
"development" -- then the fundamental premises above would require
some re-examination.

Analysis of Residuals

"Residuals" in the political system comprise the remaining
category of determinants or influences on foreign policy. Political culture, institutions, and processes are the components with
which this unit will deal. In this section some discussion of both
the domestic and international environments is appropriate since
those aspects of the environment which have most impact are
usually functions of specific institutions or processes.

Yugoslav political culture is the first and the most difficult
with which to deal. Relative to most other modern states and certainly compared with either Eastern European or most other European
states, Yugoslavia has a fragmented political culture. It is regularly challenged by sub-system identifications promoting particularistic interests and demands. On nearly all conventional scales
-- economic, social, cultural, language, or life style -- those
within Yugoslavia are remarkably heterogeneous. Apart from this
condition, against which inroads are constantly being made by the
national leadership, a few basic but crucial common bonds have
been forged. In nearly all areas, the Yugoslav leadership has
managed to legitimize and popularize its own power through a slid-
ing scale of cautious reforms and a constant expenditure of effort
and resources to improve, if only relatively, the plight of the
various groups within the state. The most recent and pronounced
example of this is in the semi-autonomous region of Kosovo where
language, educational, and industrial policy have been changed to
accommodate a persistently alienated minority. The point is simple,
in spite of limited success in political "enculturation" and
socialization across the board (24), three fundamental tenets (as
cognitions, valuations, and/or affections) have been nurtured:
  a) a respect and faith in Tito -- political and personal
  b) an amorphous belief in socialism -- principle made relevant
     to individual needs
  c) a realization and appreciation that social and economic
     well-being has improved.
Whether fused or separated the end product for foreign policy is
the same. Domestic fragmentation is offset by the above three

broadly accepted factors and is therefore less impact laden with regard to foreign policy formation or conduct. More accurately, the variations and tensions of the internal system are seldom articulated in terms which challenge or resist Yugoslav foreign policy.

An exception of serious proportions is the development of a mobile, influential, and articulate economic elite whose values and perspective are sometimes out of synchronization with conventional political policy and who are materially and acutely concerned with foreign policy relevant matters. Yet this group is linked to the other power-laden Yugoslav groups -- Party, state, intellectual -- by the advantages and positions which they hold within the system, thereby sharing their ultimate concern for its maintenance. The elite political culture which surrounds and characterizes these groups seems qualitatively different from the general political culture in just a few essential ways. The core of the contemporary culture (above "a, b, c") is basically the same except in the respect that the degree, subtlety, and commitment (interest) with which the elite embraces them are greater. For mobility, LCY membership is useful but the restraints put upon members are hardly inhibiting. The pronounced lack of any strict doctrinaire or ideological "purity" is one of the key differences between the elite political culture of Yugoslavia and its Eastern European neighbors.

Some very probing studies have been completed which include examination of the elite responsible for formulation of Yugoslav foreign policy. (25) One study by R. Barry Farrell is interesting for two reasons. It sought to identify those in the foreign policy responsible group by other then formal role identification. Among those in the sample were educators, media, and Party personnel as well as the holders of formal state foreign policy positions. It may be that the list should have included a small number of industrial and economic men. The study is also of interest because it reveals a relative biographical homogeneity with a small potential for fragmentation along Party/state lines. Other prominent work on Communist elites has been undertaken in research by Beck, Zaninovich, Welsh, Shoup, and Djordjevic.

The analytic question remains: is political culture (elite or mass) a useful variable to examine when seeking to understand foreign policy formation? It does seem at first glance to hold some potential to reveal to us something of the political dynamics of the system. However, as a factor from which to draw understanding or explanation about the specific shape of contemporary Yugoslav foreign policy, closer examination suggests it is less than fertile. The degree (or lack) of integration, enculturation, socialization, and ideological penetration in the Yugoslav state bears little patterned correlation to content, quality, or stability of foreign policy. If political culture is a force, and some reservations are evident above, it is manifest indirectly through some other dimension of the system.

It should be recognized that the concepts of elite political

culture and prescriptive influences in the leadership may be over-
lapping, and in this sense the above statement stands qualified.
Shifting the focus to political institutions is not as easy as
it might first appear. It would be simple if we were willing to
accept out of hand the proposition that, given that Yugoslavia is
a communist state, the only three significant institutionalized
features of the system are the Party, the leader, and the ideological doctrine. And if we were liberal in our interpretation we
might concede that the order is open to question. Most of our research on Eastern European politics has either explicitly or implicitly made these assumptions about relevant political institutions. It has remained a "given" of political analysis rather than
a hypothesis. Few would deny the importance of those institutions
mentioned, but to examine them to the exclusion of all others is
inadequate scholarship. This critique is more valid for those who
have failed to acknowledge many significant changes in the contemporary Yugoslav political system. One can find measures of the
same kind of change in most other Eastern European political systems -- changes toward greater plurality of articulated interests
and influences with real consequence for foreign policy formation.
    Yugoslavia is the classic frontrunner in diversification and
reform of the communist system. (26) Its institutional structure,
both formal and functional, has undergone changes of major proportions since the early Fifties. Part of the success of the institutional metamorphosis of Yugoslavia has been its patience and evolution which can be credited to the single flexible but cautious
leadership. The alternative which we have seen among the East European systems is the sharp and explosive institutional change which
is met by keen regional superpower interest and has precipitated a
number of volatile responses. (27) The case of Yugoslavia reflects
incremental changes which nonetheless warrant our full appreciation. One such development has been the increasing credibility of
the state's legislative organs. (28) These, established pragmatically enough along the lines of major interest groups or sectors
with society, are five in number and have in practice clearly been
invested with uneven power and potential. The two organs that would
most likely claim interest in and therefore power of discussion
about foreign affairs would be the Federal Chamber, far and away
the most powerful, and the Chamber of the Economy. From the Almond
and Powell scheme (29), the most appropriate functional label for
these groups would be "validator-modifiers" which connotes that
they "await initial decisions by bureaucratic agents and then
approve or revise them". While this may seem hardly impressive,
the responsibility is at least two levels above the role of "ceremonial legitimator" from which parallel Yugoslav legislatures have
evolved, and which can still be found in East Europe. Barring substantial setbacks, the trends, which can be empirically verified,
is toward these organs attaining the characteristics of policy
"energizers" which would hold out the possibility of prescribing
general areas of foreign policy priorities and insuring and super-

vising that a bureaucratic decision is made.

Can any part of the state apparatus be identified as either the "initiator" or "regulator" of foreign policy? The single most powerful unit apart from the man/leader/institution, Tito the President, is the Federal Executive Council. Dzemal Bijedic is now President of the FEC. This group of highly placed officials has institutional and functional linkages with nearly every governmental and national political bureaucracy. It is the initiator and/or regulator over the foreign office (Milos Minic-Secretary of State for Foreign Affairs) and over special "commissions" whose expertise is filtered into critical decisions. Basically it controls foreign policy although it must remain responsive to such coherent representatives of vested policy interests as the Socialist Alliance, the LCY, the industrial "direktors", the military, and the various Political and Economic Chambers of the Republics. The suggestion is clear: it is possible to perceive a substantial measure of pluralistic influences on the foreign policy decisions of the decision-making elite. This implies that the foreign policy complex has not been able to avoid being affected by a general environmental factor -- the impressive if limited de-centralization and democratization of the domestic political system. The basic environmental change toward fuller system-wide participation (in principle) is more than ten years old. Decisions to become involved with OECD and GATT, to settle the Trieste issue, to actively denounce both the US in Vietnam and the USSR in Czechoslovakia, to normalize relations with West Germany, to make the joint Romanian-Yugoslav warning to the Soviet Union following the Czech invasion, and to open Yugoslav firms to substantial foreign investment, all reflect the active influence of particular groups on foreign policy formation. This should not be over-estimated; influence and periodic success are far from raw power and control of policy. To some the most startling proposition here is that the LCY and the Socialist Alliance are not central, dominant entities in foreign policy formulation and conduct. This appears to be the case in spite of the fact that both are frequently and evidently vocal on the course of foreign policy. A tenous institutional balance seems to have developed between the "mass organizations" and interest representatives on the one hand, and the foreign policy bureaucracy on the other. The benefactor-mediator-controller of this organizational juxtaposition is the Federal Executive Council and Josef Broz Tito.

A general characteristic of the contemporary Yugoslav system specifies: a marginally effective legislature slowly moving toward greater efficacy; a dominant executive relinquishing power over marginal foreign policy decisions; a structures yet non-functioning regional power distribution (Republics, proposed leadership collegium); and a embryonic functional power distribution at the national level. Lest the adjective veil the significance, we should force ourselves to compare these attributes with those of other East European political systems. The principal leadership

has already been discussed in some length. A few additional comments will suffice. Formulae for "stability of tenure" are difficult to apply to Yugoslavia. The rotation principle is a convenient veil behind which more meaningful changes than are readily
perceived take place. Few such changes are as public as the
Rankovic removal in '66. However, we know only a few of the elite
have remained consistently at or near the apex of power -- Tito,
Kardelj, and more recently Popovic. Maneuvering and "adjustments"
in the ranks are also concealed within the system by the continuity provided by Tito himself. Recruitment is elitist with exceptions coming in specialized bureaucratic roles or at lower levels,
and there is an unmistakable element of charisma in the executive
leadership of the contemporary political system.

The structure and institutional features of the international
system -- the East-West face-off, the emergence of new citizen-
states, the Communist system, the Eastern European sub-system,
and the United Nations Organization -- collectively constitute
one of the most helpful and illuminating determinants of Yugoslav
foreign policy. The international environment has been both the
shroud and the catalyst to the greatest adventures of Yugoslav
policy in different periods of her foreign relations. Those dimensions of the external environment listed above are the most overt
of the foreign policy determinants. Clearly, there is much overlap
among them but their individual impact can be found on specific
policy outputs. Policy in the early periods was *reactive* to the
foreign political environment in which Yugoslavia found itself.
Most assessments maintain that early foreign policy was made and
implemented in a crisis milieu because the post-war environment,
especially the Soviet dominated Communist system, was not as the
Yugoslav leadership had expected it to be. (30) Later, whether
because of ingenuity or necessity (probably both), it became increasingly clear that the peculiar situation in which Yugoslavia
found herself could be used as the foundation for a distinctive
foreign policy position in international systems. Since the collapse of the Soviet-Yugoslav Reconciliation of '55 the policy-
making establishment has seized the initiative and turned more
pragmatically to shaping or manipulating the environment to further her policy objectives. Examples would read like a catalogue
of Yugoslav foreign policy. One case is the "Non-aligned" theme
which blended the emergence of new or politically evolving states
with a widespread concern over the apparent independence of superpower foreign policy behavior in the international community. The
result was prestige and leadership of a third, ad hoc bloc of
citizen-states.

The best case may be the way in which the manifestations of
the vestages of the Cold War or the Soviet-American competition,
if you like, have been parlayed into a set of Yugoslav foreign
policies whose effectiveness is indeed impressive. "No Man's
Land" is a dangerous place to be unless you are the European answer to the Turkish bazaar merchant. With independence as the watch-

word and a foot in every camp, the emphasis is "business" with
the West, "socialism" with the East, and "politics" with the Third
World. This gross simplification is, in its essence, valid. It is
better formula, of course, than it is a practical guide to policy
since these are not three separate games, but three parts of the
same game. It is possible for the Yugoslavs to approach foreign
policy in this framework, one might hypothesize, because of the
varied priorities which exist in the institutionalized societies
in the Western, Eastern and Third Worlds. Ours is not called the
"capitalist" system because of its political priorities (save for
some periods of foreign political crusades); the communists are
themselves bound by the ideological emphasis of their system; and
the Third World finds the game of politics the cheapest and most
visible to play. The result: not the tightrope one might suspect.
Rather, the Yugoslavs are on the auction platform, and, like the
auctioneer, are dependent upon the market and the competition.
Carrying the analogy just a bit further, as long as the demand
remains (a function of the international environment), the independence and political insulation upon which the Yugoslavs place
such importance can also remain.

It is disturbing that this analysis cannot deal in more tangible terms with the *political process* as a determinant of Yugoslav
foreign policy. Some process-relevant propositions have been suggested implicitly. It is a part of the frustration that the contributors to this volume share -- a consequence of having distinct
and sometimes paramount restrictions placed upon the politically
relevant research which can be undertaken in and about these countries. Political communication and information linkages would be
particularly helpful in examining Yugoslav policy. Capacities for
mobilization contingent upon levels of modernization and a full
range of propositions about decisional style based upon studies
of speed and patterned development of decisions will be necessary
before we can have any confidence in our comparative conclusions.

Cultural and organizational determinants are of substantial
importance in analyzing foreign policy. The case of Yugoslavia,
whose predominant and distinguishing characteristic is the impact
of leadership factors on policy, does, nonetheless, offer us
enough evidence of the effects of "residuals" to put forth some
basic concluding propositions. There is relative autonomy for external policy in the Yugoslav political system. It has become
fairly well insulated from public opinion or concern. The general
public's position (including the lower or non-foreign policy
elites) is one of acquiescence, flexibility, or toleration although active support is often forthcoming from the various factions within the domestic environment.

Institutions and process will most certainly change when the
Presidency is passed on to either a new person or a new organizational entity. As this happens two critical questions should demand our attention. First, will interest group access increase
and if so for which groups, and second, will ideology remain an

amorphous set of principles as opposed to rigid guidelines for policy? If either one or both factors change, the domestic political system will have been fundamentally changed. Foreign policy would not escape the repercussions. However, if the political forces which come to power recognize that the present equilibrium has produced inordinate prestige and unprecedented stability in foreign relations and has successfully mollified the impact of domestic conflict on foreign policy issues, one would anticipate a concerted effort to maintain the system or to introduce change very cautiously.

Policy Outputs

Output or policy is the fourth and final segment of this chapter. The development of the first three "determinants" section has, of course, been reliant on a charting of the substantive course of Yugoslav foreign policy. To this end, a chronology of principal events of the post-World War II period is presented followed by a brief synopsis of the central themes of policy in the Seventies. (31) Finally some effort at a synthesis of comparative conclusions is offered.

Output has traditionally been the focus of foreign policy research. In this chapter it has been relegated a clearly secondary position on the premise that our greatest analytic need is for a comparative method for examining how foreign policy is made and which "forces" or factors determine its quantity, nature, effectiveness and propensity to change.

Table 9.5 which follows indicates clearly enough that Yugoslav foreign policy is a series of shifts and maneuvers designed, or at very least responding, to the amelioration of Yugoslav needs and interests to the international environment. The finesse and credibility with which it does this is impressive especially given that it is a new, Twentieth Century (or Post-War depending on your perspective) state whose capability factors are hardly impressive. The reader must be cautioned that the categorization ("pro-Soviet, pro-West, neutralist") has restricted itself to each event's superficial significance and impact. Before one accepts the specific classifications of Table 9.5, rather more in depth investigation of single events may be warranted.

Foreign policy in the Seventies has been and will be developed and executed along five substantive central themes:
1. "Non-alignment"
2. UN oriented policies (including supplementary international organizations)
3. Role in the Communist system (heretic, model, or whatever)
4. Foreign policy specifically contributing to domestic political development
5. Foreign policy of the economic sector (EEC, EFTA ties)
The sharpest problems and most volatile political challenges will

TABLE 9.5

CHRONOLOGY OF FOREIGN POLICY EVENTS 1946-1969

1946

Jan. 30, New Constitution a-
dopted on Soviet model ('36)

May 27, Tito in Moscow for
talks with Stalin

July 1, Trieste problem temporarily "solved" by Allies

Aug. 19, Two US planes shot down
by Yugo.--US ultimatum followed

1947

Sept. 21-28, Cominform established with Belgrade headquarters

---

1948

Feb. 10, Stalin warned Yugoslavs
on Balkan Federation plans

Mar. 18, SU recalled its mil.
and techn. advisors from Yugo.

June 28, Cominform expels Yugo.
Eight other C.P.'s denounce
(July)

July 21-28, Fifth Congress Y.C.P.
Tito denies charges and receives domestic support

Aug. 20, UN committee condemned
Yugo. for aid to Greek C.P.

Dec. 31, Belgrade announced
decrease in trade with Soviets

1949

June 2, Moscow openly support
anti-Tito political forces
in Yugoslavia

June-July, "Titoists" in other
EE states were purged; all EE
broke off econ. relations.
Econ. agreements with West
(US) made

Sept. 8, Amer. Import/Export
Bank granted Yugo. $20 million
loan

Sept. 27, SU denounced Aid and
Friendship Treaty, other EE
states followed

1950

Mar., Yugo/West relations developed (econ. and political)
Yugo. opposed China entry
into Korean War. Greek and
Italian relations normalized.

May 3, Tito declared Yugo. "neutral" between East and West.

Dec. 29, Truman authorized $38 mil-
lion Marshall Plan Funds for Yugo.

Table 9.5 continued

1952

July 13, US decided to send
Yugo. heavy mil. equip.,
including jet aircraft

Oct. 11, Djilas criticized
Stalin's economic theses

Dec. 17, Yugo broke diplomatic
relations with Vatican over
church/state relations

1953

Mar. 31, Tito announced
Churchill promosed protection
of Yugo. and Yugo. promised
to resist any aggressor

June 14, USSR requested dipl.
relations with Yugo. resume

Sept. 21, Yugoslavia sent ambassador to Moscow

Dec. 21, Yugoslavia sent ambassador to Tirana

1954

Jan. 17, Djilas expelled from
Central Comm. for criticizing
the system

Aug. 9, Greece, Turkey, and Yugo.
sign twenty-year political/
military mutual alliance

Oct. 5, Final settlement of
Trieste signed with Italy

1955

Jan. 5, USSR and Yugo. signed
formal trade agreement

June 2, Khrushchev-Tito communiqué
on foreign policy agreement (issues indicate victory for Tito);
Tito and Bulganin signed declaration of friendship and co-opera-
tion.

May 26. Khrushchev in Belgrade
with apology for rift and re-
newal of close ties

July 31, Soviet trade increased
60% by agreement

1956

Jan. 3, Soviets contracted to
build reactor in Yugoslavia

June 1-23, Tito received
warmly in Moscow

June 24, Tito visited Romania and
made agreement for closer ties

Sept. 19, Tito consulted with
Russians and Hungarians at Yalta

244

Table 9.5 continued

<u>1957</u>

Aug. 3, Tito and Khrushchev met secretly in Romania

Oct. 7, Yugo. recognized East Germany, West Germany severed relations

Sept. 5, New Class not permitted in Yugo. (Oct. 5 Djilas jailed)

Oct. 8-17, Zhukov visited Yugoslavia

Sept. 12, Gomulka visited Tito

Nov. 14, Congress of 12 Ruling Parties ended with Yugo. not signing the "Peace Manifesto"

<u>1958</u>

April, New LCY Program adopted at Seventh Congress

Dec. 22, US agreed to let Yugo. purchase $95 million of surplus agricult. goods

----

<u>1959</u>

Aug., Reports indicate Yugo. has largest army in EE outside the USSR

Sept. 21, Tito speech includes, "We have revised our practices... But..we are Marxist..Leninists."

<u>1960</u>

Sept. 28, Tito and Khrushchev met in NYC. Tito perceived snub by Eisenhower-no invitation to Washington, D.C.

Dec. 26, Tito delivered anti-Amer. speech in Belgrade

<u>1961</u>

Feb. 13, Tito began African tour, foci Egypt and Ghana

Nov. 13, Tito denounced Albanians and Chinese

Sept. 1-6, Non-aligned Conference in Belgrade (anti-US tinge)

Nov. 27, LCY backed Soviet stand against China

Oct. 13, US revealed sale of jet fighters to Yugo. Also trained pilots

----

<u>1962</u>

Dec. 3-21, Tito visited USSR and was highly honored

Table 9.5 continued
_____

1963

Apr. 7, Yugo. adopts new, more flexible constitution. "Socialist Federal Republic of Yugoslavia"

Apr., US moved to drastically cut US aid to Yugoslavia

Aug. 20, Khrushchev visited Yugoslavia

Sept. 26, Yugo-USSR conclude vast trade agreement

Oct. 16, Tito visited US. Kennedy received Tito at White House; demonstrations curtail Tito's travel plans in US

Oct. 22, Tito addressed UN for non-aligned cause (themes)

Nov. 30, Gheorgiu-Dej visited Belgrade. Yugo-Romanian relations cemented with "Iron Gate" agreement

Dec. 16-20, Yugo. sends first top dipl. mission to Czech. since '48

1964

Apr. 28, US announced huge wheat deal with Yugoslavia

June 1-8, Tito visited Finland as "neutralist"

July 19, Yugo-W.Germany econ. agreements. Foreign employment for Yugo. in spite of lack of dipl. relations

Sept. 7, Tito and Gheorghiu-Dej met at "Iron-Gate"

Sept. 10-14, Tito visited Budapest

Sept. 17, Tito stated that Yugo. would participate in CMEA

Sept. 21-26, Novotny (Czech) visited Yugoslavia

Oct. 5-11, Cairo Conference of non-aligned nations

1965

Apr. 30, Professor is sentenced for anti-Soviet book

June 8, Tito visited East Germany

June 18, Tito visited USSR

Nov. 15, Gomulka and Cyrankiewicz (Poland) visited Belgrade

July 25, New economic reforms officially announced

1966

June 25, Vatican-Yugo. protocol signed re-establishing dipl. relations

Sept. 26, Ulbricht visited Yugo.

246

Table 9.5 continued

<table>
<tr><td colspan="2">1966</td></tr>
<tr><td>July 1, Rankovic removed from leadership</td><td>Dec. 20, Anti-US (Vietnam) demonstrations in several Yugo.cities</td></tr>
<tr><td>Sept. 22-25, Brezhnev visited Yugoslavia</td><td></td></tr>
</table>

<table>
<tr><td colspan="2">1967</td></tr>
<tr><td>Jan. 28, Yugo. dipl. facilities bombed in US and Canada</td><td>June 23, Soviet mil.mission in Belgrade. Soviet planes and ships used Yugo. facilities</td></tr>
<tr><td>Apr. 24, Conference of Europe Communist Parties at Karlovy Vary. Yugoslavia attended</td><td></td></tr>
</table>

<table>
<tr><td colspan="2">1968</td></tr>
<tr><td>Jan. 10, Yugo. Premier visited Italy and Vatican</td><td>Aug. 4, Tito supported Czechoslovak Party</td></tr>
<tr><td>Jan. 22-23, Conference of Mediterranean Communist Parties in Rome, Yugo. denounced all foreign military presence</td><td>Aug. 9, Tito in Prague. Enthusiastic reception by Dubcek and Czechs</td></tr>
<tr><td>Jan. 31, West Germany and Yugo. re-established dipl. relations</td><td>Aug. 30, Johnson warns Soviets as pressure put on Yugo. and Roman.</td></tr>
<tr><td>Feb. 26-Mar.-5, Yugo. boycotted communist conference in Budapest</td><td>Sept. 9, Yugo. received heavy pressure from Soviet bloc. Tito was denounced by Soviet papers</td></tr>
<tr><td>Mar. 10, Tito visited Japan, expressed desire for another non-aligned conference</td><td>Sept. 26, Yugo. became "primary" target of Soviet attacks</td></tr>
<tr><td>Mar. 12, Bulgaria and Yugo. exchanged heated attacks</td><td></td></tr>
</table>

<table>
<tr><td colspan="2">1969</td></tr>
<tr><td>Feb. 10, Yugo. and W. Germany concluded economic treaty</td><td>June 25, Poland denounced Yugo.</td></tr>
<tr><td>Mar. 10, Tito opened LCY Congress with criticism of Soviet interference in other Socialist states</td><td>July 8-11, Consultative Meeting of Non-aligned Nations convened in Belgrade</td></tr>
</table>

Table 9.5 continued

<u>1969</u>

May 26-29, Italian Foreign Minister visited Belgrade	Dec. 13, Bulgarian-Yugo. talks break down
June 5-17, Yugo. boycotted Kremlin Conference of Communists and Workers' Parties	

come when these lines of policy tangle. When a friction develops between any two or more of these "modern tradition" policy themes, the Yugoslav system seems susceptible to a polarization along any number of issue or group defined lines. This would present the single greatest danger to the contemporary direction of Yugoslav foreign policy: the polarization of foreign policy interests among domestic political groups ("perspective" vs. "will", leadership groups or economic vs. political foreign policy interests). In either case the result, the internationalization of Yugoslav foreign policy, could become a challenge of major proportions to the political system not without reverberating consequences for all of Eastern Europe.

However, to date the Seventies have averted such problems in spite of very pronounced political stands on explosive issues including the June War, the Vietnamese War, the Czech crisis, and the Soviet-West German pact. This suggests not only that the confidence and stature of foreign policy are high but also, as posited earlier, that the foreign policy of Yugoslavia has been masterfully led *and* successfully insulated from domestic anxieties.

Conclusions

In a comparative sense, one will note that Yugoslavia has developed a foreign policy with a higher degree of flexibility than has any comparable state. Certainly this is true in Eastern Europe but more importantly Yugoslavia may have surpassed most contemporary states in the international community. Implicitly this leads us to examine the balance struck between ideological and pragmatic guidelines for foreign policy. The scope of her "situational" commitments actually enhances maintenance of the domestic political system and makes a substantial contribution to the expansion of the system's "capabilities". Broached with the question of the general responsiveness of the system to foreign policy inputs (or feedbacks), one finds that while the flow of domestic inputs is limited and in many senses secondary, responsiveness is good. Reaction and adjustment to the international milieu have been and remain swift and seemingly unencumbered by "prescriptive" forces.

One explanation for the low yield of domestic foreign policy inputs is the effectiveness of the "vanguard" function of the leadership. The theoretical literature gives us the concepts of "gain" and "lead" which regulate demands put upon the system.

Through the maze of apparent and non-apparent priorities of Yugoslav foreign policy, this chapter has provided an examination which points to the need in the early stages for Yugoslavia to survive. Identity in tact, in a hostile (at least perceived as such) world. To this end, the domestic political system as well as the substance of foreign policy had to be severely altered. In the contemporary period, priorities have diversified with the decreasing challenge from the outside. Foreign policy is now directed toward bolstering the rate of political and economic development, a task to which the valuable lessons of a rocky beginning can not profitably be applied.

This chapter was propagated on the premise that we do not adequately understand Yugoslav policy because of the inhibitions and limitations of the traditional foundations of foreign policy analysis. If, through the selected comparative framework applied in this chapter, we can better contest and/or enhance our thinking about Yugoslav policy, then the door is open for further scholarly and sophisticated pursuits. (32)

NOTES

1. David Wilkinson, *Comparative Foreign Relations: Framework and Methods* (Belmont, California: Dickinson Publishing, 1969).

2. Wilkinson, op. cit., pp. 33-34.

3. Norman Pounds, *Eastern Europe* (Chicago: Aldine Publishing, 1969).

4. See Richard Farkas, *Yugoslav Economic Development and Political Change* (New York: Praeger Publishers, 1975).

5. *Economist s World Outlook 1970*, Economic Intelligence Unit (London, 1970), p. 33.

6. Wilkinson, op. cit., p. 53. Also note the discussion of D.O.N. project.

7. Wilkinson, op. cit., p. 61.

8. Wilkinson, op. cit., pp. 62-63.

9. Those "indicators" of the comparative model. Wilkinson, op. cit., pp. 33-34.

10. A sample of the growing research literature on Eastern European elites can be found in numerous publications by Zaninovich, Welch, Beck, Fleron, Farrell, and Triska.

11. The most noteworthy and rigorous study is to be found in *Comparative Communist Political Leadership*, Carl Beck, et al. (New York: David McKay Publishers, 1973).

12. Wilkinson, op. cit., p. 73.

13. Cecil Crabb's treatment of American foreign policy and Cyril Black's Russian foreign policy are just two prominent examples

of the emphasis often placed on prescriptive influences in foreign policy.

14. Interviews were conducted during the summers of 1969 and 1970 and the winter of 1970. "Political elite" is interpreted loosely. Total interviews=107.

15. Wilkinson, op. cit., p. 73.

16. Ibid.

17. Wilkinson, op. cit., p. 75.

18. Zujovic and Hebrang were exceptions and levelled challenges to Tito's policy in its early stages.

19. The interview research conducted in 1969 and 1970 yielded this very pronounced and uniform awareness. The comparative study *Values in the Active Community* finds a similar sensitivity in Yugoslavia.

20. Almond and Verba, *Civic Culture*, Chapter 4, pp. 101-114.

21. Documented development of this argument may be found in P. Auty's, *Tito: A Biography*, Part IV.

22. Phyllis Auty's, *Tito: A Biography* (London: Longman, 1970). Especially Part IV, Chapters 14-17.

23. Wilkinson, op. cit., pp. 74-75.

24. Some recent studies, M. George Zaninovich's attitudinal and value study of Yugoslav communes prominent among them, have yielded results which reflect less attitudinal heterogeneity vis-à-vis the political system in general than is tradition-ally posited. These cast a new light on assessments of Yugo-slav "enculturation" and socialization.

25. Yugoslav elite studies: Farrell, "Foreign Policy Formation in the Soviet Union and Eastern Europe", 1966, Djordjevic, "Status and Role of Executive Organs...", Grozsdanic, "Administrative Management in Public Enterprises", 1966.

26. China and Cuba on various criteria might challenge Yugoslavia for the distinction.

27. Poland, Hungary, and Czechoslovakia are outstanding examples.

28. The Yugoslav Legislature ("Federal Assembly") is divided into five chambers: Social-Political Chamber, Economic Chamber,

251

Educational-Cultural Chamber, Chamber of Nationalities, and
Chamber of Public Health and Social Welfare. By the Letter of
the Yugoslav Constitution the above descrived "legislative
organs" are technically both legislative and executive organs
of the state.

29. Wilkinson, op. cit., p. 106 and Almond and Powell, *Comparative
Politics: A Developmental Approach*, p. 158.

30. Auty, op. cit., pp. 246-247.

31. Gathered from data presented in Langer, William (ed.),
Encyclopedia of World History (Boston: Houghton Mifflin, 1968),
and George Prpic, *A Century of World Communism* (New York:
Barron's Inc., 1970).

32. A bibliography for the study of Yugoslav foreign policy could
include: P. Auty, *Tito: A Bibliography* (London: Longman, 1970);
J. Campbell, *Tito's Separate Road* (Evanston: Harper and Row,
1967); V. Dedijer, *Stalin's Last Battle* (London, 1969);
M. Dijilas, *Conversations with Stalin* (London: Hart-Davis,
1962); E. Kardelj, *Socialism and War* (London: Methuen, 1961);
Nonaligned (Beograd: Jugoslavia Press, 1961); A. Rubenstein,
Yugoslavia and the Non-Aligned World (Princeton University
Press, 1970); *Tito: Selected Speeches and Articles, 1941-1961*
(Naprijed, Zagreb, 1963); W. Vucinich (ed.); *Contemporary
Yugoslavia* (Berkeley: University of California Press, 1969);
Yugoslavia's Way (New York: All Nations Press, 1958); see also
International Problems and *Review of International Affairs*,
both journals of The Institute of International Economics and
Politics, Belgrade.

Chapter X

INNOVATION IN EAST EUROPEAN FOREIGN POLICIES

*William C. Potter**

It has become fashionable recently to emphasize the dynamic character of communist political systems. Descriptions, explanations, predictions, and even the occasional celebration of revolutionary breakthrough, system transformation, and diffusion of innovation today fill the pages of many scholarly journals and books in the field of Soviet and East European studies. (1) Domestic political structure, ideology, economics, and social policy, as well as military doctrine and foreign relations, are among the topics of change that are analyzed. Interest in the process and product of change also seems to be fairly well distributed among those who regard political analysis as an art and those who see salvation in the pocket calculator. Unfortunately from the standpoint of theory building and accumulation of knowledge on change processes, enthusiasm over the discovery that communist nations also change has not been matched by rigorous concept specification or precision of analysis. As William Welsh points out, "political scientists have begun to devote some attention to the conceptual and operational problems involved in the longitudinal comparison of observations, but it remains the case that a substantial majority of the comments made about social change are highly descriptive and impressionistic and show little understanding of what economists have long since learned, i.e. that the study of change introduces... perplexing methodological issues not encountered when one is dealing with cross-sectional data." (2)

It is the purpose of this chapter to tackle some of the conceptual and operational problems in the study of political change. Because most discussions of change in Eastern Europe have emphasized the prospects for or constraints on domestic political change, this chapter focuses on the foreign policy dimension. Specifically, it seeks to: 1) clarify and provide operational measures for the

254

concept of *innovation* as distinguished from *nonconformity* and *change*; 2) view the foreign policy behavior of the East European states within a more general framework of national adaptation to internal and external demands; 3) identify the extent of continuity and change in several dimensions of East European foreign policy between 1948 and 1973; and 4) assess the relationship between a Warsaw Pact state's receptivity to foreign policy innovation (as indicated by changes in select foreign policy outputs) and changes in its domestic and external environment.

The chapter is divided into three parts. The first part, a theoretical overview, which sets forth a framework for viewing foreign policy change. It draws heavily upon the foreign policy as adaptive behavior "theory" of James Rosenau. The second part consists of a statement of and rationale for several research hypotheses regarding the association between change in demands emanating from the domestic and international environment and change in foreign policy outputs. It also suggests a method for measuring foreign policy innovation. The third part presents data on the evolution of foreign trade, treaty, defense spending, and United Nations voting behavior of the East European states between 1948 and 1973. Based upon this data innovation scores are calculated for each of the East European nations. Alternative explanations for the observed national differences in the consistency of foreign policy behavior of the East European states are then discussed. In particular, data on the level of economic development, intrabloc conflict, and leadership attributes are correlated with foreign policy innovation scores in order to test the hypotheses in the second part.

Nonconformity, Change, and Innovation

Although most scholars agree that over the past twenty years there has been considerable change in the foreign relations of the Warsaw Pact states, the nature of these changes and the factors responsible for them rarely have been subjected to systematic study that combines historical acumen with rigorous quantitative analysis. (3) Many studies of Soviet and East European foreign relations also fail to distinguish between new Warsaw Pact relations as deviations from a nation's own past policy goals and actions and new relations as a departure from Soviet policy aims and actions. The two deviations need not be the same. Romania between 1965 and 1968 for example, regularly deviated from the Soviet Union in the seven major committees of the United Nations General Assembly at the rate of four to seven deviant votes per one hundred votes cast -- a higher rate of deviant voting than any other member of the Warsaw Pact. In this respect, at least, Romania may be termed the most "innovative" or more precisely, nonconforming member of the Warsaw Pact. Between 1965 and 1968, however, Romania's voting record (vis-à-vis the Soviet Union) was rather stable, fluctuating from a 6.3% deviance rate in 1965 to a 6.7% deviance rate in 1968. In comparison, although Poland's voting record never reached the level of Romanian deviancy, the range and annual rate of change in Poland's voting record between 1965 and 1968 surpasses that of Romania's. (4) In other words, in terms of the *magnitude of change* during a four year period (another way of viewing innovative behavior) Romanian voting behavior was more constant and less "innovative" than was the voting behavior of Poland.

This example of a nation being both less conforming and yet more constant over time in one area of foreign policy illustrates the conceptual confusion apt to occur when the term *innovative behavior* is applied to both deviations from past policy and deviations from the present policy of a global or regional hegemony. (5) To reduce that confusion this chapter distinguishes between foreign policy *conformity*, foreign policy *innovation*, and foreign policy *change*.

Conformity in foreign policy is a relational concept that refers to the correspondence in kind and degree of the foreign policies of two or more states. In the context of this chapter, high conformity generally implies an unequal relationship between a regional hegemony and a regional subordinate. It is assumed that the hegemony restricts the freedom of foreign policy maneuver of the subordinate state or at least that the subordinate state acts as though its behavior is restricted. (6) In other words, a finding that there exists a high degree of correspondence between Soviet and East German foreign trade ratios with the "West" (i.e. trade with designated Western countries as a percentage of total Soviet and East German trade) would be interpreted as high East German conformity to at least one dimension of Soviet foreign policy. (7)

While conformity suggests the lack of independence in foreign policy, *change* refers to any transformation of or deviation from a nation's own prior policy. (8) Bulgaria's defense contribution to the Warsaw Pact, for example, may over a period of several years go up or down by one, two or ten percent. The contribution as a percentage of Bulgaria's central expenditures may or may not correspond closely to the rise or drop in the percentage of Soviet governmental expenditures for Warsaw Pact defense. Regardless of this correspondence or lack of it, change in Bulgaria's defense expenditures is simply the extent to which Bulgaria's defense spending varies over time.

Change, it is suggested, refers to any deviation from past policy. *Innovation* in foreign policy, by contrast, refers to a particular type of change -- change that is of a non-incremental nature. It also implies "implementation of a policy which is institutionalized and which is generally acknowledged to have systemic significance". (9) Precisely what constitutes non-incremental policy or the institutionalization of policy is not easily discerned and makes operationalization of the term hazardous. Nevertheless, it is useful to distinguish among different degrees of change, both in their "newness" (i.e., the order in which nations adopt a policy change), the magnitude of their departure from past policy, and their systemic importance and consequences.

I have argued elsewhere that most approaches to the study of foreign policy are negligent in explaining how and why foreign policies change. (10) In some instances this neglect stems from the implicit or occasionally explicit assumption that permanently operating factors, or at least relatively immutable conditions, rather than dynamic factors account for the foreign policy behavior of states. The "essentialist" image of Soviet foreign policy now unfashionable but at one time prevalent in the works of many Western cold warriors and Morgenthau's impression of "that astounding continuity in foreign policy" (11) are illustrative of this viewpoint. In other instances, even when the premises of the model are consistent with the notion of change, a theoretical or normative interest in equilibrium, preservation of the status quo, and systems maintenance may direct the attention of the analyst away from a focus on system transformation, adaptation, and policy change. (12)

To be sure, there are certain approaches in which foreign policy change is of theoretical interest. Unfortunately, those analysts who are interested tend to be overly restrictive in their focus on the conflict dimension of foreign affairs and to adopt unicausal explanations of foreign policy outputs (or at best to assess few competing, plausible determinants of foreign policy behavior). The power-capability theory of Organski and the interaction system approach of Triska and Finely are examples. (13) Moreover, there is a tendency to study either foreign policy inputs and process, process and outputs, inputs and outputs, or simply process or outputs independently rather than examining the interaction effects of the input, process, and output variables. (14) Finally, and most devastatingly for the development of a theory of foreign policy transformation, the few theorists who are interested in foreign policy change and attempt to examine multiple determinants fail -- as do most of their less change oriented foreign policy colleagues -- to provide research hypotheses in a form amenable to empirical testing. (15) Even Michael Brecher's input-output framework (16) which is multicausal in conception, purports to be dynamic, and is demonstrably research oriented, is deficient as a framework for explaining or predicting changes in foreign policy. It recognizes that foreign policies change, but it provides no rationale for change other than to suggest that the operational and psychological environments of decision-makers are in a continuous state of interaction with foreign policy outputs.

Although most of the major frameworks for the study of foreign policy inadequately address the issue of policy change, there are a few -- very few -- monographs that deal specifically with foreign policy adaptation and change. (17) James Rosenau's imaginative essay on "The Adaptation of National Societies: A Theory of Political System Behavior and Transformation" is especially relevant to the focus of this study.

Underlying Rosenau's "theory" is the assumption that "... all

foreign policy actions undertaken by a national society stem from
at least one common source, namely, the need to keep essential
structures (18) within acceptable limits by achieving a balance
between the changes and demands from within the society on the one
hand and the changes and demands from its salient environment on
the other." (pp. 3-4). According to Rosenau, there are four basic
orientations or strategies a nation may pursue in order to adjust
to internal and external demands. They are the politics of acquiescent adaptation, intransigent adaptation, promotive adaptation,
and preservative adaptation and are distinguished by their relative responsiveness to changes and demands emanating from domestic
political, social, economic, and physical structures (i.e. internal determinants) and demands and changes emanating from the external environment. Patterns of acquiescent adaptation presumably
stem from perceptions of a preponderance of external demands,
intransigent patterns from salient internal demands, promotive
patterns from the absence of either intense internal or external
constraints, and preservative patterns from the conflict between
severe domestic and foreign demands. These adaptation strategies,
in turn, are assumed to lead to or be associated with differences
in twenty types of domestic and external political behavior and
structure. (19)

Unlike most other foreign policy framework, Rosenau's adaptation theory explicitly addresses the issue of foreign policy change.
It also combines environmental and domestic determinants of foreign
policy behavior and suggests that national adaptation strategies
mediate between foreign policy inputs and outputs. (29) In Rosenau's
words, although his "theory of national adaptation is cast at an
extremely high level of abstraction, it does lend itself to research and empirical testing." (p. 21). At a minimum, his essay
does generate hypotheses which are amenable to empirical tests.

As an explanation of foreign policy change there are two major
difficulties with Rosenau's theory: 1) a failure to specify in
unambiguous fashion where causation is located and 2) a failure to
discuss the conditions under which changes in internal and external demands occur. The remainder of this section and the propositional inventory that follows seek to remedy these deficiencies.
They draw extensively upon concepts developed by Rosenau, but try
to specify more precisely, and in a fashion conducive to testing,
the causal relationship between domestic and external demands and
changes in foreign policy outputs.

A major deficiency of Rosenau's theory of foreign policy as
adaptive behavior is the lack of precision and consistency in
identifying the causal and outcome variables. At one point (p. 5)
the four types of national adaptation are said "to lead to important differences in political behavior and form", presumably differences in the twenty categories of political behavior and form
previously identified. (Emphasis added.) These categories, however,
are identified (Figure 10.1) as "Characteristics of Four Types of
Adaptation". It is unclear whether they are meant to be indicators

of the concept "adaptation type" or the product of different
adaptation strategies. At a later point in the essay (p. 16)
Rosenau inquires as to "what conditions must be present for a society to adhere to acquiescent, intrasigent, promotive, or preservative orientations?" He suggests that the rank order of potency
of "Four Clusters of Independent Variables" will vary in each of
the four types of national adaptation (p. 16). These four variable
clusters assumed to be the sources of different national adaptation types are labeled systemic, societal, individual, and governmental. But many of the indicators of these clusters of so-called
independent variables are the same indicators that are used to
distinguish among adaptation types (p. 6) and also are assumed to
be the "result" of the four types of adaptation. (21) (p. 6) As
Figure 10.1 indicates, one thus has a causal model in which the
same factors appear not only as *indicators* of different concepts
but also as one of the *concepts*.

A modified version of Rosenau's causal model is present in
Figure 10.2. It retains his principal concepts, but specifies more
precisely the relationship believed to exist between the domestic
and external structural attributes of the operational environment,
the psychological environment of the decision-makers, and the
foreign policy behavioral outputs which identify the national
adaptation strategy. As Figure 10.2 indicates, elements in the
operational environment do not directly affect the *choice* of adaptation strategies or policy action, but rather set the parameters
for operational outcome of the decisions once they are implemented.
The psychological environment, it contrast, directly affects the
selection of an adaptation strategy and consists of decision-maker
perceptions of demands arising from the domestic and external sectors of the operational environment. In other words, it is assumed
that differences in domestic and external structure are associated
with the kind and degree of perceived demands and that differences
in perceived demands, in turn, are associated with specific adaptation strategies.

Elsewhere I have proposed a more complex framework that details
the anticipated, cause-effect relationship between specific foreign policy structural variables, decision-maker perceptions of
demands, from the operational environment and different adaptation
strategy outputs. (22) Here it is sufficient to note that one may
distinguish theoretically among adaptation strategies in terms of
a number of areas of foreign policy activity including trade,
alliance, defense spending, diplomatic contact, international organization, and interventionary behavior. These types of behavior
may be evaluated in terms of their constancy or rate of change and
their independence or conformity to the behavior of the regional
hegemon. One also may distinguish between policy change which is
dictated by another actor (most likely the regional hegemon) and
voluntary policy initiation (perhaps based upon the conscious
emulation of another state's successful policy innovation). Figure
10.3 suggests the relationship between the four types of adaptation

FIGURE 10.1

ROSENAU'S CAUSAL MODEL

	p. 16	p. 5	p. 6
CONCEPTS:	"Cluster of Independent Variables" (e.g., governmental variables)	Adaptation Type (e.g., Acquiescent)	Character of the Party System (e.g., one party dominant)
INDICATORS:	Character of the Party System (e.g., one party dominant)	Character of the Party System (e.g.,	Character of the Party System (e.g., one party dominant)
MEASURES:	(% of Vote Polled by Opposition Parties)	(% of Vote Polled by Opposition Parties)	(% of Vote Polled by Opposition Parties)*

* This is a plausible measure, although not one provided by Rosenau.

FIGURE 10.2

MODIFIED ROSENAU CAUSAL MODEL

CONCEPTS:	Operational Environment	Psychological Environment	Adaptation Strategy
INDICATORS:	Domestic and external structural variables (e.g., population, level of economic development, distance from super-power)	Decision-maker perceptions of demands emanating from the domestic and external sectors of the operational environment	Foreign trade, alliance defense, spending, diplomatic contact, interventionary behavior, etc.
MEASURES:	GNP/capita, miles, etc.	Content analysis of decision-maker records	Trade with regional hegemony as % of total trade, defense expenditures as a % of central governmental expenditures, etc.

261

FIGURE 10.3

DECISION-MAKER PERCEPTION OF

INTERNAL AND EXTERNAL DEMANDS

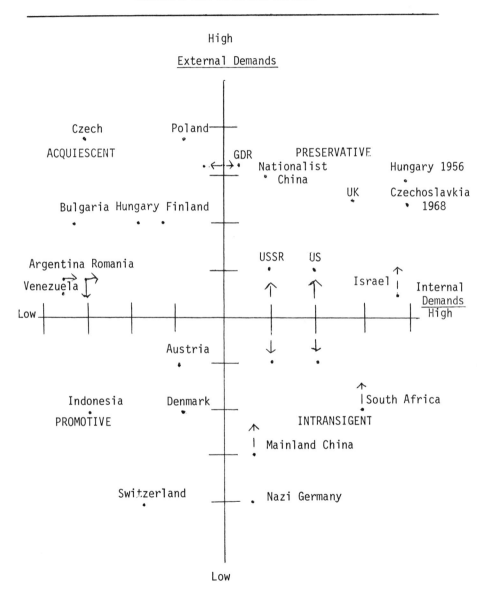

strategies and the differential demands from domestic and foreign
sectors. A number of nations are placed in the different cells for
illustrative purposes, although the validity of their assignment
spots along the two axes is yet to be empirically tested.

The Determinants of Innovation: A Propositional Inventory

If one accepts Rosenau's argument that foreign policy behavior
is a result of decision-maker responsiveness to internal and external demands (or in the case of promotive adaption, the absence
of such demands), it follows that change in foreign policy behavior, whether this be transformation from one adaptation strategy
to another or less extensive change, results from changes in
decision-maker perceptions of demands. According to our framework,
fundamental changes in the operational environment such as transformation of the economy, a change in the prevailing ideology, or
the emergence of a new political force (perhaps due to war, revolution, or sustained depression) might be expected to modify significantly decision-maker perceptions of demands and thereby lead
to a shift in foreign policy behavior. Less apparent, however, are
the conditions short of major domestic and external upheaval that
produce changes in the perception of demands associated with foreign policy innovation. The next portion of this chapter identi-
fies a number of conditions hypothesized to be associated with
foreign policy innovation. They by no means exhaust the list of
plausible determinants, but represent examples of internal and
external factors that might be expected to modify decision-maker
perceptions of demands. A brief rationale for each proposition and
a method for testing it follow the proposition. It is emphasized
that although the quantitative portion of this study focuses on
the foreign policy behavior of the East European states, the following propositions and their theoretical assumptions are not intended to be country specific. (23)
    Hypothesis One: The greater a subordinate regional state's con-
flict with the regional hegemon, the greater will be its innovation in foreign policy. (24)
    Many studies have pointed to a relationship between individual
and organizational search and policy innovation and conditions
that generate stress. (25) James Q. Wilson, for example, maintains
that "many organizations will adopt no major innovation unless
there is a 'crisis' -- an extreme change in conditions for which
there is no adequate response." (26) As Havelock et al. point out,
"The conservative forces in organizations are often such that they
can be moved significantly only by major shocks from their environment which threaten their very existence." (27) James March and
Herbert Simon also suggest that past programs of action may be
abandoned when external changes impose "deadlines" or create other
threats to organizational goals. (28) According to Donald Schon,
"In individuals and organization it is easy to underestimate the

strength of the dynamisms that tend to keep things as they are.
Only the strongest incentives can lead an organization to effective
deliberate change. Something like a state of crisis rate, its survival as it has been, is threatened." (29)

Although the effect of crisis on innovation has received some
attention in the organizational decision-making literature, there
is little empirical evidence (or speculation for that matter) in
the area of international relations to support the hypothesized
relationship between crisis -- generated by real or imagined
threats to decision-makers -- and policy innovation by organizations. Nor is there much empirical evidence regarding the relationship between degree of international conflict and decision-maker
perception of stress. It is not unreasonable, however, to hypothesize that a positive relationship exists between the amount of
interstate conflict and decision-maker perception of stress, and
that intensified demands on decision-makers as a consequence of
interstate conflict promote innovative foreign policy behavior.
The hypothesis further suggests that while the focal point of a
regional hegemon's foreign policy probably will be the behavior of
a rival hegemon, the aspiration levels and performance goals of
decision-makers of regional subordinate states are more likely to
be set in relation to the regional hegemon than in relation to non-
regional actors. In other words, the state of relations between
the regional subordinate and the hegemon is apt to be the principal source of anxiety for decision-makers in subordinate states.

Correlation analysis is used to examine the relationship between intrabloc conflict and foreign policy innovation. Methods
for calculating a nation's foreign policy innovation score are
discussed below in the section "Measuring Innovation". The degree
of intrabloc conflict is tapped by the Moses International con-
flict-cooperation scale. (30) "The Moses scale assigned to each
event involving an actor nation acting toward a target nation a
value from 1 to 30. The values near the low end of the scale are
characterized by intense conflict." (31) The Moses scale is used
to analyze the extensive Warsaw Pact nation events data set (for
the years 1948-1970) collected by Barry Hughes. (32) Average conflict intensity scores are calculated fore select intrabloc dyads.

Hypothesis Two: Foreign policy innovation is apt to be greatest
among those states which experience the greatest change in leadership attributes.

In a study of East European leadership attributes Carl Beck
examines the relationship between change and continuity in the
distribution of leadership characteristics in four East European
states and the "gross characteristics of political outcomes in
these countries in comparative and historical perspective. (33) He
finds, among other things, that basic stability in elite attributes
over time is associated with constancy of political outcomes and
political structure.

Beck's study, although very interesting and informative as a
survey of the evolution of East European elite attributes, does

not adequately test the relationship between change in elite characteristics and change in policy outputs. Nor does Beck provide a theoretical rationale for expecting changes in elite attributes to be associated with changes in particular policy outputs. The reason for the tentative nature of his findings results from the fact, readily admitted by Beck, that only elite attributes and not political outcomes are measured and subjected to statistical analysis. (34) This deficiency is less troublesome in the present study, however, since measures of change of four areas of foreign policy behavior (trade, treaty, defense spending, and United Nations voting) also have been calculated for a twenty-three year time period. The Rosenau adaptation framework in its modified form also provides a plausible explanation for the anticipated association between changes in elite characteristics and changes in policy outputs. Differences in such factors as age, party education, revolutionary and partisan activity, international background, and technical education, it is hypothesized, are apt to be associated with differences in the modal operational code or psychological environment through which decision-makers view the world. A change in elite attributes, therefore, may lead to a change in the elite's perception of the intensity of conflicting demands emanating from the domestic and foreign scene. This, in turn, may lead to a change in policy output.

The data source for the elite background analysis is the machine-readable holdings of the University of Pittsburgh's Archive on Political Elites in Eastern Europe. Nine attributes reflecting both demographic and career characteristics for Central Committee members of Bulgaria, Czechoslovakia, Hungary, Poland, and Romania are analyzed for the period between 1958 and 1970. (35) Table 10.1 presents the list of elite attributes in dichotomous form. The percentage of Central Committee members possessing each attribute for every year is first calculated. The coefficient of variability statistic is then computed in order to describe the homogeneity or constancy of each attribute over time. This statistic, used by Beck in his analysis of elite change, is simply the standard deviation divided by the mean. The lower the coefficient, the more constant or homogeneous the variable. (36) The mean coefficient of variability for all the elite attributes is then calculated for each country. By ranking nations in terms of their coefficient of variability and then correlating this ranking with one based upon foreign policy innovation scores a simple indication of the degree to which change in elite attitudes is associated with foreign policy innovation is provided.

TABLE 10.1

EAST EUROPEAN LEADERSHIP ATTRIBUTES

ATTRIBUTE	INDICATOR
Rural	Rural place of birth (under 25,000 population)
Party education, foreign	Party education in the USSR
Partisan	Partisan or underground activity during World War II
Party membership	Communist Party member prior to 1945
Revolutionary	Revolutionary activity before World War II
Technical education	Education at a commercial or polytechnical institute
International background	Member of a diplomatic mission, employee or member of an international commission, delegate to an international conference
University education	University education complete or incomplete
Age	Less than 40 years old

Hypothesis Three: There is a positive relationship between a nation's level of economic development and the degree of innovation in its foreign policy.

Many observers of organizational behavior have pointed to the relationship between an organization's relative size and wealth and its propensity to innovate. (37) In his study of "The Diffusion of Innovation among the American States" Walker also finds that "the larger, wealthier, more industrialized states adopt new programs somewhat more rapidly than their smaller less well developed neighbors." (38) Kintner and Klaiber hypothesize that nations highly developed socio-economically will be "less willing to follow blindly the foreign policy dictates of another state (i.e., they will be more immune from external demands) and more inclined directly and independently to formulate their goals and objectives." (39) If this is the case, one might predict that a change in foreign policy outputs and adaptation strategy would result if internal economic developments made the society less (or more) susceptible to external demands. This is consistent with some "convergence theories" which assume that changes in foreign policy behavior as well as social and economic policy will accompany changes in economic development. Is one justified in making inferences about nation-state innovative behavior based upon research at subnational levels of analysis? Do differences in economic development among states account for differences in foreign policy outputs? Testing Hypothesis 3 should enable one to better answer these questions.

Correlation analysis is used to determine the relationship between economic development and foreign policy innovation. Probably the most commonly employed indicator of economic development is GNP per capita. Reliable GNP (or NMP) data for the 1948 to 1973 time period for many of the Warsaw Pact states, however, are unavailable. Consequently, another frequently used indicator of economic development is employed, electric energy production (million kilowatt hours) per capita. (40)

In the theoretical overview an effort was made to distinguish between the concepts of foreign policy change and innovation. Change, it was suggested, refers to any deviation from a nation's prior policy. Innovation, by contrast, implies the adoption and institutionalization of a policy that has systemic significance and is considerably different from existing policy. Magnitude of change, duration of change, and systemic consequences of change, therefore, are regarded as the defining attributes of innovation. Admittedly, these indicators of innovation are not precise. As Braybrooke and Lindblom point out, "whether a change is called 'large' or 'small' depends on the value attached to it, and this value can vary from person to person." (41) It also may be argued that "any change is non-incremental if one counts its indefinitely cumulating consequences from here to eternity." (42) In addition, there is apt to be some disagreement over whether or not a policy change has systemic significance. Nevertheless, as Braybrooke and Lindblom note, the notion of small is not as subjective and personal as previously implied, "for in any society there develops a strong tendency toward convergence in estimates of what changes are important or unimportant." (43) Although no sharp line divides incremental from non-incremental change, one may identify as non-innovative changes that are ephemeral and erratic (i.e., of a short duration and having no apparent course or purpose) and changes that are trivial because they have little or no impact on important systemic variables (what Rosenau refers to as "essential structures").

Ideally, one would retain all of the indicators of innovation in the quantitative analysis of the evolution of East European foreign policy behavior between 1948 and 1973. Unfortunately, no meaningful operational definition of systemic impact was found. (44) Innovation scores, therefore, are calculated on the basis of two rather than three criteria: 1) magnitude of change, and 2) constancy of direction of change. A preliminary survey of the data suggested that a 3% yearly change baseline was discriminating for all foreign policy indicators but treaty behavior. That is, annual changes in foreign policy outputs of 3% or more were sufficiently uncommon to exclude fluctuations that might arise due to changes in the data's reliability over time and changes of a nonpurposive, "muddling through" or incremental character. In order to tap the institutionalization dimension of the concept of innovation only foreign policy change which is in the same direction (or more precisely, not in an opposite direction) for two or more consecutive years is counted. (45) An I score equal to the percentage change over the previous year, therefore, is assigned whenever the change is at least 3% and when there is no reversal in the direction of change for a minimum of two years. (46) The only exception to this rule is when I scores for treaty behavior are calculated. Because of the great variability in treaty activity (due in part to the small number of treaties signed each year) the 3% rule was increased by a factor of ten. A change of 30%, therefore, is necessary before a country receives an innovation score in the treaty dimension. Annual innovation scores are calculated for each country by summing the I scores for each indicator of foreign policy behavior.

One conclusion that emerged from the theoretical overview was that few studies adequately address the issue of how and why foreign policies change. A positive response to a logically antecedent question "Do foreign policies change?" was taken for granted. For many countries there seems little reason to challenge this assumption, although consensus as to the magnitude and dates of change may be lacking. In any case, data usually are available to provide empirical support for or against the proposition. In the case of Eastern Europe, however, there is a paucity of time series data and analyses which employ multiple indicators of foreign policy behavior. (47) In the absence of longitudinal and multifactor studies of foreign policy outputs, claims as to the permanence or flux in the foreign relations of the East European states can be regarded, at best, as tenuous.

The section that follows presents data which should facilitate the testing of a number of hypotheses regarding foreign policy change and innovation on the part of the East European nations. It is divided into two parts. The first part presents data and a brief commentary on East European foreign trade, treaty, defense spending, and United Nations voting behavior between 1948 and 1973. Based upon this data, innovation scores are calculated for each of the countries. The second part discusses alternative explanations for the observed national differences in the constancy of foreign policy behavior of the East European states.

Foreign Trade as an Indicator of Innovation

Foreign trade is one of several indicators of foreign policy behavior identified in our national adaptation framework. Its importance as an indicator of foreign policy intent and interdependence often has been observed. A statement from the "Report on the Political Aspects of East-West Trade" made by the Political Committee of the Consultative Assembly of the Council of Europe is illustrative of this point of view: "The problem of East-West trade is primarily a political one... Born of politics, it lives by politics and is constantly engendering political options for which, as often as not, economics merely provide a more or less useful pretext." (48) More specifically, Robert Dean notes that in order to understand the development of political relations between the Warsaw Pact states and the Federal Republic of Germany one must recognize the "great extent (to which) trade is a strategic variable in the foreign policies it reflects." (49)

Although one also may exaggerate the degree of correspondence between economic transactions and political intent, the foreign policy significance of trade is especially apparent among nations whose economies are centrally planned and whose governments exercise close control over international trade flows. (50) As this is the case for the East European nations our study of change in the foreign policy behavior of the Warsaw Pact states begins with a description of the evolution of their trade behavior between 1948 and 1973. Tables 10.2-10.5 provide data on three categories of foreign trade: 1) each East European nation's trade (combined imports and exports) with the Soviet Union as a percentage of its total trade; 2) each East European state's trade with the "West" as a percentage of its total trade (51); and 3) each East European nation's trade with West Germany as a percentage of its total trade. The rationale for selecting these particular areas of trade was a desire to include politically significant and sensitive trade partners among whom one might most expect changes in foreign trade to mirror changes in political intent.

TABLE 10.2

TRADE WITH THE USSR AS A PERCENTAGE OF TOTAL TRADE*

	Bulgaria	Czech	GDR	Hungary	Poland	Romania
1948		16.2	20.2	19.0	22.0	
1949			37.7	23.2	19.1	
1950	52.2	27.5	39.7	26.8	26.6	
1951			45.6	29.1	25.0	
1952	57.1	34.9	42.3	29.7	32.5	
1953	49.7	35.5	45.7	33.4	33.5	
1954	46.3	35.0	44.1	30.3	37.6	
1955	48.9	34.5	38.2	21.8	32.1	
1956	45.3	31.8	40.9	23.6	30.6	
1957	53.5	34.0	44.6	29.3	30.6	
1958	53.2	33.0	42.8	26.9	26.2	51.5
1959	52.2	35.6	44.9	29.7	29.8	47.3
1960	53.1	34.4	42.8	30.2	30.3	40.1
1961	52.1	33.6	43.7	33.5	30.6	40.4
1962	53.3	37.8	48.9	36.0	32.5	40.6
1963	54.0	39.0	48.6	34.3	33.7	41.9
1964	53.0	37.5	46.6	34.7	32.7	42.2
1965	51.1	36.9	42.8	35.6	33.1	38.8
1966	49.2	33.5	41.4	33.1	32.2	33.5
1967	51.3	35.0	41.9	34.7	35.2	28.2
1968	54.2	33.6	42.6	37.1	35.9	28.7
1969	55.2	33.7	41.2	35.9	36.7	27.3
1970	53.0	32.5	39.1	34.0	36.5	27.0
1971	53.6	32.7	38.2	34.5	35.5	25.0
1972	54.3	33.6	37.7	35.4	33.2	24.5
1973	53.3	30.8				

* The entries are for combined imports and exports. Figures are based on c.i.f. imports and f.o.b. exports. Percentage figures for years 1948-1969 are derived from data in Paul Marer (1972). Entries for 1970-1973 are based upon data in the United Nations annual *Yearbook of International Trade Statistics*.

270

TABLE 10.3

TRADE WITH THE WEST AS A PERCENTAGE OF TOTAL TRADE*

	Bulgaria	Czech	GDR	Hungary	Poland	Romania
1948						
1949						
1950						
1951						
1952						
1953						
1954						
1955						
1956	11.4	17.0	20.5	28.8	30.7	
1957	11.6	18.4	19.2	23.0	32.2	
1958	16.5	16.6	18.8	21.2	32.7	17.0
1959	18.2	15.7	17.9	22.4	29.4	15.3
1960	18.1	16.0	18.0	22.8	28.7	21.9
1961	11.1	17.7	17.8	21.6	29.2	25.3
1962	12.4	14.1	15.6	21.1	27.1	24.8
1963	13.2	15.0	15.7	23.3	26.1	24.1
1964	16.4	15.5	17.9	23.8	26.9	24.4
1965	16.9	16.4	19.3	23.5	25.0	26.7
1966	20.9	18.7	19.8	24.8	27.8	31.7
1967	17.5	18.4	18.5	24.1	26.7	37.1
1968	15.6	19.2	17.0	20.7	26.3	34.8
1969	13.5	20.2	18.6	24.8	25.1	34.4
1970	15.1	21.3	20.5	27.4	25.0	34.2
1971	13.9	18.9	20.8	24.0	25.1	32.2
1972	12.5	20.2	21.8	23.9	29.2	35.3
1973	13.4	19.7				

* The entries are for combined imports and exports. Data for
1956-1966 was obtained from Kintner and Klaiber (1971). Entries
for 1967-1973 are based upon data in the United Nations annual
Yearbook of International Trade Statistics.

TABLE 10.4

TRADE WITH WEST GERMANY AS A PERCENTAGE OF TOTAL TRADE*

	Bulgaria	Czech	GDR	Hungary	Poland	Romania
1948						
1949						
1950						
1951						
1952						
1953			6.8	3.3		
1954	2.7		8.8	4.6		
1955	2.8	2.1	10.9	6.1		
1956	2.8	3.5	11.0	6.4		
1957	3.4	4.2	11.3	5.1	4.7	
1958	3.7	4.0	11.2	5.3	5.0	5.2
1959	6.0	3.6	11.1	5.6	5.6	4.2
1960	4.7	3.4	10.3	5.4	5.2	6.6
1961	3.2	3.3	9.3	5.2	4.8	7.1
1962	3.3	3.0	8.5	4.6	4.1	7.5
1963	3.9	2.6	8.7	4.8	4.0	6.7
1964	4.1	3.1	9.4	5.2	4.0	6.5
1965	4.6	3.4	9.5	5.2	4.4	8.0
1966	6.2	3.2	10.2	5.6	4.0	9.3
1967	4.0	3.3	9.0	5.1	4.2	12.0
1968	3.7	3.6	8.6	4.4	4.4	9.0
1969	2.8	5.0	10.1	5.0	4.3	8.7
1970	2.6	5.5	10.2	5.9	4.9	8.6
1971	2.5	5.8	10.2	5.9	5.4	8.5
1972	2.9	5.4	10.3	6.5	7.2	9.5
1973	3.4	5.9				

* The entries are for combined imports and exports. Entries for all years are based upon data in the United Nations annual *Yearbook of International Trade Statistics*. These figures correspond closely with those compiled by Dean (1974). Exceptions are Romania in 1970 (Dean's figure is 7.3) and Poland for all years between 1962 and 1972. Dean's Polish figures are highly suspect and may be the result of a printing error.

TABLE 10.5

DESCRIPTIVE STATISTICS OF TRADE BY AREA AS
PERCENTAGE OF TOTAL TRADE (1948-1973)

	Mean Trade	Total Change*	Ave.Annual Change	Range	Max	Min	Standard Deviation
BULGARIA							
USSR	52.1	48	2.3	11.8	57.1	45.3	2.73
West	14.9	34	2.0	9.8	20.9	11.1	2.78
FRG	3.7	8	.4	3.7	6.2	2.5	1.05
CZECHOSLOVAKIA							
USSR	33.4	30	1.4	22.8	39.0	16.2	4.38
West	17.7	21	1.2	7.2	21.3	14.1	2.04
FRG	3.9	6	.3	3.8	5.9	2.1	1.11
GDR							
USSR	41.7	76	3.1	28.7	48.9	20.2	5.47
West	18.7	18	1.1	6.2	21.8	15.6	1.70
FRG	9.8	9	.5	4.5	11.3	6.8	1.15
HUNGARY							
USSR	30.9	59	2.5	18.1	37.1	19.0	4.97
West	23.6	29	1.7	8.1	28.8	20.7	2.12
FRG	5.3	12	.6	3.2	6.5	3.3	.74
POLAND							
USSR	31.3	56	2.3	18.5	37.6	19.1	4.57
West	27.9	22	1.4	7.7	32.7	25.0	2.46
FRG	4.8	6	.4	3.2	7.2	4.0	.88

continued

Table 10.5 continued

ROMANIA

USSR	35.8	33	2.4	27.0	51.5	24.5	8.60[+]
West	28.0	34	2.6	21.8	37.1	15.3	6.87[+]
FRG	7.8	15	1.0	7.8	12.0	4.2	1.91[+]

* Total change figures represent the sum of annual percentage point changes (rounded off each year to the nearest percentage point).

[+] Note that in each area of trade the standard deviation, a common measure of dispersion, is greatest for Romania.

As Tables 10.2-10.5 indicate, the countries of the Warsaw Pact are not and have not been homogeneous in their trade "preferences". Between 1950 and 1973, for example, Bulgaria consistently devotes a greater percentage of its total trade to Soviet imports and exports than any other East European country. In only five of these years does Bulgarian trade with the Soviet Union slip below 50% of Bulgarian total trade and in no instance below 45%. Czechoslovak, Hungarian and Polish trade with the USSR, on the other hand, never exceeds 40% of their total trade figures. (In the area of trade with the USSR the extremes are 16.2% of Czechoslovak total trade in 1948 and 57.1% of Bulgarian trade in 1952.) Similar disparties are apparent in the categories of trade with the West and trade with West Germany. Romania in 1967, for example, has the highest percentage of total trade in both categories, 37.1% with the West and 12.0% with West Germany. In the same year no other East European state maintained more than 27% of its total trade with the West and only East Germany, among the other Warsaw Pact countries, devoted more than 5.1% of its total trade to West German imports and exports.

More interesting, perhaps, and less often noted in accounts of East European trade are the differences in the patterns of evolution of trade among the Warsaw Pact countries. As the descriptive statistics in Table 10.5 indicate, the East European states differ substantially in the continuity of their trade behavior. Whereas the range of Bulgarian trade with the Soviet Union, the West and West Germany never exceeds 12% for a twenty-four year time span, Romania, in a much shorter period of time demonstrates a much wider range of trade behavior (27% in trade with the Soviet Union, 22% in trade with the West, and 8% in trade with the Federal Republic of Germany). The extent of fluctuation in Romanian trade vis-à-vis the other East European states is particularly noteworthy if one looks only at trade patterns after 1958, the first date for which reliable statistics on Romanian trade are available. Since 1958

the range of Romanian trade with the Soviet Union is almost two
and one-half times that of any other East European country, Romanian imports and exports to the USSR dropping from 51.5% of total
Romanian trade in 1958 to under 25% in 1972. The range of Romanian
trade with the West also is over twice that of any other Warsaw
Pact state (including the Soviet Union) and jumps from 17% of
total trade in 1958 to over 35% in 1972. (52) Finally, the range
of Romanian trade with West Germany is almost two times that of
its nearest Warsaw Pact competitor. (53) A closer look at Tables
10.2-10.4 further indicates that by far the greatest variation in
the range of trade with the Soviet Union for Czechoslovakia, the
German Democratic Republic, and Poland occured during the early
post-World War II years of communist political consolidation in
Eastern Europe.

Defense Spending as an Indicator of Innovation

One of the few dimensions of Soviet and East European foreign
policy that has received careful attention in terms of quantitative, time-series analysis is military expenditures. A number of
time-series studies, for example, focus on the interdependence of
US and Soviet defense spending or propose alternative explanations
for the size of the Soviet military budget. (54) Several recent
works also probe the dynamics of intra-Warsaw Pact defense relations, particularly the association between level of economic development and the size of defense expenditures. (55)
A difficulty that each of these studies shares -- indeed a problem common to any study of comparative Warsaw Pact defense expenditures -- is the absence of reliable budgetary information and the
lack of consensus among Western scholars as to the proper method(s)
for estimating defense expenditures. Many analysts are of the opinion that official Soviet and East European defense figures substantially and consistently understate actual military outlays. The
1973-74 issue of *The Military Balance*, for example, notes the
"implausibly static" nature of official Soviet defense spending
figures at just under 18 billion roubles since 1969 and suggests
that a more accurate estimate of defense costs should include "a
more precise allowance for manpower costs" (p. 8). Among other
things, this "more precise allowance" entails assumptions that:
1) Soviet manpower related costs resemble US costs in terms of
their share of the defense budget; 2) 70-80% of the Soviet All
Union science budget is for the defense related costs; and 3) rouble
defense figures should be converted into dollars at the rate of 0.5
roubles to one dollar. This yields as estimate of $87.2-90.6 billion
for manpower and non-manpower defense costs for 1973 (pp. 8-9).
It also yields, however, an estimate which the cumulative impact
of uncertainties is enormous. (56)
Because of these uncertainties there are instances when it
makes sense to employ official Soviet and East European budgetary

275

figures. This would appear to be the case when time-series analysis is used and a systematic bias in reporting (e.g., a regular understatement of defense expenditures) is not a principal worry. By looking at variations from the trend rather than the expenditures themselves one also can reduce the problems that stem from different definitions of defense expenditures. (57) Computing defense expenditures as a percentage of central government expenditures (in which both categories of outlays are given in local currency conversion.

Table 10.6 presents data on East European military outlays as a percentage of central governmental expenditures as well as national defense expenditures as a percentage of the total Warsaw Pact Defense budget. Descriptive statistics for these variables are provided in Table 10.7

TABLE 10.6
EAST EUROPEAN DEFENSE EXPENDITURES*

	Bulgaria	Czech	GDR	Hungary	Poland	Romania
1948						
1949						
1950						
1951					6.5(0.9)	
1952					9.6(1.5)	
1953					9.7(2.3)	
1954					8.3(2.5)	
1955					10.2(2.8)	
1956		10.1(4.1)			9.0(2.9)	
1957	(0.5)	9.5(4.2)			6.6(2.4)	8.7(1.6)
1958	(0.6)	9.7(4.2)			6.7(2.8)	7.6(1.5)
1959	(0.6)	9.2(4.1)		4.8(0.6)	7.8(3.5)	7.1(1.4)
1960	(0.6)	8.5(3.6)	(2.9)	4.5(0.7)	7.5(3.7)	6.5(1.5)
1961	(0.6)	8.5(3.6)	(2.4)	4.7(0.7)	7.3(3.4)	5.8(1.3)
1962	7.7(0.6)	8.8(3.7)	5.0(2.4)	6.0(0.8)	7.4(3.4)	5.3(1.2)
1963	7.7(0.6)	9.0(3.5)	4.9(2.1)	6.8(0.9)	8.2(3.5)	5.3(1.2)
1964	6.7(0.6)	8.4(3.5)	4.9(2.3)	6.5(1.0)	8.0(3.8)	4.7(1.2)

continued

Table 10.6 continued

1965	7.4(0.6)	8.9(3.5)	5.0(2.4)	6.0(0.8)	8.2(4.2)	4.9(1.4)
1966	6.5(0.6)	7.1(3.5)	5.4(2.7)	5.3(0.8)	7.9(4.3)	4.6(1.4)
1967	6.5(0.6)	8.7(3.7)	6.1(2.7)	5.2(0.8)	8.4(4.2)	4.0(1.3)
1968	5.9(0.6)	8.6(3.3)	9.7(3.7)	4.6(0.8)	8.4(4.0)	3.9(1.2)
1969	6.0(0.5)	7.9(3.3)	9.8(3.8)	5.1(0.9)	9.4(4.2)	4.5(1.4)
1970	6.2(0.6)	7.6(3.5)	9.7(4.0)	5.1(1.0)	9.3(4.4)	5.4(1.5)
1971	6.2(0.6)	7.1(3.5)	9.1(4.2)	4.8(1.1)	9.4(4.7)	5.6(1.6)
1972	6.1(0.6)	7.4(3.7)	9.6(4.4)	4.6(1.1)	9.2(4.9)	5.4(1.6)
1973						

* The first column entry is defense expenditures as a % of central government expenditures. The entry in parentheses is the % of WTO defense costs borne by the nation. The first set of figures is derived from official national budgetary information as reported in the 1973 edition of *World Armaments and Disarmament, SIPRI Yearbook* and total governmental expenditures (also in local currency) as reported in the *Statesman's Yearbook* (annual). The second set of figures on national contributions to Warsaw Pact defense is derived from the 1973 *SIPRI Yearbook* report of individual Warsaw Pact state defense expenditures coverted to US dollars at Benoit-Lubell exchange rates (pp. 236-237).

277

TABLE 10.7

DESCRIPTIVE STATISTICS OF DEFENSE EXPENDITURES
FOR THE EAST EUROPEAN STATES

	Mean Exp.	Total Change	Ave.Annual Change	Range	Max	Min	Standard Deviation
BULGARIA							
% Central Exp.*6.6	2	.2	1.8	7.7	5.9	.67
% Warsaw Pact+ .6	1	.1	.1	.6	.5	.04
CZECHOSLOVAKIA							
% Central Exp. 8.5	9	.5	3.0	10.1	7.1	.89
% Warsaw Pact 3.7	2	.1	.9	4.2	3.3	.30
GDR							
% Central Exp. 7.2	7	.6	4.9	9.8	4.9	2.31
% Warsaw Pact 3.1	3	.2	2.3	4.4	2.1	.82
HUNGARY							
% Central Exp. 5.2	4	.3	2.3	6.8	4.5	.72
% Warsaw Pact .8	0	0	.7	1.1	.6	.19
POLAND							
% Central Exp. 8.3	14	.6	3.7	10.2	6.5	1.06
% Warsaw Pact 3.4	8	.4	4.0	4.9	.9	1.03
ROMANIA							
% Central Exp. 5.6	8	.5	4.8	8.7	3.9	1.31
% Warsaw Pact 1.4	5	.2	.4	1.6	1.2	.15

* The first row entry is for defense expenditures as a percentage
of central government expenditures.

+ The second row entry is for the percentage of Warsaw Pact defense costs borne by the nation.

Tables 10.6 and 10.7 indicate that with few exceptions defense expenditures as a percentage of central governmental expenditures as well as national contributions of total Warsaw Pact defense costs have remained stable. The principal exceptions to this conclusion, however, are noteworthy. They involve substantial increases in German expenditures since 1957, rather wide fluctuation in Polish defense outlays in the 1950s, and a gradual but sustained increase in the proportion of Warsaw Pact expenses borne by the East European states (as opposed to the Soviet Union) between 1948 and 1972.

The jump of nearly 4% in East German governmental expenditures earmarked for defense between 1957 and 1958 represents the largest annual percentage increase for any Warsaw Pact country for the entire time period under study. During this same 1967-68 period, that percentage of total Warsaw Pact defense costs borne by the German Democratic Republic also rose by 1% and continued to climb by 2% annually through 1972. An explanation for this rise in East German expenditures is beyond the scope of this chapter. It is interesting to note, however, Starr's suggestion that the change in defense spending resulted not from new Soviet demands, but rather from the removal of Soviet constraints and the increase perception of threat from Bonn and, after 1968, from Czechoslovakia. (58)

Polish defense spending, although never experiencing as sharp a climb as East Germany's in 1968, did vary considerably in the 1950s and fluctuated between lows of 6.5 and 6.6% in 1951 and 1957 and a peak of 10.2% in 1955. Since 1955 Polish defense spending never has surpassed the 10% figure. Like East Germany, however, Poland gradually has increased its share of total Warsaw Pact defense costs. Polish contributions have soared from less than 1% in 1951 to 4.9% in 1972. During the same period Soviet military expenditures as a percentage of total Warsaw Pact defense costs have declined from 90.2% in 1951 to 83.6% in 1972. (59)

United Nations Voting as an Indicator of Innovation

The virtual unanimity of Soviet and East European voting on the floor of the General Assembly of the United Nations often is pointed to as a sign of continued Soviet bloc conformity in the foreign policy domain. It remains to be demonstrated, however, whether Warsaw Pact states are as circumspect and cohesive in their voting behavior in United Nations committees further removed from public scrutiny. Hughes and Volgy, for example, believe that voting in committee such as the Political Committee would reflect differences among the Warsaw Pact states. They refrain from such analysis, however, because "Unfortunately, it would take a small army of researchers to examine the records of the committee meetings and piece together the voting patterns." (60) Robert Weiner's study of "Albanian and Romanian Deviance in the United Nations",

however, demonstrates that this is not necessarily the case. (61)
In fact, Charles Wrigley has compiled "United Nations Roll Call
Data" (in machine readable form) for the seven main committees of
the UN General Assembly between 1945 and 1971. (62) Little effort
is required to check whether Warsaw Pact voting conformity extends
to these seven committees. (63) If it does not, the degree of
deviation from Soviet policy for different Pact members and the
change in voting conformity over time are easily calculable.
Tables 10.8 and 10.9 present data on Bulgarian, Czechoslovak, Hungarian, Polish, and Romanian deviations from Soviet votes in the
seven main committees of the General Assembly between 1948 and
1971 and the summary statistics for the change in conformity variable. Deviations as a percentage of total votes cast are indicated.
(64) It should be noted that Bulgaria, Hungary, and Romania did not
become members of the United Nations until 1955.

It is apparent from Table 10.8 that at least between 1948 and
1963 there is little evidence of nonconformity or change in the
degree of conformity on the part of East European members of the
Warsaw Pact. With the exception of Polish voting before 1949, at
no session of the United Nations did an East European state deviate
from Soviet voting more than 7.2% of the time. The few instances
when five or six deviate votes were counted -- Czechoslovakia and
Poland in 1949 and Poland in 1958 and in 1963 -- may well have
been the result of what Thomas Hovet refers to as "mixed signals".(65)

Table 10.8 also indicates that by 1965 there were signs of
Romanian nonconformity in the United Nations. (66) Between 1965 and
1968 the Romanian delegation deviated a total of twenty-three
times from Soviet votes, between 4.4% and 7.2% of the total votes
cast each year. By 1969, however, these nonconforming votes can no
longer be dismissed as inconsequential or the result of mixed signals. In that year deviant votes made up over 14% of the Romanian
total votes. This figure continued to climb to 21.2% and 24% in
1970 and 1971 respectively. In short, by 1971 approximately one
out of every four votes cast by the Romanian delegation was contrary to that of the Soviet delegation. The magnitude of the change
in Romanian behavior is further indicated by the increasingly large
number of deviations that took place in the politically sensitive
First (Political and Security) and Second (Economic and Financial)
Committees. Romanian deviations usually came on issues relating to
arms control and disarmament, the Middle East, and assistance to
third world countries through such bodies as UNCTAD.

TABLE 10.8

UN DEVIATIONS AS A PERCENTAGE OF TOTAL VOTES

	Bulgaria	Czech	GDR	Hungary	Poland	Romania
1948		3.9			7.7	
1949		3.1			3.0	
1950		0			.9	
1951		0			6.5	
1952		.5			0	
1953		0			0	
1954		1.8			1.8	
1955	1.3	0		0	0	0
1956	0	0		3,3	3.3	6.7
1957	3.1	1.0		2.1	4.1	2.1
1958	0	1.0		4.0	5.0	2.0
1959	0	0		.7	1.4	.7
1960	0	0		.7	0	.7
1961	.6	1.2		2.4	1.8	1.2
1962	1.0	0		0	1.0	0
1963	0	0		1.4	7.2	2.9
1964*						
1965	0	0		1.1	0	6.3
1966	0	0		2.2	1.1	4.4
1967	1.8	1.8		3.6	5.4	7.2
1968	0	1.3		4.0	4.0	6.7
1969	4.7	7.0		2.4	2.4	14.1
1970	1.1	3.3		1.1	6.7	21.1
1971	1.9	2.9		2.9	2.9	24.0
1972						
1973						

*Wrigley (1971) reports no records of UN roll call votes in the seven main committees for 1964.

TABLE 10.9

DESCRIPTIVE STATISTICS OF EAST EUROPEAN
DEVIATIONS FROM SOVIET VOTING BEHAVIOR IN
THE SEVEN MAIN COMMITTEES OF THE UNITED NATIONS

	Main Deviation*	Total Change	Ave.Annu- al Change	Range	Max.	Min.	Standard Deviation
BULGARIA	1.0	21	1.3	4.7	4.7	0	1.36
CZECHOSLOVAKIA	1.0	26	1.1	3.9	3.9	0	1.25
GDR							
HUNGARY	2.0	21	1.2	4.0	4.0	0	1.34
POLAND	2.9	50	2.3	7.7	7.7	0	2.52
ROMANIA	6.3	42	2.5	24.0	24.0	0	7.27

* Entries are in percentages (i.e., deviant votes as a percentage
of total votes cast).

Treaties as Indicators of Innovation

As Holsti and Sullivan note, "Treaties and agreements have
traditionally served as an index of nation's relations with other
nations." (67) They serve to make formal and to institutionalize
channels of communication and influence between states (68) (p. 137).
As such they not only reflect the prevailing foreign policy perspectives of national decision-makers, but may influence the course
of subsequent international interactions.
Triska and Slusser argue that "For Soviet Russia, a state alleg-
edly new, different and unique in the world, international treaties
have proved to be especially significant... By means of international treaties, Soviet Russia clarified, articulated, and made
concrete its relations with other states at various stages of its
development." (69) Although there are not comparable studies of
the theory and practice of East European treaties, the legitimization function that treaties perform by conferring recognition in-
ternationally would seem to apply to the new East European regimes
after the Second War much as it did to Soviet Russia after 1917.
Changes in treaty behavior, particularly treaty activity involving
members of an ideologically antagonistic alliance, might be expected to reflect more basic changes in the foreign policy perspectives of national decision-makers. By mapping changes in the
annual distribution of treaties in various international environ-

282

ments one may compute another measure of the constancy or change in a nation's foreign policy behavior. Table 10.10 presents information on East European treaties with NATO countries as a percentage of total bilateral treaties for each year. Table 10.11 provides summary statistics for the treaty variable. (70)

TABLE 10.10

TREATIES WITH NATO COUNTRIES AS A
PERCENTAGE OF TOTAL BILATERAL TREATIES*

	Bulgaria	Czech	GDR	Hungary	Poland	Romania
1948	20	32	0	14	36	14
1949	20	41	0	0	35	0
1950	23	11	0	15	8	11
1951	0	20	0	16	8	0
1952	0	11	0	0	17	0
1953	29	18	0	0	17	0
1954	0	27	0	43	7	43
1955	8	0	0	8	13	0
1956	6	5	0	11	8	8
1957	6	3	0	23	3	4
1958	19	0	0	4	16	15
1959	0	0	0	5	15	6
1960	0	6	0	13	34	36
1961	9	0	0	6	18	0
1962	0	21	0	0	14	33
1963	25	0	0	27	35	18
1964	50	23	0	7	26	45
1965	19	26	0	14	29	36
1966	25	0	0	4	30	17
1967	27	26		15	55	48
1968	45	50		14	30	35
1969						

* The data source for these computations is The University of Washington's "Treaty Information Project" data set compiled under the directionship of Peter Rohn.

TABLE 10.11

DESCRIPTIVE STATISTICS OF EAST EUROPEAN TREATIES WITH
NATO COUNTRIES AS A PERCENTAGE OF TOTAL BILATERAL TREATIES

	Mean	Total Change	Ave.Annu- al Change	Range	Max	Min	Standard Deviation
BULGARIA	15.8	251	12.0	50	50	0	14.8
CZECHOSLOVAKIA	15.2	279	13.3	50	50	0	14.9
GDR	0	0	0	0	0	0	0
HUNGARY	11.8	179	8.5	43	43	0	10.1
POLAND	21.6	200	9.5	52	55	3	13.1
ROMANIA	17.6	367	17.5	48	58	0	17.1

It is apparent from Tables 10.10 and 10.11 that treaty behavior, at least as we have measured it, is more volatile than our other indicators of foreign policy behavior. This probably is due in large part to the small total number of treaties signed annually by the East European states. Great variability in the *percentage* of treaties signed therefore appears when only minor changes occur in the distribution of the *number* of treaties concluded with different nations. (71)

All of the East European states with the exception of the German Democratic Republic have a range of over 40 percent of their ratio of treaties with NATO countries to total bilateral treaties. The greatest range of behavior is displayed by Poland which initialed at least one treaty with a NATO state every year between 1948 and 1968. Poland also exhibits the highest mean treaty percentage figure (21.6%) and the highest figures (55%) for any one year.

Although the pattern is not precise, most of the East European states appear to have changed their treaty signing behavior in the same direction on two occasions. The first major change occured in 1953 and 1954 when Bulgaria, Czechoslovakia, Hungary, and Romania all increased substantially their percentage of treaties signed with NATO countries. (This jump, by the way, was not shared by the Soviet Union.) Again in either 1962 or 1963 all of the Warsaw Pact states but Romania experienced a sharp rise in the percentage of their treaties signed with NATO countries. Although this section is intended to provide only a mapping of foreign policy change, not an explanation for change, it is intriguing to note that the marked increase in NATO treaties after 1962 coincides with a large drop in US-Soviet conflict intensity after 1962 as indicated by our Moses conflict scores.

Summary of Research Findings

Table 10.12 presents annual and cumulative innovation scores for each of the East European states in the areas of foreign trade, defense spending, United Nations voting, and treaty behavior. When data are available, average annual I scores also are indicated for three time periods representing the post-World War II Stalin era, the period between Stalin's death and the Hungarian Revolution, and the period since 1957.

TABLE 10.12

CUMULATIVE INNOVATION SCORES
(All indicators)

	Bulgaria	Czech	GDR	Hungary	Poland	Romania
1948						
1949	0	0	18	4	5	0
1950	0	3	0	4	3	0
1951	0	0	0	0	6	0
1952	0	0	0	2	11	0
1953	7	0	0	0	0	0
1954	0	0	0	0	0	0
1955	0	0	0	4	6	0
1956	0	0	3	3	3	0
1957	5	0	0	6	0	3
1958	0	0	0	0	0	0
1959	0	0	0	6	12	8
1960	0	0	0	0	0	17
1961	0	0	0	4	0	3
1962	0	4	5	0	0	0
1963	3	0	0	0	6	3
1964	3	0	0	0	0	0
1965	0	0	4	0	0	6
1966	0	0	0	0	0	10
1967	3	3	0	0	3	3
1968	3	0	4	0	0	3
1969	0	0	0	4	0	7
1970	0	0	0	0	0	7
1971	0	0	0	3	0	0
1972	0	0	0	0	0	0
1973						
TOTAL I SCORE:	24	10	34	40	55	70

The rankings of East European nations according to our quantitative measures of non-incremental change in foreign policy generally are consistent with traditional wisdom regarding Warsaw Pact foreign policy innovation. Romania clearly emerges as the state having pursued the most innovative foreign policy, the bulk of its non-incremental change occuring in the 1960s. Poland, the second highest scorer on foreign policy innovation, achieves its position mainly because of the variation of its foreign policy outputs in the years prior to Stalin's death and in 1955, 1956, and 1959. Similarly, the greatest concentration of foreign policy innovation for Hungary, the national occupying the third position in the innovation hierarchy, occurs between 1955 and 1957, a period usually identified as the time of most thoroughgoing political change. (72)

Probably the most incongruous from a traditional standpoint is the absence of any foreign policy innovation score for Czechoslovakia in 1968. The absence of any innovation score in 1968 results in part from the ephemeral nature of Czechoslovak policy changes during the Prague Spring and the failure of these changes to meet the "institutionalization" requirement of the operational definition of innovation. It is interesting to note, however, that even if one waives the "two year, same direction change" requirement little variation is apparent in our indicators of Czechoslovak foreign policy behavior between 1967 and 1969. Only in the treaty dimension where there is a shift from 26% treaties with NATO countries in 1967 to 50% in 1968 is there a significant change. Also surprising in view of Polish and East German justification for the invasion in terms of halting an incipient Czechoslovak-West German alliance, Czechoslovak trade with the Federal Republic actually rose from 3.6% of total Czechoslovak trade in 1968 to 5% of total trade in 1969.

Table 10.13 summarizes information on the degree of association between an East European state's ranking on our foreign policy innovation index and its ranking on indices of mean conflict with the regional hegemon, mean variability in elite attributes, and mean level of economic development. (73) As will become apparent in the following discussion, there are a number of methodological reasons for interpreting these findings cautiously. Like the research of Kintner and Klaiber, it is suggested that the findings be regarded as "a pilot test of hypotheses which generally 'make sense' to the student of international relations, but which may or may not be true." (74)

TABLE 10.13

RANK ORDER CORRELATION MATRIX (ALL YEARS)

	Bulgaria	Czech	GDR	Hungary	Poland	Romania	Correlation with I score r_s	Significance Level
I Score Rank	5	6	4	3	2	1		
Mean Conflict Rank	6	4	1	3	5	2	.31	.273
Elite Attribute Variability Rank	2	5		3	4	1	.60	.143
Mean Economic Development Rank	4	2	1	5	3	6	-.60	.104

Our first hypothesis is that the greater a subordinate regional state's conflict with the regional hegemon, the greater its foreign policy innovation. In other words, it is expected that those East European countries which have experienced the most conflict in their relations with the Soviet Union also will demonstrate the greatest non-incremental change in their foreign policy behavior. (75) The Spearman rank order correlation between the innovation variable and mean conflict with the Soviet Union is .31, significant at the .273 level. Although the coefficient is positive, i.e. in the predicted direction, the magnitude of the correlation is not very high and does not achieve a level of statistical significance that inspires much confidence. A possible explanation for the relatively low correlation may have been the failure to distinguish between the effects of intense and moderate conflict on innovative behavior. According to March and Simon the amount of crisis induced stress may be the critical variable affecting organizational change. (76) A moderate level of conflict may generate demands which result in more rigorous search activity and the consideration of new policy alternatives. If acceptable alternatives are not found, however, an increase in the intensity of conflict induced stress may impede the ability of decision-makers to reason and respond effectively to the perceived demands. If one categorized the degree of conflict associated with the Soviet led invasions of Czechoslovakia and Hungary as intense (rather than moderate) and excludes these conflict scores from the conflict average our correlation coefficient rises to the more respectable level of .54. (77)

Our second hypothesis is that those states which experience the greatest change in leadership attributes will demonstrate the greatest amount of innovation in foreign policy. Table 10.13 indicates that the correlation between the elite variability index and prosperity to engage in non-incremental foreign policy change is high and in the predicted direction, .60. (78) As anticipated by the hypothesis, the Romanian Central Committee experienced the greatest mean variability (.42) as well as the most variability for five of the nine indicators of elite attributes among the five East European states for which we have data. Particularly interesting in terms of the "red versus export" controversy and the interdisciplinary literature on characteristics of individual innovators is the finding that relative to the central committees of other East European countries the Romanian elite experienced much greater change in the areas of technical education, revolutionary activity prior to the Second World War, and membership in the Communist Party prior to the Communist's seizure of power. Not only has the Romanian elite experienced the greatest variability in these characteristics, but the change has been in the direction of increased representation by Party members whose expertise lies in technical skills rather than in revolutionary experience. (79)

289

TABLE 10.14

THE VARIABILITY OF ELITE ATTRIBUTES (1948-1970)*

	Bulgaria	Czech	Hungary	Poland	Romania
ATTRIBUTE					
Rural	.03	.05	.23	.05	.07
Party Education, Foreign	.40	.17	.29	.29	.26
Partisan	.12	.34	.17	.15	.54
Party Membership	.14	.15	.15	.16	.34
Revolutionary	.45	.46	.32	.35	.74
Technical Education	.56	.29	.56	.13	.70
International Background	.20	.22	.10	.20	.28
University Education	.10	.42	.09	.08	.06
Age	.90	.65	.69	.99	.76
Mean Coefficient of Variability:	.33	.23	.29	.27	.42

*The data source for this table is The University of Pittsburgh's Archive on Political Elites in Eastern Europe.

Our third hypothesis is that there is a positive correspondence between a nation's level of economic development and the degree of innovation in its foreign policy. According to this hypothesis one would expect those East European states that were most developed economically to be the most innovative in their foreign policy behavior. Table 10.13 suggests that, if anything, the opposite is the case. The correlation between our indicators of foreign policy innovation and economic development is high, .60. The direction of the relationship, however, is opposite to that predicted by the hypothesis. The two East European nations with the lowest level of economic development between 1948 and 1972 (Romania and Hungary) are among the top three in foreign policy innovation. The two states with the highest level of economic development (the GDR and Czechoslovakia), on the other hand, rank among the three least innovative states in the foreign policy sphere.

The finding that an inverse relationship appears to exist between level of economic development and degree of foreign policy innovation makes little sense from a theoretical standpoint. It certainly is not supported by most economic and organization behavior studies which point to a positive relationship between organizational wealth and prosperity to innovate. (80) There is, however, an alternative "economic explanation" for foreign policy innovation. The critical factor may be the degree of change in economic development corresponding changes arise in the intensity of domestic demands, if substantial, may alter not only the decision-makers' psychological environment but also lead to changes in foreign policy outputs. In fact, between 1957 and 1972, the period for which there is the most complete data for our indicators of foreign policy behavior, there is a .71 correlation between change in level of economic development and degree of foreign policy innovation. (81) Romania, the nation which experienced the greatest amount of non-incremental change in its foreign policy behavior also exhibited the most variability in its economic development.

Conclusions

What is one to make of our findings? Does it make sense to speak of East European foreign policy innovation as adaptive behavior and to distinguish among the concepts of innovation, nonconformity, and incremental change? Is there reason to believe that the statistically meaningful but hardly conclusive relationships we have discerned between foreign policy innovation and change in domestic and external conditions represent more than frail artifacts of our quantitative method? Finally, even if the answers to the latter two questions are affirmative, are there more adequate means to operationalize the concept of innovation and to analyze the process of continuity and change in the foreign policy behavior of the East European states?

Admittedly, the distinction between change and innovation is

not precise. Nevertheless, like Braybrooke and Lindblom we maintain that it is crucial to distinguish between political decisions
that represent only marginal and repetitive adjustments to changing circumstances and non-incremental changes in policy that are
institutionalized. (82) As Tables 10.1-10.12 indicate, a nation
may exhibit a great deal of annual fluctuation in its foreign policy outputs and yet display very little in the way of non-repeti-
tive, non-incremental, long term change. (83)

There also is a compelling reason to distinguish between foreign policy change and foreign policy conformity. As Gitelman
points out, although there has been no shortage of studies regarding change in Soviet-East European relations "it seems that whatever the method employed, the same fundamental question underlies
almost all of the research: how much cohesion... is there between
the USSR and Eastern Europe? Almost all of the literature on foreign policy of East European states has explicitly or implicitly
addressed itself to the question of whether the particular state
or states are becoming more or less independent of the Soviet
Union." (84) This is an important question and deserves (and has
received) serious attention. An exclusive concentration on cohesion and conformity, however, not only can distort one's perception of the foreign policy objectives of the East European states
but can conceal the extent of change in East European foreign
policy over time. (85) If, as Gitelman suggests, "we take seriously the notion that the East European states do enjoy some autonomy
in policy making and implementation, it would seem that East European policies and behaviors ought to be examined for their intrin-
sic interest and importance, not merely as factors which are con-
ductive to greater or lesser cohesion with the Soviet Union." (86)
Hopefully this chapter's mapping of change and innovation for
several indicators of East European foreign policy will facilitate
more detailed and informed historical and quantitative study of
the dynamic nature of Warsaw Pact foreign relations.

In regard to the issue of the reasonableness of alternative
explanations for foreign policy innovation it is reassuring to
find that the quantitative index of innovation used in this study
coincides (or at least is not inconsistent with) more traditional
accounts of East European foreign relations. This does not confirm
that either or both approaches are correct in their conclusions,
although it may raise one's level of confidence. An advantage of
our quantitative approach over highly impressionistic accounts of
political change is that its methods of analysis, however primitive, are explicit and replicable. The fact that the framework,
hypotheses, and methods are not country or alliance specific also
facilitates tests as to the generalizability of the findings.

On the debit side of the ledger is the crudeness of the measure
of innovation, the relatively low level of statistical achieved,
and the failure of the statistical tests to take full advantage of
the longitudinal nature of the data. Nonparametric measures of
association were used because of the small N size, lack of homo-

geneity, and the rank order character of certain assumptions of linear regression may yield more meaningful tests of the research hypotheses. (87)

More perplexing is the problem of refining the indicators of innovation and the coding rules for its measurement. It would be useful, for example, to develop alternative, independent measures of foreign policy innovation. One measure used by Jack Walker in his landmark study of diffusion of innovation among the American states is suggestive. (88) It involves assignment of innovation scores on the basis of the relative speed with which states adopt new policies. A comparable measure of foreign policy innovation might be the relative speed with which states establish or sever diplomatic relations with controversial nations (e.g., Chile, Bangladesh, Portugal, the Federal Republic of Germany, Cuba). Data gathering difficulties, unfortunately, precluded inclusion of this alternative measure in this chapter. (89)

Andrzej Korbonski ended a recent article in the *Slavic Review* by noting that "much work still needs to be done in the general area of political change in Eastern Europe." (90) In particular, he called for an expansion of our factual base, more precise definitions of individual variables, a paradigm for comparing the experiencec of the various countries. Echoing Montias, he also suggested that "a parallel effort should be made to correct the 'almost ubiquitous failure to test hypotheses against the available data'." (91) Recognition of the validity of these points directed the focus and organization of this chapter. Mindful of the limitations of the data and methods of analysis, it is hoped that progress has been made toward narrowing the gap between informed speculation and reality.

NOTES

*   The author is grateful to Alexander J. Groth, Robert J. Lieber, and William Zimmerman for helpful comments on an earlier version of this chapter. Thanks also are expressed to Holly Knauert for computer programming assistance and to Lee Dunsky, Kent Chadwick, and Linda Martin for help in coding the data.

1. See, for example, Andrzej Korbonski, "The Prospects for Change in Eastern Europe", *Slavic Review*, Vol. 33, No.2 (June, 1974); Kenneth Jowitt, *Revolutionary Breakthroughs and National Development: The Case of Romania, 1944-1965* (Berkeley: University of California Press, 1971); "Soviet Society in Flux", *Problems of Communism*, Vol. 23 (November-December, 1974); Zvi Gitelman, *The Diffusion of Political Innovation from Eastern Europe to the Soviet Union* (Beverly Hills: Sage Publications, Inc., 1972); David Finley, "Some International Pressures and Political Change In Eastern Europe", paper presented to the Westerns Slavic Conference, San Francisco, October 25-27, 1973; Chalmers Johnson (ed.), *Change in Communist Systems* (Stanford: Stanford University Press, 1970).

2. William Welsh, "Economic Change and East European Regional Integration" in Louis J. Mensonides and James A. Kuhlman (eds.), *The Future of Inter-Bloc Relations in Europe* (New York: Praeger, 1974), p. 107.

3. Probably the best historical studies of Warsaw Pact relations are Zbigniew Brzezinski's *The Soviet Bloc* (New York: Praeger, 1971) and Robin Renington's *The Warsaw Pact* (Cambridge: MIT Press, 1971). An interesting attempt to provide quantitative indicators of East European conformity to Soviet foreign policy between 1956 and 1967 is William Kintner and Wolfgang Klaiber's *Eastern Europe and European Security* (New York: Dunellen Publishing Co., 1971).

4. Poland's voting deviancy record between 1965 and 1968 was 0% in 1965, 1.1% in 1966, 5.4% in 1967, and 4% in 1968. See Table 10.8 for the complete record of East European "deviant votes" in the main committees of the United Nations between 1948 and 1971.

5. As Kenneth Hempel notes, a failure to distinguish the two forms of innovative behavior is one difficulty with Hughes and Volgy's quantitative study of "distance" in Soviet-East European relations. Cf. Hempel, "Comparative Research on Eastern Europe: A Critique of Hughes and Volgy's 'Distance' in Foreign Policy Behavior", *American Journal of Political Science* (May, 1973), and Barry Hughes and Thomas Volgy, "Distance in Foreign Policy Behavior", *Midwest Journal of Political Science* (August, 1970).

6. The second possibility was brought to my attention by William Zimmerman.

7. It is theoretically possible, of course, that East Germany rather than the Soviet Union is the regional pace setter in trade and other foreign policy matters. Time-series analysis of different dimensions of foreign policy (e.g., trade and treaty behavior, UN committee voting, diplomatic recognition, and defense spending) provides some clues as to which nation emulates policy and which nation initiates it. A third possibility, that both the Soviet Union and East Germany respond to the cues of another party, is more difficult to rule out.

8. Note that change and conformity are not necessarily incompatible, change in one nation's foreign policy possible reflecting a similar change in another state's external behavior.

9. Zvi Gitelman, *The Diffusion of Political Innovation: From Eastern Europe to the Soviet Union* (Beverly Hills: Sage Publications, Co., 1972), p. 12).

10. See Potter, "Continuity and Change in the Foreign Relations of the Warsaw Pact States, 1948-1973", Mimeo, Davis, California, 1975.

11. Hans Morgenthau, *Politics Among Nations*, 4th edition (New York: Alfred A. Knopf, 1967), p. 5.

12. See in particular Morton Kaplan, *System and Process in International Politics* (New York: John Wiley and Sons, 1957) and George Liska, *International Equilibrium* (Cambridge: Harvard University Press, 1957).

13. See AFK Organski, *World Politics*, 2nd edition (New York: Alfred A. Knopf, 1968) and Jan Triska and David Finley, "Soviet-American Relations: A Multiple Symmetry Model", *Journal of Conflict Resolution*, Vol. IX, No. 2 (March, 1965).

14. The failure to discuss the linkage between foreign policy inputs, process, and outputs is a major weakness of Rosenau's pre-theory. See James Rosenau, "Pre-Theories and Theories of Foreign Policy", in R. Barry Farrell (ed.), *Approaches to Comparative and International Politics* (Evanston: Northwestern University Press, 1966).

15. See, for example, George Modelski, *A Theory of Foreign Policy* (New York: Praeger, 1972); Richard Snyder et al., *Foreign Policy Decision-Making: An Approach to the Study of International Politics* (New York: Free Press, 1962); and Graham Allison, *Essence of Decision* (Boston: Little, Brown, 1971).

16. See Michael Brecher et al., "A Framework for Research on
    Foreign Policy Behavior", *Journal of Conflict Resolution*, Vol.
    13 (March, 1969).

17. Cf. James Rosenau, *The Adaptation of National Societies: A
    Theory of Political Behavior and Transformation* (New York:
    McCaleb-Seiler-Seiler, 1970); Saadia Touval, *Domestic Dynamics
    of Change from Confrontation to Accommodation Politics*, Research
    Monograph 38 (Princeton: Center for International Studies, 1973)?
    Patrick McGowan, "Adaptive Foreign Policy: An Empirical Approach"
    in James Rosenau (ed.), *Comparing Foreign Policies* (New York:
    John Wiley, 1974).

18. By "essential structures" Rosenau has in mind "four interaction
    patterns that most observers would agree are so basic as to be
    necessary to the continued existence of national societies":
    political structure, economic structure, social structure, and
    physical structure (p. 21). See the Appendix to Rosenau's essay
    for a discussion of operationalizing essential structures.

19. See Rosenau (1970), p. 6, for a list of these twenty types.

20. However, as is discussed below, Rosenau is not very precise or
    consistent in specifying the causal relationship.

21. Rosenau, for example, defines governmental variables as "those
    aspects of a government's structure that limit or enhance for-
    eign policy choices by decision-makers" (1966, p. 43). It
    seems reasonable to categorize "character of the executive",
    "character of the party system", "role of the legislature",
    etc. -- items listed as characteristics of the four types of
    adaptation (1970, p. 6) -- as governmental variables.

22. Potter, op. cit., pp. 36-48.

23. The generalizability of the findings, however, may be limited by
    the fact that most, if not all, of the East European states for
    most years would seem to fall in the same acquiescent adaptation
    type category (i.e., they are more responsive to external than
    internal demands). My colleague, Alexander Groth, suggests that
    in order to acknowledge the probable mediating effect of such
    factors as foreign policy autonomy, military capability, politi-
    cal strategic significance to the regional hegemon, etc. that
    each hypothesis in the propositional inventory should include a
    ceteris paribus clause. Although he undoubtedly is correct in
    pointing out that the impact of the variables hypothesized to be
    associated with foreign policy innovation will vary according to
    the prevailing mix of internal and external demands the small
    number of countries examined in the quantitative analysis pre-
    cludes effective statistical control for extraneous variables.

The mediating effect of such variables is considered in a lengthier version of this chapter which includes a case study of Soviet and East European foreign policy changes toward the Federal Republic of Germany. This study also extends the "correlates of foreign policy innovation" to all NATO as well as Warsaw Pact nations.

24. In order to dispel the objection that the hypothesis is tautological it is emphasized that there is no overlap in the indicators of conflict and innovation. As operational definition of foreign policy innovation in the areas of trade, treaty, defense spending, and UN voting behavior is provided below in the section "Measuring Innovation". A description of the scale used to code conflict data is provided in P. Terrence Hopmann and Barry B. Huges, "Dyadic and Multilateral Events Data" (First ICPR edition codebook, June, 1974).

25. See especially James March and Herbert Simon, *Organizations* (New York: John Wiley, 1958), p. 184 and Ole Holsti, *Crisis Escalation War* (Montreal: McGill-Queens University Press, 1972), p. 12.

26. James Q. Wilson, "Innovation in Organizations: Notes Toward a Theory", in James D. Thompson (ed.), *Approaches to Organizational Design* (Pittsburgh: University of Pittsburgh Press, 1966), p. 208.

27. Ronald G. Havelock, *Planning for Innovation* (Ann Arbor: Institute for Social Research, 1971), p. 619.

28. March and Simon, op. cit., p. 186.

29. Schon cited in Havelock, op. cit., pp. 6-11.

30. See Lincoln Moses et al., "Scaling Data on Inter-Nation Action", *Science*, Vol. 156 (May, 1967).

31. P. Terrence Hopmann and Barry B. Hughes, *Three Programs and Two Data Sets for Analyzing International Interactions* (University of Minnesota and Case Western Reserve University, 1972), p. 12.

32. Barry Hughes, "Dyadic and Multilateral Events Data", (1971). The data were provided by the Inter-University Consortium for Political Research.

33. Carl Beck, "Leadership Attributes in Eastern Europe: The Effect of Country and Time" in Carl Beck, et al., *Comparative Communist Political Leadership* (New York: David McKay, 1973), p. 87.

34. Beck's "measures" of policy outcomes consist of the observation

that "most analysts of Eastern Europe agree that political outcomes in Bulgaria have changed less than in Czechoslovakia,
Hungary, and Poland over the past twenty-five years". (p. 88)

35. Analysis of the GDR was precluded because of the absence of
Archive data for that country.

36. See Hubert M. Blalock, *Social Statistics* (New York: McGraw Hill,
1960), p. 73 for a discussion of the coefficient of variability
statistic.

37. See, for example, Lawrence Mohr, "Determinants of Innovation
in Organizations", *American Political Science Review* (March,
1969) and Edwin Mansfield, "The Speed of Response of Firms to
New Techniques", *Quarterly Journal of Economics* (May, 1963).

38. Jack L. Walker, "The Diffusion of Innovation Among the American
States", *American Political Science Review* (September, 1969),
p. 884.

39. Kintner and Klaiber, op. cit., p. 249.

40. A Pearson's product-moment correlation of .98 significant at
the .001 level was found to exist between electricity production per capita and another indicator of economic development,
steel production per capita, for the 1948-1973 time period.

41. David Braybrooke and Charles Lindblom, "Types of Decision-
Making", in James Rosenau (ed.), *International Politics and
Foreign Policy* (New York: Free Press, 1969), p. 208.

42. Ibid., p. 209.

43. Ibid., p. 208.

44. The systemic consequences dimension of innovation is considered
in the case study portion of a longer version of this chapter.

45. In other words, when calculating I scores 0% change counts as
change in the same direction.

46. The standard deviation, variance, and coefficient of variability are alternative measures of dispersion that also might be
used to tap the constancy of foreign policy behavior. They do
not provide, however, any indication of the permanence of change.

47. Recently, a number of handbooks have been compiled that provide
longitudinal data on important categories of foreign policy
behavior. They include: Ellen Mickiewicz (ed.), *Handbook of
Soviet Social Science Data* (New York: Free Press, 1973); Paul

Marer, *Soviet and East European Foreign Trade, 1945-1969*
(Bloomington: Indiana University Press, 1972); Arthur Banks,
Cross-Polity Time-Series Data (Cambridge: MIT Press, 1971).
Kintner and Klaiber (1971), Hughes and Volgy (1972), Kegley
(1974), and Welsh (1974) are among those who have displayed an
interest in the quantitative study of Soviet and East European
foreign policy. In no instance, however, do they analyze more
than three indicators of foreign policy behavior.

48. Cited by Robert W. Dean, *West German Trade with the East: The
Political Dimension* (New York: Praeger, 1974), p. xii.

49. Ibid., pp. xii-xiii.

50. One should keep in mind, as Tollison and Willett point out,
that it is possible for economic data to provide a "good proxy
for political variables without there being any causal mechanism between the two". See Robert Tollison and Thomas Willett,
"International Integration and the Interdependence of Economic
Variables", *International Organization*, Vol. 27, No. 2 (1973),
p. 256.

51. Fifteen countries were chosen to represent the West: Austria,
Belgium-Luxembourg, Canada, Denmark, Finland, France, West
Germany, Greece, Italy, the Netherlands, Norway, Switzerland,
the United Kingdom, and the United States. These are the same
countries selected by Kintner and Klaiber (1971) to represent
trade with the West.

52. The close association between changes in Romanian trade with
the Soviet Union and Romanian trade with the West between 1958
and 1971 is indicated by a Pearsons product-moment correlation
of -.95 significant at the .001 level.

53. It is interesting to note that in this same time period the
range of Soviet trade with Eastern Europe as a percentage of
total trade never exceeds nine percent. For data on comparable
indicators of Soviet foreign policy behavior between 1948 and
1973 see Potter (op. cit.).

54. See, for example, Paul Smoker, "The Arms Race: A Wave Model",
Peace Research Society (International) Papers, Vol. 4 (1966);
Frederic Pryor, *Public Expenditures in Communist and Capitalist
Nations* (Homewood, Illinois: Richard D. Irwin, 1968); John C.
Lambelet, "Toward a Dynamic Two-Theater Model of the East-West
Arms Race", *Journal of Peace Research*, Vol. 1, No. 1 (Autumn,
1973); and Franz Walter, "One More: Economic Growth, U.S.
Defense Expenditures and the Soviet Defense Budget", *Soviet
Studies*, Vol. 26, No. 3 (July, 1974)

55. See in particular Pryor (op. cit.) and Harvey Starr, "A Collective Goods Analysis of the Warsaw Pact After Czechoslovakia", *International Organization*, Vol. 28, No. 3 (Summer, 1974).

56. This fact is acknowledged by the editors of *The Military Balance*. See Appendix 8B in the 1974 *SIPRI Yearbook* for a thorough discussion of the problem inherent in estimating Soviet military expenditures and an assessment of alternative approaches.

57. This point is made by Pryor, op. cit., p. 110.

58. Starr, op. cit., p. 529.

59. Soviet contributions to Warsaw Pact defense between 1951 and 1972 are provided in the *SIPRI Yearbook* (1973, pp. 231-237).

60. Hughes and Volgy, op. cit., p. 463.

61. *East European Quarterly*, Vol. 12, No. 1 (Spring, 1973).

62. Data were provided by the Inter-University Consortium for Political Research.

63. Weinter's study suggests that at least for Romania it does not.

64. Deviations as a percentage of total votes cast rather than the total number of deviations are provided since the number of votes taken each session (and thus the number of opportunities for deviation) vary considerably over time.

65. Thomas Hovet, *Bloc Politics in the United Nations* (Cambridge: Harvard University Press, 1960). The fact that in the case of Czechoslovakia these deviant votes occured in five different committees, however, suggests that the votes were not an isolated instance of mixed signals.

66. These signs might have been detected in 1964 had committee votes been recorded that year.

67. "National-International Linkages: France and China as Nonconforming Alliance Members", in James Rosenau (ed.), *Linkage Politics* (New York: Free Press, 1969), p. 187.

68. Charles Cary, "Patterns of Soviet Treaty-Making Behavior with Other Communist States", in Jan Triska (ed.), *Communist Party States* (New York: Bobbs-Merrill, 1969), p. 137.

69. Jan Triska and Robert Slusser, *The Theory, Law and Policy of Soviet Treaties* (Stanford: Stanford University Press, 1962), p. 2.

70. Holsti and Sullivan are correct in calling for a cautious in-
    terpretation of this kind of treaty information because of the
    likelihood of serious data omissions, particularly for the
    later years, (op.cit., p. 194).

71. Extensive variability by itself, however, is not a sign that
    the measure of treaty behavior is unreliable or that treaty
    activity fails to reflect more basic changes in foreign policy
    behavior. In fact, for the entire time period for all Warsaw
    Pact countries statistical tests indicate a low but significant
    correlation between treaties with NATO countries as a percent-
    age of total treaties and deviations (.34 significant at the
    .001 level) and trade with the West (.29 significant at the
    .003 level).

72. See, for example, Paul Kecskemeti, *The Unexpected Revolution*
    (Stanford: Stanford University Press, 1961) and Paul Zinner,
    Revolution in Hungary (New York: Columbia University Press,
    1962).

73. The time period varies according to data availability. For
    mean conflict and elite attributes data are available between
    1948 and 1970; for economic development the period is 1948-1972.

74. Kintner and Klaiber, op. cit., p. 220. One of the principal
    difficulties in comparing East European nations in terms of
    their foreign policy innovation is the lack of substantial
    variation in their behavior. In the case of Romanian innova-
    tion one can speak with some confidence due to Romania's lead-
    ing scores on four of our seven indicators of foreign policy
    behavior. The position of Czechoslovakia as a laggard in for-
    eign policy innovation also is clear. Less apparent, however,
    is the accuracy of the rankings of other countries, although
    they are not inconsistent with most historical accounts of
    East European foreign relations.

75. As previously indicated, conflict is tapped by the Moses inter-
    national conflict-cooperation index. See Moses et al., (op.
    cit.), and Hopmann and Hughes (op. cit.), for a discussion of
    the coding procedure.

76. March and Simon, op. cit., p. 184.

77. The correlation is significant at the .133 level.

78. The correlation is significant at the .143 level. The elite
    variability coefficients are provided in Table A of the Appendix.

79. In their survey of interdisciplinary research findings on in-
    novation Everett Rogers and Floyd Shoemaker report empirical

support for the hypothesis that innovators are less dogmatic
than late adopters and that although innovators may not have
more education than laggards they tend to have more specialized
operations. See Rogers and Shoemaker, *Communication of Innova-
tions* (New York: Free Press, 1971), pp. 346-387. For an excellent discussion of the red versus expert dilemma see Richard
Lowenthal, "Development vs. Utopia in Communist Policy" in
Chalmers Johnson (ed.), op. cit.

80. See, for example, Mansfield(op. cit.), and Mohr (op. cit.).

81. The coefficient is significant at the .056 level. The coefficient of variability statistic was used as the measure of
change in economic development.

82. Op. cit., p. 208. Gitelman also implied this distinction when
he defines innovation "as the development and implementation
of a program which is institutionalized and which is generally
acknowledged to have systemic significance." (Op. cit., p. 11,
emphasis added.)

83. Bulgarian trade with the Soviet Union between 1950 and 1973 is
an example. During that period trade increased or declined on
the average of 2.3% each year -- only one -- tenth of one percent less than that Romanian rate of change in trade with the
Soviet Union. The direction of change in Romanian trade away
from the USSR, however, is unambiguous, dropping from 51.5% in
1958 to 41,9% in 1963 to 28.7% in 1968 to 24,5% in 1973. In
contrast, Bulgarian trade with the Soviet Union in 1973 (53.3%)
is only marginally different from trade with the Soviet Union
in 1950 (52.2%).

84. "Toward A Comparative Foreign Policy of Eastern Europe", paper
presented to the International Conference of Slavicists,
Banff, 1974, p. 7.

85. Gitelman demonstrates that the Polish policy of rapprochement
with West Germany was not motivated by a desire to move away
from the Soviet orbit, but by a strong desire to alleviate if
not solve "their most pressing foreign policy problem" (1974,
p. 9). Studies which emphasize "deviation from Soviet policy"
indicators also are apt to ignore the extent of change in
Soviet policy over time.

86. Ibid.

87. In particular one would wish to clarify the relationship between the occurrence of specific amounts of conflict, leadership change, etc. and the degree of foreign policy change
and/or innovation present. In order to explain much of the

variance in foreign policy innovation it also may be necessary to take account of the interaction effects among several plausible determinants of policy outputs. It also is conceivable that the conditions that promote foreign policy innovation are not the same in all countries.

88. Walker, op. cit.

89. No consistent order of recognition or severance was apparent in the small number of cases for which data were collected although Romania was first or last more often than amy of the other East European states (e.g., Israel, Bangladesh, Portugal, West Germany, and the Phillipines).

90. Op. cit., p. 239.

91. The citation for Montias is "Modernization in Communist Countries: Some Questions of Methodology", *Studies in Comparative Communism*, Vol. 5, No. 4 (1972), p. 413.